American Cinema in the Shadow of 9/11

Edited by Terence McSweeney

EDINBURGH
University Press

Dedicated with love to my parents

Edinburgh University Press is one of the leading university presses in the UK. We publish academic books and journals in our selected subject areas across the humanities and social sciences, combining cutting-edge scholarship with high editorial and production values to produce academic works of lasting importance. For more information visit our website: edinburghuniversitypress.com

Edinburgh University Press Ltd
The Tun – Holyrood Road,
12(2f) Jackson's Entry,
Edinburgh EH8 8PJ

Typeset in 11/13 Adobe Sabon by
IDSUK (DataConnection) Ltd

A CIP record for this book is available from the British Library

ISBN 978 1 4744 1381 7 (hardback)
ISBN 978 1 4744 1382 4 (webready PDF)
ISBN 978 1 4744 1383 1(epub)

Contents

Figures

Acknowledgements

This ambitious book would not have been possible without the help of a significant number of people, far too numerous to mention here. Most of all I would like to thank the sixteen authors who have contributed to this volume. It has been a real privilege to work with you and I hope the book lives up to all of our expectations.

I would like to thank the staff and students at Southampton Solent University, in particular the students of the 2015–16 unit 'After 9/11: Film, Television and Culture', for their interest and passion for the topic, which for me proved infectious. Thanks also to the staff of the Vere Harmsworth Library at the University of Oxford's Rothermere American Institute where some of the editing of this manuscript was done during my tenure as Visiting Research Fellow in the academic year 2015–16.

I am very fortunate to be part of a wonderful team at Edinburgh University Press. In particular I would like to thank Gillian Leslie for her belief and support in the project from the very beginning.

Special thanks are always reserved for my family, without whom this book could not have been written. Olga, Harrison and Wyatt, the three people who are the reason I am who I am. I love you now and forever more.

Foreword

Although contemporary viewers watch movies in new ways and on different devices in the digital age, film has lost none of its power to shape the way viewers understand the contours of both the present and the past. Indeed, the question of how film affects us is just as pressing today as it was for some of the cinema's earliest theorists. How does it engage viewers, transmit affect and provoke meaning-making? How does it shape understandings of the past and present? As Miriam Hansen observed, theorists like Siegfried Kracauer, Walter Benjamin and Theodore Adorno were interested less in the ontology of film than in 'the kind of sensory-perceptual, mimetic experience it enabled', which of course was contingent on social and political constellations. They were interested not so much in what cinema is, but 'in what cinema *does*' (Hansen 2012: xvii). Film offers up a seemingly material past; it invites affective engagement, evoking not just visual, aural and tactile faculties, but intellectual and cognitive ones as well. We are addressed, as Siegfried Kracauer wrote, 'with skin and hair' (quoted in Hansen 1993: 458). Because of the materiality of the filmic mode of address, the medium has the capacity to provoke us, to make us think, to fundamentally shape our ideas about both history and politics.

The essays in this volume share a commitment to the idea that film, as a cultural product, has an intimate – though by no means straightforward – relationship to its own historical moment. All films, as these essays suggest, are ideological, and in that sense they present a distorted reality, and yet they index the very real anxieties and social contradictions of their moment of creation. In complicating the idea of cultural production as simple reflection, Raymond Williams writes, 'It is not the "mere surface" or "appearances only" which are reflected in art, but the "essential" or "underlying" or "general" reality' (Williams 1978: 10).

The conflicts depicted in mass culture correspond, sometimes obviously and sometimes more ambiguously, to the social, political and economic milieus in which they were conceived. And yet, these cultural productions are at the same time deeply ideological in their attempts to manage, or fix, or contain the conflicts and problems they themselves depict. This collection helps us to see the ways in which mass culture is deeply ambivalent: both an actual register of the political landscape, an expression of the actual conditions of existence, and also a strategy for deflecting or redefining the nature of the problem or conflict. These 'ideological fixes' often work in the service of the dominant ideology, sometimes in politically reactionary ways, but at other times they offer up a vision of the way things *should* be.

Because these films, made in the shadow of 9/11, at once expose fundamental political, social and economic crises and contradictions, and attempt to solve, fix or reimagine them, they offer profound insight into our times. Because they touch us 'with skin and hair', they are potent political agents, and we need to be cognisant of both the work they do and the work they inspire in us. The essays in this volume do more than simply reflect on the present: they provide us a framework for considering future films, which will most certainly engage the new phase of the 'war on terror' in which we find ourselves.

Alison Landsberg

REFERENCES

Hansen, Miriam (1993), '"With Skin and Hair": Kracauer's Theory of Film, Marseilles 1940', *Critical Inquiry*, 19.3, Spring, pp. 437–69.
Hansen, Miriam Bratu (2012), *Cinema and Experience: Siegfried Kracauer, Walter Benjamin and Theodor W. Adorno*, Berkeley: University of California Press.
Williams, Raymond (1978), *Marxism and Literature*, New York: Oxford University Press.

American Cinema in the Shadow of 9/11

Terence McSweeney

The conflict which came to be known as the 'War on Terror', insti-
gated by the administration of President George W. Bush in 2001
and continued by his successor Barack Obama, was the first war of the
twenty-first century and an event of profoundly global reach and implication. While the majority of its military operations were undertaken in
Afghanistan (2001–14) and Iraq (2002–11), this volume turns its attention to another vitally important front of the war, the films produced by
the American film industry in the first decades of the new millennium.
Now, more than fifteen years after the events of 11 September 2001, it
is clear to see that these films not only function as a uniquely telling and
resonant cultural battleground in which conflicting ideologies were projected for all to see, but were also able to shape the cultural imaginary
of post-9/11 America in a range of compelling ways. While the 'War on
Terror' was officially brought to an end by President Obama in 2013, it
is one that is still fought in the films about the conflict which continue
to be made today.

This edited collection is an attempt to interrogate and explore the
complicated relationship between film and society in these turbulent
'War on Terror' decades. It seeks to make a contribution to the remarkable body of work which already exists that examines the symbiotic
exchange between national identity and the politics of cinematic representation (see Kracauer 1947; Wood 1986). How far films are able
to reflect and influence the cultures and times in which they are made
remains a matter for continued debate, but what is clear is that much
of the cinematic output of the post-9/11 era is deeply immersed in the
tumultuous environment which saw the films produced.

The authors of this volume, many of whom are the foremost scholars in their field, have already made considerable contributions to the
study of American film and culture. In this project they turn their attention to the shifting coordinates of post-9/11 American cinema with the
collective assertion that the events of the 'War on Terror' frequently
provided more than a modish and convenient backdrop for many of
the films produced, and that in actual fact, as Mark Lacey asserts, film
emerged as a medium in which '"commonsense" ideas about global
politics and history are (re)-produced and where stories about what is
acceptable behaviour from states and individuals are naturalised and
legitimated' (614). In this understanding of the relationship between
cinema and culture, popular film is not a shallow frivolity, but rather
an expressive socio-political artefact and a very influential part of the
way meanings are generated by society at large.

None of the authors contained in this collection suggests that films
simply reflect the times in which they were made, as the relationship
between cinema and culture is a much more complex one. Films, like
other art forms, are able to embody ideas, and both crystallise and
mobilise cultural debates. While they are able to challenge hegemonic
ideologies, given that the majority of them are created and embedded within capitalist, corporate-owned enterprises, the texts that are
most often produced therefore habitually adopt and tend to inculcate
dominant ideological perspectives. Some of the most interesting works
on the relationship between the media and culture in recent years, like
those by the scholars Alison Landsberg and Andrew Hoskins, have
attempted to examine this relationship. In what ways do films and television programmes reach beyond the frames of the screen and function
like visceral 'prosthetic memories' (Landsberg 2003) or 'media flash-
frames' (Hoskins 2004), which, according to some, are able to become
as impactful as first-hand experience itself? While their methodolo-
gies are diverse, the conclusions of many of these writers are similar:
film does much more than reflect the cultures and times in which it is
made; in fact, it is able to participate in their formation in potent and
affective ways. Indeed, in recent years an expanding body of empirical
research has also emerged on this subject which seems to confirm what
many cultural theoreticians have speculated about for decades: that
the media, and in particular film, plays a decisive role in how people
come to view the world (see Zacks 2014; Marsh, Butler & Umanath
2012). In what way the events of the 'War on Terror' became represented in the films made in the post-9/11 years and how they went on
to contribute to the discourse surrounding the war, both at the time
and for subsequent generations, is the subject of this volume.

Figure I.1 The shadow cast by the World Trade Center was a prominent one both before and after 11 September 2001. Permission granted by Nathan Benn.

The volume itself is called *American Cinema in the Shadow of 9/11*, adopting one of the most widely used metaphors for the substantial impact of 9/11 and the 'War on Terror' on American and global culture, indicative of the still-lingering presence of 9/11. Writers, commentators, politicians and filmmakers have turned to this most malleable of metaphors regularly: from Brian Michael Jenkins' and John Paul Godges' edited collection *The Long Shadow of 9/11: America's Response to Terrorism* (2011) to Kimberly Tan's article at the *Huffington Post*, 'Growing up in the shadow of 9/11'. Even more recent tragedies like the Boston Marathon Bombing (15 April 2013) and what is being called 'the 2014 Ferguson unrest' have become viewed through the prism of this flexible metaphor (see Kazianis 2013; Robison 2014). Regardless of the accuracy of the assertion, it has become an almost ever-present one and was even parodied in *The Onion Magazine*, in an article entitled 'The puppies of 9/11: Becoming full-grown dogs in the shadow of terror'. Discussing his 2005 alien invasion film *War of the Worlds*, Steven Spielberg stated, 'It seemed like the time was right for me as a filmmaker to let the audience experience an alien that is a little less pleasant than E.T. Today, in the shadow of 9/11, I think the film has found a place in society' (quoted in Hard). Several people have argued that Spielberg's film, and many genre films like it, have had a similar relationship to 9/11 and the 'War on Terror' as the cycle of alien invasion films like *The Thing From Another World* (1951), *The War of the Worlds* (1953) and *Invasion of the Body Snatchers* (1956) had to the prevailing anxieties of the Cold War era in which they were made (see Matthews 2007; McSweeney 2014). It is entirely appropriate then that all three of these Cold War-era texts have been subsequently remade in the post-9/11 era, each time reflecting the changing fears and anxieties of the decade.

During the 2016 American presidential election campaign this shadow continued to loom as potential nominees from both sides of the political spectrum evoked 9/11 to support their candidacy, as many politicians have done since September 2001. On 14 November 2015, in the second Democratic presidential debate, Hillary Clinton emphatically reminded America that she had 'represented New York on 9/11 when we were attacked' (quoted in Fox). The Republican presidential candidate Donald Trump went even further, suggesting, 'I believe that if I were running things [in 2001], I doubt those families would have – I doubt those people would have been in the country [referring to those who perpetrated the 9/11 attacks]' (quoted in Alexander). Trump also claimed that he had seen 'thousands' of Muslims celebrating the attacks in Jersey City, New Jersey (quoted in Kessler) and had even viewed people jumping from the World Trade Center from his penthouse (quoted in Tait). Donald Trump, more aware than most of the power of the image to move Americans, funded screenings of Michael Bay's *13 Hours: The Secret Soldiers of Benghazi* (2016) as part of his campaign tour in January 2016. While neither Hillary Clinton nor Barack Obama is portrayed directly in the story of a six-man security team who sought to defend the American diplomatic compound from attacks in Benghazi, Libya on 11 September 2012, the film dramatises the controversial and disputed 'stand down order', the limitations placed on the security of the compound ('Uncle Sam's on a budget right now') and the lack of air support for those on the ground, implying that the blame for the event should be placed squarely on the Obama administration. Andrea Tantaros of Fox News' *Outnumbered* (2014–), suggested that 'anyone [who] sees this movie . . . and then goes on to vote for Hillary Clinton . . . [is] a criminal' (Fox News, *Outnumbered*, 19 January 2016). However, an unnamed representative of the CIA had a very different opinion of the film, stating, 'It's a distortion of the events and people who served in Benghazi that night. It's shameful that, in order to highlight the heroism of some, those responsible for the movie felt the need to denigrate the courage of other Americans who served in harm's way' (quoted in Goldman and Miller).[1]

Critical explorations of post-9/11 film are an emerging topic in contemporary film studies, as evidenced by the growing number of monographs published on the topic with every year that passes. University courses on post-9/11 cinema all over the globe are now being taught to students who have very little memory of the events themselves and within a handful of years will be taught to students who were only born after 11 September 2001. This volume joins a multi-disciplinary body of work in an attempt to re-evaluate what '9/11' and the 'War on Terror' have come to mean both to people who lived through those years and what they might mean to generations to come. It is a disavowal of that recurring aphoristic platitude that '9/11 changed everything' but at the same time an engagement with the understanding that 9/11 was a seismic cultural event with far-reaching cultural implications. Film is far from a disposable pop culture artefact, as which it has frequently been dismissed, and has emerged as nothing less than 'the locus for America's negotiation of September 11 and its aftermath' (Schopp and Hill 13).

It has proven invaluable for many scholars to look for cinematic precedents in their examinations of how the 'War on Terror' has been portrayed on the screen. Films about the Vietnam War (with one or two exceptions) did not emerge until after the end of the war itself, whereas

Figure I.2 In the post-9/11 era both the themes and iconography of the 'War on Terror' narrative were frequently incorporated into genre films. Here *Battle: Los Angeles* (2011) draws extensively on the conflicts in Iraq and Afghanistan to give its cinematography resonance.

a significant number of films about Iraq and Afghanistan were made during the conflict, beginning with *American Soldiers: A Day in Iraq* as early as 2005, which was followed by a veritable wave of films in 2007 and 2008 including *In the Valley of Elah* (2007), *Redacted* (2007), *Battle for Haditha* (2007), *Stop-Loss* (2008) and *The Hurt Locker* (2008), all of which were made while major combat operations were still continuing. It is interesting to note that films about the Vietnam War almost entirely stopped being produced after the start of the 'War on Terror', as one national crisis seemed to have been replaced in the cultural imaginary by another.[2] However, while they stopped being made, their influence on combat films set in Afghanistan and Iraq was profound, as Paul Haggis, the writer and director of *In the Valley of Elah*, observed: 'There's a freedom I think that we got from the folks who made the films about Vietnam. We started learning from that, and we're standing on their shoulders.' He continued, 'I think if the nightly news was doing its job, we wouldn't have to do some of these films. Because we aren't getting the news of what's truly happening to our men and women' (quoted in 'Filmmakers Take a Closer Look').[3]

While many of the essays in this collection concern themselves with explicit dramatisations of the 'War on Terror', some turn to allegorical films which emerge just as, if not more, impactful than those which directly represent the conflict. For a variety of reasons allegorical texts have often had more freedom to engage politically with the eras in which they were made (see Benjamin 1977; Jameson 1981). In the cinematic arts one does not need to look far for allegorical texts of worth which often emerge as startling manifestations of the fears and anxieties of their respective eras (see Weimar-era German cinema, post-Second World War Japanese science fiction film or Cold War American science fiction film). Given the cultural resonance of the 'War on Terror', it comes as no surprise that many allegorical films were able to bear witness to this fractious period, mirroring the events of the decade in the form of alien invasions, zombie outbreaks, superhero films, disaster films or even 'torture porn', each projecting their narratives through the prism of 9/11 and the 'War on Terror'. It hardly needs to be said that the 'War on Terror' becomes manifested in science fiction films like *Children of Men* (2006), *War of the Worlds*, *Cloverfield* (2008), *Avatar* (2009), *Monsters* (2010), *Battle: Los Angeles* (2011) and *Edge of Tomorrow* (2014), just as the 1960s and 1970s became projected in the so-called 'Vietnam Westerns' like *The Wild Bunch* (1969), *Little Big Man* (1970), *Soldier Blue* (1970) and *Ulzana's Raid* (1972), which depicted the war in Vietnam allegorically, and with considerable scepticism, several years before the war was portrayed explicitly on American screens (see Pye 1981).

Figure I.3 In a reversal of a recurring visual motif in American cinema after 9/11, Bruce Wayne (Ben Affleck) runs *into* the dust and debris created by falling towers in *Batman versus Superman: Dawn of Justice* (2016).

The malleability of allegory might be regarded as one of its most appealing qualities. In this way a film like Zack Snyder's *300* (2005), despite being based on a graphic novel written in 1998 and set in 480 BC, was read by many cultural commentators as a visceral manifestation of prevailing cultural fears and fantasies of the 'War on Terror' era. The film's depiction of a heroic last stand by a small group of outnumbered Spartan warriors against a Persian horde provoked a range of different interpretations: it was read by Stephen Prince as 'an argument and a justification for waging war against Iraq and Iran' (291), whereas Slavoj Žižek saw something very different, associating the Persian 'multiculturalist different-lifestyles paradise' with American culture against the 'fundamentalist' Spartans (69). Regardless of one's interpretation, it is readily apparent that the film is bound to the decade in which it was made, and, as Hamid Dabashi memorably suggested, 'If we ever forget what G. W. Bush's America felt like, it will take only ten minutes of *300* to remind us' (quoted in James: 20).

What is certain is that *every* film is ideological, regardless of its genre or subject matter, as Jean-Louis Comolli and Jean Narboni convincingly argued in *Cahiers du Cinéma* in 1976: 'every film is political, inasmuch as it is determined by the ideology which produces it' (24–5). Films which seem on the surface easy to dismiss can be regarded as acutely revealing manifestations of ideology, whether their writers and directors intended them to be or not, as American film in the new millennium functioned as a battleground in which a war of meanings was waged. Post-9/11 cinema is a reaffirmation of the power of film to function as a cultural barometer in an age when new forms of digital media increasingly threaten its

Figure I.4 Not an actual image of the World Trade Center, but a digital re-creation of it for Oliver Stone's *World Trade Center* (2006).

pre-eminence as the dominant art form. It was in this era that US Senators Dianne Feinstein (Democrat, CA), John McCain (Republican, AZ) and Carl Levin (Democrat, MI) felt compelled to write an open letter to Sony Pictures in December 2012 in which they expressed the fear that Kathryn Bigelow's *Zero Dark Thirty* 'has the potential to shape American public opinion in a disturbing and misleading manner', and *American Sniper* was able to become the highest-grossing domestic film of the year and a cultural phenomenon in a genre which just a few years before had been labelled as 'box office poison'.[4] Just as our understanding of both the Second World War and the Vietnam War has been comprehensively shaped by the films produced about them, so will film play a distinctive role in how the 'War on Terror' comes to be remembered.

The essays contained in this volume present an interrogation of some of the defining American films of the new millennium. Collectively they attempt to discern to what extent film was not only able to trace the ideological currents of the first decade of the twenty-first century but, in very potent ways, also shape them. **Part I** of the collection considers films which dramatise the events of the 'War on Terror' directly: whether it is the day of 11 September 2001 and its aftermath (in films like *United 93* [2006], *World Trade Center* and *Extremely Loud and Incredibly Close* [2011]) or the conflicts in Iraq and Afghanistan (in *American Sniper, Zero Dark Thirty* and *The Hurt Locker* [2008]). If one has any doubts about film's ability to function as both a barometer and a catalyst of national discourse one only needs to turn to Clint Eastwood's *American Sniper*, here discussed by John Shelton Lawrence and Robert Jewett in the opening chapter of the volume. Lawrence and Jewett return to the terrain of their ground-breaking and influential works on the relationship between American film and culture, *The American Monomyth* (1988) and *The Myth of the American Superhero* (2002), in 'The Mythic Shape of *American Sniper* (2015)', in which they explore how far Eastwood's film can be regarded as reaffirming the tropes of heroic narratives about American wars, or whether it offers a challenge to them. Their lucid and multi-layered engagement with the figure of Chris Kyle – both the person and the film's vivid incarnation of him – examines the reasons why the film has resonated so profoundly with vast sections of the American public, to the extent that it was not only able to earn more money at the domestic box office than every single war film set in Iraq and Afghanistan before it combined, but as of writing is now the most financially successful American war film ever made. More complicated than many gave it credit for, *American Sniper* marks a shift in how the 'War on Terror' has come to be remembered and creates a very different vision of the conflict compared to films like *Battle for Haditha* (2007) and *Redacted* (2007). It is arguably part of a conscious effort to reframe the events of the Iraq War and reclaim the conflict in the national imaginary in a very similar way to the process in which Hollywood engaged with the Vietnam War in films like *The Deer Hunter* (1978), *Platoon* (1986) and more recently *We Were Soldiers* (2002). The cumulative effect of these portrayals, both of the Vietnam War and the conflicts in Iraq and Afghanistan, is the depiction of the American soldier as the primary victim of their respective conflicts, not, as one might expect, the Vietnamese, Iraqis and Afghanistanis who died and were wounded in their hundreds and thousands, if not millions.

In **Chapter 2**, 'Responding to Realities or Telling the Same Old Story? Mixing Real-world and Mythic Resonances in *The Kingdom* (2007) and *Zero Dark Thirty* (2012)', Geoff King also explores the specificity of post-9/11 American film by situating his two case studies in a rich cultural and historical landscape. As he argued in his seminal *Spectacular Visions: Hollywood in the Age of the Blockbuster* (2000), King maintains than many American films can be read as simultaneously of their time and as part of the American mythological tradition. While the Western genre is long gone as a cultural force, traces of its DNA remain embodied in many contemporary American films, and both *The Kingdom* and *Zero Dark Thirty* demonstrate the efficacy of the cinematic medium to embody cultural understandings of the 'War on Terror' era at the same time as they evoke the tropes of the American frontier narrative, despite being set very firmly in the contemporary Middle East. Like *American Sniper*, *Zero Dark Thirty* proved to be one of the most culturally resonant films of the period, but King largely sidesteps the well-travelled debate about whether the film endorses torture or not in favour of a detailed reading of how Bigelow's affectual drama (and also Peter Berg's *The Kingdom*) imposes fictional or mythic-ideological frameworks onto its real-world narratives (see Westwell, McSweeney, Chaudhuri).

In **Chapter 3**, 'Acts of Redemption and "The Falling Man" Photograph in Post-9/11 US Cinema', Guy Westwell, who has written his own monograph on the impact of the 'War on Terror' on American film, *Parallel Lines: Post-9/11 Cinema* (2014), takes as a starting point one of the quintessential images of the 'War on Terror' era, the photograph of the unidentified 'falling man' taken on 11 September 2001 by Richard Drew. Such has been the impact of the picture, which Mark D. Thompson described as 'perhaps the most powerful image of despair at the beginning of the twenty-first century' (63), it has been returned to in a variety of forms over the years: in art, literature, television and film. Westwell considers how the image (and the World Trade Center itself) has been co-opted by a variety of authors to function as a prism through which prevailing attitudes towards 9/11 have been projected. In a detailed analysis of two such examples, *Extremely Loud and Incredibly Close* (2011) and *The Walk* (2015), Westwell engages with questions of representation and identity, memory and trauma (both on a personal and cultural level) and argues that, as Mark Lacey suggested, American cinema in the first decades of the new millennium became 'a space where "commonsense" ideas about global politics and history are (re)-produced and where stories about what is acceptable behaviour from states and individuals are naturalised and legitimated' (614).

Chapters 4 and 5 both turn their attention to an area of post-9/11 film which has been largely neglected in studies of the topic: the cinematic representations of Muslims in American film in the 'War on Terror' decades. Both Chapter 4, Paul Petrovic's '"You be very mindful of how you act": Post-9/11 Culture and Arab American Subjectivities in Joseph Castelo's *The War Within* (2005) and Hesham Issawi's *AmericanEast* (2008)' and Chapter 5, 'Refracting Fundamentalism in Mira Nair's *The Reluctant Fundamentalist* (2012)' by Ana Cristina Mendes and Karen Bennett, explore films which offer a rare refocalisation of American cinema's habitual marginalisation, if not erasure, of Muslims from cinema screens and a challenge to what Jack Shaheen, the author of *Reel Bad Arabs: How Hollywood Vilifies a People* (2009), has called the perpetuation of stereotypes of 'bombers, belly dancers, or billionaires' (Shaheen: 13). In Chapter 4 Petrovic asserts that *The War Within* (directed by Joseph Castrello and based on a screenplay by Tom Glynn and the Pakistani American actor-writer Ayad Akhtar, who also plays the lead role in the film and went on to win the Pulitzer Prize for his play *Disgraced* [2013]) and Hesham Issawi's *AmericanEast* are two of very few American films to centralise the experience of American Muslim lives in their narratives and portray their characters with a sense of humanity and cultural sensitivity instead of crudely drawn caricatures. In Chapter 5 Mendes and Bennett argue that while Mira Nair's 2012 adaptation of Mohsin Hamid's 2007 award-winning novel *The Reluctant Fundamentalist* also places the experience of a Muslim, Changez Khan (Riz Ahmed), at the centre of the narrative, this is problematised by the compromises of adapting the complicated and morally ambiguous source on which it is based for the demands of the mainstream market. Mendes and Bennett concede that *The Reluctant Fundamentalist* is a rare example of an American film which breaks free of the America-centric view of the 'War on Terror' and in doing so destabilises the habitual privileging of American subjectivity and authority, but that adhering to many of the tropes of the thriller genre results in a film in which much of the moral relativity of Hamsin's novel becomes lost in translation.

Moving from films which explicitly dramatise the 'War on Terror' to those that are deeply influenced by it but do not, for the most part, portray it directly, **Part II** of the collection begins with **Chapter 6**, Vincent M. Gaine's analysis of perhaps the defining action-adventure series of the era (or of any era), the iconic figure of Ian Fleming's James Bond in '"Not now that strength": Embodiment and Globalisation in Post-9/11 James Bond'. In a dynamic investigation of Daniel Craig's four films as James Bond, from his first appearance in *Casino Royale* (2006) to his fourth film *Spectre* (2015), Gaine explores the thematic and stylistic variations undertaken in the Craig era. Craig's Bond, as Gaine astutely reveals, is as intrinsically connected to the post-9/11 decades as the first incarnation of the character played by Sean Connery was to the Cold War era in which the original books and films were written and set. In this chapter, Gaine proposes that the Bond franchise, more than any other, given its longevity, is uniquely placed to observe changing cultural and socio-political trends. The Craig Bond emerges as a much more complicated figure than his predecessors, both emphatically masculine and yet at the same time distinctly fallible, but a resolutely more human figure because of it. Daniel Craig's interpretation of the character, as Gaine observes, is a Bond who bleeds and one who is traumatised rather than a figure who glides almost effortlessly through his adventures with hardly a scratch, as he once did in the eras of Connery, Moore and Brosnan.

Adam Knee continues this discussion of the action/adventure genre in **Chapter 7**, 'Training the Body Politic: Networked Masculinity and the "War on Terror" in Hollywood Film', offering a detailed analysis of the representation of masculinity and agency in two Hollywood films, *Unstoppable* (2010) and *Source Code* (2011), which exhibit striking similarities at a range of levels, from their narratives to deeper structures of gendered character function, theme and geo-political perspective that, he contends, are a manifestation of distinctly post-9/11 American concerns. Like Vincent M. Gaine's chapter on James Bond, Knee analyses both the *variations* inherent in the genre in the wake of 9/11 and the *consistencies* of the parameters of American mainstream film, and, more specifically, a developing conceptualisation of modes of disciplined masculinity necessitated by the nation's 'War on Terror' narrative. Knee concludes with a comparative analysis of a pre-9/11 film and its post-9/11 remake in which these parameters are brought to the fore: the original Paul Verhoeven *RoboCop* (1987) and *RoboCop* (2014) directed by José Padilha.

Chapters 8 and 9 both look to the present by way of the past in their analysis of films which are set in the nineteenth and twentieth centuries, but are dramatised through the filter of twenty-first-century American experience. In **Chapter 8** Andrew Schopp explores the recent films of Quentin Tarantino in his '"Gettin' Dirty": Tarantino's Vengeful Justice, The Marked Viewer and Post-9/11 America', and in **Chapter 9**, in a piece called 'Stop the Clocks: *Lincoln* and Post-9/11 Cinema', Ian Scott presents an analysis of Steven Spielberg's *Lincoln*. Both chapters consider in what way films might play, as Robert Burgoyne has suggested, 'a decisive role articulating an image of America that informs, or in some cases challenges, our sense of national self-identity, an image of nation that is projected to the world' (Burgoyne: 2). Andrew Schopp argues that the representation of morality and history in *Inglourious Basterds* (2009), *Django Unchained* (2012) and *The Hateful Eight* (2015) is a particularly complicated and distinctly post-modern one, inherently connected to the American vision of the world after 9/11. His analysis of Tarantino's texts from the perspective of justice, civilisation and revenge makes an invaluable contribution to existing commentaries on Tarantino's work. He also considers their status as allohistorical narratives (commonly referred to as alternative history), which encompasses an awareness of the fact that Tarantino's films are seemingly divided into a unified diegetic world in which a significant number of his characters reside (see *Reservoir Dogs* [1992],

Pulp Fiction [1994], *Inglourious Basterds*, *Django Unchained* and *The Hateful Eight*) and the films that these characters might go to see in this alternate universe (*Death Proof* [2007], *Kill Bill: Volume One* [2003], *Kill Bill: Volume Two* [2004]). On the surface a range of inter-related strands connect his films, like the branding of Red Apple cigarettes, characters being related to each other, i.e. the Vega brothers in *Pulp Fiction* and *Reservoir Dogs*, Sergeant Donny Donowitz in *Inglourious Basterds* being the father of filmmaker Lee Donowitz in *True Romance* (1993), and recently 'English' Pete Hickox in *The Hateful Eight* being an ancestor of Archie Hickox in *Inglourious Basterds*, but this fluidity is complicated even further both by Tarantino's liberal appropriation of material from other sources as inspiration and the way the films seem to both reflect, engage and even comment on each others' narratives.

As well as its discussion of American history and cinematic tempo-rality, Schopp's work on Tarantino is connected directly to **Chapter 9**, Ian Scott's analysis of Steven Spielberg's *Lincoln*, by the presence of the enigmatic president in both of their narratives: while, of course, Abraham Lincoln plays a central role in Spielberg's *Lincoln*, the histori-cal figure of Lincoln plays a peripheral but important figure in Quen-tin Tarantino's *The Hateful Eight* through the repeated appearance of Major Marquis Warren's (Samuel L. Jackson) letter, which he claims to have received from Lincoln himself. Ian Scott's analysis of Spielberg's film reads *Lincoln* as one of the most resonant and culturally important historical films of the new millennium and explores how far it might resonate with the tempestuous political climate of the 'War on Terror' era. It was around the time of the production of *Lincoln* that several commentators began to talk of an 'Obama Cinema' (see J. Hoberman 2012; Izo 2014) and despite being set more than one hundred and fifty years before, Spielberg's *Lincoln* was released at American cinemas in the same week that President Barack Obama was elected for his second term of office. Scott offers a range of vibrant and compelling perspec-tives on the film: reading it as a challenge to traditional notions of the biopic, as a treatise on historical and cinematic time, but most impor-tantly connecting it to cinematic depictions of the iconic president from D. W. Griffith's *Abraham Lincoln* (1930), through John Ford's *Young Mr Lincoln* (1939) and even to the allohistorical fantasy 'mashup' of *Abraham Lincoln: Vampire Hunter* (2012).

The second part concludes with **Chapter 10**, a strikingly original piece by Stephen Joyce which questions the very nature of the influ-ence of 9/11 and the 'War on Terror' on the American film industry. In 'Foreshadows of the Fall: Questioning 9/11's Impact on American Attitudes' he argues that it is possible to conclude that the changes many have seen in post-9/11 American cinema, and indeed America's real-world reactions to the traumatic events which occurred on 11 September 2001, were actually comprehensively anticipated by American genre cinema throughout the second half of the twentieth century. Joyce's suggestion is not that American cinema was in any way prophetic, but that America's responses to 9/11 replicate patterns so encoded into American ideological belief systems that they have been filtered into Hollywood films for decades. Using three films made prior to 9/11 – *Pearl Harbor* (2001), *Independence Day* (1996) and *The Siege* (1998) – he traces these patterns contained within their narratives and even their mise en scène. Joyce's argument underlines the importance of avoiding the allure of simplistic connections between 9/11 and American film, the likes of which have permeated some otherwise very fine academic work on the subject. This is undoubtedly a manifestation of the apophenic desire to see 9/11 and the 'War on Terror' reflected everywhere (see Pollard).[5] It is important for scholars of post-9/11 film to remember that explosions, dust clouds and debris existed and were placed on the frames of American films before 11 September 2001. Just as important is the need to avoid hyperbole, as Kristian Verslys found it hard to do when he asserted that 9/11 represented a 'total breakdown of all meaning-making systems' (2).

Part III, the final part of the collection, focuses on allegorical representations of the 'War on Terror' and collectively argues the significance of the form's undervalued ability to represent underlying cultural tensions and contradictions often in ways more resonant than direct dramatisations have been able to. In the introductory essay to this section, **Chapter 11**, '"Daddy, I'm scared. Can we go home?": Fear and Allegory in Frank Darabont's *The Mist* (2007)', Terence McSweeney addresses the potency of the horror genre to function as a cultural barometer by engaging with some of the defining anxieties of the era in a metaphorical fashion. Discussing Frank Darabont's *The Mist*, an adaptation of the Stephen King novella, McSweeney reads the film's narrative concerning a disparate group of small-towners stranded inside a local supermarket plagued by what might be supernatural beasts outside and, perhaps even more dangerously, religious extremism inside as an articulate treatise on prevailing new-millennial fears. *The Mist* was one of many American genre films which seemed to dramatise Susan Faludi's assertion that, 'The intrusions of September 11 broke the dead bolt on our protective myth, the illusion that we are masters of our own security, that our might makes our homeland impregnable, that our families are safe in the bower of our communities and our women and children are safe in the arms of their men' (2007: 12). *The Mist* uses familiar genre tropes but localises them to the very specific coordinates of post-9/11 America in a comparable way to how the most resonant horror and science fiction films have done to their own cultures and eras throughout the decades. McSweeney argues that there is a transgressive potency in the horror genre to confront some of the myths which have been at the centre of American popular film since its inception, and in particular the 'master narrative' of the 'War on Terror' which emerged after 9/11.

Chapter 12 remains with the horror genre, but takes a broader overview of one of the defining trends of the American film industry which has progressively gathered pace in the first years of the twenty-first century: the increasing prevalence of the remake. In 'The Terrible, Horrible Desire to Know: Post-9/11 Horror Remakes, Reboots, Sequels and Prequels', James Kendrick analyses the rising cultural and commercial fortunes of the American horror film which experienced between 1995 and 2005 increases of more than 80 per cent in terms of production and 106 per cent in terms of market share ('Horror: Year-by-Year Market Share'). In the first decade of the 21st century, 2007 was the biggest year for American horror films (it was also the year of the release of *The Mist* discussed in the previous chapter), with thirty-one releases accounting for 7.16 per cent of the total market share of the US domestic box office ('Horror: Year-by-Year Market Share'), as opposed to just sixteen releases in 1995. Yet Kendrick does not dismiss this development as being purely economically motivated; rather he asks what can these modern horror films, very often remakes of classic horror films of the 1950s and the 1970s, tell us about the cultural and political climate they emerge from? In an incisive analysis of the recurrent tropes in post-9/11 American horror films, Kendrick points out that horror's persistent ties to cultural anxiety provide an intriguing insight into their times as they become increasingly darker, more graphic and deny their characters any sense of hope or redemption. Most interestingly, Kendrick observes, the contemporary horror film replaces the ambiguity of the defining horror films of the 1970s with a desire to explain which he suggests parallels American society's need to understand following the terrorist attacks on 11 September 2001. Kendrick then turns to Rob Zombie's 2007 remake of John Carpenter's original *Halloween* (1978) as an articulation of many of the tropes discussed in the first part of the essay, offering some surprising conclusions concerning the power of the horror film to reflect cultural unease.

Moving to the science fiction genre, but remaining within the field of allegory, Chapter 13 sees Christine Muller scrutinise one of the most economically successful and culturally impactful genre variations to emerge from the American film industry in the last two decades, the renaissance of the superhero film. While it is an emergence which has been criticised by many (see Alan Moore's assessment of it as a 'cultural catastrophe' in Flood 2014), its impact has been so profound that to dismiss it seems imprudent, and, as Richard Gray and Betty Kaklamanidou observed in their *The 21st Century Superhero: Essays on Gender, Genre and Globalization in Film* (2011), in many ways the 2000s were the 'decade of the superhero' (1). Indeed, one can learn a great deal about a culture by its heroic mythology. Just as the ancient Greeks had tales of Hercules and Achilles, and late nineteenth-century America turned to mythologised stories of Wyatt Earp and Davy Crockett, in the twentieth century and into the twenty-first, western culture found its heroic ideals embodied in comic-book heroes like Superman, Batman and Spider-Man. In Muller's chapter, 'Post-9/11 Power and Responsibility in the Marvel Cinematic Universe', she considers the relationship between the superhero film and the tumultuous post-9/11 era, exploring the ideological function of superhero narratives. Muller looks at how the Marvel Cinematic Universe often returned to trauma in a variety of forms in their films, which frequently emerge not as bloated blockbusters empty of resonance but texts which engage with the decade in deeply revealing ways (see DiPaolo and McSweeney). Far removed from the cartoonish fantasyscapes of Salkind-era *Superman* (1977) or the increasingly extravagant excesses of Tim Burton and Joel Schumacher's Batman years, the real-world-set Marvel Cinematic Universe films, beginning with *Iron Man* (2008), are deeply immersed in what we might call the ongoing 'War on Terror' narrative. While some writers have dismissed the genre as perpetuating hegemonic ideological systems (see Hassler-Forrest), Muller argues that they are able to, at times, offer more than the conservative world view with which they are primarily associated. The defining events of the 'War on Terror' era thus become replayed in the MCU through the melodramatic spectacle of the superhero genre.

This idea that the science fiction genre might function as a fertile way to engage with the times in which the films are made is also intriguingly explored in the two final chapters in the volume. Both **Chapter 14**, Sean Redmond's 'Nowhere Left to Zone in *Children of Men* (2006)', and **Chapter 15**, Steffen Hantke's 'Traumatise, Repeat, Finish: Military Science Fiction (Long) after 9/11 and Doug Liman's *Edge of Tomorrow* (2014)', offer a detailed analysis of two science fiction films which positively reverberate with the political climate of the decade, an example of 9/11 and the 'War on Terror' functioning as what Adam Lowenstein described as an 'allegorical moment' in his book *Shocking Representations: Historical Trauma, National Cinema and the Modern Horror Film* (2005). In **Chapter 14** Redmond contends that Alfonso Cuarón's richly symbolic dystopian drama *Children of Men* is a film haunted by the dread of both the traumatic diegetic incident that leads to the film's storyline (women not being able to conceive children for some unexplained reason) and the events of 9/11, which leaves its mark on the film's narrative and imagery in a range of ways. The collection concludes with Steffen Hantke's illuminating analysis of Doug Liman's *Edge of Tomorrow* from a variety of critical perspectives: discussing elements of self-reflexivity, star persona, the film's distinctly ludological central narrative conceit (on this point he offers an analysis of how this narrative strategy functions as a commentary on the idea of 'getting it right the next time'), to the melange of 'War on Terror' and 'greatest generation' themes presented throughout the film. Hantke makes the case that while it proved commercially underwhelming on original release, *Edge of Tomorrow* is worthy of critical reappraisal and analysis.

It is the hope of the authors of this collection that their work might be able to contribute to the growing discourse concerning the complicated interactions between media and culture in the post-9/11 period. More than fifteen years after the events of 11 September 2001, it is possible to conclude that, without fear of exaggeration, its impact is still being felt. The films produced by the American film industry in these years provide a valuable insight into the era; they are simultaneously a product of their times and frequently present us with an articulate commentary on them. If nothing else, they prove that the shadow of 9/11 still looms over American film and society and will continue to do so for the foreseeable future.

NOTES

1. It is worth noting that the role of the film *The Innocence of Muslims* (2012) was frequently discussed in relation to the motivations of those who attacked the diplomatic compound. Protests started in the US diplomatic mission in Cairo, Egypt before taking place in many countries across the Middle East.

2. American-made films about the Vietnam War slow down in the 1990s but after 2000 the only notable films about the conflict released are *The Quiet American* (2002) and *We Were Soldiers* (2002), which were both made before the wars in Iraq and Afghanistan, and *Rescue Dawn* (2006).

3. In his article 'The articulation of memory and desire: from Vietnam to the war in the Persian Gulf', John Storey provides a sustained analysis of the tropes of Vietnam War cinema which offers striking parallels to modern combat films.

4. Bill Everhart used 'box office poison' in 'Summer comes earlier to movie season', *The Berkshire Eagle,* 1 May 2009.

5. Tom Pollard does this several times in his interesting *Hollywood 9/11 Superheroes, Supervillains and Superdisasters* (2011), when he insists there is a 'subtle yet distinct post 9/11 message' (44) in Robert Zemeckis' *Beowulf* (2007), which apparently equates the three monsters Beowulf defeats with Bush's 'Axis of Evil': Iraq, North Korea and Iran.

REFERENCES

Alexander, Harriet (2015), 'Donald Trump: I would have prevented 9/11', *The Telegraph*, 18 October 2015, last accessed 6 January 2016: http://www.telegraph.co.uk/news/worldnews/donald-trump/11939480/Donald-Trump-I-would-have-prevented-911.html

Benjamin, Walter (1977), *The Origin of German Tragic Drama*, New York: Verso.

Burgoyne, Robert (2008), *The Hollywood Historical Film*, Oxford: Blackwell.

Chaudhuri, Shohini (2014), *Cinema of the Dark Side: Atrocity and the Ethics of Film Spectatorship*, Edinburgh: Edinburgh University Press.

Cinema of the Dark Side: Atrocity and the Ethics of Film Spectatorship (2014), Edinburgh: Edinburgh University Press.

Comolli, Jean-Louis and Jean Narboni (1976), 'Cinema/Ideology/Criticism', *Movies and Methods* (vol. 1), ed. Bill Nichols, Berkeley: University of California Press, pp. 22–30. (Originally printed in *Cahiers du Cinéma*, no. 216, October 1969.)

Dipaolo, Marc (2011), *War, Politics and Superheroes: Ethics and Propaganda in Comics and Film*, Jefferson, NC: McFarland.

Everhart, Bill (2009), 'Summer comes earlier to movie season', *The Berkshire Eagle*, 1 May 2009.

Faludi, Susan (2007), *The Terror Dream: Fear and Fantasy in Post 9/11 America*, Melbourne: Scribe.

Feinstein, Diane et al. (2012), 'Feinstein Releases Statement on *Zero Dark Thirty*', 19 December 2012, last accessed 7 August 2013: http://www.feinstein.senate.gov/public/index.cfm/press-releases?ID=b5946751-2054-404a-89b7-b81e1271efc9

'Filmmakers Take a Closer Look' (2007), *Associated Press*, 12 December 2007, last accessed 15 September 2010: http://www.msnbc.msn.com/id/20711050/

Flood, Alison (2014), 'Superheroes a "Cultural Catastrophe", says Comics Guru Alan Moore', *The Guardian*, 21 January 2014, last accessed 3 February 2016: http://www.theguardian.com/books/2014/jan/21/superheroes-cultural-catastrophe-alan-moore-comics-watchmen

Fox, Emily Jane (2015), 'Hillary Clinton still can't shake her Wall Street 9/11 debate Comment', *Vanity Fair*, 16 November 2015, last accessed 6 January 2016: http://www.vanityfair.com/news/2015/11/hillary-clinton-wall-street-september-11

Goldman, Adam, and Greg Miller (2016), 'Former CIA chief in Benghazi challenges the story line of the new movie "13 Hours"', *The Washington Post*, 15 January 2016, last accessed 27 January 2016: https://www.washingtonpost.com/world/national-security/former-cia-chief-in-benghazi-challenges-film-version-of-2012-attack/2016/01/15/9cf2defc-baf7-11e5-b682-4bb4dd403c7d_story.html

Gray, Richard J., and Betty Kaklamanidou (eds) (2011), *The 21st Century Superhero: Essays on Gender, Genre and Globalization in Film*, Jefferson, NC: McFarland.

Hard, Andrew (2005), '*ET* Turns Invader in *War of the Worlds*', *Fox News*, 29 June 2005, last accessed 25 June 2010: http://www.foxnews.com/story/0,2933,160952,00.html

Hassler-Forrest, Dan (2012), *Capitalist Superheroes: Caped Crusaders in the Neoliberal Age*, Washington, DC: John Hunt Publishing.

Hoberman, J. (2012), 'A New Obama Cinema?', *New York Books*, 11 February 2012, last accessed 5 February 2016: http://www.nybooks.com/daily/2012/02/11/new-obama-cinema-clint-eastwood-halftime/

'Horror: Year by Year Market Share' (2008), 30 September 2008, last accessed 8 February 2016: http://thenumbers.com/market/Genres/Horror.php

Hoskins, Andrew (2004), *Televising War: From Vietnam to Iraq*, London: Continuum.

Izo, David Garret (2014), *Movies in the Age of Obama*, Lanham: Rowman & Littlefield.

James, Nick (2009), 'Films of 2008', *Sight and Sound*, 19.1, January, pp. 16–29.

Jameson, Frederic (1981), *The Political Unconscious: Narrative as a Socially Symbolic Act*, Ithaca: Cornell University Press.

Jenkins, Brian Michael, and John Paul Godges (eds) (2011), *The Long Shadow of 9/11: America's Response to Terrorism*, Santa Monica, CA: Rand Publishing.

Kazianis, Harry (2013), 'Seeing Boston's Tragedy Through the Shadow of 9/11', *The Diplomat*, 17 April 2013, last accessed 6 January 2016: http://thediplomat.com/2013/04/seeing-bostons-tragedy-through-the-shadow-of-911/

Kellner, Douglas (2010), *Cinema Wars: Hollywood Film and Politics in the Bush-Cheney Era*, Oxford: Wiley-Blackwell Press.

Kessler, Glenn (2015), 'Trump's outrageous claim that "thousands" of New Jersey Muslims celebrated the 9/11 attacks', *The Washington Post*, 22 November 2015, last accessed 6 January 2016: https://www.washingtonpost.com/news/fact-checker/wp/2015/11/22/donald-trumps-outrageous-claim-that-thousands-of-new-jersey-muslims-celebrated-the-911-attacks/

King, Geoff (2000), Spectacular Narratives: *Hollywood in the Age of the Blockbuster*, London: I. B. Tauris.

Kracauer, Siegfried (1947), *From Caligari to Hitler. A Psychological Profile of the German Film*, Princeton: Princeton University Press.

Lacey, Mark (2003), 'War, Cinema and Moral Anxiety', *Alternatives*, 28, pp. 611–36.

Landsberg, Alison (2003), 'Prosthetic memory: the ethics and politics of memory in an age of mass culture', in Paul Grainger (ed.), *Memory and Popular Film*, Manchester: Manchester University Press, pp. 144–61.

Lawrence, John Shelton, and Robert Jewett (1988), *The American Monomyth*, Lanham: University Press of America.

— (2002), *The Myth of the American Superhero*, Grand Rapids, MI: W. B. Erdmans.

Lowenstein, Adam (2005), *Shocking Representations: Historical Trauma, National Cinema and the Modern Horror Film*, New York: Columbia University Press.

Marsh, E. J., A. C. Butler and S. Umanath (2012), 'Using Fictional Sources in the Classroom: Applications from Cognitive Psychology', *Educational Psychology Review*, 24, pp. 449–69.

Matthews, Melvin E. (2007), *Hostile Aliens, Hollywood and Today's News: 1950s Science Fiction Films and 9/11*, New York: Algora Publishing.

McSweeney, Terence (2014), *The 'War on Terror' and American Film: 9/11 Frames per Second*, Edinburgh: Edinburgh University Press.

Pheasant-Kelly, Francis (2013), *Fantasy Film Post-9/11*, London and New York: I. B. Tauris.

Pollard, Tom (2011), *Hollywood 9/11 Superheroes, Supervillains and Super Disasters*, Boulder: Paradigm Publishers.

Prince, Stephen (2009), *Firestorm: American Film in the Age of Terrorism*, New York: Columbia University Press.

'The puppies of 9/11: Becoming full-grown dogs in the shadow of terror' (2012), *The Onion Magazine*, 14 September 2012, last accessed 6 January 2015: http://www.theonion.com/graphic/the-puppies-of-911-becoming-full-grown-dogs-in-the-29567

Pye, Douglas (1981), 'Ulzana's Raid', *Movie*, 27/28, Winter/Spring, p. 79.

Robison, Gordon (2014), 'Long Shadow of 9/11 over Ferguson', *Gulf News*, 19 August 2014, last accessed 6 January 2016: http://gulfnews.com/opinion/thinkers/long-shadow-of-9-11-over-ferguson-1.1374026

Schopp, Andrew and Matthew B. Hill (2009), 'Introduction: The Curious Knot', in Andrew Schopp and Matthew B. Hill (eds), *The War on Terror and American Popular Culture: September 11 and Beyond*, Madison: Fairleigh Dickinson University Press, pp. 11–42.

Shaheen, Jack (2009), *Reel Bad Arabs: How Hollywood Vilifies a People*, New York: Olive Branch Press.

Storey, John (2003), 'The articulation of memory and desire: from Vietnam to the war in the Persian Gulf', in Paul Grainger (ed.), *Memory and Popular Film*, Manchester: Manchester University Press.

Tait, Robert (2015), 'Donald Trump says he watched people jump from Twin Towers on 9/11 from his flat – four miles away', *The Telegraph*, 25 November 2015, last accessed 6 January 2016: http://www.telegraph.co.uk/news/worldnews/donald-trump/12015344/Donald-Trump-says-he-watched-people-jump-from-Twin-Towers-on-911-from-his-flat-four-miles-away.html

Tan, Kimberly (2011), 'Growing up in the shadow of 9/11', *Huffington Post*, 11 September 2011, last accessed 6 January 2016: http://www.huffingtonpost.com/kimberly-tan/post_3878_b_1874107.html

Thompson, Mark D. (2008), 'Luther on Despair', in Brian Rosner (ed.), *The Consolations of Theology*, Grand Rapids, MI: Eerdmans, pp. 51–74.

Verslys, Kristian (2009), *Out of the Blue: September 11th and the Novel*, New York: Columbia University Press.

Westwell, Guy (2014), *Parallel Lines: Post-9/11 Cinema*, London: Wallflower Press.

Wood, Robin (1986), *Hollywood from Vietnam to Reagan*, New York: Columbia University Press.

Zacks, Jeffrey (2014), *Flicker: Your Brain on Movies*, Oxford: Oxford University Press.

Žižek, Slavoj (2009), *In Defense of Lost Causes. Welcome to the Desert of the Real*, London: Verso.

PART I

Dramatisations of the 'War on Terror'

CHAPTER I

The Mythic Shape of *American Sniper* (2015)

John Shelton Lawrence and Robert Jewett

God blew that bullet and hit him.
Chris Kyle describing his 2,100 yard kill in an interview
with the *New York Post* (Buiso 2012)

Finally, the movie [American Sniper] gives America something it's lacked since the start of the war – a war hero on a truly national, cultural scale . . . Chris Kyle has entered the pantheon of American warriors – along with Alvin C. York and Audie Murphy – giving a new generation of young boys a warrior-hero to look up to, to emulate.
David French in the *National Review* (2015)

I.

More than any other single figure, Chris Kyle, author of the auto-biographical *American Sniper* (2012), seems to have emerged as a widely recognised and respected hero of the Global War on Terror (GWOT). This essay endeavours to locate his persona among the emblems of American mythology and ideology that emerged in the wars waged against so many enemies and that still offer no prospects of ending. One interpretative option to consider was described in our study *The Myth of the America Superhero* (2002) where we advised against the seductive myth of Golden Violence enacted by superheroes, scenarios that warrant the circumvention of law and institutional safeguards as well as punishments that miraculously never injure the innocent.

In *Captain America and the Crusade against Evil* (2003), anticipating the war with Iraq, we reminded readers about the US history of religiously tinged millennial crusading whose ideological premises are so often expressed by pop superheroes. In a kind of shorthand, we called that apocalyptic crusading mentality 'the Captain America Complex' because of the Captain's recurring apocalyptic battles to save the world in the comic book pages. The canonical statement of the 'Complex' in foreign policy had surfaced at the time of the Spanish American War when Albert J. Beveridge (1898) spoke these words to his fellow US Senators: 'Almighty God . . . has marked the American people as the chosen nation to finally lead in the regeneration of the world. This is the divine mission of America . . . We are the trustees of the world's progress, guardians of the righteous peace.'

Now that a US Navy sniper has moved to centre stage of the theatre where national memories are formed and unwelcome facts shoved behind the curtains, we want to explore the implications. Does Chris Kyle, murdered by a fellow Iraq veteran at the age of thirty-eight, fit the scheme of an American superhero? Is he an agent of the Captain America Complex? If not, where does he stand on the mythic spectrum? Moreover, what does Kyle's stature say about the popular understanding of how America has used its military power? Is Kyle's story understood as a cautionary tale? Has it fed the mythic momentum for 'the guardianship of the righteous peace' to which the nation has frequently committed itself? Or is there something new in this sniper story that demands altered conceptions of the popular American mythos?

II.

Before Chris Kyle burst forth with superstar rank in late 2014, America had travelled an episodic mythic journey during the previous thirteen years. There had been a cultural search for an inspiring figure to symbolise America's aspirations to create a safe, 'never again' world. George W. Bush referred to 'this crusade, this war on terrorism' and promised, 'We will rid the world of evil doers' (quoted in Purdum 2001). Drawing on the mythic, the president evoked the cowboy Western when he styled himself as sheriff, declaring on 19 September 2001, 'I want justice . . . There's an old poster out West that said, "Wanted, dead or alive".' In this vein he said of the Taliban, 'we're going to smoke them out' (quoted in Knowlton 2001). Surprisingly, in November 2001 US Special Forces *did* ride horses to capture Mazar-i-sharif in Afghanistan (Stanton 2009).

By 2002, President George W. Bush was sitting in the White House with Vice President Cheney chortling at *Der Spiegel*'s satirical cover for a feature article lamenting the pop superhero models that apparently inspired his Global War on Terror. Apparently indifferent to or wholly ignorant about the article's excoriating content, Bush was amused by his muscular Rambo rendition, and ordered thirty poster-sized enlargements for his White House staff (*Der Spiegel* 2002). Did Bush grin in recollecting that *Rambo: First Blood Part II* was marketed with the slogan 'No man, no war, no law can stop him'? In that same cartoon, Colin Powell appeared as Batman, Donald Rumsfeld as Conan the Barbarian, Dick Cheney as the Terminator and Condoleezza Rice as Catwoman.

Figure 1.1 During the giddiest phase of Bush's programme to 'rid the world of evil', Bush grinned at his Rambo biceps and trigger finger, taking pride rather than feeling shame over the ridicule. Public Domain Image. Uncredited photographer.

However, the sheriff approach to law enforcement – bringing evil doers to the jail for trial –ultimately felt too limited as a war vision for Bush and some of his key administrators. He signalled the emergence of a global, apocalyptic vision when he declared to the US Congress on 20 September, 'Our war on terror begins with Al Qaeda but does not end there. It will not end until every terrorist group of global reach has been found, stopped, and defeated' (Bush 2001a). Then in Atlanta he declared, 'We wage a war to save civilisation itself' and 'we know that our cause is just and victory is ultimately assured' (Bush 2001b). Senator John McCain joined with a call for ferocious killing in a global extermination of America's enemies: 'Shed a tear, and then get on with the business of killing our enemies as quickly as we can, and as ruthlessly as we must . . . Only the complete destruction of international terrorism and the regimes that sponsor it will spare America from further attack' (2001).

At the staff level in the White House, David Frum, President Bush's speech writer, quickly coined for 2002's State of the Union Address 'the axis of evil' phrase to identify Iran, Iraq and North Korea as existential threats to the United States (Borger 2003). More ambitiously, Frum's *An End to Evil* (2003), co-authored with Richard Perle – a sitting Chairman of Bush's Defense Policy Board Advisory Committee – seemed intoxicated with the notion that now the US had a moral warrant to establish an entire world of freedom and peace 'brought into being by American armed might and defended by American might' (279). The pair claimed to be achieving 'an end to evil' by spreading death among national leaders that they deemed unworthy to rule. Of Iran's Supreme Leader, they said:

> Ayatollah Khamenei has . . . no more right to control . . . Iran than any other criminal has to seize control of the persons and property of others. It's not always in our power to do something about such criminals, nor is it always in our interest, but when it is in our power and interest, we should toss dictators aside with no more compunction than a police sharpshooter feels when he downs a hostage-taker. (114)

Despite such expressions of the will to assassinate whom it pleased America to kill, the authors still adhered to the thought that 'we are fighting on behalf of the civilized world' (273). The apocalyptic, global scope remained intact in the commitment that 'we must deter *all* regimes that use terror as a weapon of state against anyone, American or not' (italics in authors' text: 82). This apocalyptic duo's hit list grew to seven, including Afghanistan and Iraq – wars already underway – as well as Iran, North Korea, Syria, Libya and Saudi Arabia: 'We must move boldly against them . . . And we don't have much time' (83). Startling omissions in their proposed rampage were the associated costs or dangers to America itself in 'ending evil' across the entire world – not to mention the damage to the national reputation inherent in disregarding so many treaties.

A broad expansion of targets characterised American policy as a consensus emerged in the Bush administration that many continents would have to be pacified. While the insurgent phase Operation Enduring Freedom Afghanistan was just beginning, the US launched Operation Iraqi Freedom in early 2003, in which Chris Kyle did four duty tours in Nasiriyah, Falluja, Ramadi and Sadr City. Other 'Enduring Freedom' franchises opened in the Philippines, the Horn of Africa, Pankisi Gorge (Republic of Georgia), the Trans-Sahara, the Caribbean and Central America, and Kyrgyzstan, as well as Operation Unified Protector in Libya (Bolger 2014: xiv). The goal of these operations was to depose or neutralise powers hostile to the United States while creating stable, democratically controlled social and political orders. President George W. Bush characterised the mission at the beginning of Operation Iraqi Freedom as one in which America would help 'Iraqis achieve a united, stable, and free country'. During this invasion he also promised that 'coalition forces will make every effort to spare innocent civilians from harm' (2003). The courageous agents of such a delicate task would need to be very discrete in applying military force.

In Iraq an early candidate for treatment as an American hero appeared in the figure of Pfc Jessica Lynch, a unit supply specialist severely injured in a truck accident. In 2007 she testified before Congress that the media and the military had lied about her 2003 actions in Iraq 'for their own gain', and she dismissed the 'story of the little girl Rambo from the hills who went down fighting' (Luo 2007).[1] Then there was Pat Tillman, who walked away from a professional football contract to fight in Afghanistan, where he apparently died from friendly fire. At that same hearing with Jessica Lynch, the Tillman family, including Kevin, who served in Afghanistan with Pat, denounced the lies which falsely depicted Pat valiantly dying from Taliban gunfire. They also excoriated the commander who forbade soldiers who knew the truth from revealing it to his brother (Luo 2007). Marcus Luttrell told a remarkable story of survival in his bestselling book *Lone Survivor* (2007), but it was only a story of personal victory since all of his comrades died – and an additional sixteen perished while attempting to rescue his unit. A further irony lay in his rescue by Afghan villagers whom he was tempted to kill but refrained from doing so by his fear of the consequences (320–1).[2] The American public has not been able to settle on a commander hero either. General David Petraeus was temporarily lionised after his leadership in the Surge of 2007, but his honour was stained by a sexual affair and a conviction that sentenced him to two years' probation for sharing classified information with his mistress (Schmidt and Appuzo 2015).

And then there were the atrocious embarrassments caused by the unheroic agents of the global campaign: those who perpetrated the tortures at Abu Ghraib prison (Danner 2004) and at Bagram in Afghanistan (Philips 2010); those who murdered twenty-four Iraqi civilians in Haditha (Englade 2015); Blackwater's mercenary guns that murdered Iraqi civilians (Pelton 2006); and a variety of other abuses that steadily shamed the nation. It would take a powerful story and actor to overcome these bad associations of the 'War on Terror', but Chris Kyle finally did this for many Americans, especially those who lived in his native state of Texas.

III.

Chris Kyle's fame among Texans was conveyed by the attendance of seven thousand at his televised memorial service in the Dallas Cowboys stadium on 14 February 2013, an event followed by a 200 mile-long cortège stretching from Midlothian to Austin's State Cemetery. His murder at the age of thirty-eight by a fellow veteran he was attempting to help added a note of martyrdom to his life. A fellow SEAL eulogised: 'His spirit will live on forever. Know this: legends never die, and Chris Kyle isn't gone. He is everywhere. Yes, he is Chris Kyle. He is "The Legend"' ('One Soldier's Journey' 2014). In 2015 Texas Governor Greg Abbott declared February 2 'Chris Kyle Day' (Holley 2015). Kyle's second book, *American Gun* (2013), was published posthumously and his spouse's *American Wife* (2015) followed. The titles of these books convey the impression that he, his weapons and his wife are essentially iconic for the experience of military service in the anti-terror war.

The blockbuster successes of Kyle's autobiography and the film based upon it make it likely that Chris Kyle will emerge as the most remembered actor in the 'War on Terror'. Positive appreciations of the film came from the White House. Michelle Obama, who adopted veterans' care as a personal project, became a film commentator in praising the film's emotional content:

This film touches on many of the emotions and experiences I have heard first-hand from military families over these past few years. This movie reflects those wrenching stories I've heard, the complex journeys that our men and women in uniform endure, the complicated world, the decisions they are tasked with every day, the stresses of balancing love of family with love of country, and the challenges of transitioning back home. (Quoted in Oldenburg 2015)

The interplay between book and film

Chris Kyle's nickname 'Tex' was replaced by 'the Legend' after an exceptionally long shot in Fallujah, Iraq (Kyle 2012: 276–7). His moniker is a cautionary flag about attempting to use either his book or the film based on it as a literal transcription of his life. Before *American Sniper* became a blockbuster film, the book of 2012 that provided its template had already sold more than a million copies (Lewis 2015), thus providing significant background information for many in the film audience. Although the book accurately reflects much of Kyle's life, he used professional co-authors, masters of popular serial commando fiction – Jim DeFelice and Scott McEwen, both literary descendants of Tom Clancy.[3] With other US veterans they have co-authored dozens of serial thrillers; the genre conventions in those books feature ticking bomb plots, globally mobile protagonists, binary stereotypes of US allies and adversaries, lengthy descriptions of weapons, and hostility towards superior authority, particularly when restrictive rules of engagement are being enforced or diplomatic solutions pursued. The guns and grenades of

Figure 1.2 Before *American Sniper* (2014) became a blockbuster film, Chris Kyle had become a bestselling author and celebrity through the mammoth sales of his book. Here Kyle, accompanied by his wife Taya, signs books at Fort Pendleton in California on 12 January 2012. Public Domain Image. Taken by Corporal Damien Gutierrez.

the protagonists are righteous, killing bad guys without producing any harm to civilians. Series titles like Sniper Elite (McEwen with Thomas Koloniar), Rogue Warrior (DeFelice with Richard Marcinko) and Red Dragon Rising (DeFelice with Larry Bond) offer lone-wolf protagonists struggling against their timid commanders and agencies to defeat Chechen, Chinese, Mexican and Middle Eastern terrorists who threaten to destroy America. Paralleling the conventions of these novels through film has been the long-running *Sniper* (1993) franchise, which employed 'War on Terror' themes and locations with *Sniper* (1993), *Sniper 2* (2002), *Sniper 3* (2004), *Sniper: Reloaded* (2011) and *Sniper Legacy* (2014).

Several traits of the commando genre mark *American Sniper*. Kyle takes the stance of the warrior for the righteous nation in explaining his actions in Iraq: 'Everyone I shot in Iraq was trying to harm Americans or Iraqis loyal to the new government' (5). For the weapons-conscious audience Kyle carefully describes his guns and ammunition, their special virtues and limits. Like standard genre commandos he has more faith in killing than in politics, believing that every success in Iraq came from effective killing and the resultant threat of death for those who defied the US occupation and its chosen Iraqi government. Putting it bluntly when discussing the insurgents' incentive to negotiate, he writes, 'They only started to come to the peace table after we killed enough savages out there' (361).

Kyle repeatedly shows contempt for the rules of engagement (ROE) governing kills, rules that expressed the policy imperative, articulated by Bush, to 'spare innocent civilians from harm'. As Kyle puts it, the ROEs 'got so convoluted . . . because politicians were interfering in the process. The rules are drawn up by lawyers who are trying to protect the admirals and generals from the politicians; they're not written by people who are worried about the guys on the ground getting shot' (342). Kyle did not want to kill every Iraqi male he saw, but he wanted more leeway to kill suspects, feeling that the SEALs were being forced 'to fight with one hand tied behind their back' (342). His warrant for impatience, reiterated several times and echoed in the film, is that he was absolutely confident that every person he killed was a bad guy – even though some of his incredible shots were in the range of 2,000 yards where vision is highly inferential. He hated them and he loved killing them: 'I loved killing bad guys' (251) and 'I don't shoot people with Korans – I'd like to, but I don't' (227). These visceral outbursts against a wholly unworthy enemy were qualified by his acceptance of the role as protector of civilians (305) and his refusal to kill a child (387). This was followed by his denying that the US caused any civilian deaths in Iraq (389) – as if every warrior were as restrained as he presented himself to be. We should note that Kyle's beliefs were at variance with that of many other warriors. Marine Lieutenant Nathaniel Fick, for example, who was one of the first to enter Iraq, surveyed the invasion's wreckage with his enlisted men – the civilians carelessly killed or wounded, the looting, disrupted electricity, medical shortages, banditry – and they told him they felt the war was already lost. As he contemplated a girl struck by gunfire, Fick concluded, 'They had to hate us. If the tables were turned, if I were that father I'd be plotting the deaths of the people who'd harmed her' (Fick 2005: 318, 334).

Even though Kyle's book matches several expectations of the heroic genre, it also presents a Kyle as he expressed his military and political sentiments in post-publication interviews. What is not generic to the commando superheroic model is Kyle's unusual depiction of the home/battlefield rhythm that marked his deployment of military service during 'The Long War'. With its commitment to a volunteer professional military, the US encourages its service members to have families by providing housing, medical care and education for them. Because the 'War on Terror' is the longest declared war in US history, the warrior role had to be joined with the family role. So Kyle was not an isolated figure, matching the superheroic genre, but remained with his family despite the tensions. In the autobiography Taya Kyle, his spouse, is given a prominent voice with substantial sections of her own text in italics. She worries about Chris' silences and emotional explosions at home, and his continued distraction by the battle zones he has temporarily left. It is these struggles to accept the home/battlefield rhythm that make Taya Kyle an important part of his story. For some reason, her name as co-author was omitted, perhaps because of the convention that women do not write commando novels.

Another departure from the saviour-commando genre is the absence of any sympathetic Iraqis and Kyle's complete lack of idealism about Iraq's fate: 'I didn't risk my life to bring democracy to Iraq. I risked my life for my buddies, to protect my friends and fellow countrymen. I went to war for my country, not Iraq . . . I never once fought for the Iraqis' (240). He accepted the Bush doctrine of pre-emptive war to eliminate Iraq's weapons of mass destruction, as well as Iraq's affiliation with Al-Qaeda, and his narrative never betrays any awareness of the discrepancies that emerged early in the war. Killing enemies in Iraq was simply viewed as a way of guarding the home front by conforming to his role in the country's military. Kyle never expressed any awareness that a war founded on pretexts could create new enemies against his own country.

Despite the fact that Kyle was not playing the role of an isolato superhero, he entertained himself with the superheroic films while serving in Iraq: 'James Bond movies, some Clint Eastwood, John Wayne – I love John Wayne' (222). Especially significant was his commitment, and that of his platoon, to the Punisher, one of the most violent and anti-social of the superheroes, one who shades towards the criminal anti-hero at times. The Punisher appeared in two feature films, both of which were released while Kyle was serving: *The Punisher* (2004) and *The Punisher: War Zone* (2008). According to Kyle, the Punisher is 'a real bad-ass who rights wrongs, delivering vigilante justice' (263). His platoon adopted 'the Punishers' as their nickname and used the Punisher logo, stencilling it onto their armour and leaving it as a mark at locations where they had killed insurgents. Their message was: '*You see us? We're the people kicking your ass. Fear us. Because we will kill you, motherfucker. You are bad. We are badder. We are bad-ass*' (263: Kyle's italics). In fact, however, Kyle was not acting as a vigilante punisher but as a military officer following commands.

Unlike commando novels, Kyle's biography contains fervent statements of personal religious belief. He indicates that his crusader tattoo symbolises his commitment as a Christian holy warrior: 'I had a crusader cross inked in. I wanted everyone to know I was a Christian. I had it put in red, for blood. I hated the damn savages I'd been fighting. I always will' (250). He also believed that God was on his side, even assisting in his kills. In one long shot at 1,600 yards, he pulled the trigger despite scoffing marines: 'I took the shot. The moon, Earth, and stars aligned. God blew on the bullet, and I gut-shot the jackass' (204). Kyle seems comfortable in stating his certainty that he was a totally righteous killer: 'when God confronts me with my sins, I do not believe any of the kills I had during the war will be among them. Everyone I shot was evil. I had good cause on every shot. They all deserved to die' (430).

Another departure from the commando genre, whose pathos has contributed to the success of book and film, is that his career comes to a decisive end. During his fourth tour, Kyle's inventory of his badly damaged body (404) – knees, knuckles, broken fingers and ribs – tells him that he cannot go on. And after being shot twice, he remarks, 'I'm not superhuman. I can die' (384). He also reaches a decision that his family needs him, is important to him and that he must leave the service. And once he has left there is no prospect that he will return for more war.

The book's translation to film preserves its rhythmic structure, which alternates between stateside scenes of military training and life with Taya, and Chris' four deployments in Iraq between 2003 and 2009.

The film faithfully depicts physical injuries and the psychic pains that disorient Chris, lead to his denials about his true condition, and eventually lead to his retirement. But it also invents fictions that both magnify Kyle's aura of heroic destiny – and in the end deflate it with irony.

The fictionalisation of Chris Kyle in the film

An important narrative decision for the film was Clint Eastwood's and Bradley Cooper's introduction of classic and revisionist Western tropes – a process that substantially fictionalised some events of Kyle's life. As Cooper, who played Kyle in the film, frankly stated in his interview with Terry Gross:

> I love the idea of framing it as a Western, I thought that could be cinematically viable, ripe for cinema, and that this guy happened to be incredibly charismatic.
>
> You have a guy going into a town and there's his equivalent on the other side, another sharpshooter. He's a sharpshooter, and [it ends in] tumbleweeds, a dust storm, there's a showdown, this sort of one man and his pursuit – that idea. (Fresh Air 2015)

The classic Western story presents outsize figures who bear a sense of command and destiny that leads them to act independently in response to evil. A measure of this independence is visible in the cinematic depiction of Kyle's last battle in Sadr City. In 'the showdown' that Cooper depicts we see egregious disobedience to his commanding officer in order to take a shot that exposes his platoon's tenuous position. 'The Legend' and his companions barely scramble away from death, Chris losing his iconic Bible, American flag and gun in the dust. The battle's ending is not the chaotic carnage of Peckinpah's *The Wild Bunch* (1969), but it is disorderly and a sign that it is time for Chris to leave the battlefield.

Rites of initiation as a protector-killer

There are mythic details at the beginning of the film when young Chris symbolically discovers his destiny as a protector-killer with a compulsion to save others. Based on Kyle's report in the book that 'my dad made it clear I'd get a whuppin' if I started a fight' (11), we see his father's belt laid on the dinner table and his menacing stare as he angrily intones a fable about wolves, sheep and sheepdogs. This scene follows a playground incident in which Chris was seen fighting. His father tells him that he must respond aggressively to the aggressions of others in order to protect the weak. 'We take care of our own. And if someone picks a fight with you or bullies your brother, you have my permission to finish it.' Afterwards young Chris is shown attacking the fat bully who had tormented his younger brother. In another revelatory incident, young Chris is marked as deadly with a gun by shooting a large deer: 'Helluva shot, son. You got a gift', after which his father forces him to 'process the kill' – to slit its throat and get his hands in the blood.

The feminine challenge and the call of destiny

While Chris is a young man riding the rodeo circuit, a young woman insults his manhood and his aimless life of pleasure. Feeling despair about whether her allegations are true, he patriotically enlists with the Navy after seeing TV news about the US embassy bombings in Kenya and Tanzania (1998). Both episodes for his life are invented, if the book is to be believed. Kyle's book reports that he was getting bored with his life as a ranch hand in Texas and decided to explore several military recruitment options over an extended period, initially being rejected by the Navy because of steel pins in his arms (20–4).

The ritual cycle

In Don Siegel's *The Shootist* (1975) starring John Wayne, the dying J. B. Books (Wayne) hands his gun to Gillom (Ron Howard), who uses it to kill the cowardly bartender who shot Books from behind. Gillom has defied his mother's Christian values and emphasis on conciliation in an effort to control Books' tendency to gun people down. In *American Sniper*, Chris Kyle similarly passes a gun to his son Colton when he takes him hunting, just as his father had taken him. This suggests that there is a ritual cycle in his family, in which the legacy of learning to kill with a gun will be transmitted as a heroic legacy.

The duel with Mustafa

Mustafa, the vaunted supersniper of Iraq's insurgent terrorism, is killed by Chris in the final shootout. Mustafa functions as a symbolic figure who embodies the evil that the Iraq War is supposed to resolve. Chris recognises his signature at Fallujah, where he kills Sheikh Obedi, one of Kyle's informants. Mustafa also shows up at Ramadi, where he shoots Kyle's friend Biggles (Jake McDorman) in the face. Then he is present in Kyle's final battle at Sadr City, where the film depicts him dying from Kyle's bullet. Kyle's book merely reports that he had heard of Mustafa, but he believes that some other sniper killed him (158). The cinematic rendition with a top Olympic sniper creates a classic cowboy standoff, as Bradley Cooper reminds us. But there is another dimension here.[4] Mustafa is increasingly shown to have a life parallel to that of Kyle; we see him in his apartment with his wife and child, appearing to have his mind elsewhere; we see the worried look on the face of his wife as he packs his sniper gear to return to battle. He and Kyle are doppelgängers, skilled professionals at killing who are becoming estranged from their families. Clint Eastwood has often used the doppelgänger trope, conspicuously in *Unforgiven* (1992) where Will Munny, the ageing gunman, is paired against Sheriff Little Bill Dagget, whom he kills.

Diminishing Kyle's heroic aura

The reckless, vengeance-driven soldier in denial about Marc Lee's letter

Marc Lee (Luke Grimes) was a trusted colleague who had a background as a seminary student. Two weeks before he was killed, he wrote a questioning, philosophical letter to his mother, from which she is shown tearfully reading at the funeral: 'My question is when does glory fade away and become a wrongful crusade?' Then Chris hears in voiceover: 'When does it become an unjustified means by which one is completely consumed?' After the funeral, as he drives home with Taya (Sienna Miller), she queries, as if agreeing with the sentiments of the letter, 'Chris? I want to know what you thought of his letter.' Chris admits that because of Biggles' shooting and the desire for revenge, 'We were operating off emotion and – we walked into an ambush.' This remark comes off as a sober realisation of error, earlier underscored by the prominent appearance in the film of the Punisher logo on body armour and vehicles. Instead of reflecting on his own reckless revenge quest, Chris then indulges in magical thinking: 'But that's not what killed him. That letter did. That letter killed Marc. He let go and he paid the price for it.' He was shot, in other words, because he lost his will to believe in the war. Taya has no rebuttal she wishes to pursue at that moment because Chris seems very angry at the idea he might be part of a 'wrongful crusade'. Chris has similar moments of denial in the film about his injuries and his high blood pressure.

The man who can't keep a promise to an Iraqi

When Chris is doing house-to-house searching Fallujah, he encounters the family of Sheikh-Al Obedi. After his men terrify them, he attempts to get Obedi to help him locate 'the Butcher', an enforcer working with the Al-Qaeda leader, Zarqawi. The Butcher punishes Iraqis who cooperate with the occupying force. Obedi demands $100,000 and secrecy as his price for leading Kyle to the Butcher. At the moment in the streets when Obedi knocks on his door, the insurgents attack; the Butcher comes out and applies a power drill on the head of Obedi's son. Chris is helpless to stop the carnage, which is complete when Mustafa kills Obedi. Chris has offered protection that he cannot provide, which looks like a betrayal of Obedi's family.

Pulling a gun on the family sheepdog

After Chris has retired from the Navy, the film fictionally depicts his son Colton's sixth birthday celebration. The family's sheepdog is playing with the children while Taya attempts to have a conversation with a silent Chris: 'I just feel this dark space between us and I don't know how to reach you.' At that moment a child becomes frightened by the dog and Chris rises to wrestle with him, then pulls out his concealed .45 to kill it. The adults are horrified. The sheepdog incident symbolically conveys that Chris is close to the edge of insanity and no longer the fable's protective sheepdog. This evokes an earlier scene in which Taya had said, 'I need you to be human again.' The movie shows her weeping about his transformation as he lies emotionless in bed.

What overall impression of Chris Kyle can an audience derive from the film, where considerable effort is given to making him a more appealing figure? *American Sniper* omits Kyle's repeated expressions of contempt for the people of Iraq. It omits his bloodthirsty statements such as 'I loved killing bad guys' (251) and 'I don't shoot people with Korans – I'd like to, but I don't' (227). It omits his absolute denial that the US forces had killed civilians, which Kyle decries as 'pure bullshit' (389). It omits his understanding that he is fighting as a Christian crusader. Yet the film suggests that Chris came home as a damaged person, lacking in insight about the issues of the war, and failing to understand his own impulses. Kyle had done his job of protecting fellow servicemen extremely well. He collected numerous battle decorations for his shooting skills and leadership. But when the film takes us to the scene where he is murdered by Eddie Ray Routh (Vincent Selhorst Jones), he still seems to be travelling towards the goal of 'being human again' in the way that Taya wanted.

IV.

The shapes of heroic action and the relationships of heroes with their communities are decisive elements in identifying mythic paradigms. Sniping is a lonely task that isolates the soldier temporarily from battle mates and thus presents an impression of individuality. Captain E. J. Land, who launched the sniper programme in Vietnam, had these words for his recruits: 'When you go on a mission, there is no crowd to applaud you – no one for whom you can flex your muscles or show how tough you are. When you go on a mission, you are alone' (Henderson 1988: 95–6). Despite the tactical isolation, the sniper is still executing military orders about whom to kill and why. The Chris Kyle story relates the exploits of a well-trained governmental agent – a Special Forces operator – acting under the authority of the American government. The preference of Special Forces for the 'operator' language suggests the precise action of a cog in a bureaucratic machine. Even Chris' crusader Christian hatred for his enemies received tacit sanction within the Defense Department

Figure 1.3 After his retirement from the US Navy, Kyle formed Craft International, a security training company. He designed a logo for it that expresses the values espoused in his book – the decisive role of violence and the rejection of feminine conciliation ('momma'). The Punisher design hits the vengeance button and the cross links it to Christian crusading. Source: Craft International decal purchased on eBay.

command. Undersecretary of Defense for intelligence Lieutenant General William G. 'Jerry' Boykin appeared publicly in uniform to make such statements as 'we are in the army of God, in the house of God, have been raised for a time such as this', and he also stated that Bush is 'in the White House because God put him there' (Cooper 2003). Zealous statements were also made on Iraq's battlefield. Lieutenant Colonel Peter Newell used these words to prepare his warriors for battle at Fallujah: 'This is as pure a fight of good versus evil as we'll probably see in our lifetime' (Bellavia 2007: 60). Statements of Kyle that seem hateful and demeaning towards Iraq's people were an expression of this crusading outlook.

As we indicated earlier, Chris Kyle, despite his operator role, was inspired by pop superheroes, especially the Punisher. He even adopted it in designing a logo for the security training company he created after retiring. But Kyle, unlike the Punisher, is obviously not a vigilante killer acting on his own behalf. And his commitment to family and his retirement from the stresses of the battlefield express his normality.

As indicated in the case of *Der Spiegel*'s satirical cover, superheroic comparisons were used early in the 'War on Terror' to ridicule the Bush administration's extravagant, even metaphysical military aspirations. We had described this campaign as an expression of the 'Captain America Complex', a mix of beliefs shared by zealous religions, whether Christians, Jews or Muslims. That view is Manichaean, with conspiratorial evil doers on one side and righteous killers on the other. The belief system authorises the destruction of other human beings and their cultures. There is a faith that the utter destruction of the evil enemies will bring about an era of peace. We feared the consequences of such a simplified view and felt that many episodes of Captain America – particularly in his battles with Red Skull – illustrated the limits of the complex. As we showed in *The Myth of the American Superhero* (2002), superheroes operate outside the law and often disguise their identity so as to avoid the full responsibilities of citizenship. They emerge in times of crisis after normal institutions and laws fail to cope with an external crisis. True to the superheroic tradition, Captain America rather soon recognised the failure of the institutions, but in his post-9/11 life, those failing institutions were his own government. J. Richard Stevens, in his book *Captain America, Masculinity, and Violence* (2015), has justifiably criticised our application of the Captain America concept as we defined it in our *Captain America* book of 2003. Writing with a full knowledge of what happened in the Captain's fictional world since 9/11, Stevens characterised his opposition to Bush foreign policy:

Captain America himself actually resisted the Captain America complex that otherwise gripped America's foreign policy, and he became one of the few early critiques of the moralistic language presented by the Bush administration at a time when other media were far less willing or able to challenge the suppositions about the identity and nature of America's enemies in the war on terror. (Stevens 2015: 215)

To our surprise, we too had begun to notice examples of the Captain's alienation from and critique of American power as described in Stevens' study.[5] Soon after the events of 9/11, John Ney Rieber, the story writer for Captain America, said, 'I don't know how you could write Captain America if you weren't interested in writing about America. I feel very strongly that Cap should be about the rough questions' (quoted in Jenkins 2006: 84). As a consequence, early in the US campaign against terrorism, the Captain distanced himself from the nation's millennial fervour to take on enemies abroad. For example, a mere two months after 9/11, Cap appeared in *Spider-Man #36*, in which unspoken meditations appear against the background of the ruined Word Trade Center: 'What do we tell the children? Do we tell them evil is a foreign face? No, the evil is the thought behind the face, and it can look just like yours' (Straczynski and Romita 2002).

Encouraging critical reflection on the evil in oneself countered statements by America's leaders that the nation was wholly innocent and under attack because of its universal values. Cap also refuses Colonel Fury's order to take an assignment in Afghanistan as the 'New Deal' series begins (Rieber and Cassaday 2002: np). On assignment at a coca field in Colombia, where a US-assisted raid is directed at the workers, he protests furiously: 'they're peasant farmers. Desperate to feed their families . . . The government soldiers will burn the field and many of these people will starve.' Then reflecting on his own integrity: 'It's like having your principles crushed in a vise. I am here at the hubris of the government – I can't interfere with these soldiers . . . as they cut these impoverished people to ribbons to make us look good on TV. To help us fight "The War on Drugs"' (Priest and Divito 2005: np). One cannot imagine such utterances from the mouth of Chris Kyle. His moments of disobedience are ones of zeal for the destructive cause rather than challenging the mission itself.

With regard to his military superiors, Captain America's titles relating to the GWOT from 2002 to 2006 express anger about his military assignments that reflect paranoia and deception on the part of his leaders. In *Two Americas*, he discovers that a US Navy admiral has tried to create a more compliant, destructive 'Anti-Cap' with whom he fights while they debate the premises of the war. The Anti-Cap, who is paranoid, vicious and programmed to kill him, tells the true Cap that in 'the new war' 'America's enemies are everywhere' and that 'this war requires will . . . whoever is the most committed wins'. Cap replies, 'And, that would be you?' To which the Anti-Cap delivers a cynical taunt: 'You are a product of America's hope. I am the sum of America's fear' (Priest and Sears 2004: np).

Numerous post-9/11 episodes in many other issues of the comics, carefully documented by J. Richard Stevens, symptomise the Captain's disintegration from the conflicting vectors that arc through his conscience. As superhero he carries individualistic burdens of acute awareness and righteous moral judgement. As a US warrior he has a duty of obedience to command. Unfortunately, the hubristic premises of the GWOT echo the rhetorics of villainy that characterised his traditional foes. Those associations are reinforced by real-life news headlines about deceptive pretexts, incompetence in command, torture and secrecy.

Given these developments in the comic book culture, it appears to us that the Chris Kyle story conforms neither to the older superheroic paradigm established in the Golden Age of comics nor to the extensively revised paradigm of the Captain America that emerged after 9/11. Kyle's conscience tugs at him because he could not kill enough Iraqis. As he tells the doctor in the film after his retirement, he regrets his absence from the battlefield: 'the thing that haunts me are all the guys I couldn't save . . . I'm willing and able to be there, but I'm not. I just quit.' He is just an exceptionally lethal man with a gun who is exemplary in following commands – except in the final, fictional battle of the film when he goes rogue.

Since Kyle does not conform to prevalent superheroic paradigms, we suggest an apt historical comparison from early America is Stephen Decatur, commonly acknowledged as America's first post-Revolutionary War hero. He earned fame during the 1st Tripolitan War when he confronted the Barbary pirates and helped to end their predatory attacks on American shipping. He is famous for his toast expressing loyalty to the American nation, even when it carries out misdeeds. 'Our country – in her intercourse with foreign nations, may she be always in the right, but always successful, my country right or wrong' (Guttridge 2007: 200). Wishing for your country's success even when it pursues a wrongful policy means ultimately that loyalty trumps justice. Like Chris Kyle, who died at thirty-eight, Decatur died at the young age of forty-one. The cause was gunshots delivered by a fellow naval officer, James Barron, who had been court-martialled and sought to return to service after five years. The duel resulted from an insult Decatur had given in opposing Barron's return to service. If Chris Kyle is identified as the Stephen Decatur of the Global War on Terror, a man who supports fully the wrongful cause, this would account for his lack of vigilantism and his performance of required military duties. Since there is no tragic ambiguity in his selection of a mission or individual flaw that accounts for the mission's failure or success, it is doubtful that such figures are heroic in the sense of our popular tropes. Our interest in the implications of mythic paradigms therefore shifts from the Stephen Decatur figure to the nation he served, whether 'right or wrong'.

V.

If it is plausible to view Chris Kyle as the Stephen Decatur of the Global War on Terror, our evaluation must include the nation on whose behalf he served. In the wake of 9/11, our voices joined many others expressing fears about how the United States was being tempted to respond with its military power. For a few relatively calm days the world bestowed sympathy on America for lives lost and the national trauma. Even the mayor and city council head of Tehran sent a letter of condolence to Mayor Rudolph Giuliani of New York City which suggested that 'this act is not just against New Yorkers, but all humanity' (Purdum 2001). The temporary bafflement and hesitation of US leaders suggested that the nation might share plans and responsibility with other nations, avoiding vengeful, counterproductive actions. Instead, the nation turned to military means, of which Chris Kyle was the most effective single agent. To evaluate his stature as a heroic figure is to evaluate the nation itself.

Fifteen years after the launching of the GWOT, the world strains against the consequences of American blundering in Afghanistan and Iraq. Obama has continued the GWOT, gradually withdrawing 'boots on the ground' but compounding the world's dismay with drone strikes that kill civilians and targeted killings that often find the wrong target (Sluka 2011; Currier 2013). Trillions have been spent, millions have been displaced, hundreds of thousands have been killed (Watson Institute 2015) and the enemies of 'the chosen nation' and its 'guardians of the righteous peace' continue to multiply on several continents.

As Howard Gambrill Clark shows in a 2015 issue of *The American Interest*, activities such as sniping are now viewed as evidence of the basic narrative that ISIS shares with other terrorist groups, that '*Islam is under attack*' (italics in original). He cites the contention of the

Al-Qaeda branch in Syria that American airstrikes are a 'war against Islam'. Similarly, ISIS claims that drone strikes are 'a clear message that the war is against Islam'. Clark surveys the statements made by terrorists such as the Boston Marathon bombers to show that 'what they have in common is a grievance about the killing of Muslims', which fits this basic narrative.[6] This is why volunteers for ISIS, including significant numbers from the US (Schmidt 2014), have risen to a flood tide during 2014–15, far surpassing our capacity for targeted killings by drones and other means. The celebration of sniping, no matter how efficient or impressive as a technical achievement in lethal shooting, is obviously counterproductive in the current circumstances. In his book *Virtual War: Kosovo and Beyond* (2000), Michael Ignatieff presciently warned against the delusions that have characterised GWOT: 'We see war as a surgical scalpel and not a blood-stained sword. In so doing we mis-describe ourselves and we mis-describe the instruments of death. We need to stay away from such fables of self-righteous invulnerability' (quoted in Sluka 2011: 75).

At the time of writing, Iraq and Afghanistan along with Syria remain zones of intense sectarian strife, terrorism, insurgencies and disrupted economies. Cities in which Kyle fought have fallen back into insurgent hands that resist the central Shiite-dominated, US-backed government in Baghdad. The GWOT that Chris Kyle served now appears to have lost any semblance of the heroic. In candid reflections, several commanders have admitted serious failures in goals, policy and execution. For the audience of National Geographic's documentary *American War Generals* (2014), General Stanley McChrystal flatly called the Iraq War an error. 'Before that war, if we'd looked at the cost – not just in Americans but in Iraqis and others – if we'd looked at the distrust it created – or loss of trust – around the world for America; I don't think a rational person would have ever said, "Yeah that's worth it; we'll do that"' (Schogol 2014). No matter how many Stephen Decaturs and Chris Kyles we recruit to rectify this tragic mistake by heroic exploits, the old formula no longer holds: 'my country right or wrong' – to be supported in either case. This particular wrong is on such a scale that not only the country but its mythic identity are fundamentally challenged. This is why we find the analysis of Richard Stevens so compelling. Responding to our 2003 suggestion in *Captain America* that it was time for the Captain to take a 'dignified retirement' (9), Stevens correctly chastises us in saying that had our opinion prevailed, 'comic book readers would have been robbed of one of the few overtly critical texts of Bush-era foreign policy at a time when so many other media forms were hesitant to offer much political criticism of any kind'

(Stevens 14: 286). When the Bush administration engaged the GWOT, it did not realise its behaviour could be coded in the world of comics as megalomaniacal villainy. Or that its statements justifying the violation of treaties and falsifying evidence to create a pretext for war would fall below the standard of respectability for a comic book character who became as sagely critical as Captain America.[7]

The Chris Kyle of *American Sniper* will likely be remembered as the soldier who fervently believed his international vigilante bosses to pursue a war of dubious legality. Inspired by the vengeance of the Punisher, he gave his all, and, like so many others of his generation, came home badly wounded and failing to understand the larger meaning of what he had been through. Bonded to his guns, he was killed by a fellow wounded veteran, Eddie Ray Routh. Sensing that Routh was a strange bird, clearly signalled in the film, Kyle still had faith that taking him to a shooting range would have therapeutic value. After the killing, Taya Kyle took up Chris' Gospel of the Gun, telling the NRA convention in Houston: 'He loved his fellow man enough . . . to stop the evil coming at him', and after returning to the states 'he discovered a new use for guns: healing' (Michel 2013).

It was an irony that a man who had been so alert on the field of battle would be so trusting in a situation of lethal danger. The deluded Routh acted on the Bush premise: when you suspect that you are in danger, attack first and verify later. At his trial for the murder of Kyle and Chad Littlefield, Routh was not allowed by his counsel to take the stand. Dr Mitchell Dunn, a forensic psychiatrist, explained that at the time Routh thought he was defending himself from Kyle and Littlefield, who were planning to kill him. According to Dunn, 'If you are going to be killed, then you have a right to defend yourself . . . I'm not saying it's logical, but it was logical in his mind' (Fernandez and Jones 2015a). On his behalf, a plea of not guilty by reason of insanity was made.

The death of Kyle, discretely veiled from us in the film, should be part of our understanding of his career as a hero. We need to remember the politics that made his heroism possible and also consider the entertainment system which thrives on the depiction of remotely administered death and has so little patience with the face-to-face diplomacy and negotiation that could make such killing unnecessary. Policy makers are not granted the privilege of pleading 'not guilty by reason of insanity'. But they are ingenious in escaping through their pleas that they 'meant well'. The jury for Routh found him guilty and sentenced him to a life term without the possibility of parole (Fernandez and Jones 2015b). The public is even more warranted in rejecting the good intentions of policy makers when so much is at stake. We hope that *American Sniper* does not contribute to the feeling Kyle's death, along with the suffering of so many other veterans, somehow sacrificially atones for all the wrongs that were wrought by the war that he served.

NOTES

1. The Jessica Lynch story was quickly made into a TV movie, *Saving Jessica Lynch* (NBC 2003).
2. Luttrell's book was the basis for the film *Lone Survivor* (2013), in which Luttrell himself acted a minor role.
3. Taya Kyle's *American Wife* asserts that Scott McEwen was simply a deal maker who had no role in *American Sniper*'s authorship (113). She gives DeFelice sole credit as the professional writer who is a co-author.
4. In the film, Mustafa's legend is that he competed for Syria in the Olympics and crossed the border to fight with Iraq's insurgents.
5. See John Shelton Lawrence, 'Foreword', in Weiner (2009).
6. See also on this theme Ahmed Akbar's *The Thistle and the Drone: How America's War on Terror Became a Global War on Tribal Islam* (2013).
7. J. Richard Stevens has pointed out that much of the film franchise, particularly now that Disney has purchased control, does not express the tradition of Captain America as critic of jingoism and megalomaniacal policies. He notes, however, that 2014's *Captain America: The Winter Soldier* treats the theme of mass surveillance and 'predictive warfare' based on suspicions and probabilities (2005: 286–7), thus bringing Captain America into a dissident role for the Obama era.

REFERENCES

Ahmed, Akbar (2013), *The Thistle and the Drone: How America's War on Terror Became a Global War on Tribal Islam*, Washington, DC: Brookings Institution Press.

Bellavia, David, with John R. Bruning (2007), *House to House: An Epic Memoir of War*, New York: Free Press.

Beveridge, Albert J. (1898), 'On Expansion', *Congressional Record* (56th Congress, 1st Session), Vol. XXXIII, pp. 705, 711, last accessed 25 May 2015: www.wwnorton.com/college/history/ralph/workbook/ralprs30.htm

Bolger, Daniel (2014), *Why We Lost: A General's Inside Account of the Iraq and Afghanistan Wars*, New York: Eamon Dolan/Houghton Mifflin.

Borger, Julian (2003), 'How I created the axis of evil', *The Guardian*, 28 January 2003, last accessed 13 May 2015: www.theguardian.com/world/2003/jan/28/usa.iran

Buiso, Gary (2012), 'Meet the Big Shot', *New York Post*, 1 January 2012, last accessed 20 May 2015: http://nypost.com/2012/01/01/meet-the-big-shot/

Bush, George W. (2001a), 'President Bush Addresses the Nation', *Washington Post*, 20 September 2001, last accessed 13 May 2015: www.washingtonpost.com/wp-srv/nation/specials/attacked/transcripts/bushaddress_092001.html

— (2001b), 'President Bush on Homeland Security,' *Washington Post*, 8 November 2001, last accessed 13 May 2015: www.washingtonpost.com/wp-srv/nation/specials/attacked/transcripts/bushtext_110801.html

— (2003), 'Operation Iraqi Freedom', The White House (archives), 22 March 2003, last accessed 13 May 2015: http://georgewbush-whitehouse.archives.gov/news/releases/2003/03/20030322.html

Clark, Howard Gambrill (2015), 'Go Local', *The American Interest*, 10.6 (July/August 2015), last accessed 15 July 2015: http://www.the-american-interest.com/2015/06/10/go-local/

Cooper, Richard T. (2003), 'General casts war in religious terms', *Los Angeles Times*, 16 October 2003, last accessed 20 June 2015: http://articles.latimes.com/print/2003/oct/16/nation/na-general16

'Costs of War' (2015), The Watson Institute at Brown University, ongoing compilation last accessed on 25 May 2015: www.costsofwar.org/

Currier, Cara (2013), 'Drone Strike Tests Legal Grounds for War on Terror', *ProPublica*, 6 February 2013, last accessed 29 June 2015: http://www.propublica.org/article/drone-strikes-test-legal-grounds-for-war-on-terror

Danner, Mark (2004), *Torture and Truth: America, Abu Ghraib, and the War on Terror*, New York: New York Review Books.

Der Spiegel (2002), cover caption, 'Die Bush Krieger: Amerikas feldzug gegen das boese' (The Bush warriors' campaign against evil), 18 February 2002.

Englade, Kenneth F. (2015), *Meltdown in Haditha: The Killing of 24 Iraqi Civilians by US Marines and the Breakdown of Military Justice*, Jefferson, NC: McFarland.

Fernandez, Manny, and Kathryn Jones (2015a), 'An American sniper, his killer, and deep scars bared for a jury', *New York Times*, 19 February 2015, last accessed 8 July 2015: http://www.nytimes.com/2015/02/20/us/american-sniper-jury-hears-of-struggles-of-chris-kyle-and-eddie-ray-routh.html

— (2015b), '"American Sniper" Jury Finds Chris Kyle's Killer Guilty of Murder', *New York Times*, 24 February 2015, last accessed 8 July 2015: http://www.nytimes.com/2015/02/25/us/american-sniper-trial-jury-finds-ex-marine-guilty-of-murder.html

Fick, Nathaniel (2005), *One Bullet Away: The Making of a Marine Officer*, Boston: Houghton-Mifflin.

French, David (2015), '*American Sniper* has reached a cultural moment: here's why', *National Review*, 5 January 2015, last accessed 13 May 2015: www.nationalreview.com/corner/396668/american-sniper-has-created-cultural-moment-heres-why-david-french

Fresh Air (2015) (radio interview), 'Bradley Cooper: "Sniper" controversy distracts from film's message about vets', 2 February 2015, transcript last accessed 26 May 2015: www.npr.org/2015/02/02/383062401/bradley-cooper-sniper-controversy-distracts-from-films-message-about-vets

Frum, David, and Richard Norman Perle (2003), *An End to Evil: How to Win the War on Terror*, New York: Random House.

Guttridge, Leonard F. (2007), *Our Country, Right or Wrong: The Life of Stephen Decatur*, New York: Macmillan.

Henderson, Charles (1988), *Marine Sniper: 93 Confirmed Kills*, New York: Berkeley Books.

Holley, Peter (2015), 'Texas Gov. Greg Abbott declares "Chris Kyle Day" as "American Sniper" continues to surge', *The Washington Post*, 2 February 2015, last accessed 20 June 2015: http://www.washingtonpost.com/news/post-nation/wp/2015/01/31/texas-governor-declares-feb-2-chris-kyle-day/

Jenkins, Henry (2006), 'Captain America sheds his mighty tears: comics and September 11', in Daniel J. Sherman and Terry Nardin (eds), *Terror, Culture, Politics: Rethinking 9/11*, Bloomington: Indiana University Press, pp. 69–100.

Jewett, Robert, and John Shelton Lawrence (2003), *Captain America and the Crusade against Evil: The Dilemma of Zealous Nationalism*, Grand Rapids, MI: Eerdmans.

Knowlton, Brian (2001), 'Terror in America: "We're going to smoke them out": President airs his anger', *New York Times*, 19 September 2001, last accessed 13 May 2015: www.nytimes.com/2001/09/19/news/19iht-t4_30.html

Kyle, Chris, with Chris McEwen and Jim DeFelice (2012), *American Sniper: The Autobiography of the Most Lethal Sniper in US Military History*, New York: HarperCollins.

Kyle, Chris, with William Doyle (2014), *American Gun: A History of the US in Ten Firearms*, New York: William Morrow.

Kyle, Taya, with Jim DeFelice (2015), *American Wife: Love, War, Faith, and Renewal*, New York: William Morrow.

Lawrence, John Shelton, and Robert Jewett (2002), *The Myth of the American Superhero*, Grand Rapids, MI: Eerdmans.

Lawrence, John Shelton (2009), 'Foreword', in Robert G. Weiner (ed.), *Captain America and the Struggle of the Superhero*, Jefferson, NC: McFarland, pp. 1–7.

Lewis, Andy (2015), '*American Sniper* book sales see continued bump from movie's success', *Hollywood Reporter*, 15 February 2015, last accessed 13 May 2015: http://www.hollywoodreporter.com/news/american-sniper-book-sales-see-770901

Luo, Michael (2007), 'Panel hears about falsehoods in 2 wartime incidents', *New York Times*, 25 April 2007, last accessed 13 May 2015: www.nytimes.com/2007/04/25/washington/25army.html

Luttrell, Marcus, with Patrick Robinson (2007), *Lone survivor: the Eyewitness Account of Operation Redwing and the Lost Heroes of SEAL Team 10*, New York: Little, Brown & Company.

McCain, John (2001), 'War is hell: there is no substitute for victory', *Wall Street Journal*, 30 October 2001, last accessed 27 May 2015: www.mccain.senate.gov/public/index.cfm/opinion-editorials?ID=21e7f3d7-d14a-48fc-a44d-5f800a3feoao

Michel, Casey (2013), 'Palin, Santorum, and Perry remind the NRA convention of America's greatness and that greatness comes from a gun', *Houston Press*, 6 May 2013, last accessed 1 June 2015: http://www.houstonpress.com/news/palin-santorum-and-perry-remind-the-nra-convention-of-americas-greatness-and-that-greatness-comes-from-a-gun-6734141

Oldenberg, Ann (2015), 'Michelle Obama gives *American Sniper* two thumbs up', *USA Today*, 30 January 2015, last accessed 6 June 2015: www.usatoday.com/story/life/movies/2015/01/30/michelle-obama-bradley-cooper-veterans-american-sniper-6/22591537/

'One Soldier's Journey: The Story of *American Sniper*' (2014), bonus track of *American Sniper*, DVD, Warner Bros.

Pelton, Robert Young (2006), *Licensed to Kill: Hired Guns in the War on Terror*, New York: Crown Books.

Philips, Joshua E. S. (2010), *None of Us Were Like this Before: American Soldiers and Torture*, New York: Verso.

Priest, Christopher, and Bart Sears (2004), *Captain America and the Falcon: The Two Americas*, Vol. 1 (#1–4), New York: Marvel Comics.

Priest, Christopher, and Andrea Divito (2005), *Captain America and the Falcon: Brothers and Keepers*, Vol. 2 (# 8–14), New York: Marvel Comics.

Purdum, Todd S. (2001), 'After the attacks; the White House warns of a wrathful, shadowy and inventive War', *New York Times*, 17 September 2001, last accessed 21 May 2015: http://www.nytimes.com/2001/09/17/us/after-attacks-white-house-bush-warns-wrathful-shadowy-inventive-war.html

Rieber, John Ney, and John Cassady (2002), *Captain America: One Nation*, Vol. 4 (#1), New York: Marvel Comics.

Schmidt, Michael S. (2014), 'US steps up fight to block ISIS volunteers', *New York Times*, 8 October 2014, last accessed 20 June 2015: http://www.nytimes.com/2014/10/09/world/middleeast/us-steps-up-fight-to-block-isis-volunteers.html

Schmidt, Michael S., and Matt Apuzzo (2015), 'David Petraeus is sentenced to probation in leak investigation', *New York Times*, 23 April 2015, last accessed 31 May 2015: www.nytimes.com/2015/04/24/us/david-petraeus-to-be-sentenced-in-leak-investigation.html

Schogol, Jeff (2014), '"American War Generals" a sobering reflection on US failures', *Navy Times*, 11 September 2014, last accessed 13 May 2015: http://archive.militarytimes.com/article/20140911/OFFDUTY02/309110065/-American-War-Generals-sobering-reflection-U-S-failures-Iraq

Sluka, Jeffrey A. (2011), 'Death from above: UAVs and losing hearts and minds', *Military Review*, May/June, pp. 70–6.

Stanton, Doug (2009), *The Horse Soldiers: The Extraordinary Story of a Band of US Soldiers Who Rode to Victory in Afghanistan*, New York: Simon & Schuster.

Stevens, J. Richard (2015), *Captain America, Masculinity, and Violence: The Evolution of a National Icon*, Syracuse, NY: Syracuse University Press.

Straczynski, J. Michael, and John Romita, Jr. (2002), 'Spider-Man #36', in *The Best of Spider-Man: Volume One*, New York: Marvel Publishing.

CHAPTER 2

Responding to Realities or Telling the Same Old Story? Mixing Real-world and Mythic Resonances in *The Kingdom* (2007) and *Zero Dark Thirty* (2012)

Geoff King

I. INTRODUCTION

To what extent do Hollywood features that dramatise aspects of the so-called 'War on Terror' respond in some ways to what we can understand to be the *realities* of the situation, either directly or in more general and approximate terms? How far, on the contrary, do they seek to impose fictional, or mythic-ideological, frameworks onto this kind of subject matter? Or, in what ways might such different approaches be combined, variously, in particular examples? This chapter addresses these questions through an analysis of two films that are in some ways contrasting but that also overlap in certain respects: *The Kingdom* and *Zero Dark Thirty*. *The Kingdom* begins by emphasising the real-world context of its fictional version of the response to an attack on an American oil compound in Saudi Arabia. But it then proceeds to offer an in many ways classic example of the imposition of familiar frameworks, in its evocation of a number of characteristics associated with the long-standing mythology of the American frontier – an approach that can be seen to serve a strong ideological purpose. *Zero Dark Thirty* also includes some such resonances, but to a much lesser extent, as a result of its greater commitment to claims to offer something closer to a reconstruction of particular real-world events relating to the hunt for, and eventual assassination of, Osama Bin Laden.

Underlying such films, I suggest, we can identify at least two, sometimes rival, imperatives. One is a desire on the part of the filmmakers (whether conceived at the level of figures such as writers and directors or of producers and studio executives) to respond to the real-world context, broadly or in more specific fashion. Another is the imperative to produce work that fits into particular Hollywood commercial routines, the nature of which can also vary. The latter include options that range between the production of recuperative fantasy – offering positive, feel-good impressions that counter any disturbing implications of a context such as the 'War on Terror', often including mainstream-conventional sources of action-thrills among their major attractions – and more 'serious' modalities that offer fewer such appeals in the process of seeking to take the moral complexities of the material more greatly on board.

How exactly Hollywood films have responded to events such as the 'War on Terror', or the post-9/11 context more generally, can often be understood in terms of the outcome of alternative imperatives such as these. How far these events changed Hollywood production remains subject to much debate. Contrary to some accounts that have made sweeping and unconvincing claims of large-scale change (notably, Pollard 2011), I would argue that much also remained the same in many examples of Hollywood's output in this period, including some films that directly addressed issues such as the fight against certain forms of 'terrorism'[1] committed under the name of Islam. It is clear that some shifts of focus occurred in Hollywood, particularly in embracing specific issues and situations that either directly represented or resonated with events such as the so-called 'War on Terror'. The process through which Hollywood films typically do this is one that is considered briefly at the start of this chapter. But it is equally clear – often glaringly so, I would suggest – that plenty also remained the same and that many post-9/11 and/or 'War on Terror'-era studio films continue to draw on very familiar routines, even if examples that differ in significant ways can also be identified.

One of these routines, as found very clearly in *The Kingdom*, entails the mobilisation of a set of thematic oppositions that draw strongly on the resonances of frontier mythology, a very familiar dimension of American culture. Many post-9/11 films can be understood in these terms, particularly via the figuration of central characters in respects akin to those of the classic notion of the 'frontiersman', or that share some very similar structural oppositions. In this respect, such films can be situated in a long Hollywood tradition, one I have examined in other instances from the pre-9/11 era elsewhere (King 2000) and also in relation to some other films from the contemporary period in which the focus is on representations of the war/s in Iraq (King 2016b). The continuity between many Hollywood features before and after 9/11 in this respect is striking, I suggest, demonstrating some of the ways in which myth/ideology can be seen to function, persistently, in texts of these kinds.

Before addressing these examples in detail, it is useful to consider how, more generally, we might understand the manner in which a source of cultural production such as Hollywood takes on board aspects of real-world events or contexts, such as those of the post-9/11 era. That some studio films engage with, respond to or 'reflect' such material in general terms, as part of their appeal to a broad audience, is often taken for granted in general public/critical discourse. The interpretation of Hollywood, or other forms of popular cinema, in this way is also a well-established part of academic analysis, often traced back in particular to the work of Siegfried Kracauer (originally 1947; 2004) on the cinema of the Weimar Republic in Germany, which he views as a window onto central aspects of the socio-psychology of the period. Films are often read as offering reflections – or, preferably, more active shapings of understandings – of aspects of their times, with varying degrees of metaphorical distance from or proximity to the nature of actual events. Ryan and Kellner (1990) and Kellner (2010) use the term 'transcoding' to describe a process through which particular ideological discourses are translated into media texts, although the exact mechanisms through which this works are often less than fully explained. Many films of what he defines as the Bush-Cheney era are said by Kellner broadly to 'tap into' phenomena such as 'the events, fantasies, and hopes of an era' (2010: 4), but what exactly 'tapping into' involves is, in this case, generally left unexplored.

This is, clearly, a large and important issue, one that can only be touched on here. I propose, as a starting point, thinking at the level of the kinds of pragmatic approaches that might be expected of Hollywood filmmakers. In many cases, I suggest, filmmakers seek to offer some contemporary currency as part of the overall recipe according to which some films are put together. This might involve directly engaging in territory such as that which is the focus of this book, as in examples such as *The Kingdom* and *Zero Dark Thirty*. But it can also involve adding certain reference points, metaphors or carriers of resonances to a wider range of films. A good example of the latter is *War of the Worlds* (2005), an alien invasion fantasy that includes a number of quite direct references to the principal events of 9/11 (including the dust that coats the principal character as a result of the disintegration of victims of the Martian death rays, the displays of home-made posters appealing for sightings of missing people, and explicit references such as the question 'is it the terrorists?' asked, almost comically amid the mayhem, by his daughter). It would be mistaken, I think, to view this film as a 'product' of 9/11, in the sense of being a film that came about *as a result of* those events. It is a film that was perfectly likely to have appeared if 9/11 had *not* happened, given the various ways in which it fulfils core Hollywood industrial strategies of the time (as a spectacular blockbuster, as a pre-sold science fiction scenario, as a star vehicle for Tom Cruise, as a film with a superstar director, Steven Spielberg, and as a combination of all of these factors).

This is a question insufficiently asked in many cases by those who interpret films as productions or metaphorical expressions of this particular historical, socio-cultural context. It might be argued that specific aspects of the film were shaped by the 9/11 factor, however; the particular darkness of parts of *War of the Worlds*, for example (I am deliberately writing in broad and speculative terms, here, of how we might generally interpret such things, rather than seeking to test them against what information might be available about the specific production history of any particular example[2]). Exactly how we understand these relationships is an important, often neglected issue. We might view films, variously, as *products of* a situation (very strong linkage); as not products of but as being *shaped by* particular real-world contexts in some respects, even if they might have appeared otherwise; or as having *resonances with* something such as the discourses and practices associated with the 'War on Terror', without necessarily arguing for the existence of any direct form of determination.

It is normal practice, I would argue, for Hollywood to include references or broader resonances of these kinds to contemporary real-world material in films that are not necessarily in any way directly 'about' whatever topic is involved. To do so, in a case such as *War of the Worlds*, can be understood as a way the filmmakers seek to give an extra dimension to the work: in this case, to make the horrifying nature of the alien attack – the stuff of unlikely fantasy – seem several degrees more real, or closer to what can be imagined to be a plausible reality, by employing elements of detail that evoke the nearest equivalent that might be found to a recent real-world event. This is a question of the shaping of the operative modalities at work in the film. Some Hollywood films might be equally likely to *avoid* the inclusion of such resonances, or to make them very much more implicit, precisely to maintain a stronger balance in favour of what would generally be seen as the modality of 'escapist' fantasy that does not bring such painful contexts to bear on fictional material designed primarily as a source of entertainment.

In the case of films that include more immediate elements of contemporary geopolitical material, such as representations of the 'War on Terror', similar kinds of choices are available. This appears to be an arena in which some (variable) sense of plausible relation to real-world issues has often been favoured in Hollywood productions of the post-9/11 era. To make a film involving the activities of agencies such as the FBI or CIA in this period without including some sense of real-world resonance might be to risk too great a loss of plausibility to be desirable; at least, in films that are positioned at the relatively more serious/substantial end of the studio scale. (It is ironic that one example that generally seems to lean much more towards the implausible, in general comic modality and plotting, *The Interview* [2015], produced a storm of real-world repercussions because its scenario – however daft and detached from likelihood – entailed the imaginary assassination of a real-world geopolitical figure and thus provoked a reaction at that level.) This raises a number of questions relating to the motivations of Hollywood filmmakers/studios, including the extent to which they are driven by the desire to frame some films as relatively more 'serious' or 'substantial' than others, something I address in general at length elsewhere in terms of the notion of the 'quality' studio feature (King 2016a). If we think of the types of films that tend to be involved in the treatment of issues such as 'wars' on terrorism, they tend to fall into a particular range or combination of genres – particularly various kinds of 'thriller' (or 'espionage thriller'), which might also draw to varying degrees on other territory such as that of the 'war' or 'action' film (*Body of Lies* [2008] and *Green Zone* [2010], for example, combine a number of such components). These might, in some cases, also be combined with aspects of the 'serious' social issues films (the 'social problem film', as classically designated).

A number of different imperatives might thus be in play. These include in some cases a desire to position a film as a 'serious' representation of the kinds of issues or moral dilemmas entailed in the prosecution of a 'War on Terror'. But they can also entail the construction of scenarios that provide scope for what would conventionally be understood as more mainstream 'crowd-pleasing' dimensions, such as the staging of heroic action. It is to a large extent within or between these parameters that I situate *The Kingdom* and *Zero Dark Thirty* in this chapter. *The Kingdom* offers by far the more mainstream-conventional engagement of the two, despite some noteworthy qualifications, drawing very clearly on the kinds of thematic oppositions associated with the articulation of frontier mythology and related aspects of hegemonic ideology, and in the process producing scope for conventional forms of individual-heroic agency. *Zero Dark Thirty* is considerably more questioning or neutral in tone, particularly as far as such agency is concerned, but also establishes some similar thematic resonances, if in a more muted manner.

II. REAL-WORLD POINTS OF REFERENCE AND MARKERS OF 'SERIOUS' MODALITY

Both films establish considerable points of reference in the real-world context of the 'War on Terror', each including some relation to the *ur-villain* figure of the time, within this framework, Osama Bin Laden. These films are clearly *products of* the historical reality in this sense, as opposed to having the more diffuse types of shapings or resonances outlined in some instances above. *Zero Dark Thirty* has this status in a very obvious way, being a dramatisation of a version of what were presented as the real investigations and mission leading to the assassination of Bin Laden by the American military.[3] Bin Laden also figures in *The Kingdom*, directly in the establishment of some historical background and indirectly in the figure of a militant Islamic leader/bomb maker within the diegesis, Abu Hamza (Hezi Saddik), who is referred to at one point as an 'Osama wannabe'.[4] The real Osama makes an appearance in a sequence that opens the film, a potted background that sketches some of the history of the relationship between the film's principal setting, Saudi Arabia, and the United States. At a full three minutes, this is unusually long for such a context-setting sequence in a Hollywood feature.

A mixture of graphics and historical footage accompanied by voices from news reports – what sound like 'expert' opinions and others the implied status of which is unclear – is used to provide an account that focuses particularly on the basis of the relationship in the American need for access to Saudi oil and the opposition provided by 'fiercely anti-Western' Wahhabi Islamists within the country and the particularly antagonistic figure of Bin Laden. The sequence seems to represent a concerted attempt to establish some of the real-world context, if mostly outside the main body of the film. Neither side of the opposition between radical Islam and the alliance of convenience between the US state and the Saudi royal family is presented very positively, even if the dice are inevitably weighted overall in favour of the latter. Animated block graphs demonstrating the status of Saudi as the world's largest oil producer and the US as its largest consumer morph into the shape of the twin towers of the World Trade Center. This seems to imply a causal link between the US/Saudi relationship, and the opposition it generated, and this outcome – an implication that seems generally quite radical for a Hollywood feature (it is followed by the establishment of the fact that fifteen out of the nineteen hijackers were Saudi, another marker of the problematic nature of the superpower relationship).

Additional factual background is worked into some of the early scenes of the dramatic narrative, one that involves the sending of an FBI mission to investigate a huge bombing at an American oil company compound in Riyadh. This includes further reference to the strategy of Al-Qaeda and the sensitive nature of any American presence in the country, identified as one of the justifications used for bomb attacks of this kind. The film also dramatises a number of internal American conflicts between different state bodies, and/or their individual agents, with the FBI mission being undertaken directly against the wishes of major institutions such as the State Department and the Department of Justice (oppositions the basis of which are explored further below). The implication is that the material of the film is rooted in real-world situations and can be taken as a fictionalisation of some of the dynamics that result.

Zero Dark Thirty makes a more sustained and literal claim to real-world reference, starting with the opening title making the strong proclamation that: 'The following motion picture is based on first-hand accounts of actual events' (the term 'first hand' claims a greater immediacy than more widely used phrasings such as 'based on actual events' or 'based on a true story'). The post-9/11 context is then immediately established via a sequence in which a caption reads 'September 11, 2001' and a black screen is accompanied by a montage of voices reflecting various responses to the attacks. A stark impression is created, sustained for nearly ninety seconds, one that seeks to evoke the horror of the occasion without what might be seen as the exploitative use of any visual representation. The latter, in itself, marks a further claim to 'serious' or 'thoughtful' engagement with the subject matter. The film's version of the subsequent investigations, including the hunt for Bin Laden, is intermingled with the regular inclusion of real-world reference points, including a number of further attacks. Some of these are relegated to background while others are reconstructed in stagings that involve the central characters, notably a bombing at the Marriott Hotel, Islamabad, in 2008, during which the main CIA protagonist Maya (Jessica Chastain) and a colleague Jessica (Jennifer Ehle) are present, and a suicide bombing at a US base in Afghanistan that kills the latter. The representation of the torture of detainees, meanwhile, clearly evokes some of the notorious images of abuses at the Abu Ghraib prison in Iraq, including the fitting of a dog collar to one victim and the humiliating display of his sexual organs to Maya during one session, along with more generally controversial real-world practices such as waterboarding and the use of stress positions (the film also, later, reflects external criticism of such practices and the closure of this particular detainee programme as a result). The initial evocation of 9/11 and the representation of further attacks functions effectively in the film to imply a justification for the torture of detainees, part of the purpose of which is presented as seeking to prevent upcoming bombings, and for the general mission that increasingly comes to narrow down to the hunt for Bin Laden.

Both films also back up the claims to real-world resonance contained in this kind of content with the implicit effect of their visual style, each adopting a variant of 'shaky-cam' footage that carries with it the resonances of documentary-reality status. This is more noticeable in *The Kingdom*, where camerawork is often distinctly unstable, creating the impression of being 'grabbed' on the fly in the midst of events rather than the outcome of careful construction (which it still remains, of course; the impression is precisely a rhetorical construct). The film also employs on-screen captions to identify some of the main protagonists in the early stages, another device that creates a documentary impression, as one that would usually be employed to identify real-world rather than fictional figures. *Zero Dark Thirty* employs a more subtle version of the unsteadicam, much of its footage having a slight camera motion visible at the margins, the effect of which is a more subliminal claim to the status of something akin to reality.

III. HEROIC ACTION OR ITS RELATIVE ABSENCE

What kinds of movie scenarios and approaches are then inserted into or combined with the dimension of real-world context presented by these films? It is here that *The Kingdom* and *Zero Dark Thirty* represent considerably different tendencies, if still with some points of overlap. *The Kingdom* illustrates a very familiar Hollywood reliance on central tropes related to the inheritance of frontier-type discourse, both in itself and as a motivating framework for sequences that steer the film in the direction of the action genre. *Zero Dark Thirty* offers very much less of the latter, and none at all that is focused directly on the central protagonist, largely as a result of the nature of the stronger real-world-based scenario within which the diegesis is positioned (if its claims of first-hand authenticity are to be plausible, there are limits to how far it could go in, say, inventing some more action-oriented activities for the central character). It does, however, offer a variety of heroism of its own that shares some qualities with those associated with frontier-style action, although in a distinctly different mode.

The Kingdom sets up a classic, very familiar opposition between how it situates its hero, and some related characters, and others to which he is juxtaposed. The focus of the film is on the championing of those involved in what is characterised as direct, hands-on action, on the ground, as opposed to those situated as politically, bureaucratically or otherwise mendaciously motivated to block or interfere with such expressions of agency (for another example that mobilises the same type of opposition in broadly similar territory, see *Body of Lies*, one of the examples examined in King 2016b). It is within this frame that the main protagonist, Fleury (Jamie Foxx), is established as a figure who carries some of the resonances of the traditional frontiersman, here in the guise of an FBI agent. Fleury and his immediate colleagues want to travel to Saudi to investigate for themselves the causes of the bombing in Riyadh, motivation at a personal level being added through the fact that the dead include two agency colleagues. Their requests are denied by the various forces cited above, on the basis of what is presented as political expediency. Through what is characterised as an act of skilled backstage wrangling, Fleury manages to secure permission from the Saudis for himself and three others, without official approval from either the State Department or the White House. On the scene, the group faces further obstruction from the Saudi authorities, who initially restrict their access to the site of the bombing, and discouragement from an American embassy official, the latter presented as wheedling and pusillanimous. With the help of a positively coded local policeman, Haytham (Ali Suliman), and as a result of further initiative shown by Fleury during a meeting with a Saudi prince, they are eventually able to act more or less unconstrained, a process that leads to the uncovering of the identity of those responsible for the attack.

The hands-on, on-the-ground action dimension that forms a central component of the characterisation of modern incarnations of the frontiersman (for more on this, see King 2000) is manifested literally. It is seen in the initial demand to have 'boots on the ground', in Saudi, as opposed to operation from a distance or reliance on others. It is then developed in more specifics in the bomb-site investigation as conducted by team member Sykes (Chris Cooper), which entails an actual process of 'getting your hands dirty', as he puts it, by groping around for evidence in the muddy crater left by the principal explosion. Fleury himself, meanwhile, is established as a character who acts by 'instinct' more than anything else, another key component of this mythic figuration. The subject of acting by instinct is brought up by the prince, in

Figure 2.1 'Getting your hands dirty': on-the-ground action by Sykes (Chris Cooper) at the bomb site in *The Kingdom* (2007).

relation to one of his hunting hawks, but the context is one in which the reference is quite clearly also to Fleury. In an incident in which the team is attacked when travelling by road in a convoy, for example, we are shown intimations of what is about to happen, as seemingly picked up 'instinctively' in advance by the hero.

Central heroic qualities are shared among the team members to a significant extent, but Fleury is clearly positioned at the head of the group, both generally and in the action that leads to the conclusion of the film. One team member, the least active and least comfortable on overseas/frontier-type terrain, Leavitt (Jason Bateman), is kidnapped and about to be executed on camera, while Fleury, female colleague Mayes (Jennifer Garner) and Saudi police colonel Faris Al-Ghazi (Ashraf Barhom) fight to rescue him. A vehicle chase is followed by a prolonged sequence of firefight action in a 'hostile' neighbourhood. No time is available for a call for backup, we are told, leaving the outnumbered threesome to engage in the requisite (and largely implausible) action that results (similarly establishing the same obligatory dynamic in such cases – that of the small heroic group left to sort things out on their own – is the fact that their initial deployment in Saudi includes the presence of no supporting security force).

Heroic-action agency of this kind is largely absent from *Zero Dark Thirty*, a clear marker of its different balance of modalities. A physical separation is made between the forces which take part in the eventual

Special Forces operation to kill Bin Laden and the central character, Maya. It is notable that she is involved in no direct action heroics at all. She comes under assault on two occasions, once in the hotel bombing and once when her car is fired upon as she is about to leave the American embassy in Islamabad. In the first case, she is little more than one of many shocked survivors. In the second, her only response – realistically enough – is to slam her car into reverse, back behind the security gates. At no point does her investigative role translate into one of directly pursuing the subjects of the investigation, contrary to the popular-fictional trope (convenience) in which the two roles are often combined, as is the case in *The Kingdom* (this is an implausible device familiar from other contemporary contexts, notably the various *CSI: Crime Scene Investigation* TV series [2000–]).

Maya's heroism is framed as a form of dogged persistence, in her insistence on the fruitful nature of the one line of enquiry that eventually leads to the location of Bin Laden. She does this in the face of repeated opposition and scepticism from her superiors. This establishes something of the kind of opposition found in *The Kingdom*, although to a lesser extent. A distinction is maintained between her certainty, and her demand for action, and those who prevaricate, even after more senior colleagues eventually take on board her argument in the latter stages of the film (a key manifestation of this is the number she keeps writing on a glass partition wall between herself and her senior, noting the escalating number of days – up to and beyond one hundred – that pass without any action being taken). More senior figures, or those from other departments including the White House, are presented as cautious and sceptical, but it is notable that in this case they are given a more rounded and less negative characterisation than equivalents in *The Kingdom*. The film also implies that Maya possesses the kind of instinctive knowledge or foresight attributed to Fleury, in the certainty she maintains in her beliefs, an issue in which the dice are of course loaded for the viewer, knowing as we are likely to do that she is right because of our foreknowledge of the reported real-world outcome of the process.

Some striking differences are apparent between the nature of the final action-mission sequences in the two films, although there are also some points of overlap that lean towards the more serious modality in which some moral complexity is implied. The mission itself in *Zero Dark Thirty* is presented in a distinctly less than heroic manner. The Special Forces team (sympathetically characterised in themselves, personally) encounters very limited resistance, killing a small number of male figures and one woman and terrifying a group of children.

Figure 2.2 No sense of heroic triumph: Maya (Jessica Chastain) identifying the body of Osama Bin Laden in *Zero Dark Thirty* (2012).

Bin Laden himself is presented as being shot at close range while lying apparently defenceless in bed. The reaction of Maya to confirmation of apparent success, and when she is called upon to identity the body after the return to base, is without any hint of triumph or satisfaction. The closing stages of the film are distinctly sombre in tone, featuring muted, uncelebratory music and the quiet shedding of tears.

The Kingdom offers a much more conventional climax in terms of the nature of the conflict, as a sustained source of familiar action-movie thrills resulting from explosions and exchanges of gunfire. Some quite brutal close-quarters exchanges are also included, notably one involving Mayes as she manages to free Leavitt. The film also ends on a distinctly sombre note, however, closer here to that of *Zero Dark Thirty* than in most other respects. The action climaxes with the killing of Hamza in front of members of his family, particularly his grandson, to whom he whispers a final comment. The inclusion of family members is part of a pattern employed across the film, primarily in relation to Fleury and his relationship with others. The film begins with Fleury on a visit to the school of his young son and provides other spaces for engagements between the two that establish his status as a character with a commitment to the domestic world as well as to that of special-action thrills. This is notable given that these two dimensions are often separated out in manifestations of frontier-type mythology (for more on this, see King 2000, 2016b). Fleury also visits the young son of one of the FBI colleagues who died in the initial explosion, and the son of Al-Ghazi after he also perishes in the climactic scenes. It is notable, then, that the 'bad guys' are also given this family dimension, if to a lesser extent, as a way of seeming to humanise their general position. A similar familial status is granted to the Bin Laden contingent in their compound in *Zero Dark Thirty*, although in this case a notable contrast exists with the presentation of Maya as a mission-obsessed officer lacking any apparent domestic/family connections. If her characterisation does not fit into conventional frontier routines at the level of direct, hands-on heroic action, it shares the dimension in which a presence in this world is often set in opposition to that of settled domesticity.

Most striking in *The Kingdom*, however, is a parallel that is drawn at the close of the film. Back in the US, Leavitt asks Fleury what he had said to Mayes in the early stages of the film, to stop her crying after the initial news of the death of their colleagues in the Riyadh attack. The film then cuts to one of the women in Hamza's family group, similarly asking the young girl what her grandfather had whispered to her before he died. 'I told her we were gonna kill 'em all', is Fleury's reply to Leavitt, followed by a cut to the girl's answer, that Hamza's words were, 'Don't fear them, my child. We are going to kill them all.' To suggest such a mirroring of responses, in this context, seems a daring move for a generally mainstream-oriented Hollywood feature. Any hint of moral equivalence between the two sides might be expected to be beyond the pale of what would be likely to be entertained in a context such as this. Equally unusual is the fact that the final image of the film is from the Saudi location, a big close-up shot on the eyes of the girl, one that implies an emotional proximity to her situation.

Both films end, then, in a mood that is sombre and with events that seem likely to evoke a sense of moral disquiet. If *The Kingdom* is generally the more conventional of the two, in its provision of plenty of hands-on action heroics, it offers that one element of final moral equivalence that is unusual for a studio feature and stronger than any doubt encouraged by *Zero Dark Thirty*. These are respects in which both lean towards the 'serious' end of the Hollywood spectrum of engagement in such territory. This is a position that appears to want to go at least some way towards embracing some of the more complex aspects of notions such as that of a 'War on Terror', rather than an approach in which such material is used as a basis on which to articulate simpler, black-and-white moral oppositions. *Zero Dark Thirty* can be compared, for example, with the more mainstream-conventional TV movie *Seal Team 6: The Raid on Osama Bin Laden* (also known as *Codename: Geronimo*, *The Hunt for Osama Bin Laden*, 2012), a feature that presents a much more positive version of the assassination mission. Here, the Bin Laden compound seems to be more strongly defended, resulting in more fire-fight action and a sense of more equal conflict (and in which Bin Laden himself is portrayed as being shot while standing up and holding an automatic weapon); the assault team is repeatedly told to be careful not to shoot women or children; the equivalent of the Maya character ends up all smiles; and the upbeat closing scenes include President Obama celebrating the 'patriotism' and 'courage' of those involved in the mission. Peter Berg, meanwhile, director of *The Kingdom*, returned to this kind of terrain with *Lone Survivor* (2013), a 'mission gone wrong' feature set in Afghanistan in which a small group of Special Forces (again, typical modern frontier figures) are hugely outnumbered in 'hostile' behind-the-lines Western-type rocky hillside territory. It is a film that almost fetishistically emphasises the suffering bodies of the heroes during extended sequences of fighting action before the single survivor, having been helped by anti-Taliban Afghanis (equivalents of the 'good Indian' in the frontier tradition), is rescued by the airborne 'cavalry'.

IV. EXPLANATIONS?

How, then, do we explain the kinds of qualities found in examples such as *The Kingdom* and *Zero Dark Thirty*, and the particular balance in which they are held? Some aspects of both films seem clearly to result from an orientation on the part of the filmmakers, at some level, towards wanting to position their works as relatively serious engagements with some of the difficult issues entailed in the notion of the 'War on Terror'. This raises a number of further questions about the space that is available in contemporary Hollywood for such an approach, and from which figures such an imperative might come. Is it a question, for example, of individual filmmakers who seek to pursue such an approach – even if it might be considered to go against the commercial grain – and what opportunities are available for this attitude with the studio regime? The existence of such potential might also be dependent on financial support and/or budgetary limitations.

Films that offer less in the way of celebratory dynamics, such as *Zero Dark Thirty*, might be expected to have less commercial potential, and so to be considered viable only within limited parameters. Despite being a studio release, from the Sony division, Columbia Pictures, *Zero Dark Thirty*'s quite modest $40 million budget was provided entirely independently, by Meg Ellison's Annapurna Pictures investment fund, one that has tended to invest in less obviously commercial-seeming projects (another example from the same year was P.T. Anderson's *The*

Master), a factor that gave it scope to resist what might be expected to be more conventional studio pressures. It was also a film strongly shaped by the individual inclinations of the screenwriter Mark Boal and director Kathryn Bigelow, as suggested by numerous press reports that discuss its origins (for example, Cieply and Barnes 2012). *The Kingdom* is generally a more conventional studio picture in its overall balance, produced by Universal, although it also gained from outside funding. Its $70 million budget was shared between the studio and the financier Relativity Media, as part of a multi-film deal between the two (Garrett 2008), an increasingly frequent practice in Hollywood at the time, at both the more and less commercial ends of the scale.

The Kingdom performed disappointingly at the box office, however, grossing $47 million in the US and $39 overseas (a total of $86 million worldwide).[5] If, as the trade paper *Variety* reported, it 'could be an early bellwether of whether general auds [sic] are ready to see films addressing the consequences of the "War on Terror"', the answer appeared not to be very positive, even with the film's inclusion of plenty of familiar action-heroics (McClintock 2007). The less mainstream-conventional *Zero Dark Thirty* did substantially better, grossing $95 million domestically and $37 million overseas (a total of $132 million). This might seem to be an anomaly but can be explained by a combination of the publicity generated by the film, particularly by controversy over whether or not it was interpreted as effectively endorsing the effectiveness of torture, and by its achievement of high-profile Academy Award nominations, including that of Best Picture and Best Original Screenplay (a total of five nominations, of which it won only for Best Sound Editing).

Explaining the presence of the frontier-type dynamic, where it is found, seems easier. It is a very familiar part of American culture and as such the kind of framework upon which Hollywood films are often likely to draw, as very many continue to do, both generally and in relation to material of a potentially difficult or contentious nature. It provides a schema that seems particularly useful in contexts such as this, in that it structures a capacity to celebrate certain core traditional notions of American heroic values while *at the same time* providing a mechanism through which to acknowledge some difficulties at a wider level such as that of the politics of foreign policy either in general or in specific areas. A manoeuvre that separates out the two dimensions, in this way, permits a focus on central sympathetic characters, who can be portrayed as 'good' and well-motivated (and, as such, it is implied, representatives of 'true' American values), while others can take the blame. In the context of the issues considered in this chapter, the latter dimension is that which permits some apparent 'realism', in an acknowledgement of some of the complexities or shortcomings involved at the level of policy – even if the nature of these is often implicit more than fully developed – without losing the potential for the celebration of the actions of individual heroic protagonists.

Such a structure can be understood, then, as a mythic-ideological framework that is highly functional to the kind of treatment of such issues that might be sought by films of broadly mainstream commercial orientation that deal with this terrain. It is no accident that the same kind of myth-ideology was also deployed heavily in films of very different kinds set during the even more controversial Vietnam War (from *The Deerhunter* [1978] and *Rambo: First Blood Part II* [1985] to *Platoon* [1986]; see King 2000). In the films examined in this chapter, its mobilisation is clearest in *The Kingdom*. *Zero Dark Thirty* makes a greater commitment to something *presented as* the relatively 'unvarnished' truth, however much aspects of this were disputed in media reporting of the film (see, for example, Coll 2013) and might be questioned, the result of which is to make such oppositions less supportable. Their inevitable over-simplifications would make them untenable, in fully articulated form, in this context. Very much less is found in the way of frontier-resonant action heroism, on the one hand, and of critique of other state-related forces, on the other. Both poles of the opposition are attenuated, if not entirely absent, which makes for what is positioned as a more nuanced treatment overall.

Although with a difference in balance between the two, both films can be seen to offer some ambiguity of approach, a frequent Hollywood strategy when dealing with potentially contentious material (see, for another contemporaneous example, Elsaesser 2011 on *Avatar* [2009]). This can be understood as a way of leaving the text open to different interpretations from those in rival camps, as far as the general politics of such matters is concerned, an approach that is commercially functional to an attempt to appeal to a wide range of potential viewers (*Zero Dark Thirty* is a strong example of a production that received widely varying critical response in terms of whether it was seen as supporting or questioning the manner of prosecution of the 'War on Terror'). They fit, in this respect, into a wider category of post-9/11 films identified by Guy Westwell (2014), features that he also suggests seek mechanisms for the reconciliation of political differences, alongside others that are more straightforwardly celebratory or critical of these aspects of American policy. I would agree with Westwell that this is a process broadly 'in service of hegemonic renewal' (14), particularly as it operates in mainstream features, one that 'while acknowledging some ambiguity, restores credibility for US national identity as a whole' (178). It does this particularly, I would suggest, through the portrayal of what is presented as an essential virtue in the principal American protagonists with whom the viewer is encouraged to be aligned.

NOTES

1. I put 'scare' quotation marks around this term (along with 'War on Terror') because it tends to be employed very partially in dominant discourse, often serving in effect to close off various questions about the relative cases for or against one variety of violent action or another by one party or another.
2. Some discussion of the specifics of this case can be found in an interview with the screenwriter, David Koepp, in Rob Feld (2005). Koepp falls back on rather unhelpful blandishments, however, such as the suggestion that specific 9/11 references 'weren't put in because of 9/11; they were put in because we all lived through 9/11. We all come out of the same set of experiences, and we just decided not to censor ourselves, because that's not realistic, that's not the world we live in' (142–3).
3. This was very much the context in which the film was released and discussed, regardless of any doubt about the veracity of this version of the underlying story that was cast by some commentators in subsequent years.
4. The status of this figure himself seems somewhat ambiguous. He bears the same name as a real-world figure and shares with the film's version a degree of physical mutilation (in the film, missing fingers; in the real figure, the loss of both hands and an eye). But the real-world Abu Hamza was jailed for life in 2015 after being found guilty of supporting terrorism by a New York court, rather than being shot to death as is the fate of the figure with the same name in *The Kingdom*.
5. These and the figures below for *Zero Dark Thirty* are from the entries for the films on the website Box Office Mojo, boxofficemojo.com

REFERENCES

Cieply, Michael, and Brooks Barnes (2012), 'Bin Laden Film's Focus is Facts, Not Flash', *The New York Times*, 23 November 2012: http://www.nytimes.com/2012/11/24/movies/zero-dark-thirty-by-kathryn-bigelow-focuses-on-facts.html?pagewanted=all&_r=0

Coll, Steve (2013), '"Disturbing" and "Misleading"', *The New York Review of Books*, 7 February 2013: http://www.nybooks.com/articles/archives/2013/feb/07/disturbing-misleading-zero-dark-thirty/

Garrett, Diane (2008), 'Relativity pacts big with Universal', *Variety*, 27 February 2008: http://variety.com/2008/film/news/relativity-pacts-big-with-universal-1117981527/

Elsaesser, Thomas (2011), 'James Cameron's *Avatar*: access for all', *New Review of Film and Television Studies*, Vol. 9, No. 3.

Feld, Rob (2005), 'Q & A with David Koepp', in Josh Friedman and David Koepp, *War of the Worlds: The Shooting Script*, New York: Newmarket Press.

Kellner, Douglas (2010), *Cinema Wars: Hollywood Film and Politics in the Bush-Cheney Era*, Oxford: Wiley-Blackwell.

King, Geoff (2000), *Spectacular Narratives: Hollywood in the Age of the Blockbuster*, London: I. B. Tauris.

— (2016a), *Quality Hollywood: Markers of Distinction in Contemporary Studio Film*, London: I. B. Tauris.

— (2016b), 'Reassertions of Hollywood heroic agency in the Iraq war film', in Claire Molloy and Yannis Tzioumakis (eds), *Routledge Companion to Film and Politics*, London: Routledge.

Kracauer, Siegfried (1947, 2004), *From Caligari to Hitler: A Psychological History of the German Film*, Princeton: Princeton University Press.

McClintock, Pamela (2007), '"Game Plan" wins weekend', *Variety*, 30 September 2007: http://variety.com/2007/film/news/game-plan-wins-weekend-1117973054/

Pollard, Tom (2011), *Hollywood 9/11: Superheroes, Supervillains, and Super Disasters*, London: Paradigm.

Ryan, Michael, and Douglas Kellner (1990), *Camera Politica: The Politics and Ideology of Contemporary Hollywood Film*, Bloomington: Indiana University Press.

Westwell, Guy (2014), *Parallel Lines: Post-9/11 American Cinema*, London: Wallflower Press.

CHAPTER 3

Acts of Redemption and 'The Falling Man' Photograph in Post-9/11 US Cinema

Guy Westwell

I.

This article begins by providing context for the iconic photograph 'The Falling Man', which shows a single figure falling from the World Trade Center on 11 September 2001. It describes how the initial extremely restricted but varied experience of seeing people falling from the Twin Towers gave way to a single image: a photograph by veteran Associated Press photographer Robert Drew which has become known as 'The Falling Man'. This photograph has been the subject of considerable debate, especially in relation to trauma, national identity and aesthetics. In what follows, this debate is used to describe how 'The Falling Man' photograph gives structure to two mainstream Hollywood films: *Incredibly Loud and Extremely Close* (Stephen Daldry, US, 2011) and *The Walk* (Robert Zemeckis, US, 2015). A particular focus will be how this photograph is placed to different ends within classically constructed narratives that seek some semblance of order and resolution and also made subject to the full animating resources of the moving image. This movement – from a photograph recording a fraction of a second to a conventional narrative of longer duration, and from still photograph to moving image – enables both films to seek different forms of redemption via what Thomas Stubblefield describes as 'the cathartic power of the fall' (Stubblefield 2015: 58).

An estimated two billion people worldwide watched news broadcasts showing the 11 September terrorist attacks (Friend 2007: 32–3).

These news broadcasts contained a series of spectacular and shocking images – the planes flying into the buildings, the towers collapsing, lower Manhattan disappearing into an apocalyptic cloud of dust (Friend 2007: 32–3). Those who couldn't escape down the stairwells gathered around broken windows high in the towers, signalling for help and seeking to escape the heat and smoke. Many fell or chose to jump from the windows. According to a study conducted by USA Today, of the 2,948 people killed on 9/11 around two hundred, mainly located above the 90th floor in the North Tower, died in this way (Friend 2007: 133). Numerous amateur and professional photographers and videographers recorded their plight, including Jeff Christensen, Bill Biggart, Joseph McCarthy, Joe Scurto, Eddie Remy, Lyle Owerko and Richard Drew (Friend 2007: 29–31). However, Mikita Brottman describes how the early news coverage of 9/11 in the US, with news editors struggling to make sense of what had happened, were extremely reluctant to show photographic and film images of people falling (Brottman 2004: 176).[1] David Friend reports that executives at ABC News 'made the conscious decision *not* to broadcast sequences of bodies plummeting' and that 'NBC had reportedly aired a single body, once, then showed it no further' (Friend 2007: 130).[2] Tom Junod notes that at 'CNN, the footage was shown live [. . .] then, after what Walter Isaacson, who was then chairman of the network's news bureau, calls "agonized discussions" with the "standards guy," it was shown only if people in it were blurred and unidentifiable; then it was not shown at all' (Junod 2003). Instead, news coverage privileged and repeated footage of the planes hitting the World Trade Center, long shots of the buildings on fire, and the Twin Towers' eventual collapse.

Friend notes that in the US, film and photographs of people falling were 'generally kept out of circulation, as if by an unspoken compact among editors, art directors and picture editors' (Friend 2007: 137). This self-censorship – what Junod calls an instinctive 'cultural resistance' to the images – was largely retained in newspaper content on 12 September and in the days following (Junod 2003). Also proscribed were explicit images of death and dismemberment, a prohibition that extended to any image of the consequences of falling to the ground from such a great height (Sontag 2003: 61). As Stephen Prince observes, media 'gatekeeping'[3] ensured that '[t]he carnage on the streets below the towers, with hundreds of burst and shattered bodies strewn about the pavement, has never been written about or substantively photographed' (Prince 2012: 502). As such, where video or photographs of falling people existed these were uncoupled from explicit images of the consequences of falling, a separation that, as will be shown, had significant consequences.

Thomas Stubblefield observes that on a day of almost unparalleled horror, replete with spectacular and disturbing imagery, the experience of falling people was handled with extreme circumspection by the media because it carried a singular 'intense, unruly affective charge' (Stubblefield 2015: 58). This 'charge' was so powerful that despite the work of 'gate-keeping' and self-censorship the images have been relayed and amplified via a series of representations, including mainstream cinema.

9/11, directed and produced by French filmmakers Gédéon and Jules Naudet, was screened commercial-free on CBS on 10 March 2002. The film, which shows firefighters entering the Twin Towers after the planes have struck, contains a sequence in which they hear the sound of falling people hitting the ground. No visual images of the bodies are shown (and perhaps not even recorded). At a press screening, the film's executive producer explained that the number of sound recordings of bodies impacting were reduced on the grounds that '[t]o have that incredible crush of sound every twenty or thirty seconds would have been very tough for the audience' (quoted in Craps 2007: 199–200). This editorial decision follows the one taken by the news media: ameliorating the experience of the people falling via a turning away and a carefully calibrated reduction. Already this decision errs from the deaths of two hundred people to a reduced and more 'manageable' figure. 9/11 stitches the experience of these indicative falling people into a narrative that, as I argue elsewhere, ultimately endorses the resolve to wage war, with one of the firefighters pledging to join the military (see Westwell 2014: 39–59).[4]

In Memoriam – New York City, 9/11/01 was shown on HBO on 25 May 2002. Although the film is composed of footage of 9/11 gathered from sixteen news organisations and 118 New Yorkers, the variety of footage is subject to considerable editorial work and presents the day in a clear, chronological order orchestrated in relation to Rudy Giuliani's point of view (Giuliani was Mayor of New York at the time of the attacks). The film opens with oft-reproduced shots of the Twin Towers at sunset, with the World Trade Center golden and burnished against the wider cityscape. In voiceover Giuliani reflects on how he considered the World Trade Center a symbol of a particular type of egalitarian and specifically American 'freedom', defined as the ability to succeed through hard work. Giuliani then counsels that 9/11 must be looked at in all its awfulness so that it might fuel the resolve to defend this 'freedom'. Following this, the film shows photographs of people falling, a photograph of a body after the fall, and film of Giuliani reacting in horror to the sight of people falling. In its willingness to show these images *In Memoriam* is distinctive and potentially controversial. However, framed by the opening comments about the need to look at the true horror of the event, focalised via Giuliani's (rightward-leaning and jingoistic) point of view and carefully calibrated in terms of screen time, the film places the proscribed images in such a way as to align them with the dominant discourse. Martin Montgomery profiles this discourse, whereby in the media the terrorists' murderous acts became evil acts, then barbaric acts and then acts of war, and how the attack on New York quickly became an attack on the US and that this subsequently became an attack on civilisation (Montgomery 2005: 155–6). Montgomery argues that this 'movement from concrete, verifiable entities to large abstractions serves in practice only to mystify the underlying event by immediately embedding it in larger discourses of patriotism, the homeland, and the imagined community of the nation' (Montgomery 2005: 158). *In Memoriam* is similar in this way to the dramatised documentary *DC 9/11: Time of Crisis* (2003), in which a key scene shows George W. Bush (Timothy Bottoms) visiting a hospital treating burn victims and amputees. Both films show serious injury in order to justify retributive wars in Afghanistan and Iraq, with injury to the individual presented as injury to the body politic.

Alongside these two mainstream responses, and their careful balancing of ongoing self-censorship and the clearly politically motivated activation of the sounds and sights of falling people, were other direct approaches, chiefly by artists and artist-filmmakers. For example, falling figures appeared in a number of artworks, including Carolee Schneemann's *Terminal Velocity* (December 2001), a collage of digitally enhanced (enlarged, decontextualised) press photographs, Sharon Paz's *Falling* (2002), an installation of cutouts of falling figures silhouetted on the windows of the Jamaica Center in Queens, New York, and Eric Fischl's sculpture, *Tumbling Woman* (September 2002), which shows a falling woman just prior to hitting the ground. Without clear alignment with the dominant narrative, and in contrast to the mainstream documentaries, this work was subject to considerable ire, with Paz's and Fischl's work removed from public spaces following hostile press coverage and vociferous complaints (Swartz 2006).

Aligned more with this artistic response, González Iñárritu's contribution to the omnibus film *11'09"01 September 11* uses photographs and film footage of the falling people. The wider portmanteau film brings together eleven directors from as many countries, each contributing a film lasting eleven minutes, nine seconds and one frame, and was released in late 2002 in Europe, and early 2003 in the US. Iñárritu's film begins with a long sequence consisting only of a black screen. Myriad voices and an incantation fill the darkness. Alison Young identifies this 'found sound' as news coverage of the events of 9/11 from a diverse range of countries, including Vietnam, South Africa, Poland, Germany, Canada and the United States, set alongside a prayer for the dead chanted by the Chamulas Indians of Chiapas, Mexico (Young 2007: 42). Against this aural backdrop we see an almost subliminal shot of a few frames of a person falling. The shot increases in duration and becomes more intelligible. This shot, and others, are then layered with key moments of the wider event conveyed mainly via sound recordings of radio news broadcasts, onlookers' reactions to the airplanes' collisions and their witnessing of people falling, the sound of bodies hitting the ground, phone calls from the towers, and the noise of the towers collapsing. Although this is mainly presented chronologically, the images of falling people continue as through-line and counterpoint. The film's ending consists of a montage of the towers collapsing and a return of the prayer for the dead. A black screen fades to grey then white and Arabic writing poses the question: 'Does God's light guide us or blind us?'

Young writes that the opening sequence with black screen connotes 'a failure of cinema, evidence only of the disappearance of the image' and that the film's 'accelerated repetitions have the character of trauma, dwelling on and in a memory without resolution or respite' (Young 2007: 41). Yet, for Young, the film also 'retains a strong narrative structure, progressing through the before-during-and-after of the event, and deploying the Indians' prayer, the orchestral music and the progression from black screen to white as a means of generating a redemptive narrative for the viewer' (Young 2007: 42). Marie-Christine Clemente notes that the spatial and temporal presentation of the images of falling shifts as the film progresses. As the duration of each shot increases, the film of the falling people loses its photographic and redemptive quality and the awkwardness of the fall – graceless, without agency, desperate – becomes unmistakable. Whereas the 'falling men and women could previously be envisaged as in control of their destiny in the first flashes [they later] appear to be in utter distress' (Clemente 2011). For Clemente, this shift marks a return of the repressed and, in contrast to Young's interpretation, she argues that the non-linear construction of the event – with the jumpers shown falling before, during and after the attacks – positions the film more as traumatic symptom rather than redemptive act. She concludes that '[r]esting on the traumatic 9/11 figure of the "jumpers" and based on a structure uncannily similar to trauma's *modus operandi*, Iñárritu's short film appears to rely on a traumatic mode' (Clemente 2011). As we shall see, the tension pointed to by Young's and Clemente's readings, and between trauma and its overcoming, remain a theme of further representation.

Another reading can be set against Young's and Clemente's. First, following the logic of the voices at the film's start, we are encouraged to take the falling people as representative of all, as signalling a worldly cosmopolitanism. Renate Brosch argues that the film imagines the World Trade Center as a notional Tower of Babel, thereby prefiguring Iñárritu's later film *Babel* (2006) which explores similar themes of inter-relatedness (Brosch 2011: 116). Read thus, Iñárritu's film is in tune with the wider logic of the collection of which it is part, which Stef Craps claims actively seeks a 'decentring' of the events of 9/11 by bringing together a range of views from around the world (Craps 2007: 195); Second, the film's non-chronological structure and fixation on the falling people makes their experience the focal point of the viewer's attention and empathy. This decision is deeply humanist when set alongside the inclusive gesture of the film's soundtrack and in comparison with *9/11, In Memoriam* and better-known 9/11 photographs such as 'Ground Zero Spirit', which were racially homogenous and replete with a jingoistic nationalism (Helmers and Hill 2004: 4–14). Third, the film's use of (a non-monotheistic) religious prayer for the dead intimates some kind of after-life for the falling people and points to a divine or spiritual dimension to the fall. The film here can be taken as an early example of the activation of a redemptive logic found within images of falling people, who, the film wishes to claim, sought a form of salvation in their decision to leap from the towers.

Read thus, the film neither solely retains the structure of trauma nor fully squares away traumatic experience via neat resolution but rather acknowledges the horror of the event and celebrates a certain inclusive and indomitable human spirit in the face of terror. Iñárritu's film is a brave attempt to go beyond self-censorship and the amplification of the dominant discourse. Predictably, *11'09"01 September 11*, and Iñárritu's film in particular, was widely criticised, with *Variety* denouncing the film as 'stridently anti-American' (Godard 2002). Yet, rather than being lambasted for its perceived lack of propriety and disrespect for a conservative vision of national identity or taken as merely a symptom of a damaged collective psyche stuck in a post-traumatic condition, as in Young's and Clemente's readings, the film can be seen as an early example of the desire to seek redemption via the experience of falling, a quest that, as we shall see, gives shape in different ways to both *Extremely Loud and Incredibly Close* and *The Walk*.

Susie Linfield writes that in the years immediately following 11 September photographs of falling people constituted a taboo and that they were 'among the least reproduced, least seen images of 9/11: indeed, they [were] despised' (Linfield 2010: 253–4). Yet, as we have seen, film and photographs of falling bodies were not completely absent from post-9/11 US cinema. It is true that these early engagements were varied and subject to considerable pressure around the proper way to depict people falling and that they also lack any clear consensus of how to relate to these images. However, from mid-decade the taboo noted by Linfield began to lift, and a cultural relation was established through the selection of one specific photograph which displayed a singularity and aesthetic design that was deemed somehow acceptable and which gave shape to further representation, including mainstream film.

II.

As already noted, along with others, photographer Richard Drew shot numerous images of people falling from the Twin Towers on the morning of 11 September (Friend 2007: 138). Drew recalled how one particular photograph from a sequence of twelve showing a single falling man stood out 'because of its verticality and symmetry' (quoted in Junod 2003). Initially titled 'A Person Falls Headfirst From the North Tower of the New York World Trade Center, Sept. 11, 2001', Drew's photograph appeared in many US newspapers on 12 September, including on page seven of *The New York Times*. A wave of complaints were received by those newspapers and it was rarely printed again, becoming paradoxically both 'iconic and impermissible' (Junod 2003). Indeed, Drew is reported as saying that the image is 'the most famous picture nobody's ever seen' (quoted in Friend 2007: 136).

On 23 September 2003 an article examining Drew's photograph by journalist Tom Junod was published in *Esquire* magazine with the title 'The Falling Man'.[5] In the article Drew reports that the falling man was initially thought to be Hispanic, then African-American, and likely a kitchen worker. These facts located the experience of falling in relation to racial and social diversity – something that later representations would need to negotiate – and reinforced the widely pressed claim that 9/11 affected the whole of America. The desire to name also elicited a complex, often negative, reaction to the photograph from possible family members of the falling man, with the decision to jump often judged according to concerns related to the moral (and often religiously inflected) question of whether suicide is ever an acceptable choice

(Junod 2003). In all this, Junod's article indexed how the experience of around two hundred people falling from the Twin Towers (craving air, falling by accident, deciding to die, being pushed by others) had been reduced to a single image of the individual experience of one man.

Following Junod's article, and the related documentary film, *9/11: The Falling Man* (Henry Singer, UK, 2006), the image gained traction and considerable comment. Three observations help frame analysis of my chosen films.

First, the initial self-censorship of the images had been predicated on protecting the 'dignity' of the falling people as fellow citizens, thereby protecting the sanctity of the nation during an attack by an external force. Friend observes that this impulse is 'protective of [. . .] culture, values, common decency' (Friend 2007: 133). The photograph's return was required to negotiate this. On the cover of *Esquire*, Junod's article was given the byline: 'Honoring September 11's Unknown Soldier', and Leon Wieseltier observes that the falling man 'looks like nothing so much as a [inverted, marching] soldier' and that '[r]egarded in this way, his testament [of the need to wage war] is plain' (Wieseltier 2002). Junod also observes that the composition of the photograph, in its original aspect, could be taken as a national symbol, with the falling man 'the essential element in the creation of a new flag, a banner composed entirely of steel bars shining in the sun (Junod 2003).[6] Across these responses we can see that the image is able to sustain a nationalist and jingoistic interpretation consonant with the way the experience of the falling people was appropriated by *9/11* and *In Memoriam*.

Second, the photograph drew comment in relation to its refined and appealing aesthetic. Junod observes, 'For all the horror of its conception, Drew's photo had an aesthetic component – a beauty – that many viewers found disconcerting' (Junod 2014). Seeking to describe this 'beauty', Rob Kroes notes that in the photograph the falling man 'is perfectly vertical, head down, seemingly poised and in full control of his posture. The image shows him in perfect accord with the lines of the buildings behind him. He splits them, bisects them' (Kroes et al. 2011: 12). This coherent aesthetic – the man's inverted pose, the photograph's vertical symmetry – has been criticised for its elision of the out-of-control experience of falling. It is widely noted, for instance, that in the series of Drew's photographs 'not augmented by aesthetics' that the man 'fell desperately, inelegantly' (Junod 2003). For many the photograph constitutes a turning away from the truth.[7] The selection of this particular image, it is argued, facilitates a wholesale shift in register from that of

denotation, news reportage, current affairs and the wider fields of politics and history, to one of connotation, of aesthetics, symbolism, art and
myth. Stubblefield writes that this level of abstraction, and especially
the lack of any indicator of the wider cityscape or proper sense of scale/
movement, results in a figure that 'is no longer foreseeable beyond the
instant in which it is frozen, the fall is characterized less by objectivity
than indeterminacy' (Stubblefield 2015: 58).[8]

Third, 'The Falling Man' photograph is also widely recognised as
having a redemptive quality. Junod notes that the photograph shows
'something like order; instead of showing victims of a mass murder
tumbling helplessly to their deaths, it showed one man, upside down
and bracketed by the gleaming vertical beams of both towers, in the
grip of something like grace or, at the very least, acceptance and resolve'
(Junod 2014). Readings such as this are governed by a metaphorical or
allegorical interpretation of the man's fall, and possible ascent, that
draws deeply on Christian mythology. But we might ask here, redemption from what? Friend speculates that Drew's photograph was selected
for publication, and later for wider cultural validation, 'because of its
graphic power and because it seemed *less* exploitative than photos
that showed individuals plummeting in groups or [people] in contor-
tions' (Friend 2007: 137). The 'exploitation' Friend perceives in the
deselected photographs is that of showing a process of unbecoming.
As Junod notes, these images signify 'our [America's, claimed here as
universal] vulnerability, our diminished agency, our brokenness, our
loss, and, yes, our defeat' (Junod 2014). In contrast, 'The Falling Man'
photograph has the potential to be read as showing agency, bravery,
mastery and (religious) transcendence. By this logic the photograph has
the potential to redeem not just the cruel facts of the falling people but
the ways in which the experience of 9/11 profoundly challenges US
national identity. But, as further analysis will demonstrate, this is not
a one-dimensional process: US identity can be secured, or redeemed, in
different ways, and with differing political consequences.

III.

Extremely Loud and Incredibly Close was given a limited release on
25 December 2011, and a full theatrical release on 20 January 2012.
However, the film, based on Jonathan Safran Foer's 2005 bestselling
novel of the same name, has its origins mid-decade (not long after the
publication of Junod's article in *Esquire*), when director Stephen Daldry
and producer Scott Rudin optioned the novel and began work on the

adaptation. The film tells the story of a hyper-intelligent, hyperactive, and by some accounts autistic, eleven-year-old boy, Oskar Schell (Thomas Horn), who is seeking to find the meaning of a key (marked with the label 'Black') that belonged to his father, Thomas Schell (Tom Hanks), who died in the World Trade Center on 9/11. Grief-stricken, Oskar suffers intrusive thoughts resulting from hearing the desperate phone messages left by his father as he was stuck in the North Tower, and especially Oskar's failure to answer his final phone call.

Oskar's intrusive thoughts consist of variations on the theme of 'The Falling Man'. In the film's opening title sequence a man with dark hair and wearing a business suit and smart shoes is shown falling. The images are out of focus and consist of fragmented close-ups set against a blue backdrop. The man is inverted and seemingly suspended, with only the feint sound of wind and his hair blowing signifying that the figure is travelling through physical space. There are no markers of the World Trade Center. Poignant music lends the scene an introspective and even peaceful air. An optical effect in which the image of the falling man appears to tear into vertical strips and flutter reveals a close-up of Oskar, his face lit with a torch. In voiceover, Oskar shares an abstract thought about death and the film cuts to his father's funeral and then to a flashback of Oskar and his father interacting playfully.

In a later scene, after a tiring and fruitless day of searching for the owner of the key, Oskar hides in his bathroom in despair. A close-up of water dripping from the tap provides a sensual demonstration of gravity's ineluctable pull. Oskar glances at a sun-blanched curtain and vase and a point-of-view shot and graphic match show images of a second falling figure. Again the shot is abstract and blurred, but in the left of the frame can be seen the straight vertical lines of a skyscraper and alongside it a small inverted falling man. Here the blurring of the image (which recalls earlier editorial 'gatekeeping' decisions to blur photographs to protect the anonymity of the subjects), the overexposed sun-bleached cinematography and the subjective sound design emphasise that this is Oskar's internal vision.

After Oskar's paternal grandfather (Max von Sydow) joins his search, Oskar confides that he has gathered from the internet a number of photographs of falling people and magnified them to see if they might contain his father. The photographs in this sequence are material objects shown clutched in Oskar's hands but are similarly treated in a guarded way, with Oskar's attempts at magnification leading to a blurring. One photograph – possibly taken from a sequence by photographer

Lyle Owerko – is seen relatively clearly and shows a large man without a shirt. Oskar states that 'probably other kids think that this is their Dad too'.

Towards the end of the film, as Oskar discovers that the key is, in fact, a false lead and has no direct link to his father, a final intrusive thought shows a man falling quickly and dramatically straight towards the ground (and the camera) surrounded by flames and the falling building. Although the image is blurred, Oskar's father's face can be clearly seen.

In the final scene, Oskar's mother (Sandra Bullock) discovers a scrapbook Oskar has made to record his quest to find the owner of the key. The final page is constructed in such a way as to allow the falling man to be manipulated via a tab so as to trace an arc upwards to safety.[9] This redemptive reverse image is cross-cut with a scene showing Oskar approaching a swing in Central Park that he has previously been too fearful to ride. He finds a note here left by his father and thus reassured he overcomes his fear and rides the swing.

These sequences work in concert with the film's wider narrative and overall aesthetic to re-enact and reconfigure 'The Falling Man' photograph. In the opening credits the motif of a falling man, with broad correspondences with Drew's photograph, is further abstracted and aestheticised via cinematography and use of close-ups. The motif is also, via the editing regime of the opening scenes, clearly positioned as a figment of Oskar's consciousness and then relayed to the wider narrative of his relationship with his father (cutting next to the funeral, and from there to a flashback of a playful father/son scene). The plasticity of the fluttering edit permits the animating and magical properties of the cinema to work in concert with the ordering processes of classical narrative. As a result the question of identity and of redemption so central to the meaning of 'The Falling Man' is restaged here as an enigma to be solved within the framework of Oskar's grief and his relationship with his father.

The quest narrative, and especially the diversity of Oskar's search, including ethnic minorities, cross-dressers, a range of social groups, and the young and old, establishes a cosmopolitanism that has already been noted in relation to Iñárritu's film and 'The Falling Man' photograph. Here the film acknowledges difference, and yet seeks universality. The sorrow displayed by the people Oskar visits is used primarily as a way of conveying empathy and sympathy for Oskar's loss, of matching their grief and his. Here the film avoids (divisive) claims against heterogeneity – with New Yorkers united in their pain – in preference for the stable coordinates of whiteness, with Oskar's father placed centrally as everyman. Here the film calls on Oskar's father's profession as the owner of a small jewellery business (it is significant he is not a stockbroker), the comfortable but not wealthy middle-class milieu of the family and Tom Hanks' star persona. As a consequence the film redirects the variegated experience of falling people and the ways in which 'The Falling Man' photograph activated a sense of ethnic and social diversity and contradiction, and instead conducts a deracination: in the final instance, the film is not interested in falling people, or even 'The Falling Man', but instead in Oskar's father.

This is confirmed by the intrusive thought showing Oskar's father's face, and then framed in a redemptive way via the film's final scene. Oskar's struggle to ride the swing is prefigured by an earlier scene that has Oskar's father recounting how he enjoyed jumping from the same swing as a child. This frames Thomas Schell's (imagined) jump from the Twin Towers as a desire to return to a sensation of pure childish pleasure and to his son. As Oskar's mother returns the falling man to safety – following a widely held belief that 'The Falling Man' photograph can be inverted to make the man ascend, thereby achieving salvation and a state of grace (see Wieseltier 2002) – Oskar rides the swing, eliciting a cathartic feeling made possible by his father's fall. Hence, the experience of swinging (now replacing falling) is replete with a reassurance stemming from his father's continued patriarchal authority. The film's final freeze frame of Oskar on the swing, which shifts back to the photographic from the filmic, is a positive image of transcendence, a salve to his traumatic intrusive thoughts, and to the viewer's wider cultural experience of the fall and 9/11.

Figure 3.1 The opposite of falling: patriarchal reassurance and redemption in *Extremely Loud and Incredibly Close* (2011).

The locating of the image in the subjective realm – through carefully choreographed point-of-view shots – makes meaning associated with 'The Falling Man' photograph malleable, available to be dramatised according to the different stages of Oskar's therapeutic journey. This journey is initially formed via an increasing specificity to his intrusive thoughts, with his father's face becoming clear. And the final redemptive image then shifts away from Oskar's intrusive thoughts to a more tactile form of protocinematic mechanical paper animation. Here, Oskar's father's fall becomes part of the film's rich, mannered and highly designed mise en scène, and in doing so makes the transition from intrusive thought to a now manipulable element of everyday life. This completes a multiple shifting of 'The Falling Man' image, from photograph to Oskar's mind, from a shared experience into the particular narrative of Oskar's grief for his father, and from the realm of history and politics into the realm of the film's aesthetic and its conveyance of order (via Oskar's journal and Oskar's world view) on the experience of 9/11.

These varied strategies for containing 'The Falling Man' photograph, and the wider experience of 9/11, can be related to what Pat Aufderheide calls '[t]herapeutic patriotism', a post-9/11 discourse whereby the media assumed 'a therapeutic role as grief counsellor [. . .], nurturing insecure viewers who had been stripped of their adult self-assurance by the shock of the attacks' and providing 'emotional reassurance' (Aufderheide 2001). The film's focus on the grief-stricken experience of a child, and his overcoming of this grief, is closely aligned with this logic. Rather than simply a registering or repetition of traumatic symptoms – that some claim for Iñárritu's film, for example – *Extremely Loud and Incredibly Close* seeks a therapeutic overcoming (see Westwell 2014: 110–25). As noted, to reach this destination involves considerable work across the film's cinematography, editing, production design and classical narrative form. By these means 'The Falling Man' become a normative everyman located within a specific family context where grieving is (eventually) successfully undertaken and where the decision to jump is taken to be a positive, paternal act that restores order. The film contains no explicit or implicit pleas for retribution or military action, but the desire for redemption via the return to the status quo remains fully reconcilable with the dominant discourse.

IV.

A similar reworking of 'The Falling Man' photograph can be seen in *The Walk*, though with a very different outcome. Directed by Robert Zemeckis and released in October 2015, the film continues a long-standing cultural interest, especially after 9/11, in French high-wire artist Philippe Petit's unofficial wire walk between the Twin Towers on 7 August 1974. Petit's staggering act – his 'coup' to use his words – has been represented in his memoir, *To Reach the Clouds: My High Wire Walk Between the Twin Towers* (2002), and in a range of other literary and visual texts, including David Chelsea's short graphic narrative, 'He Walks on Air' (2002), Mordicai Gerstein's children's story, *The Man Who Walked Between the Towers* (2003), Owen Smith's artwork for the cover of the 22 September 2006 edition of *The New Yorker*, and a high-profile and commercially successful documentary, *Man on Wire* (James Marsh, 2008). Petit's walk is also referenced in Don DeLillo's *Falling Man* (2007) and Colum McCann's *Let the Great World Spin* (2009).

The Walk's opening scene has Petit (Joseph Gordon-Levitt) standing on the highest platform of the Statue of Liberty. In the background is a majestic view of lower Manhattan, centred on the World Trade Center. Close-ups show Petit's earnest face and agile body as he delivers a monologue describing his fascination with the Twin Towers. The film returns to this set-up numerous times to advance the story via expository monologue and to set the action against this very specific view of New York. In the final scene, on the completion of his walk, and after the World Trade Center building manager has given him a free pass to the observation decks of both towers, Philippe addresses the camera and informs us that the expiry date on the pass has been amended to read 'forever'. The view of the Twin Towers in these scenes, and the use of voiceover narration, have correspondences with the opening sequence of *In Memoriam* but Petit is a very different cipher to Giuliani, and *The Walk* seeks a radically different relation to 'The Falling Man' and to 9/11. Petit is shown driven by a singular purpose – to walk on a tightrope between the Twin Towers – a desire he refuses to articulate in relation to rational questions of 'why?'. The enigmatic nature of his quest subverts the ways in which the Twin Towers had been presented as a positive symbol of American values in films such as *In Memoriam* and instead posits them as beacons drawing an individual to an abstract, not to mention dangerous and illegal, calling.

Via his accent, self-proclaimed Frenchness and perhaps also the national origin of the Statue of Liberty, Petit's opening monologue also points to his foreignness. And although the film largely focuses on Petit's actions, focalised via the sequences described above, the film also layers in point- of-view shots from a number of other characters, including his girlfriend, his vertigo-suffering friend (with some implication of homosexual attraction), his ragtag group of accomplices, the people of New York who witness his walk, the construction workers working on the Twin Towers and the police. Petit's vision is unique but also quickly adopted and celebrated by his fellow maverick artists and anti-authoritarian accomplices, as well as New Yorkers, and, eventually, the general public and the authorities. There is an expansive and inclusive quality to these different perspectives, and to the film as a whole. Here the film seeks a populist cosmopolitanism that contrasts markedly with Oskar's subjective point of view and preferential position in relation to difference in *Extremely Loud and Incredibly Close*.

These opening and closing scenes also point to the ways in which the film's story is governed by a complex engagement with the equilibrium, disequilibrium, restoration of equilibrium structure associated with classical narrative (Lacey 2009). In most respects the plot is conventional. It follows the conventions of the biopic, beginning *in media res* and with flashbacks to Petit's earlier life story: his training as a high-wire walker, his burgeoning romance with Annie (Charlotte Le Bon) and his alienation from his family, especially his father; in these scenes a disequilibrium originates in the disruption of family life and in Petit's unspecified but ineluctable desire to wire walk between the Twin Towers. Once his goal is set, the film follows the conventions of the crime caper sub-genre as Petit and his accomplices overcome a number of hurdles to attain their goal. Ruth Mackay observes a similar structure to the documentary *Man on Wire* (Mackay 2011). The attainment of the goal allows close bonds to develop within the group who form a surrogate family as well as consolidating a profound relation between Petit and his wire-walking mentor Papa Rudy (Ben Kingsley). In all this, the film follows a restorative, goal-oriented classical narrative structure similar to *Extremely Loud and Incredibly Close*.

The plot of the film is also structured via a further state of disequilibrium running alongside the one originating in Petit's life story; namely, the incompleteness of the Twin Towers, with construction teams shown hard at work and the final floors yet to receive their silver cladding. As well, the film shows a historical context replete with division and the political crisis of the Watergate scandal: one of Petit's accomplices criticises Nixon in favour of Kennedy and the film articulates a maverick, anti-authoritarian sensibility via its secondary characters that suggests a society subject to critique. For example, an insurance broker who works in the World Trade Center is drawn to the illegal, subversive nature of the plan.[10]

The attainment of the goal of walking the wire establishes equilibrium in relation to these elements; for example, a newsstand has front pages showing Petit's act set alongside news of Nixon's resignation, the accomplice states that Petit has helped New Yorkers learn to love the World Trade Center, and in the final scenes the towers are shown completed. Thus, 'the walk' is here a positive counterpoint to, and even salve for, the politically divisive history of the construction of the towers and for political division more generally.

Of course, *The Walk* also engages a story on a larger scale. The film's scenes on the Statue of Liberty, its layered, flashback structure and its knowing ending pull into play what might be called a 'structure of retrospect' that actively engages the viewer's knowledge of 9/11.[11] In its claim that Petit can revisit the World Trade Center 'forever', the final scene activates an irony: the viewer knows that the Twin Towers will be destroyed. Thus, the equilibrium reached in 1974 is subject (in the mind of the viewer, and implicitly) to the further (future) disequilibrium of the terrorist attacks. As such, Petit's walk, via a circular narrative logic, provides an affirmation of the World Trade Center in 1974 and again (with the film's release) in 2015. Compared to *Extremely Loud and Incredibly Close* this narrative schema engages more broadly and politically, driven by a more inclusive and ambitious redemptive impulse than the insular and individualised story of Oskar's recovery.

In relation to film form, the different phases of *The Walk*'s narrative are governed by three distinct schema. In the flashback sequences set in France the film shares much with *Extremely Loud and Incredibly Close*, activating the animating (and redemptive) possibility of the moving image. The world is shown subject to the full force of Petit's childlike zeal, talent as a performer and sense of humour, and Zemeckis has claimed inspiration from Gerstein's children's book in this. Petit, like Oskar, has a tendency to build models and to animate his desires with puppets and magic tricks, which the film emulates with a plastic and playful mise en scène. In this, both films are self-conscious about the way that the cinema can re-enact and reconfigure the world via the imagination; cinema is in itself a redemptive act. Once in New York, and following the generic template of the crime caper, this whimsy segues with a realist aesthetic consonant with 1970s crime films such as *Dog Day Afternoon* (1975): the city is a divided mix of high-end real estate, colourful local neighbourhoods and wasteland. The bleached-out cinematography and lived-in period cars and clothes convey historical verisimilitude. The final sequences of the film, as with the falling sequences in *Extremely Loud and Incredibly Close*, are subject to a high level of abstraction: plan views of the city are seen from a great height, with the stark vertical depiction of the towers and the dramatic geometric angles of the wire combining to frame Petit's walk. These sequences call directly on the formal composition of 'The Falling Man' photograph and form the film's dramatic focal point. In addition, the peril of Petit's wire walk is intensified by two earlier sequences that prefigure his act with the spectre of falling. In one, while evading security guards, Petit imagines that an accomplice falls into a lift shaft (the scene is modelled on the falling sequence in Alfred Hitchcock's *Vertigo* [1958]). In another, Petit drops his costume – a black shirt – which people below fearfully believe to be a falling body. These sequences, set against the general aesthetic design of the wire-walk sequence, also clearly engage 'The Falling Man' photograph.

Reviews of the film were mixed but all celebrated the wire-walking scenes as powerful and captivating. The form of many of these shots has a religious quality, with the stark cruciform patterning of the wire and the *cavaletti* holding it in place positioning Petit as a Christ-like figure on a cross (this imagery was used in a number of marketing posters for the film). There are also attempts to signal to viewers that an appropriate response is one of epiphany, with the broken weather patterns as a storm approaches offering shafts of sunlight through dark clouds. Here, the production design maps Petit's act onto 'The Falling Man' photograph so as to pull into play connotations of ascent, grace and redemption.

Figure 3.2 In defiance of falling: redemption through the sublime act in *The Walk* (2015).

The sequence has Petit as the focal point of a complex configuration of elements, including the full realisation in plan view of a distinct, historical New York cityscape, the eliciting of a range of emotions in the viewer, including concern and admiration (via those looking up), vulnerability and excitement (via Petit's accomplices on his level), mastery (in Petit's calm physical grace and literal point-of-view shots), and a sense of the magnitude of Petit's achievement. The latter is conveyed especially via the spectacular omniscient point-of -view shots and the depth perspective offered by the film's use of 3D. Indeed, the compositing of computer-generated images with live action and the harnessing of the full resources of 3D cinema bring an operatic grandeur to the sequence that seeks to reveal the full significance of Petit's act.[12] One shot during Petit's walk has the camera rushing towards the ground as if falling, taking us to a view of the crowd looking on. The image of people staring upwards at the World Trade Center is a familiar one from 9/11, associated with incomprehension and terror. But in this scene the fall (and the tension replete in 'The Falling Man' photograph) culminates in a crowd of people revelling in and inspired by Petit's walk.

In all this there is an overall celebration of the defiance of gravity, a resistance to falling, a refusal to be drawn to earth, that allows the film to engage 'The Falling Man' photograph and to complete its design: shifting it from a redemptive image of falling to a celebration of mastery and transcendence. The film's final scenes form a palliative, what novelist Colum McCann describes as 'a spectacular act of creation' in direct opposition to 'the act of evil and destruction of the towers disintegrating' (quoted in Mackay 2011: 10). As Petit crosses and recrosses the wire in ever-more elaborate ways, including kneeling and lying down, the film seeks to articulate via the placing of a single vulnerable human body in space what McKay calls 'a transcendent, and sublime, moment' (Mackay 2011: 3).

But what are we to make of the redemptive move as it appears in *The Walk*? The film's tag line reads 'Every dream begins with a single step', and while this might appear like typical Hollywood marketing it raises the question of the specificity of Petit's dream and why it has caught and retains the public imagination. Crucially, Petit is not following the narrative of the American Dream, leading to personal fulfilment via the attainment of wealth and power (see Emmett 2007). Instead, he pursues a dangerous, illegal, abstract, anti-authoritarian and fantastical quest. *The Walk* celebrates this quest at a time (especially following 9/11) when such desires were proscribed, where citizens were encouraged to be fearful, security-aware, conformist and governed by the dictates of the economy: to commit to the fearful maintenance of our capacity as resilient workers and consumers. The film's closing credits end with the words 'Be Moved', suggesting that the film seeks to activate a sense of possibility captured by Paul Auster's observation that 'High-wire walking is not an art of death, but an art of life – and life lived to the very extreme of life' (Auster 1997).

Richard Gray argues that 9/11 has become 'a defining element in our contemporary structure of feeling' (Gray 2009: 129). This chapter has shown that a significant part of this structure of feeling is that of falling, with the falling bodies a 'primary nodal point' around which the memory and experience of 9/11 has materialised (Stubblefield 2015: 59). Visual culture, and post-9/11 US cinema, has engaged with this experience in a range of ways, including, in the early part of the decade, the use of the experience and representation of falling people to reinforce the dominant discourse of nationalist jingoism, as with 9/11 and *In Memoriam*; and, in Iñárritu's film, via a more cosmopolitan response that finds salvation in the experience of those who fell. From mid-decade, 'The Falling Man' photograph and the redemptive possibility immanent in its design, gave structure to *Extremely Loud and Incredibly Close* and *The Walk*. These films undertake varied re-enactments of 'The Falling Man' photograph and bring to bear the full resources of the cinema, especially via the operations of classical narrative and the animating resources of cinematography, production design, editing and special effects. In doing so they seek redemption and resolution, but differentially so. *Extremely Loud and Incredibly Close* reinforces a 'therapeutic nationalism' , but *The Walk* refuses to be limited by what Roger Luckhurst calls a predetermined 'post-traumatic afterwardsness' (Luckhurst 2008: 211–12). Didier Fassin and Richard Rechtman argue that, as a cultural phenomenon, focus on the traumatised individual tends to offer an ahistorical and apolitical reading of any event that 'obliterates experience' and 'operates as a screen between the event and its context' (Fassin and Rechtman 2009: 281). Set against this, and the earlier patriotic and jingoistic appropriations of 'The Falling Man', the celebration of Petit's act signals a desire to refuse victim status and to reclaim human agency defined beyond the strictures of 9/11 and post-9/11 discourse, and, even more than that, beyond the neoliberal paradigm.

NOTES

1. Brottman notes that the explicit violent images related to 9/11 could be accessed via websites such as Ogrish.com (now no longer accessible) that did feature film of people falling from the towers.

2. By way of contrast, European and world news channels and non-US newspapers were more likely to show video footage and publish photographs of the falling people.

3. 'Gate-keeping' is a term used to describe the process of selecting and deselecting images in compliance with an institutional, commercial and ideological set of precepts.

4. Falling bodies are also heard and not seen in this way in *World Trade Center* (Oliver Stone, US, 2006), and this film has a similar structure to *9/11* in its account of heroic perseverance and bravery, and the binding of this experience to a call to arms.

5. The article was republished with a revised introduction and a podcast featuring an interview with Tom Junod on 5 October 2015; see http://classic.esquire.com/the-falling-man/

6. A related observation is made by Rob Kroes, who compares the composition of the photograph with the iconoclastic work of artist Jasper Johns. Paradoxically, by this comparison 'The Falling Man' is understood as resisting nationalism.

7. Conspiracy theories related to 9/11 also question the veracity of the photograph, especially in relation to sense of scale, with the man presumed not to be in a proper relation of scale to the building and hence the photograph displays evidence of manipulation.

8. Here 'The Falling Man's stark symmetrical aesthetic is somehow set against, and offers respite from, the detailed, complex mise en scène of the photographs of prisoner abuse at Abu Ghraib which came to public prominence at around the same time as Junod's article was published.

9. This image resembles Lyle Owerko's photograph, which is said to have influenced Jonathan Safran Foer when writing the novel upon which the film is based. However, while there is no single image in the film that is directly modelled on Drew's photograph, there is clearly an emphasis across the range of falling man images on maleness, inversion and singularity, as well as aesthetic abstraction.

10. McCann's novel goes further and actively engages with the recent memory of loss in relation to the Vietnam War as well as wider senses of social inequality related to New York's diverse population.

11. Zemeckis has stated that the film avoids referencing 9/11 in any explicit way 'because we all bring our own history to this, we don't have to comment on it' (Fleming 2015).

12. The film was given an early release in IMAX 3D format.

REFERENCES

Aufderheide, Patricia (2001), 'Therapeutic patriotism and beyond', last accessed 24 January 2013: http://web.archive.org/web/20030417152041/http://www.televisionarchive.org/html/article_pa1.html

Auster, Paul (1997), 'On the High Wire', *The Art of Hunger*, New York: Penguin, pp. 249–60.

Brosch, Renate (2011), *Moving Images, Mobile Viewers: 20th Century Visuality*, Münster: LIT Verlag.

Brottman, Mikita (2004), 'The fascination of the abomination: the censored images of 9/11', in Wheeler Winston Dixon (ed.), *Film and Television After 9/11*, Carbondale: Southern Illinois University Press, pp. 163–78.

Clemente, Marie-Christine (2011), 'Representing 9/11: Alejandro González Iñárritu's short film in 11'09"01: September 11', *E-rea: Revue électronique d'études sur le monde anglophone*, 9:1.

Craps, Stef (2007), 'Conjuring trauma: the Naudet Brothers' 9/11 documentary', *Canadian Review of American Studies*, 37:2, pp. 183–204.

Emmett, Winn J. (2007), *The American Dream and Contemporary Hollywood Cinema*, London: Continuum.

Fassin, Didier and Rechtman, Richard (2009), *The Empire of Trauma: An Inquiry Into the Condition of Victimhood*, Princeton: Princeton University Press.

Fleming, Mike (2015), '*The Walk*'s Robert Zemeckis On A High Wire Directing Career: Deadline Q&A', last accessed 11 January 2015: http://deadline.com/2015/09/robert-zemeckis-the-walk-joseph-gordon-levitt-new-york-film-festival-1201551050/

Friend, David (2007), *Watching the World Change: the Stories Behind the Images of 9/11*, London: I. B. Tauris.

Godard, François (2002), 'Canal Plus 9/11 Pic Courts Controversy', *Daily Variety*, 21 August 2002, p. 20.

Gray, Richard (2009), 'Open Doors, Closed Minds: American Prose Writing at a Time of Crisis', *American Literary History*, 21:1, pp. 128–48.

Helmers, Marguerite, and Charles A. Hill (2004), *Defining Visual Rhetorics*, Lawrence Erlbaum Associates.

Junod, Tom (2003), 'The Falling Man: Honoring September 11's Unknown Soldier', *Esquire*, 5 September 2003.

— (2016), 'James Foley: The Fallen Man', last accessed 8 February 2016: http://classic.esquire.com/editors-notes/the-fallen-man/

Kroes, Rob, Miles Orvell and Alan Nadel (2011), 'The Ascent of the Falling Man: Establishing a Picture's Iconicity', *Journal of American Studies*, 45:4, pp. 1–19.

Lacey, Nick (2009), *Image and Representation: Key Concepts in Media Studies*, Basingstoke: Palgrave Macmillan.

Linfield, Susie (2010), *The Cruel Radiance: Photography and Political Violence*, Chicago: University of Chicago Press.

Luckhurst, Roger (2008), *The Trauma Question*, London: Routledge.

Mackay, Ruth (2011), '"Going Backwards in Time to Talk About the Present": *Man on Wire* and Verticality after 9/11', *Comparative American Studies*, 9:1, pp. 3–20.

Montgomery, Martin (2005), 'The Discourse of War After 9/11', *Language and Literature*, 14:2, pp. 149–80.

Prince, Stephen (2012), 'American Film After 9/11', in Cynthia A. Barto Lucia, Roy Grundmann and Art Simon (eds), *The Wiley-Blackwell History of American Film*, Oxford: Wiley-Blackwell, pp. 495–513.

Sontag, Susan (2003), *Regarding the Pain of Others*, London: Hamish Hamilton.

Stubblefield, Thomas (2015), *9/11 and the Visual Culture of Disaster*, Bloomington: Indiana University Press.

Swartz, Anne K. (2006), 'American Art After September 11: A Consideration of the Twin Towers', *Symploke*, 14:1–2, pp. 81–97.

Westwell, Guy (2014), *Parallel Lines: Post-9/11 American Cinema*, London: Wall-flower Press.

Wieseltier, Leon (2002), 'The Fall', last accessed 8 February 2016: https://newrepublic.com/article/66449/the-fall

Young, Alison (2007), 'Images in the Aftermath of Trauma: Responding to September 11th', *Crime Media Culture*, 3:1, pp. 30–48.

CHAPTER 4

'You be very mindful of how you act': Post-9/11 Culture and Arab American Subjectivities in Joseph Castelo's *The War Within* (2005) and Hesham Issawi's *AmericanEast* (2008)

Paul Petrovic

I.

In his coda to *The 'War on Terror' and American Film: 9/11 Frames a Second*, Terence McSweeney laments 'the absence of American films that explicitly portrayed the war on terror on the screen from critical perspectives, a counter-narrative as opposed to the master narrative' (2014: 204). The ideologies embedded in mainstream American film often privilege stories of America's national victimhood in the wake of 9/11, but victimhood is a status that is sanctioned only under certain conditions. Indeed, many post-9/11 mainstream narratives legitimise the uniformity of America's cultural sufferings, so that differences on the level of national perspective, such as the differences generated by minority races and ethnicities, are altogether eliminated. After 9/11, the majority of the American independent film industry also raised little challenge to this hegemony, despite existing apart from the dominant ideology generated through Hollywood's centralised body of investors. In turn, this master narrative of 9/11 remained codified. However, a few American independent films do position themselves as critical counter-perspectives to this mono-narrative, and they are authored and directed by minorities who chronicle the abuses and caricatures placed upon the whole community of Arab Americans.

Against America's larger post-9/11 monomyth that includes films such as Paul Greengrass' *United 93* (2006), Oliver Stone's *World Trade Center* (2006) and Kathryn Bigelow's *The Hurt Locker* (2008), which highlight an American will to recover and a single-minded impression of Muslim extremism, Joseph Castelo's *The War Within* (2005) and Hesham Issawi's *AmericanEast* (2008) operate as dynamic counter-narratives. *The War Within* was co-written by Castelo, Tom Glynn and the Pakistani American Ayad Akhtar, who is the lead actor and a playwright who has since written the Pulitzer Prize-winning *Disgraced* (2013), among other plays exploring contemporary American Muslim identity. *AmericanEast* was co-written by Issawi and lead actor Sayed Badreya, and both Issawi and Badreya are Egyptian American. These two early post-9/11 films pivot on the real and imagined threat of Muslim terror in America, but, crucially, criticise American governmental and media systems. Furthermore, they erect multiple subjectivities and narratives for the Arab American beyond the master narrative's narrow conscript of the radical terrorist, which also dominates the television series *24* and Iraq War films, including Clint Eastwood's *American Sniper* (2014). Developing a multiplicity of Arab American identities is necessary for the expansion of public perception because only cultural exposure to a range of Arab American experiences can combat the Islamophobic decree of American politicians such as Donald Trump's calls to 'bar all Muslims from entering the country', and to track Muslims through the creation of a government database (Healy and Barbaro 2015). South Asian literary scholar Aroosa Kanwal chronicles that 'as a result of ongoing Islamophobia debates in the West, negative images of Muslims have continued to shape Western attitudes and speech in such a way that the figure of a Muslim has become a metaphor for barbarism and violence, meaning that Muslimness has become synonymous with terror' (2015: 3). *The War Within* and *AmericanEast*, then, deconstruct the rhetorical allegiance that the West has placed on these false synonyms, and assert the radical necessity of bringing those located in the margins into the center. Castelo's and Issawi's films thus resist the narrative endemic in much of Hollywood cinema to uncover Islamophobia, ideological resistance and the limits of American exceptionalism.

Arab Americans have generally used their texts to record the regulatory practices of American Islamophobia. Even if not reified at a bureaucratic level, America's discriminatory measures nonetheless operate as an implicit distrust of Arab Americans' otherness. Reporter Stephan Salisbury, for example, asserts this causal link, noting that 'Fear fertilizes the public soil, governmental power drives the plow' (2010: 23). That is, government agencies influence the perceptions of reality regarding Muslim identity, and those perceptions of fear crystallise within the public consensus and propagate racial hatred. Arab Americans, then, struggle to escape from the confines of American fundamentalist patriotism that delimit and marginalise Arab American subjectivity. Arab Americans suffer under widespread surveillance, scrutiny and stereotypes in these films, and they record the ideological ease with which others suspect and justify judgement against all Arab Americans. At the same time, *The War Within* and *AmericanEast* record how discriminatory judgement further alienates and isolates, and so the films exist to advocate for a deeper, more expansive project of social justice.

Castelo's *The War Within* fits the paradigm of post-9/11 cinema most cleanly. The film tracks Hassan's (Akhtar) trajectory of forced conversion to a radicalised Islam abroad, so that he slips back into America to execute terrorist activity. The film ends with him detonating a suicide bomb at the historic Grand Central Terminal, a railway station in Manhattan, and it adheres to the generic conventions of a post-9/11 thriller by framing the fatalistic dangers of Islamic extremism. However, the screenwriters position Arab American identity as something more than a simplistic caricature of Muslim otherness; the film thus raises up Arab American counter-narratives to America's master narrative. *The War Within* is one of the more adventurous examples within the corpus of Arab American cinema. Directors such as Castelo who transgress against the standards of identity discourse and mount appeals to intercultural exchange apart from their own autoethnographic identity offer new perspectives and readings on Arab American identity. The script dynamically represents minority characters, and *The War Within* never limits or artificially abridges the imagery of American Muslims.

Hassan is abducted in France by American intelligence services and imprisoned for his suspected ties to Islamic radicalism. During his time in jail, though, Hassan ends up being transformed into the embodiment of that which he was originally suspected of being. The US attempt at counterterrorism, the film suggests, runs the risk of doing nothing but fomenting radicalism. When Hassan re-enters the US through clandestine means, he takes shelter in the New Jersey family home of Sayeed Choudhury (Firdous Bamji), a childhood friend. There, Hassan directs Sayeed's American-born son, Ali, in an extremist version of Islam, and constructs the materials to execute a suicide bomb in Manhattan's

Grand Central Terminal. Castelo's film dramatically represents Hassan's battle against the ephemeral nature of western normality in the face of radical jihad. However, the film also situates how Sayeed's citizenship is questioned and spectacularised by the American media after Hassan succeeds in detonating his bomb. The film underscores the need for the Arab American community to be able to talk seriously about the dangers of Islamic radicalisation, but also for the larger American community to demonstrate belief in the virtue of Arab Americans without retreating into scripts of hysterical Islamophobia.

The War Within reveals how arduous it can be to combat the scaffolding of Hassan's radical transformation. Although Hassan questions his mission, the conditioning he receives induces him to gloss over the damage the suicide bomb would generate. After identifying the hypothetical question governing his art, namely, 'in a post-9/11 landscape, where the Muslim "other" is even more pejoratively defined, what is the role of a Muslim American artist of some visibility in that discursive environment?', Akhtar offers his authorial position in an interview accompanying *The Who & the What* (2014): 'I'm not an apologist. I'm not involved in PR about correcting some impression that people have of Islam. My position is that, as an artist, I have to have the freedom to wrestle with my demons and my raptures and those of my community, and to celebrate and criticize in equal measure' (2014: 98). Castelo's film explores in minute detail the richness with which Sayeed lives a normal American life, adhering to the same celebratory and critical spirit that Akhtar locates in his solo plays. In Hassan, Akhtar's impact is equally felt. US interference has tainted Hassan's ability to conceptualise value in America, given his own barbaric treatment without due process, and this wrongdoing prevents him from seeing the raptures of Muslim Americans. *The War Within* thus highlights Hassan's apprehensions about American exceptionalism as dependent on an extremist ideology that would not have been possible without America's forceful intervention in his life.

As a result, Hassan is unable to entertain any purpose to the quotidian nature of American existence anymore. Signalling his dissatisfaction as he leaves for a suicide attack that he later aborts, Hassan narrates in a letter he has written to Sayeed:

You are Americans now, and America has been good to you. It has become your home, the country you love. But the life you live is born from the blood of our brothers and sisters throughout the world. Your government takes actions of which its people are unaware. But ignorance is not innocence.

This rhetoric is decidedly monologic in its intentions. Hassan's monologue, as Mikhail Bakhtin writes about the monologic narrative, 'pretends to be the *ultimate word*. It closes down the represented world and represented persons' (1984: 293). Nonetheless, Castelo's film attempts to contextualise the hostility and antagonism towards America that undergirds extremist ideology. Rather than presenting the terrorist as a faceless enemy, as those Hollywood films do that make up the master narrative of 9/11, *The War Within* works to understand the rationale that afflicts radical Islam. That extremist attitude, however, is not present in Sayeed, his wife or his two children. Analysing the Choudhury family's assimilation into US culture, Stephen Prince contrasts Sayeed with Hassan, noting that Hassan 'cannot reconcile' American values 'with the violent fundamentalism that he has adopted, and the irony is that his brand of Islam, which is secretive and deceptive in its relations with Sayeed and the family', damages Sayeed and those who welcome him; as a result, Hassan 'also destroys the family that had adopted him' (2009: 99). Hassan's self-destruction, then, damns the Choudhurys – falsely – with the stigma of betraying America for an ideology with which they have no wish to engage.

Sayeed's attempt at aiding Hassan extends also to reintegrating him into the larger American community. Gabe, a friend of Sayeed's, offers Hassan a job as a driver as a courtesy to his friend. As Gabe drives Hassan back from a school event that his and Sayeed's children have attended, the film's only direct reference to the atrocity of 9/11 occurs. Pointing across the dusky skyline, Gabe reflects that people 'Used to be able to see the Twin Towers right there. You'd be able to get your bearings wherever the towers were.' This rumination is more than an incidental time stamp on the film's production. Gabe's comment situates how the Twin Towers, while operating as the hypervisible icon of western commerce and industry, also served a private function, grounding spectators and offering them access to the city's coordinates. In that respect, the Twin Towers were a locus that enabled citizens of the world, regardless of language, to negotiate New York City. The destructive acts of terrorism are thus contrasted against the architectural magnificence that offered itself up to native and immigrant Americans equally. The Twin Towers existed not just as the symbol of American exceptionalism par excellence; for many like Gabe, their function offered vitality and idealism, integrating immigrants into the city and, by extension, the nation.

The War Within does not simply ascribe vitality to American assimilation from Arab Americans; rather, through Sayeed, the film also questions the practices and fundamentalist rituals of Islam. Even as Sayeed asks Hassan to instruct his son, Ali, in the teachings of the Quran, he also betrays suspicion about the value embedded in Hassan's religious conviction. Sayeed observes that Hassan 'wasn't always' devout, and his tone implies a scepticism about Hassan's new-found investment in Islam. *The War Within* does not smear or discredit Islam, but Sayeed does raise the spectre of compulsion as a disciplinary mechanism within religious circles. In an interview accompanying his play *The Invisible Hand* (2015), Akhtar personally identifies as a 'cultural Muslim' (2015: 117). Sayeed himself likewise appears to subscribe to this affiliation, finding value not in 'The practice of particular rites and rituals [. . .] it was really more about the performance of those things' (ibid.: 116). Sayeed appears similarly decentred from the foundation of radical Islam that governs Hassan's life, privileging instead a more moderate reading of Islam. Sayeed's moderate stance with regard to Islam affords him the ability to assimilate more easily into American cultures.

The War Within documents this multi-dimensional, polyphonic Arab American community, one that navigates between political and cultural modalities. The film explores a multiplicity of national perspectives as Hassan and Sayeed listen while their fellow country-men Naved (Ajay Naidu) and Abdul (Aasif Mandvi) debate whether America has benefited the Arab American community. Naved criti-cises Pakistan as an untenable home for Sayeed's family, especially Ali, arguing that 'This is a great country where he has a chance to make a good life without worrying about corruption and violence.' For Naved, the US's economic stability offers Arab American children respite, despite the factious and discriminatory policies that America adopted after 9/11. Abdul counters, however, by highlighting the US's moribund interest in third-world countries as evidence of its bloated narcissism. Mocking the myth of American exceptionalism as the rea-son for America's regulatory practices, Abdul criticises how America 'is a greedy tyrant and has wasted the resources of the world, and profits on the poverty of nations poorer than itself'. Hassan listens, silent, and internalises both of these positions and the politics that guide them. While consensus is not reached, Castelo's film does not merely subscribe to the tyranny of American domination. Nor does it accept the premise of America as a benevolent utopia for Arab refu-gees. Instead, the praises and flaws all comingle, evidencing the film's dialogism.

The promise of political dialogism is further substantiated when Sayeed confronts Hassan over Hassan's belief that Sayeed is no longer guided by his culture nor his faith. As Sayeed gestures around him, denouncing such assumptions, he says,

I haven't forgotten my heritage. I'm not saying things are perfect here, OK? I know they're not perfect. I walk into an airport, I get into an airplane, I see the way people look at me. Look around you, yaar. Even this restaurant. There are Jews, Christians, Muslims, everyone sitting here eating comfortably, safely, peacefully. Going to school together, businesses together. What's wrong with that?

Sayeed casts the film's strongest ideological defence of America here, grounding his vindication of the US state apparatus not in some mythic justification, but in the principled reality of his surroundings. People of different faiths and creeds gather together in the city and celebrate together. For Sayeed, this multicultural assembly vindicates the national persecution that he experiences in moments. Further, Sayeed is quick to note that America's racialised fear is not altogether absolved. He qualifies that his willingness to sacrifice himself is situated around his realisation that the larger community breaks bread with one another, rather than judges one another.

Here Sayeed also recognises that some form of internal conflict is working in Hassan, and he struggles to connect with Hassan. Sayeed pleads, 'Talk to me. I'm your best friend. If you're not gonna talk to me, who are you gonna talk to?' Although Sayeed does not yet suspect the depths of Hassan's radicalisation, he is conscious of how Hassan's silence constricts him from testifying to private insecurities. Sayeed offers to bear witness to Hassan's trauma, offering to be the receptacle for whatever pain Hassan bears, and even pushes Hassan towards his sister, Duri (Nandana Sen), whom Hassan had once desired. During a last-ditch effort to engineer the explosives, though, Hassan steadfastly denies the comfort that she would provide. When Duri approaches him, Hassan adheres to the strictures of his faith, asserting, 'I can't be with you because . . . because you have been with other men, okay?' Hassan disputes Duri's bodily and Sayeed's communal offerings, and instead insists on inflicting damage on that community. Moreover, he depends upon a legalistic discourse in order to sustain his belief in jihad and draws on verbal abuse to justify his barbarism.

As Hassan distances himself from emotional contact, he readies himself for jihad, perpetuating the doctrine of self-annihilation. Hassan uses Ali's investment in him to access a basement room to complete preparations for the bomb. After hearing suspicious noises, Sayeed staggers into the room and asks, aghast, 'This is your Islam?' In this question, Sayeed indicts the extremist practices within radical Islam, denunciating how religion rationalises murder, thus epitomising the moderate

Muslim. When Hassan forces his way past Sayeed, it is Sayeed who immediately dials an American hotline number to report his friend's terrorist activity, even as Duri starts after Hassan. As such, Sayeed affirms his place, and fealty, within the US state apparatus. However, the US government officials who arrive function within the regulatory practices of American exceptionalism, arresting Sayeed for obstruction of justice and placing him under suspicion as an accomplice. As Donald Pease writes, officers such as those in *The War Within* operate as they do because 'State fantasies have played these constitutive roles within US political culture [. . .] by inciting within the citizens who take them up the desire to organize their identities out of the political antagonisms within US national culture' (2009: 4). These government officials expect the political actors they fight to fit the caricature of the synonymous Muslim terrorist and to be distinct from their allies, and so they make arrests such as Sayeed's based on that erroneous logic. Sayeed is thus led away simply because of his Muslim identity. The political antagonisms that determine US ideology preclude an accurate examination of individual character and undermine due process, just as they originally happened to Hassan.

Because the government's primary response is to Sayeed, Hassan is able to navigate to the site of his presumed deliverance. As Hassan enters Grand Central Terminal, Khalid, who has been working with him, has a change of heart and disengages the wiring to the explosives wrapped about his body. Implicit in Khalid's refusal to detonate himself is an admission that all of his preparation for the next life cannot compare with the wonder and bustle omnipresent in this life. Hassan himself discerns this wonder at strategic moments throughout the film, tracking the quotidian experiences of Muslims walking the New York and New Jersey streets, and thereby questioning the systemic incentive in perpetrating violence against American people, including his own people. Hassan, however, has received too much training and self-punishment, and sublimates his doubts through the guiding lens of jihad. Detonating the bomb, Hassan kills himself and scores of others, including Duri, who has raced to Grand Central to try to stop this violence.

The War Within thus straddles two contradictory messages. On one hand Castelo's film highlights how, as John Markert notes, national security within the 'United States must remain eternally vigilant' against Islamic terrorism (2011: 94). However, the more subliminal symbolism is the image that the film returns to after Hassan's death, when the film relies on a *cinéma vérité* treatment of news coverage documenting Sayeed's capture, and the human collateral that those images have,

Figure 4.1 Hassan observing the visible Arab American minority throughout *The War Within* (2005)

especially on Sayeed's wife and Ali. Samuel W. Bettwy emphasises how the US's detaining of Sayeed is precisely the wrong counterterrorism strategy, arguing that 'The film therefore ends where it began with the arrest and interrogation of an innocent who will be taught to resent America and become vulnerable to radicalization' (2015: 48). Furthermore, this vulnerability is not merely about Sayeed. The film closes on Ali retreating from the television screen and going into another room in the Choudhury home to pray. While misidentifying Ali's family relationship, attributing his father as Hassan rather than Sayeed, Corey Creekmur astutely analyses how Castelo's camera lingers on Ali's submission to prayer and Islam, and portends the possible 'continuation of both faith and violence, now typically conjoined, in successive generations' (2010: 88). America's supposition of Arab Americans harbouring extremist ideology and hate against the nation marginalises legitimate US citizenship within this community. Furthermore, such a mindset endangers radicalising Arab Americans when they see their community treated like suspects rather than subjects. Castelo's film, then, addresses the double-bind of Arab American subjectivity, where honourable Muslims are projected as the terrorist threat and this stigma becomes so regulatory that it closes down all other perspectives.

II.

Mainstream American entertainment continued to monopolise the representation of Arab Americans, showcasing them as extremists and as the threat against which America must remain vigilant. Director Hesham Issawi's *AmericanEast* (2008) is an attempt to contemporise with an Arab American lens Spike Lee's 1989 classic *Do the Right Thing*, where the Arab threat is policed against and where that policing ironically precipitates the crisis. In the film, Homeland Security has placed the National Terrorism Advisory System at a high terror alert, and the summer heat in Los Angeles is only further escalating national and ethnic tensions. Here, *AmericanEast* adheres to the common trope, as scholar Carol Fadda-Conrey defines it, of placing Arab American characters 'against a post-9/11 backdrop that compels them to become deeply self-conscious of their Arab identities' (2011: 542). Issawi's film chronicles how white, Jewish and Arab Americans traffic in their separate stereotypes and miscalculations, so that the only constant is the threat of abject victimhood. Issawi balances his characters' cultural judgements, mediating between antagonistic and mollifying rhetoric within the Arab and Jewish American communities. As such, the biggest threat to Arab American success comes from the white community, whose predetermined and overzealous judgement systematically aggravates *AmericanEast*'s Arab Americans. Mustafa, Omar and other ensemble characters endure discriminatory practices and finally lash out against a cultural apparatus focused on constraining their ethnic and religious identities.

AmericanEast embraces modalities of melodrama to make a larger cultural critique about the struggle to sustain a unified Muslim subjectivity. This treatment of melodrama draws on Linda Williams' work on the relationship between temporality and futility, triggering 'not just the sadness or suffering of the characters in the story but a very precise moment when characters in the story catch up with and realize what the audience already knows' (1991: 77). Mustafa Marzoke (Sayed Badreya) is an entrepreneur who dabbles in multiple business ventures, including cabs and a Middle Eastern falafel café. His family and extended network of relations have all assimilated, positively or negatively, into the American experience, becoming a nurse, an actor and a pot-smoking teen. Meanwhile, his adolescent son, Mohammed, is feeling the pull of more traditional American practices, swayed by the outreaches of Christianity in school, and is questioning the value of Islam. Ronnie Scheib offers one of the few comments on Issawi's *AmericanEast* to date, assessing how it orchestrates 'a palpable tension between social point-making and workaday soap opera' (2007: 39). These melodramatic touches surface most clearly during the film's opening, when Mustafa takes Mohammed to Los Angeles International Airport to greet their Egyptian cousin Sabir. Mohammed disappears from Mustafa's side, and the latter's fears over losing his son in the airport are escalated by the panic that the public experiences when Mustafa cries out his son's name repeatedly. The pall of 9/11 and Muslim extremism are omnipresent even years later, and as federal agents swarm Mustafa and drag him to the ground for the terror that he is inciting, Issawi's film layers the social irony by showing Mohammed's confused face reappear next to a man in the airport handing out balloons with Christian inscriptions on them. As the film underscores, Muslim identification, whether it be physical or merely the threat of a spoken Arabic name, endangers the perceptions of national security, complicating any notion of equal citizenship rights, and due process, in America. While Mustafa sees his son's interest in Christianity as a failing on his part as a father, Issawi's film questions why anyone should subject themselves to the constant persecution and prejudice that unfolds from an embracing of Islam.

AmericanEast frames this racial judgement of Arab Americans as precautionary, but the film is not simplistically adversarial or flippant about the US's security measures. Federal Agent Stephens (Ray Wise), who interviews Mustafa in a holding room at the airport, offers his sympathy but justifies the country's security measures, stating,

> You have a very rich culture, Mr Marzoke. Now imagine if some fundamentalist Christian nut jobs from the US flew a jet passenger plane into the Muhammad Ali Mosque, or another one of your renowned monuments, killing thousands of innocent Egyptians. I'm sure that you'd be busting every infidel stupid enough to go around screaming English in the Cairo airport, wouldn't you?

Stephens' defence, framed around the assumption that foreign countries enact the same restrictive national protocols and constraints, allows him to operate with immunity, especially once they search Mustafa's vehicle and find a copy of the Quran. These provisions generate a narrative of legal consensus and exempt his operatives from any liability as they profile potential threats without discretion. Such attitudes are mirrored in Yaser Ali's research on Islamophobia after 9/11, noting that 'American Muslims were viewed as presumptively disloyal noncitizens who were not entitled to the rights of citizenship' (2012: 1047). Muslim identity was therefore racialised by US authorities at airports or in congested communities, and the stigma that followed scarred whole Arab American communities who were fundamentally innocent of any transgression. In an era where the national terror alert has escalated, though, America disregards citizenship rights. Stephens frames all of his dialogue with Mustafa around this exclusionary discourse, even conjoining himself rhetorically with the Egyptian national police.

When Mustafa is released, Agent Stephens' final farewell is a reproach that warns Mustafa of the implications of an Islamophobic society. As Agent Stephens cautions, 'Let me give you a word of advice. You be very mindful of how you act and speak in public. When we're under high alert, people get trigger-happy.' Stephens' statement highlights the peril faced by many Arab Americans, whose vulnerability is newly understood. Kanwal puts forward a socio-historical lament that 'the Islamic doctrine of jihad after 9/11 came to define the Muslimness of all Muslims, irrespective of their religious, social or cultural background. Such reductionism has institutionalised the fear of Islam both as a religion and as a culture' (2015: 5). In Issawi's film, Agent Stephens' foregrounding of American fear masks the real threat of violence that can be executed under the veil of patriotic vigilance. While federal observance is necessary to protect the security of the nation and its citizens, it can also perpetuate a hyperawareness that sacrifices American diversity. Mustafa, that is, realises that he needs to be aware of American Islamophobic fear and the threat – real and imagined – that he poses to others.

As Mustafa perceives all of this context, he returns to his restaurant, Habibi's Café, to think and recalibrate his expectations as an Arab American caught in an uneasy alliance with post-9/11 America. Given this juxtaposition, Holly Arida contends that *AmericanEast* highlights how 'assimilation into American culture has become all the more difficult for Arab immigrants in the post-9/11 era' (2012: 211). Even those like Mustafa who have been naturalised face discrimination and economic repercussions as a result of America's post-9/11 environment. Middle Eastern enterprises offer little in the way of mobility or cultural exchange. Habibi's Café has regular customers, but it is fundamentally a dingy and dilapidated restaurant, frequented by immigrants alone and lacking the interior and aesthetic design to be the fine dining experience that Mustafa dreams of owning. Amid the stable of customers, though, is Fikry (Erick Avari), an Egyptian Christian. As Fikry counsels upon learning of Mustafa's anger over his day, 'We've had enough explosions.' This phrase works metonymically to advocate against both sectarian violence and needless retribution. Although Arab Americans

suffer under contested preventive policies, Fikry's position is fundamentally one of passive resistance. He advances a narrative of submission to a political reality that prejudges and demeans him, all in the
name of defusing the culture fomenting Islamophobia. Mustafa himself subscribes to this position, even identifying a sign in the restaurant
that proclaims that there is to be 'No politics or religious [sic] allowed
in this establishment.' Despite the omitted word, which neglects to
identify political and religious *discussions* as the specific issue being
regulated, Mustafa highlights his preference for order and community
among Arab Americans, not ethnic division or discord.

Another customer, Murad (Anthony Azizi), a paranoid Muslim
who suspects the Jewish people of orchestrating a Zionist takeover in
America and abroad as well, contrasts Fikry and offers further range
of Arab American subjectivities. Issawi's film acknowledges the work
that needs to be done to help Arab Americans purge their vitriol of
Jewish people. Murad acts as a mouthpiece for the more vituperative
and malicious nationalism against Israel operating as a Jewish nation-
state, uttering how the war in Iraq and Afghanistan is 'all about the
oil. It's not about this democracy shit they keep feeding us. It's about
the oil. And Israel.' When Sam (Tony Shalhoub), a Jewish business-
man with whom Mustafa wants to partner to open a more extravagant
Middle Eastern restaurant, enters Habibi's Café, Murad belittles him
and his culture. Holly Arida identifies how this approach enables
Issawi's film to broaden its cultural critique apart from merely documenting the dangers of Islamophobia, since 'it not only tackles Arab
American stereotyping but, through a confrontation between two of
the main characters, addresses anti-Semitism in the Arab Muslim community as well' (2012: 211). By revealing the exclusionary practices
present in American Muslim communities, *AmericanEast* preaches
empathy and global service, not merely Arab American victimhood.
Amid Murad's diatribes, Fikry encourages patience, noting, 'You act
as if we're the only ones, huh? It's part of a hazing process, you know?
It happened to the Irish, the Japanese, before us. We're the newcom-
ers now. That's all.' Fikry argues for a radical submission to America's
regulatory and racialised practices as the ultimate way out of national
persecution.

Issawi's film also criticises the insularity of Hollywood's entertainment industry. Omar (Kais Nashef) works as both the driver of the
cab Mustafa owns and as an actor, but the media conglomerates that
operate in Hollywood default to stereotypical views of Arab identity.
Although Omar is engaged to Kate, a white woman who is expecting
their first child, he sees little opportunity to diversify his acting portfolio.

Omar's most known performance to date is as a Muslim extremist terrorising America, and he is disturbed by the systemic typecasting he has received. Consequently, he is thrilled when he is cast in a network show, *American Safety*, where he will play a doctor who is only incidentally Muslim. Arriving on set, however, Omar is notified of last-minute script changes and informed that his character has been cut. However, the producers have tried to salvage a role suitable for him: it is, unsurprisingly, as an Islamic terrorist, bitterly revealing that, within the hegemony of American media systems, American safety is understood not by complicating precepts of Arab American identity but by repeating the mono-narrative of the Muslim extremist. When Omar questions the illogic behind the script's demand that a Muslim terrorist take over a hospital, the show's director artlessly suggests, 'terrorists want to strike fear in the heart of America. That's what the episode is about. So they go to the hospital, there's a lot of people, very little security. OK?' Given the financial loss of being a series regular, Omar's performance is initially disconsolate, and it is only after the director prods him to further accentuate his accent and anger in stereotypical fashion that the crew look on with satisfaction at the façade they have perpetrated. In doing so, *AmericanEast* indicts a hegemonic enterprise where the media markets and economies in Hollywood fail to offer multiple perspectives of Arab Americans. Arab Americans as a people are sacrificed for America's master narrative of Muslim extremism, but by recording the process through which this practice is embodied, Issawi's film simultaneously condemns it and advances itself as a counter-narrative to that orthodoxy. *AmericanEast* accuses Hollywood producers and crews of having no interest in offering true subjectivity to Arab Americans or validating their experiences with the psychological complexity that might legitimise the treatment of a terrorist, as Castelo's *The War Within* does. Instead, *AmericanEast* indicts Hollywood as perpetuating Muslim barbarism.

One of the smartest concepts that *AmericanEast* articulates is the degree to which the image of the Arab terrorist is disseminated across the country, and how the Arab American community can only grimace as these images circulate. Issawi cuts from the individual, with Mustafa watching earlier television footage of Omar in-character raging and pledging his fealty to Islamic terrorism, to a multitude of cable satellites and the platform of mainstream media broadcasting these images, and finally back to the individual, with Omar relegated to serving as a taxi driver, a small actor – in both senses of the word – in a larger matrix of economic, cultural and industry factors. In sum, then, the Arab American is frozen as an individual figure, marginalised in a larger community, so that only the threatening image is nationally depicted. Media studies scholar Deepa Kumar highlights this mindset, writing that 'the domestic War on Terror is not really about keeping Americans safe as much as it is about creating a spectacle of fear' (2012: 154). Indeed, the Arab American as spectacle is omnipresent throughout *AmericanEast*. When Omar stops in at a coffee shop and sets down his backpack before going to order, Issawi frames the scene so that one of the white college-age patrons takes notice of the abandoned backpack and nudges a friend worriedly, saying, 'I saw him before, man, like on the news or something, but with the whole raghead business.' The media effect of Omar's fictional terrorist image is totalising, and it overpowers any countervailing cultural impression of Arab Americans. In this respect, then, *AmericanEast* admonishes media practices that impress narrow ideologies onto a prejudicial populace. America's surplus of circumscribed news and media images have conditioned the public to regard any isolated Arab American figure as a danger, and so caution is abandoned under the supposed peril of the terrorist threat. By codifying surveillance as an omnipresent necessity and institutionalising fear as an appropriate countermeasure to terrorism, Omar's rights of citizenship are forfeited. Furthermore, Omar is conscious about how his participation in the manufacturing of these propagandist images is itself damaging to Arab American culture.

Figure 4.2 Omar in-character as the Muslim terrorist stereotype, perpetuated and broadcast into homes in *AmericanEast* (2008).

When the college-age patrons confront him about the backpack that they suspect to be a suicide bomb, Omar refuses to consent to the ease with which American preconceptions and biases are levelled at him, and intensifies the situation until police arrive. While Omar is let off with a warning, he comes to understand that America expects Arab Americans to swallow their self-respect and yield to the public interrogation simply because of their Muslim identity. This incident detains him long enough to miss an audition his agent had secured that could have helped him navigate out of such restrictive roles. As such, Omar is imprisoned by his need to support Kate and his unborn child, but the coffee shop awakens his new social consciousness. Upon arriving on the *American Safety* set, he declares that he cannot continue to perform as the terrorist and takes the moral stance that 'Those lines, I can't say them.' Complaining that the episode airs the following week and that they don't have time for his tantrum, one assistant offers the dramaturgical advice that Omar's character is 'a terrorist. He's full of hate. That's all you have to play.' *AmericanEast*, however, criticises this notion. The showrunner and other assistants participate in the ideological consensus of Hollywood, and their affirmation to Omar that Muslimness is 'played' synonymously with Islamic extremism reveals their dependency on stereotype. The crew is not interested in challenging or complicating American politics of multicultural identity. Rather, they subscribe to the typology of characters already reified in American media. In writing about depictions of the Muslim terrorist onscreen, Kerem Bayraktaroğlu contends that the power of 'The stereotype was, in an instance, substantiated and legitimized because it appeased the viewers and maintained a trauma that had been inflicted upon an American audience' (2014: 352).

Framing this encounter as another melodramatic incident, Issawi's film tracks how Omar's dissent is misread as a fundamentalist attack by *American Safety*'s producer. When Omar refuses to leave the studio, the producer labels him a 'maniac' and, since the producer wields the capital that makes the whole operation run, security officials show up and begin to physically drag Omar off the set, effectively silencing his protest. After the prior confrontation in the coffee shop, Omar snaps and scuffles with the security guards. During the brawl, Omar knocks a security guard's gun loose and amid the wrestling to recover it, the gun discharges, wounding the leg of one of the security officials. At that point, Omar realises how the scenario will play out in the media and picks up the gun, reluctantly becoming the terrorist threat that he had refused earlier. Yet his grievance is still fundamentally misunderstood, as an assistant justifies America's ideological position with the childlike plea to Omar: 'It's just a TV show, okay? It doesn't mean anything.' However, *AmericanEast*'s praxis unmasks Hollywood's belief in innocuous racialised caricatures as deeply incredulous. American media practices establish and delimit Arab American subjectivities, and the public then harnesses this perspective until Arab American culture feels both defensive and defenceless against narrow representations as a threat.

The news media responds to Omar's spectacle, positioning it within a larger narrative threat about reports of Muslim extremists in Los Angeles, and Agent Stephens also reappears, foreshadowing his earlier fatalistic warning to Mustafa. Mustafa and those in Habibi's Café watch in horror as the television news unfolds in real time, framing the reportage so that Omar is perceived as the terrorist threat that his fictional extremist performances already affirmed to the public. Meanwhile, Agent Stephens arrives on the *American Safety* set to try to negotiate with Omar. Omar has not, up to this point, directly hurt anyone and is simply looking for a way to extricate himself from this crisis, fielding a phone call from Kate, who is calling from the hospital and pleading with him to end the standoff. As Issawi navigates between quick cuts of Kate, Omar and Agent Stephens, the federal agent affirms to Omar that 'The SWAT guys are on their way. They will not hesitate to kill you. You have my word on that.' Omar struggles with himself, still believing that he can escape this quagmire unaffected, but such a belief is impossible in post-9/11 America. As Omar moves in acquiescence, a shot rings out and Omar crumples from a sniper's bullet. Agent Stephens turns, distraught, and gazes up at the trigger-happy sniper, but the film underscores how Hollywood, the public and the FBI and the attendant American bureaucracies all escalate the sense of national antagonism that is perpetrated against Arab Americans. This narrative moment also returns to Williams' theoretical comment about the temporality and futility inherent in melodrama, since Omar's fate is inextricably anchored to the spectator's knowledge of America's political climate.

The news media's tactless hive-mind immediately swarms upon Mustafa's restaurant after Omar's death, displacing the sense of community in the café that had mediated political disagreements about Arab American identity. As Murad, Fikry and Mustafa struggle to comprehend the news of Omar and the sense of powerlessness that they wield in American society, reporters arrive, reveal Omar's death, and position Omar as a member of a larger terror syndicate, asking, 'Did he have extremist political or religious views?' and 'Do you know if he has any connection to any of the other Middle Eastern men being arrested tonight by police?' The reporters engineer their interrogations to unnerve the Arab American patrons; significantly, the journalists never extend any sense of empathy or grief to them. Instead, the reporters use politics to frame an anarchic narrative about Omar's life and to undermine his humanity. Mustafa sees that the American media does not care that Omar was 'a friend' but only seeks to codify Omar's downfall, and so he lashes out and trashes Habibi's Café in a desperate attempt to banish the journalists. In the fallout, the 'No politics or religious allowed in this establishment' sign joins the debris on the ground, symbolic collateral in the struggle for Arab American citizenship that does not allow them to distinguish themselves in any other way.

Against this fatalism, though, *AmericanEast* orchestrates a reconciliatory note. The coda finds appeasement not in the words of a mainstream American, a Muslim or an Egyptian Christian, but in the Jewish American Sam, who agrees to fund Mustafa's more expansive restaurant. Sam affirms that 'We can change things. Maybe show that the catastrophes are not a foregone conclusion. The everyday act of breaking bread together is more powerful than all the hate.' Despite the many cultural and religious differences between Jewish and Arab Americans, Sam refuses to acquiesce to the schisms that divide them. Together, Sam and Mustafa commit to the breaking of new ground, co-owned by both parties, and Sam and Mustafa are thereby resolutely committed to one another. While Issawi's film portends future conflict as the Jewish and Arab American families bicker over who has earned the right to enter the establishment first, the film also highlights how in this political climate the young and elderly are those most qualified to compromise as Sam's elders and Mustafa's son, Ali, bond as they walk towards the restaurant. *AmericanEast* suggests that if the feud between Jewish and Arab people can be settled, so too can the master narrative of radical extremism.

The War Within and *AmericanEast* thus track the state of Arab Americans, and specifically American Muslims, in post-9/11 culture. These two films work to complicate the easy binary between America and the Islamic threat, exposing the biased manner with which American government and media treat the cultural Other. In turn, these independent films highlight how violence can be a reactionary measure. The Arab Americans in these films act out, but only after cultural oppression and Islamophobic surveillance subject them to little but the status the nation-state already fears. *The War Within* and *AmericanEast* both operate, as Akhtar expresses in an interview included in his play *Disgraced*, as a 'confrontation with the recalcitrant tribal tendencies we all harbor' (2013: 95). The victims in Castelo's and Issawi's films are victims most often due to the political antagonisms that treat them as members of a militia, that reify them within the regulatory politics that label Arab Americans as synonymous with Islamist fanaticism. Rather than perpetuate the master narrative of the Muslim extremist embedded in Hollywood cinema, the films expose the dangers of that narrative and reveal the cultural fears that Arab Americans face today.

The War Within and *AmericanEast* are part of a larger corpus of post-9/11 narratives that exemplify the contemporary struggles of Arab American subjectivity. Elsewhere, I argue that Arab American authors construct texts that 'contextualize themselves apart from the extremists even as they catalog how they have had to regulate their bodies so as to better assimilate into an American body politic now apprehensive about their ethnicity' (Petrovic 2015: xiv). Similarly, *The War Within* and *AmericanEast* work cinematically to counter the national master narrative of Arab American experience. These films document a range of subjectivities so that the true multiplicity of the Arab American can be understood, emphasising the need for diverse perspectives to come together, break bread and pursue cultural negotiation. The films do acknowledge the real violence and harm done by Islamic terrorism, but they complicate the reasons behind that terrorism as well as demonstrate how Arab Americans themselves are repelled and hurt by that violence. While these films indict the fearful manner in which minorities are perceived as little other than barbarous extremists in a post-9/11 climate, they also serve as cultural artefacts that record the aspiring hope that America can repeal its exceptionalist discourse in favour of one that recognises the Arab American community that struggles to be seen as synonymous with the history of countless other American refugees and immigrants who embody the American experience rather than terrorists who seek to destroy it.

REFERENCES

Akhtar, Ayad (2013), *Disgraced*, New York: Back Bay.
— (2014), *The Who & the What*, New York: Back Bay.
— (2015), *The Invisible Hand*, New York: Back Bay.
Ali, Yaser (2012), 'Shariah and Citizenship – How Islamophobia Is Creating a Second-Class Citizenry in America', *California Law Review*, 100:4, pp. 1027–68.
Arida, Holly (2012), 'The Arts', in Anan Ameri and Holly Arida (eds), *Daily Life of Arab Americans in the 21st Century*, Santa Barbara: Greenwood, pp. 193–222.
Bakhtin, Mikhail [1963] (1984), *Problems of Dostoevsky's Poetics*, Caryl Emerson (ed. and trans.), Minneapolis: University of Minnesota Press.

Bayraktaroğlu, Kerem (2014), 'The Muslim Male Character Typology in American Cinema Post-9/11', *Digest of Middle East Studies*, 23:2, pp. 345–59.

Bettwy, Samuel W. (2015), 'Evolving Transnational Cinematic Perspectives of Terrorism', *Perspectives on Terrorism*, 9:2, pp. 42–60.

Creekmur, Corey K. (2010), 'The Sound of the "War on Terror"', in Jeff Birkenstein, Anna Froula and Karen Randell (eds), *Reframing 9/11: Film, Popular Culture, and the War on Terror*, New York: Continuum, pp. 83–93.

Fadda-Conrey, Carol (2011), 'Arab American Citizenship in Crisis: Destabilizing Representations of Arabs and Muslims in the US after 9/11', *MFS Modern Fiction Studies*, 57:3, pp. 532–55.

Healy, Patrick, and Michael Barbaro (2015), 'Donald Trump Calls for Barring Muslims from Entering US', *New York Times*, 7 December. Web.

Kanwal, Aroosa (2015), *Rethinking Identities in Contemporary Pakistani Fiction: Beyond 9/11*, New York: Palgrave.

Kumar, Deepa (2012), *Islamophobia and the Politics of Empire*, Chicago: Haymarket.

Markert, John (2011), *Post-9/11 Cinema: Through a Lens Darkly*, Lanham: Scarecrow Press.

McSweeney, Terence (2014), *The 'War on Terror' and American Film: 9/11 Frames a Second*, Edinburgh: Edinburgh University Press.

Pease, Donald (2009), *The New American Exceptionalism*, Minneapolis: University of Minnesota Press.

Petrovic, Paul (2015), 'Introduction: Emergent Trends in Post-9/11 Literature and Criticism', in Paul Petrovic (ed.), *Representing 9/11: Trauma, Ideology, and Nationalism in Literature, Film, and Television*, Lanham: Rowman & Littlefield, pp. ix–xvii.

Prince, Stephen (2009), *Firestorm: American Film in the Age of Terrorism*, New York: Columbia University Press.

Salisbury, Stephan (2010), *Mohamed's Ghosts: An American Story of Love and Fear in the Homeland*, New York: Nation Books.

Scheib, Ronnie (2007), 'AmericanEast', *Variety Movie Reviews*, p. 39; Film & Television Literature Index with full text, 25 November 2015. Web.

Williams, Linda (1991), 'Film Bodies: Gender, Genre, and Excess', *Film Quarterly*, 44:4, pp. 2–13.

CHAPTER 5

Refracting Fundamentalism in Mira Nair's *The Reluctant Fundamentalist* (2012)

Ana Cristina Mendes and Karen Bennett

I. INTRODUCTION

Until recently, Islamic fundamentalism seemed to be so remote from the western capitalist mindset that it could only be grasped through a process of othering, which emphasised difference and reinforced damaging neo-Orientalist stereotypes. Yet in the last decade or so, there has been a shift in focus. The meta-narrative of Islamic terrorism as a foreign threat emanating from non-western cultures and motivated by a barely intelligible barbaric agenda has started to give way to another story centred upon the actions of home-grown western jihadists.

Unsurprisingly, this has provoked a complex set of conflicting responses among the opinion-makers within those countries. Particularly influential in this respect are the in-depth human-interest news stories about disaffected citizens of western nations who have joined terrorist associations and moved to Iraq or Syria (such as, for example, the leads that followed the widely circulated online video of US journalist James Foley's beheading by militants of ISIS, or the Islamic State of Iraq and ash-Sham in 2014).[1] Narratives about Europe's home-grown Islamist movements now include processes designed to bridge cultural fissures by familiarising viewers with the life trajectories of individuals who have succumbed to the discourse of Jihad Cool and thus been 'led astray'. Such representations encourage identification with the terrorists, as well as revealing *the* identification *of* them by suggesting that behind the dark mask might lurk someone we grew up next door to or who we went to school with, maybe even someone who looks and talks just like 'us'.

The anguished debate provoked by such home-grown westernised terror forms the real-life backdrop for Mira Nair's film *The Reluctant Fundamentalist* (2012), which recounts the story of a young Pakistani who becomes a suspect in the wake of 9/11 merely because he is brown and bearded (the Oriental Other incarnate). Nair's source text, Mohsin Hamid's novel of the same name, reflects the tensions of the post-9/11 historical moment when the world seemed to be living in a permanent state of global emergency, a situation naturalised by Proclamation 7463 ('Declaration of National Emergency by Reason of Certain Terrorist Attacks') issued by George W. Bush on 14 September 2001.[2] Nair wanted her film to destabilise our cultural memories of that period, and indeed the work does make a significant contribution to the politics of remembering and forgetting.[3] The film is not only an adaptation of Hamid's 2007 novel, but more relevantly an *updating* of it, based on a geopolitical narrative that had evolved since the publication of the 'source' text. After a decade of politicised memorialising of 9/11, this film redirects the focus from the domestic to the foreign, away from the personal and collective trauma resulting from the wounds inflicted on one nation's sense of identity.[4]

In a context of global securitisation and a 'new American exceptionalism' (Pease 2009), of emergent exceptionalisms inside globalisation-as-Americanisation, and of the 'cellular' (networked) model of global capitalism (Appadurai 2004), Nair's adaptation of Hamid's *The Reluctant Fundamentalist* aims to offer a counter-narrative to earlier Hollywood productions such as Oliver Stone's *World Trade Center* (2006), Paul Greengrass' *United 93* (2006) and Stephen Daldry's *Extremely Loud and Incredibly Close* (2011), which effectively nourished a cultural amnesia behind the commemorative and memorialising culture of 9/11.[5] It was the one-sidedness of the post-9/11 trauma depicted in these cinematic narratives that Nair attempted to balance.[6] By enabling us to think of 9/11 as a culturally and racially encoded event,[7] this adaptation challenges the seemingly unruffled façade of the collective memorialisation and forces a welcome displacement of the trauma narratives (and their analysis) away from the Euro-American contexts.[8]

II. THE SOURCE TEXT

Hamid's tale of how a young Princeton graduate becomes disaffected with the American Dream in the wake of 9/11 itself attempts to counter the dominant narrative with another that emphasises similarity rather than difference. This is achieved by deconstructing the very process of stereotype construction through an unsettling interpellation of the implied reader. As Hamid himself put it:

> And because it is a lot for the reader to imagine, it seems to me that one of the interesting things a novel can do is to explore the way in which readers imagine – to reveal to the reader how they imagine, and to show through the imagining, to reflect it back to the reader what they believe, and what their predispositions are and what their presumptions are. (Hamid in interview, Singh 2010: 156)[9]

The ambivalence of Nair's source text resides in the fact that the profiled subject is presented as 'partly internalizing the suspicion, partly gazing back into the oppressive eyeball' (Banita 2010: 249). In fact, the book challenges the implied readers' deep-rooted preconceptions in a variety of ways. For example, we learn only halfway through the novel that the 'fundamentalism' in the title is not, after all, Islamic fundamentalism. Hamid asks readers to confront the stereotypical terrorist-associated definition of fundamentalism: there is no evidence whatsoever that the narrator, Changez, has become a jihadi after becoming disillusioned with the west. Rather, the term refers to the slogan 'Focus on the Fundamentals' used by his New York employer, the valuation firm Underwood Samson, to justify the brutal cuts imposed on the companies they assess and streamline. Changez's job involves assessing the value of companies and shutting them down if they fall short of the 'fundamentals' of capitalist financial analysis. Hence, his growing 'reluctance' to participate in the elimination of jobs and destruction of old family companies is symptomatic not of a fanatical disposition but of his very human compassion for the victims of the radical capitalism typified by American economic policy. The fact that we, the readers, presuppose otherwise becomes the basis for a game of mirrors in which Changez's story comes to us filtered through our own fears.

Ultimately we are left not knowing exactly what happens at the end of the novel. Has violence occurred? Or is the doom we sense no more than the product of our own paranoia, a plot that we ourselves have woven by piecing together signs that seem ominous when viewed in the light of our preconceptions, but which could just as easily prove to be entirely innocent? As Hamid declares in an interview:

> I certainly was working toward an ambiguous ending, one that would reflect the reader's own view of the world back at him or her. Depending on how the reader views the world in which

Figure 5.1 Changez Khan (Riz Ahmed), the eponymous reluctant fundamentalist of the film's title, watches the collapse of the World Trade Center in *The Reluctant Fundamentalist* (2012). Yet the significance of the title is one which is only revealed later in the narrative and is a challenge to the audience's deep-rooted preconceptions.

> the novel takes place, the reader can see the novel as a thriller or as an encounter between two rather odd gentlemen. Because the journey I am asking readers to undertake is emotional and troubling, I knew I wanted a strong narrative pull, a mystery that would add urgency to their reading. The ending, I hope, is the culmination of those efforts. (Quoted in Blankenship 2007)

The novelist wants readers to engage in moral decisions – '[t]he form of the novel is an invitation to the reader' – and if the reader accepts Hamid's invitation (or perhaps challenge), then s/he is called upon to 'judge the novel's outcome and shape its ending' (quoted in Blankenship 2007).

In the last chapters of the novel, our perceptions of who is a fundamentalist and what characterises fundamentalist behaviour are challenged. This destabilising effect is achieved through the use of certain literary mechanisms that highlight the unstable relationship between events and the narrated versions of them. The most startling of these is an artful framing device by means of which Changez's love affair with America and subsequent disillusionment is recounted in the first person by the protagonist himself at a café in Lahore to an unnamed American whom he meets in the street. The American remains a shadowy figure: we never hear his voice directly, and aspects of his physical appearance that could perhaps offer clues to his identity (such as the short-cropped hair, muscular physique and apparent bulge in the jacket pocket) are filtered through a consciousness that is itself aware of the dangers of stereotyping and consistently offers us alternative readings: 'It seems an obvious thing to say, but you should not imagine that we Pakistanis are all potential terrorists, just as we should not imagine that you Americans are all undercover assassins' (Hamid 2007: 209). In view of this absence, the reader merges with the American as the narrative's addressee, sharing his doubts about the narrator's identity and the reliability of his story, and not knowing whether or not to be alarmed by the ominous-looking figures that appear to be lurking in the shadows or the power cut that suddenly plunges the café into darkness.

Changez's voice is also unsettling. He pretends to acknowledge others' voices – these are the 'tricks' the critic Peter Morey (2011) identifies in Changez's monologue. He is anachronistically polite and formal like many educated members of the British former colonies – 'like Pakistan, America is, after all, a former English colony, and it stands to reason, therefore, that an Anglicized accent may in your country continue to be associated with wealth and power, just as it is in mine' (Hamid 2007: 42) – but we sense irony in his tone. How far does that irony go? Does it harbour menace? Undoubtedly, he is playing some kind of cat-and-mouse game with his American addressee but possibly also with us, his reader, to wrong-foot him (and us) and subvert expectation and stereotype. While the narrator's voice is always one of ostentatiously sweetest reason, it is simultaneously highly coercive and manipulative, clearly by authorial intention:

> Excuse me, sir, but may I be of assistance? Ah, I see I have alarmed you. Do not be frightened by my beard: I am a lover of America. I noticed you were looking for something; more than looking, in fact, you seemed to be on a mission, and since I am both a native of this city and a speaker of your language, I thought I might offer you my services. (Hamid 2007: 1)

There are moments, however, where the hostility is not perfectly disguised, and where Changez is shown to lose his courteous manner:

> We [Pakistanis] built the Royal Mosque and the Shalimar Gardens in this city, and we built the Lahore fort with its mighty walls and

wide ramp for our battle elephants. And we did these things when your country was still a collection of thirteen small colonies, gnawing away at the edge of a continent. But once more I am raising my voice and making you rather uncomfortable besides. I apologize; it was not my intention to be rude. (Hamid 2007: 102)

For just a flash the contempt and frustration over lost glories comes through, but the hostility is abruptly sheathed again, control reasserted under the guise of formality and over-politeness once more. It is a highly strategic narratorial device which simultaneously builds suspense, while constantly attempting to lull the reader into a knowingly false sense of security.

The predatory imagery is illustrative: he tells us that his boss at Underwood Samson considered him (approvingly) to be a 'shark' (Hamid 2007: 80), that his American interlocutor jumps in his presence as if he were 'a mouse suddenly under the shadow of a hawk' (Hamid 2007: 69). Is this just a wry game like a child shouting 'Boo!', designed to draw attention to the nervousness underpinning western/Muslim interactions in the post 9/11 context – 'But listen! Did you hear that, sir, a muffled growl, as if of a young lion held captive in a gunnysack? That was my stomach protesting at going unfed. Let us now order dinner' (Hamid 2007: 114)? Or is there indeed a covert operation under way, a terrorist and a CIA operative circling each other – 'your senses are as acute as those of a fox in the wild' (Hamid 2007: 88) – getting ready to pounce – 'I hope you don't mind me saying so, but the frequency and purposefulness with which you glance about . . . brings to mind the behavior of an animal that has ventured too far from its lair and is now, in unfamiliar surroundings, uncertain whether it is predator or prey!' (Hamid 2007: 35)? In fact, in the novel, we do not actually ever get answers to any of these questions. The ambiguity is maintained till the end, every sinister interpretation countered by an innocent one, until ultimately it is the reader's choice which narrative to go for.

Drawing on self-reflexivity and self-consciousness (Srivastava 2012: 179), the book draws attention to our deep-rooted prejudices, questions the foundations on which they rest, and even raises the possibility that this kind of inter-cultural distrust may ultimately become a self-fulfilling prophecy, generating conflict in situations where none may otherwise have existed.

Unfortunately, however, there is less subtlety in the 2012 film version. The adaptation, co-authored by Nair, Hamid and screenwriters Ami Boghani and William Wheeler, was billed as a political thriller and displays all the marks of that genre from the outset. In the adaptation, the menace and suspense is imparted by the tension of the plotline, rather than Changez's tone or stance, as in the novel. The use of Gillo Pontecorvo's *The Battle of Algiers* (1966) – a reference work of documentary-like fiction filmmaking that narrates the story of the Algerian resistance movement against the French occupiers in the 1950s – is particularly apt, considering the topicality of the neo-imperialist US occupation of Afghanistan and Iraq. Pontecorvo's film inspired Nair for decades, and the aesthetic of the newsreel footage was perfect for the tension she aimed at throughout her film.

III. THE CINEMATIC REFRACTION

Nair's adaptation of Hamid's novel is motivated by the cognisance that it should mirror the nostalgic patriotism running through the post-9/11 years alongside a belligerent sanctioned US militarism (with worldwide intelligence units) and malleable racial profiling (Lau and Mendes 2016). It begins with a dramatic cold open in which we witness first-hand the brutal kidnapping of an American aid worker, counterpointed, *Godfather*-style, with shots of an upper-class Pakistani soirée. As in Hamid's novel, we are left in doubt as to Changez's complicity in these actions. However, he does receive text messages throughout the assault, and later in the café seems to be giving orders to the students amassing threateningly in the vicinity.

Figure 5.2 Changez's conversation with the journalist and CIA operative Bobby Lincoln (Liev Schreiber) attempts to set up a dialogue about the tragic events by showing both perspectives.

This then provides the pretext for the explicit CIA presence in Lahore, manifested not only in the person of the American interlocutor who is given a name, Bobby Lincoln (Liev Schreiber), and whose story is fleshed out to make him into Changez's equal and opposite, a man caught between cultures who is forced to choose sides in the wake of 9/11, but also the marksmen in the opposite building with their sights trained on the café, and, later, the helicopters circling overhead.

The heavily illustrated tie-in book for Nair's film, *The Reluctant Fundamentalist: From Book to Film*, promises 'an exclusive behind-the-scenes look' into the adaptation. The opening words, in crimson serif-font letters in the middle of the second of two black pages, present the plot as a post-9/11 coming-of-age story: 'In the ten years between 9/11 and the killing of Osama Bin Laden, a young man grows up. This is the story of that young man' (Nair et al. 2013: xvii). This is followed by two strikingly juxtaposed black-and-white photographs of Changez, played by Riz Ahmed, the British Pakistani actor and rapper (Nair et al. 2013: xviii–ix). Both pictures showcase his culturally constituted and racially profiled body. The left-hand picture presents the clean-shaven pre-9/11 Changez looking to one side, while the right-hand one shows him after the event, looking away (perhaps disengaging) and proudly displaying a beard, the symbol of his maturity and Islamisation, which he wears as a badge of foreignness, conscious that this is one of the strongest markers of difference that racial profiling is predicated upon: 'It was, perhaps, a form of protest on my part, a symbol of my identity' (Hamid 2007: 130). Reflecting the two timeframes of the cinematic narrative, the pictures foreground Changez's identity transformation, which provides the affective structure for the film, also emphasised in the promotional material.

While in Hamid's dramatic monologue the reader hears only the Pakistani side, Nair's film sets up a dialogue about the tragic events by showing both perspectives. Indeed, the filmmaker stresses cultural negotiation when discussing her adaptation. During a 2013 fundraising gala dinner of the Asia Society in Mumbai, she voiced her concern regarding 'what has happened in the last 12 years in terms of the monologue we've continued to hear from America with the rest of the world' (Padmanabhan 2013). Adapting *The Reluctant Fundamentalist* gave her the opportunity to turn the monologue into a dialogue. Understanding Hamid's novel as 'about the mutual suspicion that the two men and the two countries, America and Pakistan, have of each other' (Kaplan 2013), she intended her film to be 'not only about contemporary Pakistan but also about a *dialogue* with America' (Padmanabhan 2013, emphasis added). This, notably, sets out from a novel which is a *monologue* by a Pakistani, spoken to (and almost spoken *at*) an American.

The casting of Riz Ahmed (who before *The Reluctant Fundamentalist* had starred in Michael Winterbottom's 2006 film *The Road to Guantanamo*) as Changez is significant. Nair takes advantage of Ahmed's high cultural capital as a performer who, like the character he plays (and also like Nair and Hamid), can relate to the idea of growing up between two worlds:

> I attended a university [Oxford] where my cultural background was very different to those around me. But the film is about getting rid of those labels and stereotypes – or at least stretching the labels wide enough so that we can live inside them comfortably. (Quoted in Brooks 2012)

While the novel arguably stresses the gulf between the two realities,[10] Nair wanted 'to create a bridge between worlds that will not know each other unless we have a dialogue' (Nair et al. 2013: xii). She describes the film as a 'conversation between two cultures that goes beyond the prejudices that contaminate us' (Brooks 2012), expressing the wish to contribute to 'some sense of bridge-making, some sense of healing, basically a sense of communication that goes beyond the stereotype' (Anon. 2012). The continuous emphasis on the trope of the 'dialogue', used interchangeably with 'bridge' and 'conversation' in promotional interviews, demonstrates a more conciliatory approach on her part. The fact that Nair seems intent on building bridges is recurrent in her filmography: in her film adaptation of Jumpa Lahiri's *The Namesake*, bridges literally abound, and she has commented on the symbolism of this in various interviews.

Nonetheless, the story-within-the-story loses its subtlety in the film when juxtaposed with the novel. Changez's disillusionment with American culture (in particular his reflections on US militarist and imperialist expansion, its continuing belief in a Manifest Destiny and the brutality of its neo-colonial capitalist system, which he holds responsible for his growing disaffection) are treated very heavy-handedly. In the novel, Changez voices his anger thus: '[a]s a society, you [America] were unwilling to reflect upon the shared pain that united you with those who attacked you. You retreated into myths of your own difference, assumptions of your own superiority' (Hamid 2007: 168); and a few pages later he denounces 'the advancement of a small coterie's concept of American interests in the guise of the fight against terrorism, which was defined to refer only to the organized and politically motivated killing of civilians by killers not wearing the uniforms of soldiers' (Hamid 2007: 178).[11] In the film, his American girlfriend Erica (Kate Hudson), who is now a photographer and, significantly, his boss's niece (an extended metaphor of America) betrays his trust by proclaiming their most intimate moments to the world in an art installation entitled 'I had a Pakistani once'; and in the aftermath of 9/11 he suffers a series of indignities in his new adopted homeland, including a full-body search at the airport, questioning by the FBI, arrest for a crime he did not commit, and violent insults from strangers.

The turning-point in Hamid's novel (which comes when he learns of the Christian boys known as Janissaries, who were kidnapped by Ottomans and brainwashed into destroying their culture of origin) now takes place in Istanbul instead of Valparaiso and is triggered by a Turkish publishing chief who incites him to take a stand ('Young men don't make good mercenaries; they need a cause to fight'; 'When you decide where you stand, the colour will return to your world'). Hence, when Changez returns to Pakistan it is unequivocally to fight for his people against what he perceives as American domination. He takes a job as a university lecturer but uses his rhetorical skills to stir up the students. One day he is approached by the leader of a militant cell who persuades him to join them. The scene is thus set for the violent climax, when, after hours of long negotiations with the CIA operative in the café over the release of the kidnapped aid worker, all hell breaks loose as the students start to riot and the Americans open fire. The incident culminates in the death of a young student, which offers the excuse for a philosophical reflection about the dangers of fundamentalism on either side, as Changez renounces violence and takes to preaching messages of peace and love with prophetic solemnity.

We might speculate about the reasons for this change using the concept of 'refraction', developed by André Lefevere in the context of translation studies to refer to the changes that a text undergoes in its passage through different cultures (Lefevere 1982). The medium of film, with its emphasis on the visual, clearly does not lend itself easily to a faithful reproduction of a novel that is essentially a monologue recounted in a static scenario.[12] The (perhaps financially motivated) desire to produce a mainstream film will certainly have dictated the director's decision to recast the story as a political thriller and to abandon all nuance in favour of a sexier and more clear-cut tale. Nair probably felt that it was necessary to hammer home the parallelisms between Changez and Bobby Lincoln, the CIA operative who is his interlocutor, and to use obvious injustice to generate sympathy for the Princeton-graduate-turned-terrorist. Yet that same target public also constrains the possibility of seeing this narrative through to its logical conclusion. Indeed, in the present political climate, it would probably have been dangerous for Mira Nair to have tried to retain our sympathy for Changez once he had become radicalised. Having him convert to pacifism was thus the only way she could end the tale coherently without alienating her target public.

IV. FURTHER REFRACTIONS

Other curious refractions can also be found in the various reviews of the book that appeared in the press in 2007, the year of its publication. *The London Review of Books* and *New York Review of Books,* as befits their literary bent, focus on the formal aspect of the work and its relationship to other literary genres (respectively Chaudhuri 2007 and Kerr 2007). However, Chaudhuri, who is himself an Indian-English writer of renown, frames his comments with an autobiographical account of a similar encounter that he himself had had some twenty years earlier, and reflects upon his own relationship to the identity conflict suffered by the protagonist of the novel (he concludes, as the title of his article suggests, that Changez is 'not entirely' like him).

Reviews in newspapers from the Indian subcontinent also explore this identity dimension, seeking points of contact with Changez's experience. *The Hindustan Times,* in an article entitled 'Politics as personal' (Sharma 2007), vouches for the verisimilitude of the account: 'What makes him so believable – especially to the urbane subcontinental reader – is that he is like us: one foot firmly set in the cultural ground of his own backyard, modern Pakistan; another foot in the globalised world of Americana where one knows one's Paltrow from one's Spears.' The Pakistani-based journal *The News,* focusing on the politics of the monologue device used in the novel, concludes that the fictional interaction is 'healthy for Pakistani literature as well as Pakistani identity' because 'for the first time in Pakistan's intricate and messy relationship with the United States of America, we have a scenario, though fictional, where the American listens to the Pakistani for such a long time' (Saeed Ur Rehman 2007).

American reviews, on the other hand, tend to approach the book as an example of the 9/11 subgenre, and discuss the work in the light of that event or the literary and social ruptures brought about by it. Marina Budhos (2007), writing in *The Brooklyn Rail,* claims that fiction sales plummeted in the United States after 9/11 because people wanted reality, 'as if somehow, in such a difficult, gloomy moment for Americans, fiction became frivolous and indulgent, once we were stunned awake from our complacent slumber to realize we are a superpower hated by many'. She praises the novel for its capacity to interact with the real, but claims not to 'swallow all of it with incredulity' (an interesting phrase in the post-9/11 climate of distrust): 'As an American, one finds one-self arguing with the narrator (is Pakistan entirely vulnerable and weak during the face-off with India in 2002? Is business consulting really the same as janissaries – captured Christian boys – used by the Ottoman Empire?).'

Paula Bock in the *Seattle Times* presents the story as a case of the American Dream gone wrong, and uses rhetorical questions to anticipate her reader's response to the narrative ('Of course, on 9/11, America was the bombing victim. So why is Changez lashing out against America?'). Like Budhos, she seems to have only recently woken up to the reality of how America is viewed in the wider world, and seems to find the book helpful as a way of trying to understand that ('That 9/11 should trigger rage – against America – in the soul of a Princeton soccer star who once embraced America is Hamid's seeth-ing commentary on America's reputation in the non-western world today'). However, despite the apparent soul-searching, for her, as for some of the other American reviewers, Changez remains resolutely foreign: she finds his voice 'extraordinary', which of course a British reader would not, and seems to lament the fact that he is not allowed to live up to stereotype at the end ('It's too bad Hamid decided to punt on the last page with an ambiguous ending worthy of a freshman fiction-writing seminar').

V. CONCLUSION

To sum up, then, Hamid's skilful subversion of received ideas about the western self and the Islamic other does not survive the work's various refractions. Critics, translators and film directors are obliged, by the various constraints under which they operate, to pass the story through a new lens in order to reach new publics, and it is inevitably coloured and changed in the process. Hence, these new texts only partially achieve what Hamid has done, and, indeed, there are those that go some way to reversing it. An extreme example of this is a French review of the film (which is of course a double, or even triple, refraction), whose headline proclaims 'Kate Hudson, brune et séduite par un ambitieux Pakistanais Intégriste malgré lui' ('Kate Hudson, brown-haired and seduced by an ambitious Pakistani reluctant fundamentalist') (Anon. 2013). By focusing on the Hollywood actress who plays the part of Changez's girlfriend Erica, and reducing the story to the tale of her supposed seduction by an 'ambitious Pakistani fundamentalist' (itself a curious collocation), this headline plays into that most atavistic of masculine cultural fears: the vulnerability of their womenfolk to the sexual charms of enemy males and the need to protect their purity at all cost. The fact that this normally blonde all-American actress has now dyed her hair brown is presented almost as if it were the first stage of assimilation into Islam. The headline invites us to speculate: had she indeed married Changez and gone to live with him in Pakistan, what would have become of her? Veiled up and kept in purdah, no doubt.

NOTES

1. The perlocutionary effect of these narratives is enhanced by the fact that the global news market has narrowed considerably in recent years and is now controlled by a limited number of news providers, namely the Associated Press, Reuters and Agence France-Presse. This has resulted in a streamlining of narratives. The repeated staging of Foley's decapitation gave hyper-visibility to this horrific event, while US covert actions, such as the drone strikes in Pakistan, Somalia and Yemen, continued to take place out of the view of the cameras in the murky realm of the hyper-*invisible*.

2. In 2013, *Foreign Policy* magazine nominated Hamid one of the '100 leading global thinkers', '[f]or painting a disquieting picture of Asia's rise'. While this selection was occasioned by the publication of *How to Get Filthy Rich in Rising Asia* that year, Hamid's two earlier novels, *Moth Smoke* (2000) and *The Reluctant Fundamentalist*, had already shown him to be 'a master critic of the modern global condition' (available at 2013-global-thinkers.foreignpolicy.com, last accessed 29 February 2016). See Mendes (2016: 224–7) for a consideration of how Hamid's textual representations, despite issued from the south, are inevitably coloured by western representations.

3. Understanding memory as a performance allows us to regard memory and memorialising as a process of dealing with the past (sometimes a traumatic past) in the present, linking a present to a past and, most relevantly, to a future. These, in turn, are shaped by the process of remembering. In this framework, cinematic representations are constantly reconfiguring ideas of the nation, not only mirroring but also influencing discourses and practices of nation.

4. Nair had already dealt with the subject of 9/11 in the portmanteau work *11'9"01 September 11* (2002), in which eleven filmmakers from around the world were invited to adopt alternative perspectives on 9/11 away from the atavistic mourning gripping America in the direct aftermath of the attacks. Producer Alain Brigand had included her as the representative of India.

5. As Dominick LaCapra (2004: 95) puts it, the stories we choose to tell, read and watch reflect the 'sociopolitical uses and constructions of trauma'.

6. These films are examples of the cinematic memorialising of 9/11. Marc Redfield describes 'the ambiguous injury inflicted by the September 11 attacks as mediated events' (Redfield 2009: 2). Redfield's concept of 'virtual trauma' is helpful for understanding the ways a notion of collective trauma has been incorporated into cultural memory through Hollywood blockbusters such as these.

7. The metonymic short-hand term '9/11' effectively reifies a very complex event. See theorists such as Jean Baudrillard, Slavoj Žižek, Paul Virilio, Noam Chomsky, Jürgen Habermas and Jacques Derrida on the US reaction to it and the overarching geopolitical consequences.

8. Previous South Asian cinematic representations of the post-9/11 zeitgeist, set against the backdrop of the 'War on Terror' and featuring Muslim characters who move between Delhi, Mumbai, Lahore and the US, seem to be haunted by the spectre of the migrant South Asian as suspect of terrorism. Some of the Indian and Pakistani films that have taken up this trope include *Kurbaan* (dir. Rensil D'Silva, 2009), *New York* (dir. Kabir Khan, 2009), *My Name is Khan* (dir. Karan Johar, 2010), *Khuda Kay Liye* (dir. Shoaib Mansoor, 2007) and *Tere Bin Laden* (dir. Abhishek Sharma, 2010).

9. Elsewhere Hamid writes: 'There is another character in the story, which is the reader . . . In a way the story is not just about Changez and the American and Erica but it's about how you are reacting to your world' (interview with Harriett Gilbert, *World Book Club*, BBC, 3 April 2009).

10. Notwithstanding the protagonist's early love affairs with America, he finds that 'America was gripped by a growing and self-righteous rage . . . the mighty host I had expected of your country was duly raised and dispatched' (Hamid 2007: 107).

11. The protagonist's words echo Elleke Boehmer's argument that 'terror [has been] viewed not only as the manifestation of the imperial state, but also as the expression of an anti-colonial modernity [. . .] which allows us to examine its occurrence in the reciprocally violent historical contexts of colonialism and global neo-colonialism rather than the ahistorical "War on Terror" which is viewed simply as savage and irrational, an irruption of the primitive' (Boehmer 2007: 6).

12. Hamid seems to anticipate the difficulty of translating his novel into an essentially visual medium in a 2010 interview: '*The Reluctant Fundamentalist* is read differently by different readers, and so that's why I think it's a rich space. And it's something that I think that fiction has a unique power to engage in. Unlike a film or a television program, where the acting is done for you, in a novel we are just seeing visual characters. And the translation of those characters into words, into thoughts, into imagery, into feelings is one that has a larger imaginative component on the part of the reader' (Singh 2010: 156).

REFERENCES

Anon. (2012), '*The Reluctant Fundamentalist* opens Venice Film Festival', 30 August 2012, last accessed 29 February 2016: http://www.bbc.com/news/entertainment-arts-19421160

Anon. (2013), 'Kate Hudson, brune et séduite par un ambitieux Pakistanais Intégriste malgré lui', 21 February 2013, last accessed 29 February 2016, http://www.purepeople.com/article/kate-hudson-brune-et-seduite-par-unambitieux-pakistanais-integriste-malgre-lui_a116035/1

Appadurai, Arjun (2006), *Fear of Small Numbers: An Essay on the Geography of Anger*, Durham, NC: Duke University Press.

Banita, Georgiana (2010), 'Race, Risk, and Fiction in the War on Terror: Laila Halaby, Gayle Brandeis, and Michael Cunningham', *Lit: Literature Interpretation Theory*, 21:4, pp. 242–68.

Bock, Paula (2007), 'An American dream turns to dust in the rubble of the twin towers', 14 April 2007: last accessed 3 March 2016, http://old.seattletimes.com/html/books/2003659505_fundamentalist10.html

Blankenship, Michelle (2007), 'Interview with Mohsin Hamid', *Media Enquiries*, n/d, last accessed 29 February 2016: http://www.harcourtbooks.com/reluctant_fundamentalist/interview.asp

Boehmer, Elleke (2007), 'Postcolonial Writing and Terror', *Wasafiri*, 22:2, pp. 4–7.

Brooks, Xan (2012), 'Venice film festival opens with 9/11 drama The Reluctant Fundamentalist', 29 August 2012, last accessed 29 February 2016: http://www.theguardian.com/film/2012/aug/29/venicve-film-festival-reluctant-fundamentalist

Budhos, Marina (2007), 'Runes of ruin', May 2007, last accessed 4 March 2016: http://www.brooklynrail.org/2007/5/books/runes-of-ruins

Chaudhuri, Amit (2007), 'Not entirely like me', *London Review of Books*, 19:19, pp. 25–6.

Halaby, Leila (2007), 'Return of the Native', 22 April 2007, last accessed 4 March 2016: http://www.washingtonpost.com/wp-dyn/content/article/2007/04/19/AR2007041903000.html

Kaplan, Fred (2013), 'Crossing dangerous borders: Mira Nair on *The Reluctant Fundamentalist*', 19 April 2013, last accessed 29 February 2016: www.nytimes.com/2013/04/21/movies/mira-nair-on-the-reluctant-fundamentalist.html?_r=0

Kerr, Sarah (2007), 'In the terror house of mirrors', 11 October 2007, last accessed 4 March 2016, http://www.nybooks.com/articles/2007/10/11/in-the-terror-house-of-mirrors/

LaCapra, Dominick (2004), *History in Transit: Experience, Identity, Critical Theory*, Ithaca: Cornell University Press.

Lau, Lisa, and Ana Cristina Mendes (2016), 'Post-9/11 Re-Orientalism: Confrontation and Conciliation in Mohsin Hamid's and Mira Nair's *The Reluctant Fundamentalist*', *The Journal of Commonwealth Literature* (forthcoming).

Lefevere, André (1982), 'Mother Courage's Cucumbers: Text, System and Refraction in a Theory of Literature', *Modern Language Studies*, 12:4, pp. 3–20.

Hamid, Mohsin (2000), *Moth Smoke,* New York: Farrar, Straus & Giroux.

— (2007), *The Reluctant Fundamentalist*, London: Hamish Hamilton.

— (2013), *How to Get Filthy Rich in Rising Asia,* New York: Riverhead Books.

Mendes, Ana Cristina (2016), 'The Marketing of Postcolonial Literature', in Lucia Krämer and Kai Merten (eds), *Postcolonial Studies Meets Media Studies: A Critical Encounter*, Bielefeld: Transcript, pp. 215–31.

Morey, Peter (2011), '"The rules of the game have changed": Mohsin Hamid's *The Reluctant Fundamentalist* and post-9/11 fiction', *Journal of Postcolonial Writing*, 47:2, pp. 135–46.

Nair, Mira et al. (2013), *The Reluctant Fundamentalist: From Book to Film*, New Delhi: Penguin Studio.

Padmanabhan, Deepika (2013), 'Mira Nair's Post-9/11 Film: A Conversation with "The Other Side"', 11 May 2013, last accessed 29 February 2016: http://asiasociety.org/india/mira-nairs-post-911-film-conversation-other-side

Pease, Donald E. (2009), *The New American Exceptionalism*, Minneapolis: University of Minnesota Press.

Redfield, Marc (2009), *The Rhetoric of Terror: Reflections on 9/11 and the War on Terror*, New York: Fordham University Press.

Rehman, Saeed Ur (2007), 'Success of Understatement', 29 April 2007, last accessed 4 March 2016: http://jang.com.pk/thenews/apr2007-weekly/nos-29-04-2007/lit.htm#1

Sharma, Aasheesh (2007), 'Politics as personal', *Hindustan Times*, 16 April 2007.

Singh, Harleen (2010), 'Deconstructing the terror: interview with Mohsin Hamid on *The Reluctant Fundamentalist* (2007)', *ARIEL: A Review of International English Literature*, 42:2, pp. 149–56.

Whitehead, Anne (2004), *Trauma Fiction*, Edinburgh: Edinburgh University Press.

PART II

Influences of the 'War on Terror'

CHAPTER 6

'Not now that strength': Embodiment and Globalisation in Post-9/11 James Bond

Vincent M. Gaine

In *Skyfall* (2012), the twenty-third James Bond film, released on the fiftieth anniversary of the Bond franchise, M (Judi Dench) quotes the poetry of Lord Alfred Tennyson before a government board of inquiry. M argues that MI6 still has a role to play in national security. Her speech is intercut with Bond himself (Daniel Craig) racing to intercept the film's villain Silva (Javier Bardem), the editing giving truth to M's words. This sequence epitomises the tropes that have characterised the Craig-era Bond, as Craig's incarnation of the character has reshaped the franchise over the course of *Casino Royale* (2006), *Quantum of Solace* (2008), *Skyfall* and *Spectre* (2015). I discuss these four films in relation to other franchises as well as earlier Bond, and argue that the Craig-era Bond responds to specific concerns of the post-9/11 period. In particular, I identify the Bond of a post-9/11 era of globalisation, where national concerns are in tension with those of global capitalism, and where borders and institutions are more vulnerable to penetration than in previous decades.

I. BODIES OF BOURNE, BATMAN AND BOND

The Craig-era Bond constitutes a reconfiguration of the Bond brand within a historical and industrial context characterised by ongoing franchises, recognisable brands and films that play to established audiences. Since 2000, the box office success of such titles as *Spider-Man* (2002–), *The Lord of the Rings* (2001–3), *Harry Potter* (2001–11), *Star Wars*

(1977–) and *Toy Story* (1995–) have demonstrated the industrial logic of continuing franchise productions aimed at pre-existing markets (Singh 2014: 31). The Bond franchise's audience has been established since the 1960s, but faces competition within a crowded blockbuster schedule. Obvious rivals for Bond fans' attention include other spy films, especially the Jason Bourne series (2002–), as well as the superhero genre (Purse 2011: 104). While *Skyfall*, the most commercially successful Bond film to date, grossed over $1 billion worldwide, several superhero films including *Iron Man 3* (2013), *The Avengers* (2012) and *The Dark Knight* (2008), have surpassed that figure, while two of the Bourne films were among the top ten box office hits of their respective years (Box Office Mojo). The success of such films demonstrates the cinematic opposition that Bond's producers Eon must respond to.

Sinclair McKay claims that while preparing *Casino Royale*, Eon 'were answering the tremendous popularity of the *Bourne* spy films. . . . It was the huge success of the second film, *The Bourne Supremacy*, helmed by British Paul Greengrass, that especially made Eon sit up and take note' (McKay 2008: 349). The initially unassuming Jason Bourne transformed Matt Damon into an action hero and made Greengrass and Doug Liman, the director of *The Bourne Identity*, blockbuster directors. Both filmmakers subsequently delivered high-profile films such as *Captain Phillips* (2013) and *Edge of Tomorrow* (2014), while what was initially a trilogy spawned a spinoff/sequel *The Bourne Legacy* (2012) and a fifth entry reuniting Damon and Greengrass (2016).

The significance of Bourne is evident in critical responses both academic and popular: 'By the time Daniel Craig's name emerged as the new Bond, the franchise faced generic competition, especially from the Jason Bourne series' (Dodds 2014: 119); 'post-Jason Bourne, will the villain be James Bond's alter ego – his inner demon?' (Frayling 2015: 77); 'The brains behind Bond should take note, for the Bourne series has proved itself the smartest spy franchise around' (Empire 2004). Based on these responses, Bourne can be seen as altering expectations of what a cinematic secret agent would deliver: Bond's previous strategy of destroying every vehicle he gets into (according to Pierce Brosnan's Bond in *Goldeneye* [1995]) is too simplistic. McKay highlights the contrast between Bond's flamboyance and Bourne's more reserved approach:

[Bond's] is repeatedly a triumph of physicality and superior technology. From jet-packs to laser beam watches, the old spirit of heroic improvisation is missing. Which is presumably why the makers of the *Bourne* films made their main character such a dab hand at turning household implements into lethal weapons. (364)

McKay's claim about technology is borne out by the earlier films, as pre-Craig Bond is always well equipped by MI6's Q branch. These devices frequently save Bond's life, including a wrist-mounted dart launcher in *Moonraker* (1979) and an explosive key ring in *The Living Daylights* (1987). Such scenes are absent from *Casino Royale* and *Quantum of Solace*, and receive a new twist in *Skyfall* as well as a regressive treatment in *Spectre*. *Skyfall* uses a radio transmitter, ironically referred to as 'the latest thing', while *Spectre* features an exploding watch in a seeming concession to convention. However, previous Bonds also outwit their over-confident adversaries. Roger Moore's Bond poses as a mannequin to deceive Francisco Scaramanga (Christopher Lee) in *The Man with the Golden Gun* (1974) and Timothy Dalton's Bond takes advantage of petrol-soaked clothes to immolate Franz Sanchez (Robert Davi) in *Licence to Kill* (1989). Unarmed combat occurs across the series, such as a fight aboard a train in *From Russia with Love* (1963) between Sean Connery's Bond and SPECTRE agent Grant (Robert Shaw), as well as Bond's fight with Alec Trevelyan (Sean Bean) inside a giant satellite dish in *Goldeneye*. However, these moments stand out as exceptions, whereas the physicality of Craig as Bond is repeatedly emphasised, much like that of Bourne: in an early scene in *The Bourne Identity*, the unconscious Bourne is stripped for medical examination, exposing Matt Damon's muscular physique, which appears again later during a love scene. Similarly, in *Casino Royale* and its descendants, 'Emphasis is placed on Daniel Craig's exposed muscular torso rather than his sexuality, libido, and conquest' (Funnell 2011: 462). Craig's physique is most explicitly emphasised in the opening titles of *Spectre*, where Bond's bare torso is a central spectacle of the surreal, dreamlike images. Undulating female bodies have long been a staple of Bond film credit sequences, but Bond himself is rarely so exposed. This almost fetishistic display of Bond destabilises 'the Bond Girl in the film as the locus of visual spectacle' (Funnell: 464), suggesting a greater interest in the male body than the female. A key spectacle of the Craig-era Bond, therefore, is Bond himself, and this spectacle expresses the films' interest in bodily responses to trauma.

Trauma is central to the Bourne films (Gaine 2011: 160; Everett 2012: 106; McSweeney 2014: 23) and critics have identified post-9/11 trauma across multiple texts (see Kaplan 2005; Markovitz 2005; Hammond 2011). Furthermore, British audiences especially have the trauma of 7 July 2005: '*Skyfall* may well be akin to a distinctly post-7/7 movie, a chronological invention that highlights the emotive and material consequences of four near simultaneous attacks on the London transport system' (Dodds: 118). Trauma also informs many superhero films, as superheroes are often haunted by the loss of parents and other loved ones. The superhero genre has largely replaced and superseded Bond in terms of fantastical flamboyance, such as cloaked jets in *X-Men* (2000), pseudo-scientific explanations for Spider-Man and the Hulk, and a vigilante secret society in the Dark Knight Trilogy. Whereas Bond went into space in *Moonraker* (1979) and drove an invisible car in *Die Another Day* (2002), now the Avengers repel alien invaders and the X-Men battle giant robots. The most significant superhero film in relation to Bond is *Batman Begins* (2005), released the year before *Casino Royale*. *Batman Begins* 'places visual focus on the development of Wayne's muscular torso; his bullet-proof vest simultaneously covers and attracts attention to his muscular chest' (Funnell: 461). As well as having a similar chest, Bond dons a costume for his role: 'Bond's superhero costume becomes the tuxedo [which] personifies, to paraphrase from *Batman Begins*, a symbol people can understand' (Arnett 2009: 13). Indeed, this tuxedo is tailored to Bond's specific measurements, i.e. made for his body. Across these films, there is narrative and stylistic emphasis upon the construction of an action body, complete with appropriate attire. For Bourne, Batman and Bond, the constructed body is both traumatised and a bulwark against trauma.

Total Film's review of *Casino Royale* describes Daniel Craig as 'the first 007 who genuinely looks like he could kill a man with his bare hands' (2006). Craig's Bond owes much to the unpredictability of Bourne and Batman, all three of which are embodied with a sense of physical danger. In *The Bourne Identity*, Bourne is as surprised as the viewer when he knocks two Zurich policemen unconscious. Similarly, Bruce Wayne (Christian Bale) attacks without warning in *Batman Begins* both in a Chinese prison and later in the headquarters of the League of Shadows. Lisa Purse's analysis of *Casino Royale* highlights the film's stylistic emphasis upon Bond's physical prowess (Purse: 37–40, 49–50), with sudden cuts, short takes, confined mise en scène and the sounds of 'extreme exertions' (50). *Total Film*'s comment that 'Moore didn't fit this much action into his entire seven movies' (2006) highlights Craig's physicality as a unique selling point of the film. Of the 144 minutes of *Casino Royale*'s running time, forty-three are devoted to action sequences. Much like the action sequences of Bourne and Batman, these set pieces involve Bond's physical capability but also, crucially, his physical *limitations*. In *Casino Royale*'s parkour sequence, 'Mollaka's fluid running and jumping contrasts sharply with Bond's less agile movements, making 007's mastery of the environment seem tenuous rather than certain' (Purse: 47). Where Mollaka leaps through a small opening in a plasterboard wall, Bond bursts right through it, his physicality one of brute force rather than exceptional agility. Bond is a human specimen, not a superhero, and is therefore only capable of human exploits. Whereas Superman can fly and Wolverine is indestructible, Bond must rely on his limited physical abilities, which paradoxically serves to emphasise how physically adept he is *without* the assistance of superpowers. This absence of abilities is true of Batman as well, but technological assistance fills the Dark Knight Trilogy and is a constituent part of Batman's heroic identity – without his devices, Wayne is severely weakened in *The Dark Knight Rises* (2012).

What distinguishes Bond from Batman and other costumed crusaders are the Bond action sequences' 'authenticity' (McKay: 2), such as 'realistic-looking levels of gravity and physical resistance' (Purse: 46). In the context of digitally generated spectacles, the Bond franchise has continued with this authenticity, with emphasis upon physicality both within and beyond the diegesis. The discourse around Craig's body parallels that of other performers in action franchises, such as Hugh Jackman in *X-Men* (2000–) and Henry Cavill in *Man of Steel* (2013). The contemporary action body is physically developed, and promotional as well as journalistic discourse covers the work involved in building that action body. Publications such as *Men's Health* and *GQ* detail the workout regime Craig uses to get into the condition of Bond (see Editors 2015; Henderson 2011), demonstrating that the interest in Craig/Bond's physicality is broader than the films' diegeses. The studio participates in this discourse as well with ancillary materials for the films' home release. A featurette on the UK Blu-ray release of *Casino Royale* is entitled *James Bond: For Real*, in which the production staff repeatedly emphasise practical effects over digital. Digital effects allow the fantastic spectacle of superhero films such as flight, energy weapons and inhuman agility – Bond is explicitly distinguished from that type of spectacle by physical, feasible action sequences, as seen in the Miami sequence of *Casino Royale*.

The sequence begins with Bond pursuing Alex Dimitrios (Simon Abkarian) from the Bahamian resort of Nassau to Miami, where Dimitrios passes materials to bomber Carlos (Claudio Santamaria). The exchange between Dimitrios and Carlos at a Gunther Von Hagens exhibition 'highlights the living human body evident in Craig's frequent displays of physicality' (Cox 2014: 191). Bond demonstrates his superior physical prowess by killing Dimitrios in a knife struggle, punching Dimitrios to gain control of the knife long enough to stab the other man. Bond then pursues Carlos to the airport. As panicked people evacuate the terminal, Bond and Carlos are both seen in tracking shots as they move through the crowd. This repeated shot draws a parallel between the two men: both are equally capable and dangerous. In an overhead tracking shot, Bond runs up a boarding staircase to jump onto Carlos' tanker, similar to the earlier Madagascar sequence when Bond and Mollaka jumped between cranes. Bond is in rapid motion, attains height and jumps onto a moving vehicle and almost falls off. The sequence has multiple close-ups of Bond's face as well as the sounds of his exertion, making his endeavour relatable for the viewer. When Bond and Carlos struggle in the cab, there is no swift overpowering but multiple punches and kicks, including one that sends Bond out of the cab. In an unstable overhead shot, Bond hangs out of the cab as his gun spins away. Without his gun, Bond has only his physicality and adaptability, which includes his observation that Carlos' keyring is a bomb. Pulling himself back into the cab, a close-up shows Bond's hand on Carlos' belt, foreshadowing Bond's placement of the small bomb there. Bond's face is now bloodied and grazed, and he receives further injuries as he fights to control the tanker. Having stopped the vehicle, Bond collapses from apparent exhaustion and dizziness, the use of overhead shots emphasising his fall, before he is subdued by airport police in a tight shot that precludes any warning of these attackers approaching. The powerful and adaptable body is overpowered with shocking speed and without resistance, 'all his bodily potential constrained by over-enthusiastic police officers' (Purse: 45). The overpowering emphasises Bond's limits: he cannot overcome superior numbers when he is spent.

As part of demonstrating Bond's limitations, this sequence as well as others highlights that Bond is far from invulnerable. Back on Nassau, Bond still has visible injuries on his face and utters a very audible 'Oww!' when implanted with a tracking device. When Le Chiffre (Mads Mikkelsen) later tortures him, Bond again has a bloodied face and is stripped naked for an assault upon his genitals. This interest in Bond's vulnerability continues in the later films (see Dodds: 122; Funnell: 468; Hasian 2014: 579), the body of Craig/Bond repeatedly figured as both vulnerable and potent. A shot to the shoulder in *Skyfall*'s opening sequence leaves Bond with visible scarring, and his face is again scratched and grazed in *Quantum of Solace*. In *Spectre*, Bond is tortured, this time by Franz Oberhauser/Ernst Stavro Blofeld (Christoph Waltz). The manner of torture in *Spectre* is striking, as Blofeld uses tiny drills to penetrate Bond's skull. Bond faces sexually charged dangers in *Casino Royale* with Dimitrios' knife (Cox: 191) and Le Chiffre's assault on his testicles, and in *Skyfall* Silva (Javier Bardem) taunts Bond homoerotically. Blofeld's attack is also sexually charged because of the phallic drills, his continued success at manipulating Bond, and his target of Bond's brain. Blofeld almost literally 'fucks' Bond in the head, targeting Bond's memory and therefore identity, as Blofeld believes Bond did to him when they were children. The films' attention to the body emphasises armouring, much like the increased security measures of western governments following the terrorist attacks of 9/11. Bond's musculature visually signifies a last line of defence against attack when precautions and technology fail. However, Bond's repeated injuries and the display of his body for visual subjugation as much as for prowess and capability demonstrate the fallibility of physicality and the inevitability of trauma.

Nor is this trauma solely physical, as Bond is emotionally traumatised by the death of Vesper Lynd in *Casino Royale*. With the exception of *On Her Majesty's Secret Service* (1969), every Bond film prior to *Casino Royale* ends with Bond united with a lover. Craig-era Bond's omission of this trope reconstructs Bond as distinct from what came before, a Bond characterised by his vulnerability. This Bond contrasts with the near invulnerability of previous incarnations – the only time a bullet enters Roger Moore is when he accidentally swallows one in *The Man with the Golden Gun*, while Pierce Brosnan's shoulder injury in *The World is Not Enough* (1999) is highly unusual as the character suffers no long-term effects from his months of torture in *Die Another Day*. Instances of Bond suffering emotionally are few and far between: the mourning of Tracy (Diana Rigg) in *On Her Majesty's Secret Service*, as well as her fleeting mentions in *The Spy Who Loved Me* (1977) and *For Your Eyes Only* (1981); Timothy Dalton's furious quest for vengeance in *Licence to Kill*. The repeated emphasis upon physical and emotional vulnerability in Craig-era Bond demonstrates a consistent interest in trauma, which as noted above is a common feature in post-9/11 cinema.

As McKay and Jeremy Black (2001) argue in their respective analyses of the James Bond series, the franchise has developed in accordance with contemporary historical events: 'According to producer Michael G. Wilson, at the very start of pre-production on any Bond, when story ideas are being thrown around, he always asks himself: "What is the main worry in the world right now?"' (McKay: 319). Following 9/11, the main worry in the world has been the threat of terrorist attacks, as evidenced by increased airline security, the creation of the US Department of Homeland Security in 2002 and the invasions of Afghanistan and Iraq. *Casino Royale* especially engages with post-9/11 concerns, despite only a brief mention by M. However, *Casino Royale* also restages the event in Bond's own terms. Much like the seemingly impregnable United States, Bond operates with absolute patriotic loyalty and confidence in his own ability. His arrogance causes him to lose the poker game against Le Chiffre, suggesting that his confidence is also naïve. The CIA's Felix Leiter (Jeffrey Wright) funds Bond to continue the game and ultimately win. Despite being captured and tortured by Le Chiffre, Bond and Lynd have a happy union and are set to live happily ever after, seemingly lending credence to Bond as a conquering hero. But the film climaxes with a loss of Bond's innocence and blasé naïvety, a loss that crucially takes place in a collapsing building, the location echoing the destruction of the World Trade Center. Long shots of the ruin recall footage of Ground Zero, a visual echo also used in *The Dark Knight* (Pheasant-Kelly 2012: 123). Close-ups of Bond's face display his confusion and non-comprehension, expressing his traumatic loss of confidence.

This loss of confidence also manifests itself in the visual aesthetic of *Quantum of Solace*. While not featuring flashbacks like the Bourne series (Gaine: 160), *Quantum of Solace* uses rapid cuts, unsteady cinematography and a frenetic, frantic pace. Broadly speaking, this style is indicative of Hollywood cinema's 'intensified continuity' (Bordwell 2006: 120–1), but it also recalls amateur footage of 9/11 itself, when New Yorkers used camcorders to capture the collapse of the Twin Towers. Greengrass uses this aesthetic again in *United 93* (2006), as do other films that self-consciously echo the events of 9/11 like *Super 8* (2011), *Man of Steel* and *Cloverfield* (2008). The uncertainty created by these 'Unsteadycam chronicles' (Bordwell 2007) expresses a post-9/11 traumatised cultural consciousness. Craig's Bond exists within this consciousness: a wounded, troubled and traumatised figure in contrast to the flippant jollity of his predecessors. Bond's vulnerability expresses that of post-9/11 western democracies, especially post-7/7 Britain. Indeed, Bond is a paradoxical symbol of both British defiance and her irrelevance. As M states in her Tennyson quote, Bond, MI6 and Britain are 'not now that strength which in old days moved earth and heaven, that which we are, we are.' What they are is a nation and its agents within globalisation.

II. GLOBALISATION AND BRITAIN/BOND'S PLACE IN THE WORLD

McKay identifies a significant absence in the Craig-era Bond: 'Daniel Craig seems thus far to have steered clear of Islamist terrorists. But *Casino Royale* could not help but reflect a certain unease about the new threats the world faces, and about Britain's place in that world' (xi). This uncertainty is nothing new – when Ian Fleming published his novels in the 1950s, 'British influence in the real world was starting to wane rather sharply' (McKay: 25). This real-world waning did little to assuage Eon Productions, as across the series Bond and Britain are repeatedly shown to be of global importance: *You Only Live Twice* (1967) presents 'the profoundly erroneous impression that the only country that both America and Russia will listen to is good old Blighty' (McKay: 101); *Live and Let Die* (1973) proposes that 'the world ceaselessly trembles on the brink of crime-fuelled anarchy and that only the assured Establishment Englishness of Bond can hold such horrors at bay' (McKay: 160). More recently, however, Eon presented Bond's England as less stable and more peripheral than ever before, reflecting the contemporary geopolitical stage. This is especially apparent in *The World is Not Enough*, in which 'the diabolical villain's scheme [to disrupt the oil supply to Europe through former Soviet states] was rather ahead of its time' (McKay: 319). *Die Another Day*'s use of North Korea also demonstrates engagement in contemporary geopolitics. *Casino Royale*'s explicit reference to 9/11 is indicative of the rebooted franchise's engagement with contemporary events, but there is a crucial difference in the *stakes* of the film's drama, a difference that runs throughout Craig-era Bond. *Die Another Day, Goldeneye, Moonraker* and *Diamonds Are Forever* (1971) all feature threats to the free world in the form of satellites that the villains use to target major cities. In *Casino Royale*, Lynd warns Bond that if he loses the British 'government will have directly funded terrorism'. Rather than destroying superweapons, Bond must protect British interests and his country's reputation, something that is no longer guaranteed.

The diminished importance of MI6 and Britain did not begin with *Casino Royale*, though it becomes increasingly prevalent over the subsequent films. Since *Goldeneye*, Judi Dench's M is frequently at odds with the British government, a conflict continued by her successor Mallory (Ralph Fiennes) in *Spectre*.[1] The increased role of M complicates the place of Bond and MI6 within the British state apparatus. McKay identifies that in *Tomorrow Never Dies*, 'M . . . has to pit herself not merely against [villain] Carver, but also the mulish mess of the Admiralty and the politicians who listen to it' (McKay: 318). In *Die Another Day*, M must contend with 'brash Yankee bullies and emphatically does not have to follow the commands of her ghastly counterpart' (McKay: 339). McKay and Black note that the USA and the CIA have enjoyed a prominent if rather unconvincing role in Bond's history: various films take place in the US and Felix Leiter is one of Bond's (very few) actual friends; Bond even serves as best man at Leiter's wedding in *Licence to Kill*. Leiter is the only consistent CIA representative in Craig-era Bond, appearing briefly in *Casino Royale* and *Quantum of Solace* and referred to once in *Spectre*. In *Casino Royale*, Leiter provides Bond (a better poker player) with the funds to continue the game in exchange for the CIA apprehending Le Chiffre before MI6.

Somewhat paradoxically, the reduced role of the CIA both focuses attention on Bond and MI6 and has the effect of diminishing British importance. This allows for more inward focus, not least on Bond himself. His trauma following the death of Lynd in *Casino Royale* informs *Quantum of Solace*, while his damaged physical state is central in *Skyfall* (see Dodds: 118). Similarly, in Craig- era Bond, Britain comes under greater threat than ever before. London is threatened with an electromagnetic pulse attack in *Goldeneye* and a booby-trapped briefcase detonates inside MI6 in *The World is Not Enough*, but these are specific and isolated attacks rather than a sustained campaign. In the aftermath of 9/11 and 7/7, domestic security concerns make for dramatic material, as evidenced in such films as *The Sum of All Fears* (2002), Christopher Nolan's Dark Knight Trilogy (2005–12), Marvel's *The Avengers* and TV series such as 24 (2001–14), *Homeland* (2011–) and *Spooks* (2002–11). These concerns are especially apparent in *Skyfall*, where Silva hacks MI6 to cause a gas explosion, attacks a government inquiry in the heart of Whitehall, and uses the London Underground to stage an attack much like the bombers on 7/7.

This emphasis upon threats to Britain's national security can be seen as conservative reactions to global terrorism. The ubiquitous and malevolent 'Other' that Bond opposes may not be Al-Qaeda or Daesh, but 'terrorism' is repeatedly referred to: M describes Le Chiffre as 'private banker to the world's terrorists', and Bond's mission in *Skyfall* is (initially) to find a stolen list of NATO agents embedded in terrorist organisations. Strikingly, however, *Skyfall* takes the conservative conceit further by abandoning its geopolitical dimension in its final act to become ever more inward-looking as Silva wages a personal vendetta against M. In response, Bond withdraws with M to his family home Skyfall and the film's final act is a defence of this manor. The domestic defence that forms the climax of *Skyfall* attracted (unflattering) comparisons with *Die Hard* (1988) and *Home Alone* (1990) (see McG 2012; Stack 2012), with improvised, low-tech defences against the sophisticated weaponry of Silva's team. International terrorists, it seems, *are* interested in attacking British homes, making the home the last line of defence against the credible threats to Britain.

In *Skyfall* especially, Bond himself 'reflects and refracts an Anglo-American form of imperial nostalgia that harkens back to a time when individual spies and other social agents really could make a difference' (Hasian: 572). Resilience in the face of Silva's cyber attacks is manifested by MI6's relocation to Winston Churchill's underground bunkers, echoing British fortitude during the Blitz of the Second World War, while the recurring presence of M's china bulldog also echoes Churchill and resilient Britishness, despite the evident vulnerability of British institutions (Hasian: 580). Silva describes the failed British Empire as a 'ruin', but is thwarted by Bond's 'metaphysical strengths that he gets from his ties to ancient roots and antiquated imperial ideals' (Hasian: 572). These roots and ideals once again suggest conservative notions of traditional British fortitude, the only reliable bulwarks against global terrorism. Bond's physicality adds to this, his body representing British resilience despite (or because of) its vulnerability. Indeed, *Skyfall* ends with a reassertion of the British Establishment, Bond 'at the top of a British building, standing near a waving Union Jack as he surveys postcolonial London' (Hasian: 584). Subsequently, Bond meets with newly appointed M, Mallory, and they discuss getting 'back to work', in an office identical to that of M in films prior to *Goldeneye*, i.e. prior to Dench's M. Arguably, MI6's problems were caused by the previous M, and her death allows the restoration of (the old) order. *Skyfall*'s regressive gender politics also consign former field agent Eve Moneypenny (Naomie Harris) to the position of secretary:

> What *Skyfall* ends up suggesting is that in order for Britain to be safe in these disquieting times, it needs middle-aged to late middle-aged men (wearing well-cut suits) in charge of the office and the field. Young men and women, in this nostalgic division of labor, can either be part of the technological avant-garde (Q) or personal assistants (Miss Moneypenny). (Dodds: 130)

Through its presentation of Britain as under threat and in need of the traditional values of Bond and middle-aged masculinity in order to ensure national security, *Skyfall* appears to resolve the vulnerability of *Casino Royale* and *Quantum of Solace*. Bond is back on top, literally at the end of this fiftieth-anniversary appearance, *Skyfall* performing a meta-textual celebration with its end credits emphasising the longevity of this enduring character of conservatism.

There is a problem with this conservative reading, however. Bond, along with M and Kincade (Albert Finney), may kill Silva and his henchmen, but Bond's mission is ultimately a failure as M dies. Furthermore, the apparent British stronghold of Skyfall is destroyed, suggesting that the destruction of the British Establishment that Bond defends may be inevitable. The nostalgia for Britain's imperial past has little practical relevance as Britain's role on the global stage is consistently shown to be insignificant. This minor role also explains the films' focus on more domestic concerns, and the reduced presence of a previously prominent ally.

Britain, it appears, is of minor concern to America and the CIA. This is apparent in *Quantum of Solace*, in which Leiter and his station chief Gregg Beam (David Harbour) meet with villain Dominic Greene (Mathieu Amalric) and his associate Elvis (Anatole Taubman). Greene describes Bond as a 'pest' and requests that the CIA deal with him, in a scene that repeatedly sets Leiter against the official interests of the CIA. Beam's black suit visually aligns him with Greene and Elvis, whereas Leiter wears a tan suit that distinguishes him from the other men, and is presented as an opposing figure. Leiter says only one word, 'Sorry', when asked to identify Greene's 'pest'. Otherwise, Leiter observes the conversation between Greene and Beam, his narrowed eyes and ironic smile at one point expressing cynicism and even contempt. A two-shot of Leiter and Elvis presents them as adversaries, facing each other across a table, while a close-up of Beam features Elvis in the background, both men smirking in agreement. Three shots of Beam and Greene are taken over Leiter's shoulder, placing the viewer in Leiter's position so as to share his opposition to these two figures as they agree on Bond's removal. Beam's swift disregard of Bond as 'British secret service' indicates the lack of concern the CIA has for MI6, as does his earlier dismissal of M's official inquiry between supposedly partnered intelligence services.

The visual alignment of Beam with Greene and Elvis also indicates the erasure of divisions between state and private enterprise, Beam representing US interests in Bolivia and agreeing to Quantum's arrangement of a regime change in exchange for oil rights. Leiter provides an easily quashed protest:

> Leiter: You know who Greene is and you want to put us in bed with him.
> Beam: Yeah, you're right. We should just deal with nice people.

As Bond's friend and ally, the film supports Leiter's perspective and condemns Beam's political expediency. But the British are no better, as M is summoned to a meeting with the British Foreign Secretary (Tim Pigott-Smith), who orders M to halt Bond's mission so that Britain can also access Bolivian oil. The Foreign Secretary explicitly states: 'the world's running out of oil . . . Right and wrong doesn't come into it.'

Thus the British and American governments ignore the protests for justice and decency from Bond, M and Leiter, because of First World dependence on oil. *Quantum of Solace* develops *The World is Not Enough*'s conceit about access to oil, presenting the interpenetration of criminal capitalist operations and state machinery (a conceit that also informs *The Bourne Supremacy*). This interpenetration is made even more apparent when Quantum's actual plan is revealed to be the domestic provision of *water* to Bolivia rather foreign access to oil. Greene's description of Quantum's work practice indicates the flexibility and ubiquity of twenty-first-century capitalism:

> You should know something about me and the people I work with. We deal with the left and the right, dictators or liberators. If the current president had been more agreeable, I wouldn't be talking to you.

Bond's antagonist is no longer a remote megalomaniac bent on world domination, but western capitalism, which is ironic considering Bond's history as a figure of consumption (see Bell-Metereau 2004: 158–9). Despite the scarred faces and exotic accents of Le Chiffre, Silva, Blofeld and Greene, the enemy has become more banal and mundane. The human manifestations of evil may be Other, contrasted with the middle-class, middle-aged, heterosexual white male of the British Establishment that Bond epitomises, but what these men serve is far more insidious and pervasive. As Beam and the Foreign Secretary point out, if governments did not deal with 'villains' they would have no trading partners. Le Chiffre's betting on stock prices and Silva's cyber-manipulation of stocks and elections demonstrate the ubiquity of villainy, made mundane and everyday by globalisation. Furthermore, this enemy indicates the reduced role of states and increased influence of multinationals, as Quantum and SPECTRE are not crude purveyors of evil, but merchants of all manner of commodities. The meetings of SPECTRE's senior members in *Thunderball* (1965) and *Spectre* demonstrate this change.

In the earlier film, villain Largo (Adolfo Celi) uses a remote control to open two sets of concealed, mechanical doors, in order to enter a bunker-like chamber. Concrete and steel form the walls, floor and furniture, where men sit in low-slung chairs around a chrome catwalk. Blofeld (Anthony Dawson) looms above the rest on a raised platform, obscured by a steel shutter. The meeting includes discussion of assassination, narcotics distribution and ransoming NATO. Furthermore, one member is executed by an electrified chair controlled by Blofeld, which sinks out of site at the touch of a button for convenient body disposal.

The mise en scène, dialogue and technology all emphasise that this is a meeting of sophisticated criminality, linked into explicitly and exclusively criminal activities, including advanced methods of murder. The equivalent meeting in *Spectre* seems far less advanced, taking place in the Palazzo Cadenza, a dignified Roman building with no more sophisticated equipment than a microphone. The building appears old and established, a giant sandstone edifice to civilisation rather than a nefarious secret headquarters of modern steel and concrete. The members of SPECTRE sit around a vast wooden table, much as the board of any multinational might. There is an execution of a member, but this is done by hand, the enormous Mr Hinx (Dave Bautista) snapping the neck of his victim to demonstrate his capability as an assassin. Most tellingly, however, are the reports of the members about the activities of SPECTRE. These include lawful business such as the supply of drugs to treat AIDS in Africa, demonstrating the blurred lines between legitimate and criminal enterprise. *Spectre* portrays the apotheosis of globalisation's villainy, the film named for the omnipresent organisation. Mr White (Jesper Christensen) describes the mysterious figure at the head of the organisation, later revealed to be classic Bond villain Blofeld, as being 'everywhere,' and so the influence of SPECTRE proves to be, the octopus insignia apt as the organisation's many tentacles reach into all manner of business and government institutions. This is most apparent in the Joint Security Service.

In *Spectre*, the state itself in the form of the new Joint Security Service, headed by Max Denbigh/C (Andrew Scott), becomes an adversary for Bond. This is a development of the politicking that appeared in earlier films. Repeatedly, Bond's exploits necessitate explanations to ministers and senior civil servants, such as the Foreign Secretary in *Quantum of Solace* and whom M describes as the 'self-righteous, arse-covering prigs' of Westminster in *Casino Royale*. Threats to MI6 in *Skyfall* come both from Silva and from Westminster as a board of inquiry is convened to review M's competence. Furthermore, in *Spectre* it appears that the reassertion of MI6 at the end of *Skyfall* has failed, as British intelligence is merged into the JSS and the oo programme is discontinued. Bond's defiance of and rebellion against the JSS in *Spectre* again suggests reactionary individualism – a lone man doing what he knows to be right regardless of government regulations. Bond effectively becomes a rogue agent, something he has done previously, most obviously in *Licence to Kill*, but this time he actively works against the British Establishment. Except, crucially, he does not. Britain remains Bond's cause, as evidenced by the support he receives from Mallory,

Figure 6.1 From *Thunderball* (1965) (upper) to *Spectre* (2015) (lower) as SPECTRE evolves from a meeting of criminal masterminds to a consortium of global capitalism.

Moneypenny, Q and Tanner (Rory Kinnear), similarly genuine servants of Her Majesty who are also threatened by Denbigh and the JSS. SPECTRE is the true enemy, represented by the JSS and its *privately funded* National Security Centre, a high-tech surveillance hub beside the Thames. Denbigh boasts that Her Majesty's government would not fund such a facility and that private donors are responsible for its construction, highlighting the increased role of private enterprise in national and global security. This aspect of the film expresses post-9/11 fears about the privatisation of security services that appears in such films as *State of Play* (2009) and *Shooter* (2007) (for more on this, see Gaine 2016). Most tellingly, the film echoes a recent super-hero film that utilises aspects of the spy and conspiracy thrillers:

> [T]he edifice that houses Scott's Centre of National Security resembles nothing so much as Stark Tower. The influence of Marvel is felt elsewhere too: a plan to combine the world's intelligence capabilities into one all-seeing, all-knowing supersnoop bears striking similarities to *Captain America: The Winter Soldier*. (Smith 2015)

A more apt comparison for the NSC than Stark Tower would be the Triskelion, headquarters of SHIELD in *Captain America: The Winter Soldier* (2014), the control centre for a new security and intelligence initiative that will place the world's population under surveillance. Both films feature malevolent organisations with insignia of tentacled creatures to suggest their multi-stranded reach, but there is also a crucial difference. *The Winter Soldier* expresses fears about government surveillance and the potential for oppression by the state, which must be opposed by reactionary individualism in the form of exceptional individuals, especially the truest patriot of all, Captain America (Chris Evans). James Bond could be seen as a comparable British figure, but what he and his allies oppose is penetration of state machinery by private enterprise, making Bond a curiously individualistic figure that supports the state. SPECTRE, through the security initiative Nine Eyes, threatens absolute surveillance, described by Mallory as 'Orwell's worst nightmare'. What this stands for is globalised capitalism, making *Spectre*'s politics more complex than its seemingly conservative appearance. Whereas Captain America and his allies bring down the state apparatus of SHIELD entirely, Bond and his allies prevent the inception of Nine Eyes in favour of law and democracy. Denbigh describes Nine Eyes as a new 'superpower', which Mallory highlights as 'unelected', emphasising the film's valorisation of democracy. This valorisation becomes most apparent at *Spectre*'s conclusion.

As noted above, Bond is not alone at the finale of *Spectre*. He meets with Mallory, Tanner, Q and Moneypenny who actually perform the assault on Denbigh at the NSC. This sequence includes an interesting restaging of Bond's opening scene in *Casino Royale*, as Denbigh pulls a gun on Mallory only to realise that it is not loaded, much like the interchange between Bond and Dryden (Malcolm Sinclair) in the earlier film. The similar tactics of Bond and Mallory further underline the similarities between them – these are the men who should be protecting us (Dodds: 130). Meanwhile, Bond desperately searches for Dr Madeleine Swann (Léa Seydoux) before the old MI6 headquarters is demolished. His success in rescuing Swann, in contrast to the failed rescues of Lynd and M, is compounded by his final encounter with Blofeld. Injured and helpless, Blofeld goads Bond to shoot him and 'finish it'. But as Mallory mentions earlier to C, a licence to kill is also a licence *not* to kill, and Bond ejects the ammunition from his gun. This is one of very few moments in the Bond franchise when Bond opts not to kill, and as such is a remarkable demonstration of non-violence. Bond flippantly excuses himself from killing Blofeld because he is 'out of bullets' and 'has something better to do'. The former is only true because he disarmed himself, and the latter is Bond choosing a positive human bond (no pun intended) with another person, something he previously avoided, as *Spectre* is the first Craig-era film to conclude with a romantic union. Bond chooses his love for Swann over his hatred for Blofeld, and in doing so the film abnegates violence. A common argument about military and terrorist as well as anti-terrorist action is that violence begets violence. Bond's abstention from violence closes a cycle and suggests an alternative for Bond and perhaps for Britain as well.

Significantly, Blofeld's helicopter crashes onto London Bridge, right outside the Houses of Parliament. During the final confrontation between Bond and Blofeld, the shot/reverse-shot sequence captures a London Underground sign behind Bond and a red London Bus behind Blofeld. This brief sequence features iconic London images, including two that were attacked by terrorists on 7/7. Also, Blofeld's aircraft does not crash *into* the British Establishment but outside it; Parliament, and London as a whole, are resilient in the face of this terrorist attack. As Bond embraces Swann, Mallory takes over to, significantly, *arrest* Blofeld. This criminal mastermind who argues that information provides ultimate power is finally contained by the rule of law, the film underlining the significance of the law by the presence of Parliament. *Spectre*'s uses of this London landmark symbolises democracy and the law, taking the place of Bond's gun that he tosses away. The film is remarkable in this respect, opting for non-violence and the rule of law over a supposedly righteous execution. Earlier, the death of Denbigh is carefully constructed so as not to cast Mallory as executioner, as Denbigh is killed in a fall. Typically for Bond villains, Denbigh and Blofeld's downfalls are the result of their own hubris, but in neither case do they die because of Bond.

Bond's embrace of Swann at the end of *Spectre* seems less a concession to franchise convention than a moment of redemption. In *Quantum of Solace*, Camille (Olga Kurylenko) describes Bond's mind as his prison, but Swann, it seems, has freed him from the trauma of Lynd's and M's deaths. Bond is redeemed from his grief and trauma by his choice to love

Figure 6.2 James Bond (Daniel Craig) is forced to confront his history of violence in *Spectre*.

Swann, and the coda of *Spectre* implies that Bond has left MI6 to start a new life with her. Bond's redemption in *Spectre* provides closure, at least for these four films.

III. CONCLUSION

Craig-era Bond has delivered a complete arc of the character, from promotion to oo status through trauma and loss to eventual redemption and possible retirement. Along the way, the franchise has reconfigured Bond in relation to competition and post-9/11 concerns. Some elements of the franchise have remained, such as practical stunts and Bond's ingenuity, while sexual innuendos and elaborate gadgets have been largely replaced with embodied pain and vulnerability, while Bond has become increasingly politicised. No longer does oo7 simply prevent the deployment of superweapons by megalomaniacs – now he operates in a globalised world of instant communication and the interpenetration of private and public enterprise. This realpolitik is what makes Craig-era Bond distinct, as Bond and his allies must contend with political and economic concerns. The presence of such concerns indicates filmmakers' willingness to use such topics as dramatic material, demonstrating the engagement of popular entertainment with wider political discourse. Terrorism, oil and water supply, cyber-crime and surveillance culture are hot topics for discussion, and Craig-era Bond contributes to these debates, perhaps suggesting that old establishments like Skyfall should be destroyed, violence may not be the answer and there is something to be said for the rule of law. In an era where real-world governments vote to bomb a self-proclaimed Islamic state despite the risk to civilians, it seems sadly ironic that an abnegation of violence comes from the man described as Mr Kiss Kiss Bang Bang.

NOTE

1. To avoid confusion, I refer to Dench's character as M and Fiennes' as Mallory.

REFERENCES

Arnett, Robert P. (2009), 'Casino Royale and Franchise Remix: James Bond as Superhero', Film Criticism, Spring, 33:3, pp. 1–16.

Bell-Metereau, Rebecca (2004), 'The How-To Manual, the Prequel, and the Sequel in Post-9/11 Cinema', in W. W. Dixon (ed.), Film and Television after 9/11, Carbondale: Southern Illinois University Press, pp. 142–63.

Black, Jeremy (2001), The Politics of James Bond: From Fleming's Novels to the Big Screen, Westport, CT: Praeger.

Bordwell, David (2006), The Way Hollywood Tells It: Story and Style in Modern Movies, London: University of California Press.

— (2007), 'Unsteadicam chronicles', Observations on Film Art, 17 August 2007, last accessed 5 January 2016: http://www.davidbordwell.net/blog/2007/08/17/unsteadicam-chronicles/

Box Office Mojo, last accessed 5 January 2016, http://www.boxofficemojo.com

Cox, Katharine (2014), 'Becoming James Bond: Daniel Craig, rebirth, and refashioning masculinity in Casino Royale (2006)', Journal of Gender Studies, 23:2, pp. 184–96.

Dodds, Klaus (2014), 'Shaking and Stirring James Bond: Age, Gender, and Resilience in Skyfall (2012),' Journal of Popular Film and Television, 42:3, pp. 116–30.

Editors (2015), 'Try the Daniel Craig Workout', Men's Health, 24 March 2015, last accessed 5 January 2016, http://www.menshealth.com/fitness/workout-daniel-craig

Everett, Anna (2012), 'Movies and Spectacle in a Political Year', in T. Corrigan (ed.), American Cinema of the 2000s, Piscataway: Rutgers University Press, pp. 104–24.

Frayling, Christopher (2015), 'No, Mr Bond, I expect you to die', The New Statesman, 31 July–13 August 2015, pp. 74–7.

Funnell, Lisa (2011), '"I Know Where You Keep Your Gun": Daniel Craig as the Bond–Bond Girl Hybrid in Casino Royale', The Journal of Popular Culture, 44:3, pp. 455–72.

Gaine, Vincent M. (2016), 'It's Only a Film, Isn't It? Policy Paranoia Thrillers of the War on Terror', in A. A. Klein and R. B. Palmer (eds), Cycles, Sequels, Spin-offs, Remakes, and Reboots, Austin: University of Texas Press, pp. 148–65.

— (2011), 'Remember Everything, Absolve Nothing: Working Through Trauma in the Bourne Trilogy', *Cinema Journal*, 51:1, pp 159–63.

Hasian Jr, Marouf (2014), '*Skyfall*, James Bond's Resurrection, and 21st-Century Anglo-American Imperial Nostalgia', *Communication Quarterly*, 62:5, pp. 569–88.

Henderson, Paul (2011), 'The James Bond workout!', *GQ*, 2 August 2011, last accessed 5 January 2016: http://www.gq-magazine.co.uk/entertainment/articles/2011-08/02/gq-sport-james-bond-daniel-craig-workout-fitness-file

Internet Movie Database, The, last accessed 5 January 2016: http://www.imdb.com

Kaplan, E. Ann (2005), *Trauma Culture: The Politics of Terror and Loss in Media and Literature*, London: Rutgers University Press.

Markovitz, Jonathan (2004), 'Reel Terror Post 9/11', in W. W. Dixon (ed.), *Film and Television after 9/11*, Carbondale: Southern Illinois University Press, pp. 201–25.

McG, Ross (2012), '*Skyfall* isn't the best Bond ever, it's actually quite pants . . . Here's 007 reasons why', *Metro*, 7 November 2012, last accessed 5 January 2016: http://metro.co.uk/2012/11/07/skyfall-isnt-best-bond-ever-its-actually-quite-pants-heres-007-reasons-3816648/

McKay, Sinclair (2008), *The Man With the Golden Touch: How the BOND Films conquered the world*, London: Aurum Press.

McSweeney, Terence (2014), *The 'War on Terror' and American Film: 9/11 Frames Per Second*, Edinburgh: Edinburgh University Press.

Pheasant-Kelly, Fran (2011), 'Ghosts of Ground Zero: Fantasy Film Post-9/11', in P. Hammond (ed.), *Screens of Terror: Representations of war on terrorism in film and television since 9/11*, Bury St Edmunds: Arima, pp. 111–32.

Purse, Lisa (2011), *Contemporary Action Cinema*, Edinburgh: Edinburgh University Press.

Singh, Greg (2014), *Feeling Film: Affect and Authenticity in Popular Cinema*, London: Routledge.

Smith, Neil (2015), '*Spectre* Review', *Total Film*, 22 October 2015, last accessed 5 January 2016: http://www.gamesradar.com/spectre-review/

Stack, Tim (2012), 'Is *Skyfall* basically James Bond meets *Home Alone*?', *Entertainment Weekly*, 17 November 2012, last accessed 5 January 2016: http://www.ew.com/article/2012/11/17/skyfall-home-alone

Tennyson, Lord Alfred (1833), 'Ulysses', *Poems*.

Thomas, William (2004), '*The Bourne Supremacy* Review', *Empire*, August 2004, last accessed 5 January 2016: http://www.empireonline.com/movies/bourne-supremacy/review/

Total Film (2006), '*Casino Royale* review', *Total Film*, 19 November 2006, last accessed 5 January 2016: http://www.gamesradar.com/casino-royale-review/

Training the Body Politic: Networked Masculinity and the 'War on Terror' in Hollywood Film

Adam Knee

Released within a few months of one another, the train-themed Hollywood action thrillers *Unstoppable* (2010) and *Source Code* (2011) exhibit striking similarities at a range of levels, from surface features of narrative to deeper structures of gendered character function, theme and geopolitical perspective.[1] This essay takes the position that we can fruitfully read these twinned films in tandem as symptomatic of certain distinctive post-9/11 American concerns and, more specifically, a developing conceptualisation of modes of disciplined masculinity necessitated by the nation's 'War on Terror'. It will work from close readings of these two texts with a particular interest in the ways post-9/11 male heroism is figured as requiring some level of individual agency (in keeping with classical Hollywood convention) but also submission to a militarised logic of networked media surveillance and bodily incorporation. The analysis will then move on to an examination of a still more recent Hollywood action film, 2014's *RoboCop*, which will be read with reference to the 1987 film of the same name that it reboots, in order to demonstrate the persistence of the modes of masculinity identified in the two train-themed films.

In taking this tack, I am plainly concurring with such analysts of post-9/11 film as Prince (2009), Kellner (2010) and McSweeney (2014), who assert the soundness and utility of reading these works in relation to proximate historical events if done with caution and attention to the specific textual and historical evidence at hand; I also concur with these writers' assertions that filmic responses to 9/11 and its aftermath, even within Hollywood alone, show substantial variety in political bent and cinematic approach – although in the examples explored in this essay I would claim there is a remarkable and suggestive consistency in narrative and representational patterns, surface differences in style notwithstanding. I am furthermore interested here to connect the broader post-9/11 proclivities such analysts have identified with the loaded significations of the body itself in such productions, 'the way the body, individual and social, is employed to *make sense* of terror, conflict, and warfare', as has been highlighted in Rendell and Redmond's anthology *The War Body on Screen* (2008: 1); but in so doing, I will also be concerned to keep foregrounded the ways in which the 'war body' is a gendered body.

Unstoppable and *Source Code* trace out a distinctive perception of the active and necessary networks of power and how they are deployed in a new era of security consciousness and, moreover, what the repercussions of this new context are for individual autonomy. More specifically, both of these films are in some sense concerned with asserting the importance of the disciplined, media-controlled young male body to a post-9/11 American military-industrial complex. While on the one hand both of these Hollywood films allow some degree of (inoculating) critique of the power inequities of such a military-corporate system (acknowledging, as it were, ongoing debates about the cost of national defence in terms of individual civil liberties), on the other they also suggest that 'homeland security' needs to take precedence over such concerns. Indeed, in each film a key protagonist becomes a hero precisely in allowing his body and cognition to be subject to military-corporate discipline, largely by way of new media technologies, which in turn enables him to thwart a potentially apocalyptic explosion – an explosion in both films ironically threatened through the corporate network of the national rail system. One further paralleled, more global double-edged corporate network in both films is that of the new media technologies themselves, which the protagonists utilise in order to achieve their goals while at the same time being subject to the controls of their surveillance. These young men's goals of supporting homeland security moreover become narratively interwoven with efforts to negotiate certain axes of social difference – in terms of gender, race, age and class – in order to ensure a unified national front against security threats. That is, as these men are themselves subject to corporate-military training and discipline, so must they work to discipline the diverse limbs of the American body politic, by persuasion or force if need be, to support the same national ends.

I.

While at first glance *Unstoppable* appears primarily 'just' a runaway train thriller, a variation on the theme of director Tony Scott's previous film *The Taking of Pelham 1 2 3* (2009) (which also featured Denzel Washington), enough cues are offered to make it clear it is also positioning itself as a post-9/11 parable. Yes, the plot is primarily driven by a chemical cargo-laden train moving out of control in rural Pennsylvania and the efforts of some heroic employees to stop it in order to obviate the risk of a deadly explosion in a populated area. But with the train described (in a line also quoted in much of the film's publicity) as 'a missile the size of the Chrysler Building', with (potential) injury and death to the local residents described as 'collateral damage', and with multiple war veterans (including a twenty-two-year-old Marine, just back from Afghanistan) among those enlisted to head it off, it is clear that this can also be read as a battle for 'homeland security' transported right to the American heartland – all the more so given the track record of 20th Century Fox studio's parent company (News Corporation) in actively supporting the 'War on Terror' (see Broe 2004).

However, for the sake of Hollywood entertainment value, such a post-9/11 subtext is also somewhat de-emphasised – there is, after all, no explicit 'enemy' in this film but rather just a certain lack of vigilance and preparedness which has created the conditions to allow the train to become a danger. *Unstoppable* offers a seemingly self-conscious exercise in the techniques of classic masculinist blockbuster filmmaking, deeply enmeshed in a range of allegorised efforts towards phallic mastery, the central and most obvious being that of the machinations of not one but two machismo protagonists to rein in the runaway locomotive (the mother of all cinematic phalli) while also reining in the uncooperative women in their respective personal lives – with control over the 'unmanned' train simultaneously yielding control over the women for both protagonists. The narrative achievement of such mastery requires the male bonding (here trans-generational and trans-racial) typical of the action genre, but, in a highly technologised context, also requires access to surveillance data and communications technology, which are embodied in images of cell phone communications, television news reports (with their various aerial images and computer-generated diagrams), and a master system map at the train yard. This plot immediately resonates at an extra-textual level in a narrative of muscular directorial mastery by a Hollywood personality (Scott) over technically challenging dimensions of mise en scène (e.g. the coordination of numerous action sequences involving actual locomotives), as well as in a narrative of financial and administrative mastery by 20th Century Fox over a potentially runaway production (the company aptly referenced in the Fox News helicopters that continuously track and record the train in the later parts of the film, acquiring some of the data that the protagonists so need for their own mastery).[2]

At a more micro, dramatic level, Will Colson's (Chris Pine) difficulty with mastering the tools of surveillance and communication are indicated from the film's very opening, where he covertly keeps watch over his family as his estranged wife sends his children off to school (a gesture that prefigures the later need for surveillance information), then unsuccessfully attempts to reach his wife via cell phone. It is subsequently revealed that Will's state of affairs arises from an earlier instance of cellular ineptitude, wherein he mis-reads his wife's text-messaging a female relative as a covert communication to a supposed male lover; the upshot is that he hot-headedly loses control and confronts the man he suspects (in fact an officer of the law) with a gun (like the train, an old but nevertheless potentially lethal technology, rendered dangerous by inadequate regulation), resulting eventually in a protection order for his wife. Will's youthful lack of discipline and of technological prowess is suggested again as he starts his new railroad work assignment (with veteran engineer Frank Barnes, played by Denzel Washington) and slips up in allowing too many cars in their train (in part owing to his distraction by another technology, the cell phone once again); he must learn that, as another veteran rail system worker keeps repeating, 'It's all about precision'.[3] It is through his tutelage from the experienced engineer that this young conductor is eventually able to learn to properly acquire and coordinate data and communications to achieve control of the train – and in turn, by virtue of this, control over his estranged spouse.

That it is a gender-specific bodily struggle that underpins this technologised drama is suggested through opening images of Will's bare and muscularly toned body as he awakes before heading off to keep watch on his family. Subsequently, while technological skill is part of what is required to keep the errant train from shooting its deadly load into a populated area, the protagonists' efforts still remain a distinctly physical (and masculine) endeavour, requiring Will, for example, to repair the coupling of two train cars by hand (an effort which indeed yields a bodily injury) and also to jump from the train to a speeding pickup truck and back (the pick-up driver encouraging him with the words 'Do it, you pussy!' and thus aptly driving home the gender-specific dimensions of his efforts). If what is instrumental in averting disaster, then, is the fit and regulated young male body, what poses the greatest danger in contrast is the unfit and unregulated body, exemplified quite clearly in the character of Dewey (Ethan Suplee), the pudgy and unkempt fast-food eating engineer whose sloth, indifference to standard operating procedures, and lack of physical dexterity lead directly to loss of control over the train to begin with. Significantly, the other 'villain' of the piece, the middle-aged Vice President for Operations (Galvin, played by Kevin Dunn), also appears more heavy set, distinctly less fit than others, giving the impression of someone who has been long-removed from the more physical, hands-on work of actual train operations and focusing rather on the corporate bottom line, as evidenced in crisis decision making more concerned with financial losses than human ones.[4]

The role of Frank is somewhat exempted from this schema that values the fit, disciplined body, with Washington costumed and filmed in such a way that the characteristics of his physical build are not clearly discernible. While the same mid-fifties age as Galvin and presumably with similar years of experience, Frank remains in the rank-and-file as an engineer, and thus in effect embodies the hands-on physical know-how that Galvin appears to lack; Frank's superior knowledge becomes evident in particular as his predictions about what will happen to various corporate efforts to stop the train are borne out by the unfolding of events. Equally important is the fact that Frank is himself the chief agent of the disciplining of Will's body, his superior knowledge and instincts eventually eliciting the younger man's respect and obedience. And when physical action is required of Frank, as when he must head out to brake individual train cars by hand, his younger colleague having been injured, he is fully able to meet the challenge (the representation of Frank's running along the roof of the speeding train and jumping from car to car finessed largely through stunt work in extreme long shot) – though the coup de grâce will require the further assistance of the still- capable Will.

It might be tempting to read the relatively uneroticised figuration of widower Frank (in comparison with his beefcake white counterpart) as a residual form of Hollywood's erstwhile uneasiness with the eroticisation of African Americans, but in terms of the broader organisation of the text, this would appear to have more to do with the protagonists' age difference than their racial difference; Washington, after all, is a veteran mainstream star with numerous romantic lead roles under his belt. And the film does not hesitate to present Frank's two daughters – who are in Will's age bracket – in a form that is commensurately eroticised; indeed, a number of shots of the two young women at work as waitresses at a Hooters restaurant highlight the erotic display of their bodies and function in effect as the formal parallel of the eroticised shots of Will's body at the film's opening. Like Will, the film implies, these young daughters must learn discipline, having gone astray (perhaps owing to a lack of motherly guidance) and therefore exhibiting inadequate deference to their father (one won't speak to him because he is late to wish her happy birthday) and accepting a less than salubrious form of employment.

The eventual halting of the unmanned train coincides with a three-fold structural resolution across the film's three main axes of social and bodily difference – those of gender, age and race – suggesting, on an allegorical level, the necessity of building a consensus across American society in the face of post-9/11 threats to homeland security. The heroism displayed by Frank and Will, with both their lives put at risk, wins over (and yields masculine control over) the former's daughters (who at least temporarily leave the gawkers at Hooters to come join their father) and the latter's wife (who now returns to her husband's arms, presumably forgoing all other potential suitors). And Frank's wisdom and character has already won over the racial and generational other who shares the train with him, disciplining the young conductor and allowing the two men to function in effect as a single amalgamated protagonist – an entity which subsumes intra-national social tensions to stand in as the (male-dominated) American body politic.

Figure 7.1 In *Unstoppable* (2010), Frank Barnes (Denzel Washington) and Will Colson (Chris Pine) function as an amalgamated protagonist with the veteran engineer's training of the novice conductor.

This amalgamated male protagonist, interestingly, has a hybrid female counterpart, the control room supervisor Connie (Rosario Dawson), who, while already subject to the discipline of corporate regulation (working as boss in a train yard operations centre, not out on a train, and regularly given orders from higher management through various electronic means), is nevertheless also aware of and sympathetic to the actual conditions of hands-on train yard work (a fact which puts her at odds with her corporate superior Galvin and allows her to effectively support the trainmen in their efforts). Connie is positioned as a mediating and intermediate figure not only in terms of corporate hierarchy (as described), but also in terms of gender (a woman working alongside men in an overwhelmingly male organisation), age (she is neither as old as Frank nor as young as Will), and even race as well (she is portrayed by an actress whose star discourse is centrally one of racial mixing).[5] She is presented, moreover, as being astute, quick thinking and assertive, and she therefore functions well as the male protagonists' contact on the inside of the rail system's operations, playing her own crucial role in the film's gender-imbalanced endeavour of preserving homeland security. Ironically, however, these qualities of intelligence and independence also position her as a potential threat to the film's deeper trajectory of phallic mastery – she is, in the sexist language of one of her subordinates, a 'ballbuster'. The film's close, however, where Frank and Will are celebrated for having stopped the runaway train in time, somewhat allays these concerns in suggesting that Connie, like the other key female characters, has been brought into the orbit of the protagonists' masculine control, as she rushes up to them to say, 'I can't decide which one of you I'm going to kiss first.'

This plainly has all the elements of classical Hollywood closure, with dangers averted and romantic union effected. Yet achieving this requires submission to the logic of a corporate-military system which, elsewhere in the film, has been revealed as flawed, as built upon inequities of power and lacking proper leadership. That this framework remains largely intact is naturally not something emphasised at the film's feel-good close – though similar kinds of frameworks requiring loss of individual (male) agency are arguably rendered somewhat more visible in the two later Hollywood films to be discussed below, films which may have something more of an oppositional edge.

II.

Source Code's release so soon after *Unstoppable* in combination with such strong similarities in theme quite readily calls for some form of symptomatic reading of their shared properties. At a most fundamental level the second film is again structured around a young man's struggle to take control of a train that threatens explosive mass destruction – though this time the train is not functioning as a metaphorical stand-in for a bomb but rather contains one (planted by a terrorist), and protagonist Colter Stevens (Jake Gyllenhaal) needs to try to find the device and prevent its detonation (and find the bomber, who is planning more explosions) lest many lives be lost. (The fact that the plot features a public conveyance converted to a potential weapon of mass destruction as it hurtles towards a major US city (Chicago) provides ready 9/11 resonance as well.) The 'War on Terror' is rendered more literal here not only in that in this case the bomb has been planted by a 'home-grown terrorist' of some kind, but also in that Colter is a member of the US armed forces, a soldier closely following orders. The scenario bears comparison to that of Fox TV's terrorism-themed series 24 (2001–10), not only in that the protagonist has a strict time constraint on his mission (as the bomb is set on a timer) but also in that we see him on occasion act with brutality and violence towards others on the train (and also use racial profiling) in the hope of achieving his aims with all due speed (and the question of civil liberties and the ethics of brutality in the 'War on Terror' is thus broached, if only in passing).

A key difference from that scenario soon becomes clear to the spectator, however: the soldier is able (and compelled) to return to his efforts to find the detonating device, even after failing at this more than once (and experiencing the start of the bomb's explosion each time), owing to some form of (science-fictive) military program which allows his consciousness to inhabit another man's body but also to receive instructions from a military commander between attempts.[6] His effort to prevent the explosion, then, is also an effort to improve upon his earlier performance, both through developing greater self-awareness and self-control and through submitting to the instructions of his handler in the field; as she implores him, 'I need you to discipline yourself on this next pass.' And we do see Colter further discipline himself on each iteration, train himself to operate exactly as is required by the imperatives of the given mission – to position himself advantageously, to question the right people and cover the most useful ground, and so on until he succeeds in identifying the bomber and preventing the detonation.

The plot thus bears strong affinity to that of *Unstoppable* in that the young male protagonist must learn to take difficult instruction to discipline himself and improve his performance, in order that the American public may be protected. However, the loss of individual male autonomy, of the protagonist's control over his cognition and in particular over his body, while akin to that in the earlier film, is soon demonstrated to be of

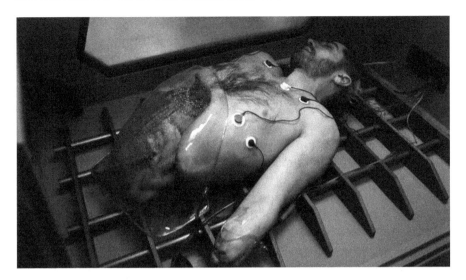

Figure 7.2 The horrific 'reveal' of Colter's (Jake Gyllenhaal) networked remains in *Source Code* (2011).

a far greater degree and kind, as Colter learns that his space-time travel abilities have been made possible in part because he had months previously given up his body (and indeed his physical mortality as usually conceived) in battle in Afghanistan, and that he now physically exists only as a partial torso hooked up to an experimental apparatus in a secret military facility. The horrifying images of the protagonist-as-torso, only presented towards the close of the film, naturally further extend the film's implicitly critical discourse about the ethics of the 'War on Terror', in this case as regards not those suspected of being terrorists, but as regards the disempowered citizens enlisted in the fight.

Another way this aligns with the earlier film's schema is that the subordination and disciplining of the male is facilitated by connections to media communications systems, and arises as a partial function of his being 'networked'. In the case of *Source Code*, that medium is a science-fictive one, a device which somehow allows the consciousness linked to what remains of Colter's torso to send messages to his handler, messages which he perceives as being in his own voice although (from what we gather) they appear to his handler as text messages. Colter's networking is thus cellular in both senses of the term – in that he is evidently sutured to the apparatus at a profound (cellular) level and in that he communicates with another networked 'cell' at a spatial (and, in the film's science-fictive framework, also temporal and dimensional) remove. And yet, while this military-built cellular network is the instrument for his disciplining and subordination, information and communication provided through networked cell phones is key to his successfully completing his railroad mission. And Colter also puts such networking to use, finally, to allow his own self-actualisation and peace at the close of the film: while on misson, against the wishes of his commanders, he uses a cell phone to communicate a (posthumous) message to his estranged father and thereby achieve a measure of resolution for both father and son, and he subsequently uses the military's communication network to facilitate his escape at the film's close (with the collusion of his immediate commander) into one of the alternative planes of reality that the apparatus appears to open up for him.

Still another continuity with *Unstoppable* is that achieving mission success involves developing an ability to negotiate with people from a cross-section of American identities so as to win them over, to have a diverse American public stay in line and function as a single unified body to support the ends of homeland security. The cross-section is here comprised of the men and women of varied ages, races and classes on the train where Colter carries out his mission, and things finally go smoothest for him not when he is struggling with the group through brutality, but coaxing them along with good humour; the film reaches a happy resolution when Colter, on a bet, convinces a Chicago comedian to try to make everyone in their train car laugh, which he does manage to do in a final moment of 'feel good' unity.

As in *Unstoppable*, the most significant 'others' the protagonist must negotiate with in order to develop some sway over them are the women he encounters on his mission. The force of the feminine is in the first instance a woman he finds himself sitting next to in the repeated train scenario and whose aid he enlists in a variety of ways – as he describes her out loud (while he is still apprehending the rules of the repetition game), 'you're the pretty girl, the distraction'. In point of fact, however, the 'distraction' (Christina Warren, played by Michelle Monaghan) proves an important one, as his growing affection for her over the course of the repetitions is part of what eventually motivates him to do whatever he can to prevent the train's explosion.

Still another woman Colter must negotiate with in order to achieve the desired control of his world is his commander in the field (Colleen Goodwin, played by Vera Farmiga), though she eventually proves (as the two soldiers grow more attached) not purely an agent of the military establishment which exploits him, but also a personal ally who works with and aids him, indeed in defiance of the orders of her own superior. In most of these characteristics Colleen is strikingly similar in narrative function to Connie from *Unstoppable* – a more senior employee of the system to which the protagonist is also beholden, whose job it is (in both films) to issue orders from a network control centre to the protagonist out in the field, but also one willing to turn against that system in the name of decency to aid the protagonist. That it is a thirty-something woman in both films who gives this needed push-back to the system, and who is seen in both films interacting with multiple higher levels of (older) male authority, plainly suggests a feminist critique of the transport/corporate/military network as (literally) an old-boy net-work that functions at the cost of exploiting the socially disempowered: the young, the female – and, in *Unstoppable* at any rate, the non-white, as represented in Connie's character and in Frank's as well.

The racial politics of *Source Code* are in fact a bit more obscure and difficult to read than those of *Unstoppable*. While the female com-mander who in her minor way rebels against the system is white (as are, for that matter, Colter and the home-grown terrorist), the organisa-tion man (indeed, the project's leader) she disobeys is an older African American man, Dr Rutledge (Jeffrey Wright). One could interpret this casting as suggesting the system has evolved so thoroughly as to encom-pass erstwhile insiders and outsiders alike, but the film also offers mul-tiple cues to read the figure as an outsider despite his seniority, such as the fact that he is evidently a non-military employee of the army, one who (it is implied) is struggling for influence and funding for his proj-ects within the system; indeed, the man's name might appear an allu-sion to the John Ford film *Sergeant Rutledge* (1960), which concerns a black American soldier at odds with and oppressed by the military system of which he is a part (being unjustly court-martialled for rape and murder). *Source Code*, then, seems to make the effort to reference institutional racism. And yet there is also a range of details given in the portrayal of Rutledge which in the aggregate plainly put him in a negative light – though their textual motivations are sometimes difficult to divine. There is most damningly his relative callousness in terms of his consideration of the ethics of his experimentation and its repercus-sions for Colter, in particular in contrast to the caring streak evinced by Colleen. This becomes linked, moreover, with repeated allusions to his preoccupation with reputational and funding successes within his organisation. The concern over reputation is moreover seemingly critically allegorised in a certain fussiness over personal appearance, a certain vanity, pointedly emphasised in unflattering shots of Rutledge attending to his coiffure. *Source Code* does leave a little space to read these details more sympathetically: as the historical outsider in a white-dominated organisation, naturally Rutledge needs to be canny in deal-ing with organisational politics and reputation in order to counter bias and to thrive. But he does not have the aura of heroism and integrity, for example, that adheres to Frank – whom he structurally echoes as a senior African American male with long experience and inside knowledge of the system/organisation who works with a younger white male protagonist.

Still another highly charged and suggestive detail in the figuration of Rutledge which, however, frustrates any attempt at definitive interpretation, is his representation as having physical difficulty negotiating the space of the military facility, owing to some form of disability which requires him to use a crutch. This might most sympathetically be taken to suggest the barriers and difficulties he faces within the military and/or more negatively be taken to prejudicially imply a lack of fitness or ability in his work (and, given the issues raised in the film, in his ethical decision making). Yet while the signifying thrust of this representational choice remains somewhat opaque, what it does at a deeper structural level is create a parallel with Colter as another male beholden to the military system and not in full control of all of his body; again, it is also difficult to know how to read that structural linkage, though for the purposes of this particular comparative analysis it is interesting that it creates a bi-racial protagonist-pair narratively positioned much like the earlier pair of Will and Frank.

The kind of thematic opaqueness in evidence here is hardly so surprising considering how common political incoherence has been found to be in Hollywood productions broaching controversial issues related to the 'War on Terror', as noted by a number of commentators; Holloway, for example, characterises Hollywood films touching on such issues as embodying the storytelling mode of 'allegory lite' – a form which may allude to controversy but is ultimately evasive and incoherent in dealing with it, due to fundamentally commercial motivations (2008: 82–4). *Source Code*, typically, while demonstrating an impulse to index topical issues, ends up prioritising generic entertainment aims. We focus primarily on the subjective experience of Colter as, even in his out-of-body state, he manages to keep Chicago safe from terrorists, circumvent the more cavalier orders of uncaring military bureaucrats, reconnect with his estranged father, and spark the romantic interest of two putatively strong and independent women (Christina and, it is clearly suggested, divorcée Colleen as well) owing to his deftness and masculine heroics; and through some science-fictive narrative sleight-of-hand, moreover, he finds a way to escape into one of the experiment's parallel universes in order to achieve able-bodied romantic closure with Christina at the film's conclusion.[7]

Ultimately, then, while *Source Code* manages to retain a classical commercial narrative structure, it highlights many elements which make its closure unstable and questionable, not least being a close immersed deeply in the realm of the fantastic. As in *Unstoppable*, the heroism (and US national security) requires a young man's self-discipline and sacrifice, but in the case of this film that sacrifice is presented as grotesque and extreme, and even open to manipulation for cynical/selfish purposes; Colter's out-of-body mission itself also appears to tend towards injustice in the casual brutality he is prepared to mete out in the name of security. Colter indeed directly questions the legality of the programme into which he has been inserted, but Rutledge affirms that 'in fact it was reviewed and sanctioned by a military court'. Given its context in this film, however, that assurance more readily lends itself to being read as evidence of the wrongness of military court judgements than as vindication of the programme; indeed, from a post-9/11 perspective, the line readily brings to mind the US government's defence of a range of seemingly inhumane policies on the basis of technicalities (such as the incarceration and abuse of prisoners at Guantanamo Bay).[8]

While it could be argued that *Source Code* and *Unstoppable* sit at modestly different points within the political spectrum, their overall thrusts – and, more centrally, their distinctive visions of the status of the young male in a time of perceived homeland vulnerability – are remarkably similar. The young male is able to help us (the US) achieve homeland security through his willingness to submit to physical and mental discipline and ultimately incorporation, becoming part of a military-corporate system which operates (and is enforced) by way of a range of transit, communications, information, surveillance and security networks, old (repurposed) and new, physical and virtual. The loss of individual agency, the rise of various kinds of brutality, are made to be seen as an acceptable price to pay for security for the larger public.

III.

Just how widespread these particular tendencies are would require further surveying of the action film corpus, but I would like to close with another example to suggest the continued salience of the patterns I have teased out, and their applicability to a more recent film that happens not to feature a young protagonist on a dangerous train. More specifically, I will offer a brief comparison of a pre-9/11 action film with its very recent post-9/11 remake to highlight the ways the more recent film would appear to have been moulded along the lines of some of the principles argued for *Unstoppable* and *Source Code*. The 1987 and 2014 iterations of *RoboCop* are especially germane to this discussion in that they are self-consciously about the construction of gender – that they quite literally detail what is involved in putting a (robo-)man together. The main narrative line of the 1987 film concerns a policeman (Alex Murphy, played by Peter Weller) in a dystopic near-future Detroit who, after suffering catastrophic injuries in a shooting, is resurrected in cyborgian form to serve a new corporatised police department operating at the behest of the monolithic Omni Consumer Products (OCP). RoboCop, as he is now called, ends up crossing paths again with the very gang responsible for his shooting, who also, it turns out, have connections to certain corrupt elements of OCP, and resolution comes both as the cyborg is able to expose and arrest or neutralise the various criminal and corporate villains and, simultaneously, to recall and reclaim some of his pre-trauma identity, taking on the name of 'Murphy' once more at the film's close.

The 1987 robotised version of Murphy projects a certain 'masculine' heroism and effectiveness not only, most cursorily, in his imposing size and deep voice, but also in his forceful (machine-driven) movements, his metallic imperviousness to penetration, and his protective and violently punitive instincts. But at the same time, this robotic man is characterised by a certain slowness and clumsiness and machine-like nature to his movements, by a lack of fluidity and grace. RoboCop's (stereotypically masculine) lack of nuance is, moreover, not just physical, but also emotional and communicative: he initially struggles to retrieve pre-trauma memories of his family and indeed of his own identity as 'Murphy', and he is cold and dismissive when his former female police partner (Anne Lewis, played by Nancy Allen) attempts to engage him on an emotional level.

Murphy is able to reclaim status as a hero in a fight against a corporate-corrupted quasi-military police state not only in developing anew control over his physical capabilities, but just as much so by retrieving his earlier subjectivity.[9] The film suggests that his mind has been taken over, his earlier memories 'wiped' in computer disc fashion, but as with his body, this colonisation has only been partial as it turns out, and his original identity can be substantially retrieved. In visual/technological terms, we see his mind represented as being like a VCR, able to record and play back what is perceived, and these perceptions are even shown to us in a scanned and pixilated video-style image. But Murphy's pre-technologised memories are still present, and these, in contrast, are presented with the same cinematic resolution as the remainder of the film's narrative information, suggesting again the persistence of the 'real' Murphy behind the corporate/state tampering, a native subjectivity that remains discrete from the newly recorded data and input corporate commands.

A comparison with the post-9/11 remake of *RoboCop* (2014), which retains the same basic plot concerns of the earlier film, reveals a striking shift in keeping with the tendencies in figurations of masculinity in the 'War on Terror' evidenced in *Unstoppable* and *Source Code*. For starters, while the earlier film does make some passing reference to global political frameworks, the later film centres such contexts – and more specifically a global 'War on Terror' – from its very opening, which comprises a broadcast of an American right-wing tabloid television show as it goes 'live' on location to 'Operation Freedom Tehran' to demonstrate the effectiveness of OmniCorp's new ED209 robots in surveillance of local residents. The 2014 Murphy (Joel Kinnaman) is also represented as being somewhat younger than the 1987 Murphy, indeed close to the age bracket of the young protagonists of *Unstoppable* and *Source Code* and thus in keeping with the new narrative pattern of young men being called upon to discipline their bodies for the sake of homeland security. (Pine and Gyllenhaal were each twenty-nine during the filming of their respective films, while Kinnaman was thirty-two years old for most of the shooting period of his *RoboCop*, and Weller, in contrast, was thirty-nine when the 1987 version was filmed.) Perhaps more substantively, in Murphy's transformed 2014 cyborgian form, the uncomfortable, clunky intersection between man and machine, the visible gaps in the joints between body and limbs which point to an unsettled amalgam of different categories in the earlier film (a soft body clad in metallic armour) are largely effaced. The new robotic Murphy (especially after some initial design modifications) is more streamlined and smooth, with less visible indication of any kind of interstitial nature: it is in visual terms a more fully unified entity, suggesting (following the patterns of *Unstoppable* and *Source Code*) an identity more fully subordinated to corporate/state needs, with traces of hybridity or amalgamation effaced.

This change from lumbering machine to deft, lightning-fast avatar is driven not only extra-textually, by the shifting capabilities of special effects technology (as they transition from analogue to digital), but also narratively, as it is revealed in a number of particularly disturbing shots that there is now less 'meat' left to the body of the subject who had been Murphy than in the earlier film, less biological material that needs to be integrated into the new product. The images echo strongly the similarly horrific 'reveal' shots of the maimed reanimated protagonist of *Source Code*, not only in their strong grotesquerie, but also in the shock they engender – in both instances in part because the protagonist-warrior had not previously been aware of the loss of his bodily integrity and wholeness, had misrecognised in the perceptions of a hybrid (and largely technological) entity the subjectivity of his former integral self.[10] This, again, is notably different from the scenario and the representation in the earlier *RoboCop*, where viewer and protagonist are kept far more cognisant of the awkward realities of human-machine amalgamation, down to the infantilising details of the cyborg's baby-food-like diet. In the later film, on the other hand, the merging is so seamless that the doctor who has worked on the cyborg has to explain this to him to dispel his disbelief: 'It's not a suit, Alex, it's you.' The line rhymes strikingly with one uttered furtively by Lewis in the earlier film to her partner-turned-robot – 'Murphy, it's you' – but while that earlier line intended to awaken the protagonist to the persistence of the human within him, in the later case it serves to apprise him of its loss.[11]

This shift between 1987 and 2014 to a masculinity more profoundly beholden to corporate-military forces, the apotheosis of the tendencies in the depiction of young masculinity directed towards the imperatives of the 'War on Terror' evident in *Unstoppable* and *Source Code*, occurs here not only in the literal remaking of the technologised body, as noted above, but also in the reconstruction of mind. While in the 1987 film, OCP's scientists have managed to (ineffectively) 'wipe' Murphy's memory at a surface level, in the 2014 film the protagonist's subjectivity has been much more profoundly compromised, as his mind has been surgically and pharmacologically altered in such a way that he is not aware of the military-industrial colonisation of his thought processes that has taken place. In particular, his cognitions have been modified so as to prevent too much experience of emotions, as this has been found to hamper the maximally efficient functioning of his cyborgian technology demanded by corporate logic. In this, the 2014 Murphy again bears strong affinity to *Source Code*'s Colter, who likewise (due to surgical and pharmacological manipulations) is no longer able to perceive the larger (military-regulated) context of his perceptual frame of reference – and again, in both films, the subtext is that such loss of young male autonomy and emotion is the necessary price of effective national defence.

The higher level of cognitive control that applies to 2014's cyborg as compared to 1987's arises not only from a differing surgical/pharmacological regime, but also from shifting technologies of monitoring and networking. The human/machine/computer entity that is 1987's RoboCop interfaces with, but to a large extent remains autonomous from, the various literal and figurative networks that he connects to and in some cases struggles with: OCP's computer system, the military-police-industrial complex, the political system. His 'owners' are only able to monitor him through a few clunky devices, such as the computer mainframe he is hooked up to in his resting hours (scientists need to look at paper-based printouts of his brain activity) and some portable proto-GPS location monitors. And, correspondingly, corporate directives, both acknowledged and covert, need to have been programmed into him in advance, or when he is 'plugged in' to the system at police headquarters. In contrast, 2014's RoboCop is much more fully networked, monitored and controllable in real time, though like his 1987 predecessor (and, for that matter, 2011's Colter) is finally able to act heroically by autonomously countering some of that control.

The 2014 RoboCop's move to a more fully networked consciousness is emblematised in images of his own point of view when in policing mode. These images comprise a main view of what is being monitored and an inset panel of dozens of security camera views and streaming data from a global surveillance network and a range of databanks, set up to allow the apprehension of correspondences and the automated deduction of guilt. This is in strong contrast to the 1987 counterpart's view of visual evidence: a single-screen time-shifted video-style playback. (The 1987 film does have some scenes of scanning of databanks, but this is shown on the monitor of a mainframe computer, not in RoboCop's mind's eye.) The revised imagery again links the 2014 cyborg to Colter as policing agents whose consciousnesses are underpinned by, indeed partially constituted by, global corporate-military data networks, and dependent upon those networks to determine appropriate military or policing actions.

Another significant realm of change for the later *RoboCop*, a realm in which it ends up less like the 1987 film and more like the 2010–11 films discussed here, is that of gender dynamics. Again, a case could be made that in some ways the 1987 film is, by the standards of its genre(s), at the least self-aware, if not in fact progressive, in terms of its gender politics. The partnership dynamic of the pre-robotic Murphy and his female working partner Officer Lewis (albeit short-lived due to Murphy's narrative misfortunes) shows a refreshing ease, assumed equality, and mutual communication and respect. It is presumably owing to the closeness of the pair that it is Lewis who is later able to detect that her newly introduced robotic colleague is really her erstwhile partner transformed and who helps him redevelop his targeting skills and his emotional memories. It could be pointed out that the film avoids the complications of heterosexual romance between Murphy and Lewis by having Murphy be a devoted father and husband (which

Lewis clearly admires); and although Murphy's only briefly seen wife has left him in the second part of the film (assuming him to be dead), RoboCop now appears largely beyond any human interest in a new love relationship.

In the 2014 film, on the other hand, Murphy no longer has a female working partner and his wife Clara (Abbie Cornish) re-emerges as a very significant and problematic character throughout the film, one who now has strong affinities in narrative function to the female protagonists of *Unstoppable* and *Source Code* in the sense of at once being an ally and working (either unwittingly or out of necessity) for the 'enemy'. Even before Murphy's mishap, Clara is figured as unhappy, a source of difficulty, seemingly scowling about her husband's working hours and about his taking time to bond with his son. After Murphy is incapacitated, it is Clara who gives the go-ahead for the RoboCop transformation (having been swayed by others who have their own best interests in mind), and when Alex sees and is revolted by what transformation he has undergone, it is out of concern for Clara that he agrees to try to manage with his new form; worse still, when Clara later goes to the media to complain about OmniCorp not providing her access to her husband, this motivates the corporation to try to assassinate him to simplify their problems (these efforts at killing him being what leads to the film's 'third act'). So unlike in the earlier version of *RoboCop* but very much as in the 2010–11 films, women, even when designated as allies, are nevertheless at a deeper level positioned as a problem that needs to be brought under control through the heroism of the male protagonist. Indeed, the attempted romantic close of the 2014 film is so problematic that the film in effect hides it from view. After Murphy has dispatched the villains who run OmniCorp, his handlers (now evidently working for a reformed police force separated from Omni's influence) have repaired his armour and arranged a visit from his wife and son. We see the woman and boy tentatively walking towards the cyborgian father as two steel lab doors slide shut to block the (obscene) reunion from our view before cutting to a final tabloid television show excerpt. It is almost as though the filmmakers are aware that it would too thoroughly try belief to show the physically and chemically altered killer interact tenderly with his family, or to image the robot-man in a physical embrace with his wife.[12]

In her overview of action films after 9/11, Lisa Purse notes a growing preoccupation with the problematic nature of American heroism and also, in relation to this, the rise of certain action films that 'locate their heroes in explicitly impossible or futile situations where bravery and patriotic sacrifice are the only options' (2011: 153). Such a description does indeed resonate with the post-9/11 films that have been analysed here, films that on the one hand would appear to offer a traditional Hollywood view of a powerful male protagonist making change in the world – but at the same time, and just as clearly, that demonstrate how in a post-9/11 environment such masculine mastery itself requires new modes of profound self-disciplining and a certain loss of autonomy in terms of both mind and body, the forms of which are dictated through various networks of military-corporate control. In all three films, a young man's body and mind must be brought under control, the self denied, in order to allow defence of the public in the 'War on Terror'. Acknowledgement is made of sacrifice and of loss of individual liberty, but these are largely seen as necessary and inevitable. At a subterranean level, threats are also seen as coming from the non-white and non-male, who are shown as potential allies in the 'War on Terror', but also as potential problems, who must be monitored and kept in place. Women in particular are figured as problematic in their potential to lure young men away from the needs of defence, to put the body to uses that are personal rather than strategic, but in the narratives presented here the hero-protagonists are already so caught up in networks beyond their apprehension that such risks have been negated.

NOTES

1. Internet Movie Database is the source for release dates, credits and cast member birth dates referenced in this essay. The website lists a 12 November 2010 US release date for *Unstoppable*, a 1 April 2011 date for *Source Code*.
2. Efforts by the studio to rein in the costs of production even before it was underway were widely reported in the trade press (see, for example, Zeitchik 2009).
3. The first time railroad old-timer Ned (Lew Temple) utters this line, the film's thematic link between railroad operations and the 'War on Terror' is made manifest: 'I don't care if you're talking about a spot weld on a class three rip track or ground operations in Afghanistan, it's all about precision.'
4. While length considerations prohibit a full discussion of issues of class in the film, as this description might suggest, class is another axis of social difference that comes into play here. The majority of characters in the film might be described as working or working-to-middle class, and even Galvin, despite his powerful position in the corporate hierarchy, retains very strong working- class associations, owing to both his train yard career origins and his style of dress and manner of speech. He ends up in stark contrast to the 'real' ruling class, embodied in the corporate leader from whom he is briefly shown taking orders (via cell phone) in one scene – a slender, grey-haired gentleman whose golf game continues despite the threat of a locomotive disaster.

5. For commentary on Dawson's mixed-race discourse, see Beltrán (2009: 154–71). Dawson's star image is also one of open bodily eroticism, perhaps best exemplified in her appearance wearing only bullets on the cover of an issue of *Rolling Stone* (19 April 2007). This association is completely effaced in *Unstoppable*, however, with her costuming largely hiding her bodily contours and her no-nonsense character focused entirely on the concerns of the job at hand. This is in keeping with her being positioned as in a separate (intermediate) generational category than that of Frank's daughters and of Will; hers is not an exposed, eroticised body requiring discipline, but one that has already been appropriately trained to support the smooth operations of the American (rail) system.

6. As Mark Fisher has commented, this nightmarish repetition scenario makes the film 'something like an existential version of 24' (2012).

7. Indeed, so fantastic and uplifting is the conclusion that we might be prompted to read it as a wish fulfilment, an attempt to overcome trauma by constructing a fantasy, much as McSweeney (2014: 28–9) reads the narrator's fantastic reimagining of his traumatic voyage in *Life of Pi* (2001) as akin to America's effort to 'construct a fantasy after 9/11'. This is all the more so as the repetition game which constitutes the bulk of the narrative evokes the kind of 'repetition compulsion' known to afflict those suffering the after-effects of trauma (see McSweeney 2014: 16–30; Randell and Redmond 2008: 6–7).

8. As McSweeney concordantly asserts, the film expresses 'anxieties about the effects of the USA Patriot Act and the expanding powers of executive authority' (2014: 15).

9. This reading of RoboCop's emotional regeneration is fully concordant with Susan Jeffords', where she positions the figure as emblematic of certain trends in 1980s Hollywood masculinity: 'It is only when Robocop rediscovers his identity – that he is/was Alex Murphy, that he is/was human – that he moves from being a mere hard body to being a hero. And that discovery hinges not on file information that his computerized brain can absorb but emotions' (1994: 112).

10. In his review of *Robocop*'s DVD release, Nick Jones also notes an echo of *Source Code* in these images, arguing that the films share a certain 'ambivalence over the integration of fleshly bodies and computerised consciousnesses' (2015: 421).

11. Clara does however revisit this line one more time later in the 2014 film, when she tells her husband, 'Alex, listen to me, I know you're in there.'

12. This closing gesture of a (highly problematic) return to the nuclear family – a gesture not even hinted at in the 1987 film – would seem to jibe with Bell-Metereau's observation that the events of 9/11 spurred a cinematic regression towards earlier traditional gender roles (2004: 142–3).

REFERENCES

Bell-Metereau, Rebecca (2004), 'The How-to Manual, the Prequel, and the Sequel in Post-9/11 Cinema', in Wheeler Winston Dixon (ed.), *Film and Television after 9/11*, Carbondale: Southern Illinois University Press, pp. 142–62.

Beltrán, Mary C. (2009), *Latina/o Stars in US Eyes: The Making and Meanings of Film and TV Stardom*, Urbana: University of Illinois Press.

Broe, Dennis (2004), 'Fox and Its Friends: Global Commodification and the New Cold War', *Cinema Journal*, 43:4, pp. 97–102.

Fisher, Mark (2012), '"Source Code": Present-Tense Trauma', *Film Quarterly*, August 2012, last accessed 14 September 2012: www.filmquarterly.org/2012/08/source-code-present-tense-trauma/

Holloway, David (2008), *9/11 and the War on Terror*, Edinburgh: Edinburgh University Press.

Jeffords, Susan (1994), *Hard Bodies: Hollywood Masculinity in the Reagan Era*, New Brunswick, NJ: Rutgers University Press.

Jones, Nick (2015), 'RoboCop', *Science Fiction Film and Television*, 8:3 (2015), pp. 418–22.

Kellner, Douglas (2010), *Cinema Wars: Hollywood Film and Politics in the Bush-Cheney Era*, Chichester: Wiley-Blackwell.

McSweeney, Terence (2014), *The 'War on Terror' and American Film: 9/11 Frames Per Second*, Edinburgh: Edinburgh University Press.

Prince, Stephen (2009), *Firestorm: American Film in the Age of Terrorism*, New York: Columbia University Press.

Purse, Lisa (2011), *Contemporary Action Cinema*, Edinburgh: Edinburgh University Press.

Randell, Karen, and Sean Redmond (eds) (2008), *The War Body on Screen*, New York: Continuum.

Zeitchik, Steven, and AP (2009), '"Unstoppable" Hits Budget Snags', *The Hollywood Reporter*, 29 June 2009, last accessed 14 February 2016: www.hollywoodreporter.com/news/unstoppable-hits-budget-snags-85962

'Gettin' Dirty': Tarantino's Vengeful Justice, the Marked Viewer and Post-9/11 America

Andrew Schopp

In Quentin Tarantino's *The Hateful Eight* (2015), a criminal masquerading as the local hangman reflects upon the vexed nature of American justice. Oswaldo Mobray (Tim Roth) first explains how 'civilised society' defines justice: the accused is tried by a jury and, if found guilty, a 'dispassionate' official carries out the sentence. Mobray then presents the idea of 'frontier justice', when people take the law into their own hands, playing judge, jury and executioner. He explains that 'the good part about frontier justice is it's very thirst quenching. The bad part is it's apt to be wrong as right.' Mobray's comments prove ironic for the film in question since several characters manipulate 'civilised' justice in order to carry out the 'frontier' kind. However, they also speak to Tarantino's post-9/11 body of work, films that offer the satisfactions of 'frontier justice' by depicting the film's oppressors brought to a violent ending commensurate with their crimes. And yet, while his revenge fantasies do appease our desire to see the bad guys 'get theirs', they also ask viewers to recognise 'the impossibility of a "just" equilibrium' (Schlipphacke 2014: 114), especially given a filmic formula that achieves 'its ends when it reveals its own failure, its inability to produce equilibrium in an unjust world' (123). By cultivating and then compromising the desire for vengeful justice, Tarantino's films invite audiences to interrogate the ways that moral definitions and ideas of justice shift, mutate, evolve, but also fail in a post-modern, now a post-9/11, culture. His most politically charged films – *Inglourious Basterds*

(2009), *Django Unchained* (2012) and *The Hateful Eight* – must be understood as both products of, and inquiries into, a post-9/11 America in which the desire to see those who deserve it 'get theirs' has undergirded everything from cultural fictions and media representations to debates about 'appropriate' interrogation methods and domestic/foreign policy.

In what follows I deconstruct Tarantino's 'moral vision' vis-à-vis justice, arguing that while his works are often disturbingly humorous, their post-modern play with morality is quite serious. In fact, when understood as exercises in politically savvy post-modern art, Tarantino's investigations of American morality remind us that we likely need such pleasurable filmic exaggerations, at least if we wish to experience a critical catharsis, the kind that does not merely satisfy the desire for a 'just' ending, but that also calls that desire into question.[1] His post-9/11 films invite a playful *and* critical interaction that 'marks' the viewer in important ways, implicating her/him in the very violence that cultivated the desire for justice in the first place.

These films also remind us that our need for such a vexed critical engagement has become more palpable after 9/11. Slavoj Žižek argues that America's 'passion for the Real' has long framed our vision of ourselves; as such, the 9/11 attacks did not signify 'the intrusion of the Real which shattered our illusory Sphere, . . . it is not that reality entered our image: the image entered and shattered our reality (i.e., the symbolic coordinates which determine what we experience as reality)' (2002: 16). For Žižek, the images that contributed to such shattering included films that fantasised the attacks long before they ever occurred (15–17). In order to avoid just 'fantasising' our post-9/11 reality, we need to determine whether, and which of, our culture's subsequent films invite us to wrestle with both the fraught and violent culture that came before 9/11 and the one we are forging in response. We also need to assess how audiences respond to any such invitation.

Susan Rubin Suleiman contends that for many post-modern theorists, 'political meanings reside in the works, not in their readings' (1991: 324), and she encourages displacing 'the political effect from the work to its reading', because doing so moves 'the debate from the question of what postmodernism "is" . . . [to] what it does – in a particular place, for a particular public, . . . at a particular time' (324). Thus, as scholars we should not ignore the text and its potential politics, but analyse both within a consideration of how readers/spectators function critically. In order to facilitate such a practice, we can adapt Judith Butler's idea of a 'national subject' and delineate a post-9/11 collective subject that 'has been instated at the national level' (via political discourse, media and cultural narratives), 'a violent and self-centered subject' that 'seeks to reconstitute its imagined wholeness, but only at the price of denying its own vulnerability' (Butler 2004: 41). This compulsion to reconstitute wholeness is crucial, since it defines this subject as believing that it is lacking and incomplete. I would further posit that this post-9/11 subject can be characterised as ontologically and epistemologically lost. It has not merely had a 'reality' shattered, as Žižek might put it; instead, it believes it has lost any definitive way of understanding the 'reality' it currently inhabits, let alone of knowing how to proceed within it. With their promise of justice at any cost, Tarantino's recent films would be appealing for such a lost, incomplete subject, and yet, as we will see, these films hardly provide the wholeness this subject desires.

Suleiman's exhortation that we consider what post-modern works do for a given audience, in a given place and time also proves relevant for Tarantino's films since they ask the viewer to engage with the present regardless of the time frame within which the text's action takes place. While it is true that Tarantino does not situate his post-9/11 films in the era in which they were produced and released, Jeffrey Melnick has claimed that the most significant works that interrogate the attacks and their cultural impact do not explicitly depict the event at all (Melnick 2009). We can extend that idea and suggest that contemporary films that temporally, geographically or generically displace the action and characters from the present might afford the best opportunities for exploring our current culture. In an interview about *The Hateful Eight*, Tarantino explains that he values the Western genre precisely because 'there's no . . . film genre that better reflects the values and the problems of a given decade than the Westerns made during that specific decade' (Tarantino 2015: 32). Genre, then, becomes a means of placing the present world into a different frame that can foster social/political critique. As my argument illustrates, when his already genre-bound films further displace the action temporally and/or geographically (situating it, say, in antebellum or post-bellum America, or in Nazi-occupied France), they ask the audience to question the moral and ethical complexities inherent in our present culture, and they compel audiences to consider the extent to which the horrors of America's past speak to, reinforce and undergird America's post-9/11 present.

II.

Quentin Tarantino's films situate characters within groups/institutions that are morally suspect (e.g. drug dealers, hit men, assassin squads, Nazi Germany, American slavery); as a result, his films interrogate the parameters within which we frame moral codes. We can trace such moral inquiry back to *Pulp Fiction* (1994) where mainstream prohibitions against crime, murder and drug use/trafficking hold no sway but hit men pause to debate the morality of massaging your boss's wife's feet, of keying a car (an act that warrants immediate execution), or of bringing an accidentally murdered victim to your friend's house right before his wife arrives home. Moral codes dominate this filmic world – they are simply not the moral codes that mainstream America privileges. *Jackie Brown* (1997) furthers Tarantino's exploration of malleable morality. Forced to negotiate a culture in which 'the law does not provide justice for black people' (Speck 2014: 8), Jackie (Pam Grier) knows that her survival entails moral compromise. As she explains to bail bondsman Max Cherry (Robert Forster), after he accuses her of rationalising in order to carry out her plan to steal Ordell Robbie's (Samuel L. Jackson) illegally acquired money, 'that's what you do to go through with the shit you start, you rationalize'. The fact that Cherry, arguably working on the side of the law, aids and abets Jackie's 'crime' only underscores the fluid morality of this filmic world.

Robert von Dassanowsky explains that while Tarantino might borrow 'the simplistic binary of good and evil . . . from B-movies, exploitation films and Hollywood propaganda film' (Dassanowsky 2014: 18), he eventually obliterates that binary (27). The moral stakes of such obliteration have become increasingly significant as his films have taken on Nazism in *Inglourious Basterds,* American slavery in *Django Unchained*, and post-bellum American race relations in *The Hateful Eight*. These films remind audiences that we might all be capable of atrocity, and they therefore undermine the reductive, binary morality so prevalent in the filmic history upon which his films draw and equally prevalent in the years following 9/11, when politicians and cultural leaders asked that Americans embrace a host of oversimplified binaries like 'friend/enemy' and 'good/evil'. Tarantino's films undermine such naïve binaries because they are almost textbook examples of post-modern theory in practice, a fact that becomes evident if we examine the way his films deploy specific post-modern techniques such as those theorised by Linda Hutcheon: first, a realigning of cultural centres and margins in order to exploit the ex-centric; second, a use of historiographic meta-cinema that reminds us that history, cinema and fiction have important ideological interconnections; and finally, an evoking of post-modern complicity and critique, manifest especially in depictions of violence that implicate the viewer.

Because Tarantino's films tend to focus on the world of the criminal, the ex-centric might initially appear to mean just moving marginalised figures into the centre. Most of his film plots do involve characters who have been culturally marginalised (women, Second World War Jews, American slaves) or who inhabit society's margins (criminals, assassin squads, bounty hunters). In fact, his films present an overlapping progression of the marginalised. While *Reservoir Dogs* (1992) through the *Kill Bill* films (2003, 2004) frame their action within a criminal world, the films from *Jackie Brown* through *Death Proof* (2007) place women, especially victimised women, into the narrative centre. *Inglourious Basterds* (2009) and *Django Unchained* manipulate centre and margin vis-à-vis historically determined victims/oppressors (Jews/Nazis and slaves/slave owners), and although *The Hateful Eight* would seem to place audiences once again in the midst of a criminal world, the film makes the line between centre and margin almost impossible to identify: a former 'rebel renegade' is the new sheriff, a black ex-cavalry officer who was once a Confederate prisoner is now a bounty hunter, and the purported local hangman turns out to be both British and part of a criminal gang.

Just as Tarantino's films draw upon traditional moral binaries in order to explode them, their use of the ex-centric never simply reverses focus or political poles. When the post-modern text plays with centre and margin, the centre is not destroyed or replaced, but critically examined through the lens of the marginal: 'postmodernism does not move the marginal to the center. It does not invert the valuing of centers into that of peripheries and borders, as much as *use* that paradoxical doubled positioning to critique the inside from both the outside and the inside' (Hutcheon 1988: 69). As a result, 'the center becomes a fiction – necessary, desired, but a fiction nonetheless' (58). Cultural centres do not become imaginary, but their inherent centrality gets revealed as a construction. More important, however, is 'the ex-centric, the off-center: ineluctably identified with the center it desires but is denied. This is the paradox of the postmodern and its images are often as deviant as this language of decentering might suggest' (60–1). Given their embrace of various 'deviant' spaces, Tarantino's films clearly exploit the ex-centric and create the 'paradoxical doubled position' that enables critique 'from both the outside and the inside'.

Pulp Fiction's emphasis on the morality of the foot massage, for example, would not be as meaningful were it not examined within such a paradoxical space, where our culture's central and normative moral prohibitions become evident precisely in their absence. Jackie Brown's moral rationalising would not carry the same significance were it not framed within a context defined by the moral norms her planned actions both violate and exploit. Similarly, while *Django Unchained* moves the marginalised slave into the narrative centre, the cultural centres that have created that marginalised subject position (i.e. capitalism and the legal institution of slavery) are interrogated from beginning to end, especially given the film's emphasis on slavery's economic foundations and on the laws that undergird and protect it (see Kaster 2014). Consistently, Tarantino's films use the ex-centric to foreground that the centre and its normative morals are culturally sanctioned constructs, thereby destabilising that centre/morality for the spectator.

However, Tarantino's post-9/11 works manipulate the ex-centric in significantly different ways than his pre-9/11 films, both because they make the desire for vengeful justice more dominant and because they begin to situate the action outside an exclusively criminal world. Revenge plays a minor role in *Pulp Fiction* and *Jackie Brown*, but in his post-9/11 works, especially the *Kill Bill* films and *Inglourious Basterds*, revenge drives the action and/or serves as the primary means by which his characters find their justice. *Django Unchained* and *The Hateful Eight* might seem like exceptions, since neither has a plot driven primarily by a character seeking revenge. However, in *The Hateful Eight*, Chris Mannix (Walter Goggins) speculates that when Major Marquis Warren (Samuel L. Jackson) burned down the Confederate prison in which he was held, killing both white southerners and white northerners, he was 'kill crazy' and motivated by revenge, and the Domergue Gang's hyper-violent effort to rescue Daisy (Jennifer Jason Leigh) illustrates Mobray's definition of 'frontier justice' quite well. Similarly, in *Django Unchained*, Django's (Jamie Foxx) final attack on Candieland can be considered the fruition of a revenge fantasy – the ex-slave finding his justice by destroying the plantation and all that it signifies. At the same time, those films that take place outside a criminal setting (*Inglourious Basterds* and *Django Unchained*) don't seem that different from those that take place inside one (the *Kill Bill* films, *Death Proof, The Hateful Eight*). The latter film makes the point clear: by manipulating the conventions of the 'drawing room mystery' (the film was reportedly inspired by Agatha Christie's *Ten Little Indians* [Mitchell 2015, v]), it complicates any easy way of knowing which characters are, and which are not, criminal. As a result, the film's primary location, Minnie's Haberdashery, becomes a microcosm of the outside world both past and present, a world in which the line between criminal and law-abiding citizen remains fluid.

Of course, centre and margin, and the power dynamics involved, exist everywhere, so moving between 'inside' and 'outside' comes to mean very little. And yet, while Tarantino's pre-9/11 films might convey this general idea, because his post-9/11 films combine the revenge fantasy with the idea that criminality exists everywhere, including our historical past, they could easily reflect a post-9/11 anxiety about how to conduct, say, a 'just' war on terror without crossing the boundary that separates 'non-criminal' from 'criminal'. More importantly, since they also give a voice to those who have traditionally been silenced, his films place the post-9/11 subject into that 'paradoxical doubled position', forcing the viewer to recognise several things: that revenge seldom actually proffers justice, that pursuing revenge usually results in an egalitarian amount of suffering, that whether one exists inside or outside the privileged half of a moral binary, one can desire vengeful justice and can use 'criminal' means to achieve 'just' ends, and that the cultural norms that rely upon maintaining such binaries might be strong but, since they are constructs, they remain vulnerable.

III.

If the trajectory in Tarantino's films includes works that manipulate centre and margin for historically determined victims/oppressors (Jews/Nazis and slaves/slave owners), then history here refers not only to social history but to film history. As such, and to see why Tarantino's recent 'historical' films bring a deeper level of meaning to the post-modern interrogation his body of work offers, we must consider them as examples of historiographic metafiction, or in this case, meta-cinema. Historiographic meta-cinema reminds us that our understanding of history is always shaped by narratives and is thus subject to various forms of construction. In such a work, the 'theoretical self-awareness of history and fiction as human constructs' constitutes a basis for the 'rethinking and reworking of the forms and contents of the past' (Hutcheon 1988: 5). These fictions 'ask us to recall that history and fiction are themselves historical terms and that their definitions and interrelations are historically determined and vary with time' (105). Perhaps most importantly, this kind of art 'suggests that to re-write or re-present the past in fiction and in history is, in both cases, to open it up to the present, to prevent it from being both conclusive and teleological' (110). This last claim underscores why historiographic meta-cinema is a more effective concept than the oft-used 'allohistory' for approaching Tarantino's films.

Allohistory implies a fictionalised *alternative* history. It is understandable that scholars would apply the term to *Inglourious Basterds* since the film depicts events, especially the demise of the Third Reich's leadership, which never occurred. But the term's emphasis on alternative history risks implying that even that which we know did occur might fall within the parameters of that alternative, and fictional, frame. The film opens with a family of Jews hunted and slaughtered, and while they are fictional characters, the hunting and slaughtering of Jews, the oppression by the Nazis, the propaganda effects of film, are not part of an alternative history but of our own. Similarly, with *Django Unchained*, while the various characters are fictional, calling the text an allohistory risks claiming that the horrific violence enacted against slaves is also part of an alternative history, and given American culture's demonstrated willingness to excise the parts of our past we don't like to face (see Loewen 2015), the term affords a disturbing political potential.

Such potential escalates for a post-9/11 culture in which the Pentagon and the Bush administration could respond to the attacks by seeking advice from Hollywood about how to create fictions that would get across the 'right ideological message' (Žižek 2002: 16), and in which a top Bush adviser could declare: '"We're an empire now, and when we act, we create our own reality. And while you're studying that reality . . . we'll act again, creating other new realities . . ."' (cited in Suskind 2004: 44). *The Hateful Eight* self-consciously examines the political exigencies of 'creating realities' by bringing together figures from both sides of the Civil War whose memories of shared events differ radically, by depicting criminals masquerading as innocents, and by showing that both criminals and lawmen can fabricate reality to further their agendas. Major Marquis Warren, for example, carries a fake letter that he claims Abraham Lincoln wrote to him, and that he uses to 'disarm white folks' since, as he says, 'the only time black folks is safe is when white folks is disarmed'. Still, whether used by an African American to negotiate a hostile post-bellum America, or by ex-Confederate soldiers to justify hunting down emancipated blacks, or by a criminal to pass himself off as a local public servant, 'created realities' are exposed as manipulative efforts at gaining power.

Using a term like 'allohistory' to describe Tarantino's films obfuscates their political potential, suggesting that they are just one more example either of not respecting historical authenticity or of revising history to serve one's own (or one's party's) agenda. Historiographic meta-cinema offers a way to understand the fictional play with history as a political technique that asks the viewer to take a more critical approach to both fiction and history, and precisely because it foregrounds both that history is subject to narrative construction (often by those with the agency to enforce their version, as that Bush adviser's infamous comment reminds us) and that fictions contribute, for better and worse, to how we understand the past. In this sense, Tarantino's films are just as valuable as those works that strive to offer historical authenticity but precisely because they do not try to do so; instead, his works play with the past in order to open that past up to the present. For example, Michael D. Richardson concludes his assessment of

Inglourious Basterds by claiming that 'the film's message of justified torture and its Manichean worldview is not very far afield from other post-9/11 glorifications of sadism and brutality' (2012: 108), a claim that could also be made about *Django Unchained* and *The Hateful Eight*. However, we could also argue that all three use their formal interrogations of the past to ask the viewer to consider how present 'real life' manifestations of sadism and brutality (that is, everything from terrorist decapitation videos to Abu Ghraib to police abuse that results in the 'accidental' death of suspects) not only fit into a historical trajectory of such brutality, but might have been facilitated by historical narratives, both social and filmic – for example, war films that have perpetuated naïve binaries by painting the Nazi as the ultimate evil and America as the ultimate good (see Meyer 2012).

Several scholars have shown that such a binary falls apart if we interpret *Inglourious Basterds* and *Django Unchained* as part of a dialectic. Not only do the ethical heroes of the first film (the Americans) become the morally suspect figures of the second, but the same actor, Christoph Waltz, portrays both Colonel Hans Landa, the Nazi 'monster' of the first film, and Dr 'King' Schultz, arguably the second film's 'ethical hero'. As Dana Weber explains, in the second film, after listening to Beethoven's *Für Elise* and reflecting on the horrors he has seen committed against Calvin Candie's (Leonardo DiCaprio) slaves, Schultz refuses to shake Candie's hand, a refusal that leads to his death. Schultz is 'reincarnated' as Colonel Landa in the first film and his first action 'is to shake farmer Perrier LaPedite's (Dennis Menochet's) hand', accompanied by an adaptation of Beethoven's *Für Elise*, the music that helped send Schultz over the moral edge (Weber 2014: 66). 'In a different historical context, then, Schultz proves himself as Candie's worthy foil' (66). Understanding the films as dialectically engaged foregrounds that the line dividing ethical hero from ethical villain is often slippery, easy to cross and subject to change over time. This idea illuminates a post-9/11 culture in which we spent a decade trying to bring to 'justice' our former Mujahideen ally, who became America's new 'greatest villain', and we did so in part by violating our own professed codes of ethical behaviour. At the very least, these films ask us to consider to what extent our extra-cinematic (im)moral actions have been informed by a whole host of historical narratives.

IV.

When Tarantino's films use the ex-centric, they reveal that the present margin can critique the seemingly absent centre – a centre that it may reject but also desires. As examples of historiographic meta-cinema, his films affirm the historical while exposing its constructed nature. But it is when his films depict violence that they offer the most effective example of post-modern complicity and critique. For Hutcheon, complicity and critique is inherent in post-modern parody: the post-modern text 'may be complicitous with the values it inscribes as well as subverts, but the subversion is still there' (Hutcheon 1989: 106). This post-modern trait can help to explain why so many assessments of Tarantino's works use the same material to reach diametrically opposed conclusions, especially about the meaning of his films' violence. For the post-9/11 American subject, no matter how violently its 'reality' might have been shattered, violent imagery seems to be a compelling draw, perhaps because despite our fear of it, violence is something we understand. By examining key sequences from *Inglourious Basterds* and from *Django Unchained* along with their critical responses, we can see how each film's manipulation of violent imagery implicates the viewer, thereby asking her/him to consider the moral imperatives involved.

According to Imke Meyer, *Inglourious Basterds* 'forces us to face up to our fascination with evil, and to the erotic charge with which we invest it' (Meyer 2012: 24). She argues that the film's final scene in which the Nazis are destroyed while watching a propaganda film 'signals the indictment of a cinema that . . . refuses to let go of narrative conventions . . . that reaffirm a victim-perpetrator dichotomy that condemns Jews to eternal powerlessness' (19), and that secures the Nazis' place as the twentieth-century's ultimate evil. For Meyer, the final violence clearly offers an important critique of twentieth-century film and culture. In contrast, while Michael Richardson agrees that the film's 'violence . . . engages audiences on an emotional level . . . [and] brings this engagement to bear on rational and ultimately moral questions', he insists that the use of violence 'remains superficial' because the viewer never identifies with either victim or perpetrator (Richardson 2012: 105). He then questions whether, especially in that final climactic scene, viewers are detached enough 'to critically engage' with the spectacle, and he concludes that they are not (107). Both readings raise important – if opposed – perspectives to which we can add a third.

Neither critic mentions that this climactic sequence is also the only moment in any Tarantino film in which the viewer witnesses an audience watching a film. We watch the Nazis taking intense pleasure in viewing the violent destruction of their enemy (American soldiers) in a film (*Nation's Pride* or *Pride of a Nation* – an allusion to Griffith's *Birth of a Nation*?)[2] that depicts a single German soldier, Frederick Zoller (Daniel Bruhl) playing himself, massacring three hundred Americans from a tower.[3] The film builds suspense not only by cutting to the action taking

Figure 8.1 The Nazi audience cheering the deaths of American soldiers while watching *Pride of a Nation* in *Inglourious Basterds* (2009).

place in the projection room between Shosanna and Zoller, or to the ongoing negotiations between Aldo Raine (Brad Pitt) and Hans Landa, but by showing the Nazi audience shouting and cheering, relishing the violence they are witnessing and precisely because their 'enemy' is being destroyed. Given the inferno that will soon consume this 'inside' audience, this meta-moment invites the 'outside' audience, especially an American one, to take pleasure in the violence depicted and in the ultimate destruction of the great evil of the twentieth century, while also forcing the viewer into the subjective position of that ultimate evil as its representatives take pleasure in the violent destruction of its own enemy – that is, America.

The subjective slippage that this moment provides parallels the kind of split subjectivity that Americans have been negotiating due to 9/11, our invasion of Iraq and our seemingly endless war on terror. The moment confronts the audience with questions it might find hard to answer in our current culture: how different are Americans, or American actions, from those we have defined as evil or those whose actions we have denounced? Are we the 'good' guys or the 'evil' guys, and if we *are* the 'good' guys, then why are we so hated? Why would any individual, group or culture cheer, just like this fictional Nazi audience, at images of violence perpetrated against us? The Nazis taking such pleasure in the destruction of Americans might seem historically anachronistic, as America was not the Nazis' only enemy and did not enter the Second World War until fairly late. This anachronism could be high-lighting America's tendency to view itself as the hero, as any 'evildoer's' ultimate nemesis, an ironic notion here since it is really Shosanna who orchestrates the demise of the Nazi leadership. However, the film might be using the Nazis as a surrogate through which the audience can play out America's present conflict with what so many would identify as the 'great evil' of the twenty-first century – that is, terrorist organisations that see the west, led by America, as a threat that must be brought down, and that have also broadcast their pleasure over the losses inflicted by successful attacks against us.

Much has also been made of the film's final moment when Lieuten-ant Raine carves a swastika in Landa's forehead and declares, 'This may just be my masterpiece', with scholars interpreting this comment as Tarantino speaking through his character about his own film (see Fujiwara 2012; Schlippake 2012). However, if the comment *does* sig-nify the director speaking vicariously through his character, we need to consider the implications of the actions involved. Is *Inglourious Basterds* Tarantino's masterpiece because, like Lieutenant Raine, it uses violence to mark its victim (the viewer) with evidence of who s/he really is (that is, capable not only of wallowing in the violent destruc-tion of those we have coded as enemy but also capable of desiring that destruction), a role that s/he, much like Hans Landa, plans to shed as soon as s/he is able? If the film *does* mark the post-9/11 sub-ject in this way, there are at least two effects. First, the viewer must recognise that s/he prefers violence in 'harmless' fictional fantasies, much like what Žižek has shown we consumed readily before 9/11. But second, and ironically, the viewer loses the 'safety' inherent in being the cinematic spectator because, just as Landa's scar swastika means he cannot remove evidence of his role as a Nazi just because he removes his uniform and leaves Europe for America, we cannot shed our knowledge that we desire such violence just because we leave the theatre. If the film does mark the viewer, then its message must somehow remain. Tarantino's recent films strive to mark the viewer in such a way, but the implications for understanding post-9/11 America become more potent when we consider *Django Unchained*'s use of spectacle and violence.

In *Django Unchained*, the concept of pleasurable violence is thwarted more than in any of Tarantino's other films. Clifford Thompson claims that 'where the comedian leaves off, the moralist seems to take over and ask: How much can you laugh at? . . . How much do you like violence' (Thompson 2013: 56)? For Geoffrey O'Brien, we reach the limit of 'amusing' violence when the film depicts two Mandingo fighters battling to the death for the pleasure of their owners (O'Brien 2013: 31). I would argue that the most disturbing sequence of violence comes when the runaway Mandingo fighter D'Artagnan (Ato Essandoh) gets torn apart by dogs. How these scenes of violence function, however, is subject to critical debate.

Samuel Perry argues that 'Tarantino chooses to enact very realistic violence on the black characters' while 'white characters suffer mostly fantastic harm', and he concludes from this that 'black people experience real harm' while 'white people suffer little, and the audience is tempted to laugh at the ridiculousness of the violence visited on them' (2014: 220). For Perry, this produces 'spectacle without agency' (221) and diminishes a history of actual violence that African Americans have suffered.

The film does depict violence against blacks and whites in two radically opposed fashions – the violence against the slaves is brutal, unyielding and also not fully visible. In fact, the scenes in which whites commit violence against the slaves are, for Tarantino, remarkably restrained: we see the whipping scars that Django and Broomhilda (Kerry Washington) bear, but not the actual rending of flesh; the Mandingo fighting sequence spends more time on the spectators, and Django refuses to watch; we do see Broomhilda branded with an R below her eye, but these moments are never as vividly depicted as the violence enacted against the whites, the cartoonish quality of which does make it seem far less 'real'.

This contrast in violence can have a different meaning, however, as it underscores that historically, while any such actions against white Americans could only be a fantasy, the violence against the slaves was not. In other words, the violence against the whites had to be grossly excessive, even comic, to emphasise that it was, historically speaking, not possible. The horrific violence against the slaves need not be depicted as visibly because, no matter how much we might wish to 'create a new reality' so that we can forget our collective past and its horrors, we know the truth and can fill in the blanks. Thus, the contrast between the fantastic and the brutal violence drives home that we know historical reality – we simply prefer the pleasure of the fantasy. In this way the film reminds us that we love to fantasise about things, even dreadful things, and even if we know that such dreadful things have real-life precedents and/or future potentials.

Confronting the viewer with her/his desire for that pleasurable fantasy proves significant if we also consider those sequences in *Django* that foreground how spectacle and performance frame the violence we witness. When Schultz discusses the kind of slave he wants to buy as his Mandingo fighter, he emphasises the spectacular, i.e. he wants a showman, a black Hercules. In the Mandingo fight sequence, violence is 'reflected back to us in watching slave owners take pleasure' in the same event, and thus we are again implicated in the viewing of this violence (Temoney 2014: 134). Django himself is 'bound by the chains of the metacinematic; that is, he is always "in character"' (Waldron 2014: 152), and thus Django exists as a living spectacle, constantly performing for and examined by a black and white audience that cannot make sense of him, and from which he cannot escape.

Still, the sequence with D'Artagnan is the most significant violent spectacle because the film emphasises the various audiences and their viewing practice as much as the event itself. We witness Candie's white workers enjoying the violence (and in this way they signify a 'white' audience and its pleasure), but we do not view the event through their eyes. In fact, though the film shows Schultz and the other slaves watching in horror, the brief violence it depicts is clearly framed as the camera's point of view – that is, we are not sutured into any character's subjective position – until the end when a shot-reverse shot shows D'Artagnan's torn body from Django's perspective, after which he puts on a pair of sunglasses, symbolically blocking out the horror. Aside from that, the sequence depicts Candie watching Schulz watch the scene, and Candie and Django staring at each other. The dialogue here is especially important, and seldom discussed, though the scene's emphasis on sound – we hear the brutal sounds of dogs ripping a man apart and that man screaming – reminds us that we should pay attention to the words:

> Calvin Candie: Your boss looks a little green around the gills for a blood sport like nigger fighting.
> Django: Nah, he just ain't used to seein' a man ripped apart by dogs is all.
> Calvin Candie: Hm. You are used to it?
> Django: I'm just a little more used to Americans than he is.

By equating this violence so directly with Americans, Django implies that Americans are both capable of, and inured to, horrific violence, and he foregrounds that for an American profit trumps everything. After all, Candie throws D'Artagnan to the dogs because he will no longer fight and thus Candie will lose money on his investment. This characterizsation of the American national identity reminds the post-9/11 American subject that s/he inhabits a culture in which profiting off the suffering of others (e.g. profiting off a war America began) has become something of a norm.[4] It also complicates the critical tendency

Figure 8.2 In *Django Unchained* (2012), after Candie (Leonardo Di Caprio) asks whether Django (Jamie Foxx), unlike Schultz (Christoph Waltz), *is* used to seeing a man ripped apart by dogs, Django replies: 'I'm just a little more used to Americans than he is.'

to view Schultz (the only fully non-American character), rather than Django, as the film's ethical hero.

Several scholars have argued that Schultz functions as the easy out for the white viewer, even going so far as to interpret him as a 'Magical Negro' (see Weaver et al. 2014; Dassanowsky 2014). These analyses claim that Schultz reflects white guilt over the horrors of slavery and martyrs himself for Django, thereby enabling the white viewer to feel good about her/himself. The problems with this interpretation outweigh the strengths, especially since Schultz's 'martyrdom' actually results in Django and Broomhilda being recaptured, Django nearly losing his genitals, and Django being sent to a labour camp. In fact, if anything, the film uses Schultz to make the viewer recognise the political problems inherent in indulging this kind of 'white guilt'. From early on the film depicts Schultz believing that the law justifies his own acts of violence and his own profiting off the bodies of others. Although he claims to despise slavery and though he acknowledges that bounty hunting is also a 'flesh for cash business', somehow his profession's legal backing makes his actions different from those of the slaver, a notion that the film undermines by reminding us that the law authorises and empowers the slaver as well (see Kaster 2014). In fact, despite his foreign nationality, Schultz deploys a rather American brand of rationalising here, considering how America's past and present efforts to protect itself and/or to police other countries has at times risked blurring, if not outright crossing, the line that distinguishes ethical from non-ethical behaviour, and often within the framework of 'legally sanctioned' actions (e.g. Iran/Contra, National Security Agency wiretapping, waterboarding prisoners).

Django confronts Schultz about his moral hypocrisy shortly before the scene with D'Artagnan. When Schultz asks Django to tone down his 'performance' and stop abusing Candie's slaves, Django retorts:

> Django: I recall the man who had me kill another man in front of his son and he didn't bat a eye. You remember that?
> Schultz: Yeah, of course I remember.
> Django: What you said was that this is my world, and in my world you gotta get dirty. So that's what I'm doin', I'm gettin' dirty.

'Gettin' dirty' is precisely what Schultz won't do when it counts the most, presumably due to his honour and to his disgust over the violence he has witnessed (the film shows him remembering D'Artagnan's slaughter). As a consequence, he refuses to shake Candie's hand and then shoots him, an act that brings about his own death. He does not martyr himself for Django; he indulges his moral anguish and ruins their entire enterprise. Django must be unchained, not just from a slave master, but from this representative of white guilt who insists on believing that he and his livelihood somehow exist outside the system that fosters the very actions he finds so morally repulsive. Only with Schultz gone can Django begin to enact his own liberation, although even here the film provides a contested finale.

On the one hand, the film again implicates the viewer as we witness Broomhilda's pleasure in watching the spectacle of Candieland being destroyed, a pleasure that likely mimics the audience's. Yet what marks *Django Unchained* as perhaps more significant than Tarantino's other films is that Stephen's (Samuel L. Jackson) final monologue reminds us that any cinematic pleasure we may take in such cathartic violence and destruction is essentially as meaningless as Django's 'liberation'. If Candieland symbolises the larger institution of slavery, then it is crucial that, as he dies and as Candieland crumbles around him, Stephen reminds Django: 'You can't destroy Candieland. We've been here and we're always gonna be here.' Any liberation is thus both individual and temporal since slavery, and the laws and economics that have enabled it, remain firmly in place. Because the film uses the past to speak to the present, it asks its audience to question the extent to which the moral vision that facilitated such laws and their concomitant practices still endures in the 'Candieland' that is post-9/11 America.

The film's release in 2012 would seem especially timely, then, as the conflicts between African American males and figureheads of the law not only raise questions about the ethical abuse of legal force, but also suggest that America remains chained to a kind of moral rationalising that sadly has not progressed very much. In that same interview

about *The Hateful Eight*, when asked whether the events surrounding the police shootings of unarmed black men in Ferguson, MO and
Baltimore, MD made their way into the final script, Tarantino replies:
'It was already in the script. It was already in the footage we shot.
It just happens to be timely right now. We're not trying to make it
timely. It is timely' (Tarantino 2015: 32). At least two examples support the director's claims: Oswaldo Mobray's discussion of 'dispassionate justice' and Major Marquis Warren's manipulation of General
Sanford Smithers (Bruce Dern). When discussing why state-supported
legal justice morally trumps 'frontier justice', Mobray explains that the
executioner is a dispassionate figure with no vested interest in the individual he executes. As he says, 'that dispassion is the very essence of
justice. For justice delivered without dispassion is always in danger of
not being justice.' The fact that Oswald is later revealed as a member of the Domergue Gang might complicate how the viewer assesses
his argument, but his idea speaks to a contemporary culture in which
Americans have questioned whether police actions can, should and do
spring from such a dispassionate position, and if not, whether their
actions qualify as justice. Similarly, when Major Warren goads General
Smithers with the story of how he tortured and then sodomised Smithers' son (perhaps yet another 'created reality'), he does so in order to
compel Smithers to pick up the gun he has placed before him. Once

Figure 8.3 In *The Hateful Eight* (2016), Oswaldo Mobray (Tim Roth) explains
to John Ruth (Kurt Russell) and Daisy Domergue (Jennifer Jason Leigh) the
differences between 'frontier justice' and that of civilised society, noting that 'the
good part about frontier justice is it's very thirst quenching. The bad part is it's
apt to be wrong as right.'

Smithers (Caucasian) reaches for the gun, Warren (African American) can legally shoot him in self-defence. This moment offers an especially ironic spin on the self-defence arguments so often made by white men (e.g. policemen, George Zimmerman – Trayvon Martin's killer) in the shootings of black men.

It is clear, then, that both *Django Unchained* and *The Hateful Eight* speak to and about racial tensions in America, tensions that were evident while these films were in development and production and that subsequently escalated. However, these filmic depictions of America's history of violence speak to more than just our ongoing tensions between white and black America. To remind us of this fact, *The Hateful Eight* offers a significant flashback to what Minnie's Haberdashery was like before the Domergue Gang arrived. The film depicts an almost utopian post-bellum America in which blacks and whites can intermarry and live in harmony, and yet the audience views this sequence knowing what Major Warren had told Bob the Mexican (Demian Bichir) a few scenes earlier: that Minnie (Dana Gourrier) 'sure don't like Mexicans' and bars them from her establishment. This knowledge ruptures the utopian vision before a single gun is fired, and it reminds us that the depicted tensions between whites and blacks also reflect the tensions between Americans and any people of colour Americans conveniently define as 'enemy'.[5]

V.

I began by claiming that we need the kind of viewing pleasure exaggerations that Tarantino's films provide, and precisely because we so often prefer our fantasising to facing a 'reality' that makes us uncomfortable. Yet if, as Žižek says, 9/11 signified the image shattering that comfortable lie, then Tarantino's films remind us that our 'reality' is, to expand upon what Ta-Nehisi Coates has claimed, inextricably bound up with a dangerous dream about manifest destiny, profit and 'progress', a dream that undergirds America, that has throughout our history been facilitated by the plunder of black bodies, and that now invites us to plunder 'the Earth itself' (Coates 2015: 150). 'Getting' dirty', and then pretending our hands are clean, has helped to make America what it is today, and Tarantino's films drive that idea home. Yet if Minnie's Haberdashery does function as a microcosm of the extra-filmic world, then with *The Hateful Eight*, Tarantino implies that 'gettin' clean' may no longer even be possible since every character, whether 'good' or 'evil', dead or dying, ends up saturated in carnage.

Given the moral inquiry they invite the viewer to enact, Tarantino's films entertain spectators into a reflection upon our past atrocities; but thanks to their post-modern play – and to our ability to join in that play – they also mark the post-9/11 subject, inviting her/him to recognise how those past atrocities likely buttress our present ones.

NOTES

1. Special thanks to Zachary Snyder, whose comments about an early version of this essay helped me to refine my argument about why the sensationalism in Tarantino's films is so valuable.
2. That this might be an allusion to Griffith's film makes more sense after the release of *Django Unchained*, with scholars exploring the many ways these two films exist in an ideological dialogue that addresses America and its values.
3. The Nazi film's narrative structure is also oddly American: on the one hand, it invokes a perverse manifestation of the American ideal of rugged individualism; on the other, it recalls Charles Whitman's 1966 rampage from a tower at the University of Texas at Austin, the kind of gun violence massacre we would never openly celebrate – except perhaps in film.
4. *The Hateful Eight* takes the idea of profiting off the bodies of others to a grisly extreme as Daisy Domergue (Jennifer Jason Leigh) bargains for her life by offering Chris Mannix (Walter Goggins) the bounty of her slain comrades.
5. Recent reports chronicle a growing presence of middle-aged white males, identifying with American colonial revolutionaries (Three-Percenters), holding armed protests at Muslim mosques in Texas. See 'Armed "Three Percenters" Movement now Confronting Muslim Americans' (2015).

REFERENCES

'Armed "Three Percenters" Movement now Confronting Muslim Americans' (2015), *The Huffington Post*, 11 December 2015, last accessed 16 December 2015: HuffingtonPost.com
Butler, Judith (2004), *Precarious Life: The Powers of Mourning and Violence*, New York: Verso.
Coates, Ta-Nehisi (2015), *Between the World and Me*, New York: Spiegel & Grau.
Dassanowsky, Robert von (2014), 'Dr "King" Schultz as Ideologue and Emblem: The German Enlightenment and the Legacy of the 1848 Revolutions in *Django Unchained*', in Oliver C. Speck (ed.), *Quentin Tarantino's Django Unchained: The Continuation of Metacinema*, New York: Bloomsbury, pp. 17–37.
Fujiwara, Chris (2012), '"A Slight Duplication of Efforts": Redundancy and the Excessive Camera in *Inglourious Basterds*', in Robert von Dassanowsky (ed.), *Quentin Tarantino's Inglourious Basterds: A Manipulation of Metacinema*, New York: Continuum, pp. 37–55.
Hutcheon, Linda (1988), *A Poetics of Postmodernism: History, Theory, Fiction*, New York: Routledge.
— (1989), *The Politics of Postmodernism*, New York: Routledge.

Kaster, Gregory L. (2014), '*Django* and *Lincoln*: The Suffering Slave and the Law of Slavery', in Oliver C. Speck (ed.), *Quentin Tarantino's Django Unchained: The Continuation of Metacinema*, New York: Bloomsbury, pp. 75–90.

Loewen, James (2015), 'Why do people believe myths about the Confederacy? Because our textbooks and monuments are wrong; False history marginalizes African Americans and makes us all dumber', *Washington Post*, 1 July 2015, last accessed 31 July 2015: washingtonpost.com

Melnick, Jeffrey (2009), *9/11 Culture: America Under Construction*, Oxford: Wiley-Blackwell.

Meyer, Imke (2012), 'Exploding Cinema, Exploding Hollywood: *Inglourious Basterds* and the Limits of Cinema', in Robert von Dassanowsky (ed.), *Quentin Tarantino's Inglourious Basterds: A Manipulation of Metacinema*, New York: Continuum, pp. 15–35.

Mitchell, Evan (2015), 'Foreword', *The Hateful Eight: A Screenplay* by Quentin Tarantino, New York: Grand Central Publishing, pp. v–viii.

O'Brien, Geoffrey (2013), 'Heart of Dixie: *Django Unchained* Mixes the Spaghetti Western with some Blaxploitation and Gives Us . . . History,' *Filmcomment*, 49.1, pp. 30–3. Web, filmcomment.com (last accessed 1 January 2015).

Perry, Samuel P. (2014), 'Chained to It: The Recurrence of the Frontier Hero in the Films of Quentin Tarantino', in Oliver C. Speck (ed.), *Quentin Tarantino's Django Unchained: The Continuation of Metacinema*, New York: Bloomsbury, pp. 205–25.

Richardson, Michael D. (2012), 'Vengeful Violence: *Inglourious Basterds*, Allohistory, and the Inversion of Victims and Perpetrators', in Robert von Dassanowsky (ed.), *Quentin Tarantino's Inglourious Basterds: A Manipulation of Metacinema*, New York: Continuum, pp. 93–112.

Schlipphake, Heidi (2012), '*Inglourious Basterds* and the Gender of Revenge', in Robert von Dassanowsky (ed.), *Quentin Tarantino's Inglourious Basterds: A Manipulation of Metacinema*, New York: Continuum, pp. 113–33.

Speck, Oliver C. (2014), 'Introduction: A Southern State of Exception', in Oliver C. Speck (ed.), *Quentin Tarantino's Django Unchained: The Continuation of Metacinema*, New York: Bloomsbury, pp. 1–13.

Suleiman, Susan Rubin (1991), 'Feminism and Postmodernism', in Charles Jencks (ed.), *The Post-Modern Reader*, New York: St Martin's Press, pp. 318–32.

Suskind, Ron (2004), 'Without a Doubt: Faith, Certainty, and The Presidency of George W. Bush', *The New York Times Magazine*, 17 October 2004: 44, NYTimes. com (last accessed 9 December 2015).

Tarantino, Quentin (2015), 'In Conversation: Quentin Tarantino', interview by Lane Brown, *New York Magazine*, 24 August–5 September 2015, pp. 30–6, 39.

Temoney, Kate E. (2014), 'The "D" is Silent, but Human Rights are Not: *Django Unchained* as Human Rights Discourse', in Oliver C. Speck (ed.), *Quentin Tarantino's Django Unchained: The Continuation of Metacinema*, New York: Bloomsbury, pp. 123–40.

Thompson, Clifford (2013), 'Rev. of *Django Unchained* by Quentin Tarantino', *Cineaste*, Spring 2013, pp. 56–7. Web, cineaste.com (last accessed 1 January 2015).

Waldron, Dara (2014), 'Hark, Hark, the (dis)Enchanted Kantian, or Tarantino's "Evil" and its Anti-Cathartic Resonance', in Oliver C. Speck (ed.), *Quentin Tarantino's Django Unchained: The Continuation of Metacinema*, New York: Bloomsbury, pp. 141–60.

Weaver, Ryan J., and Nicole K. Kathol (2014), 'Guess Who's Coming to Get Her: Stereotypes, Mythification, and White Redemption', in Oliver C. Speck (ed.), *Quentin Tarantino's Django Unchained: The Continuation of Metacinema*, New York: Bloomsbury, pp. 243–68.

Weber, Dana (2014), 'Of Handshakes and Dragons: Django's German Cousins', in Oliver C. Speck (ed.), *Quentin Tarantino's Django Unchained: The Continuation of Metacinema*, New York: Bloomsbury, pp. 51–73.

Žižek, Slavoj (2002), *Welcome to the Desert of the Real: 5 Essays on September 11 and Related Dates*, New York: Verso.

CHAPTER 9

Stop the Clocks: *Lincoln* and Post-9/11 Cinema

Ian Scott

If you can look into the seeds of time and say which grain will grow and which will not, speak then to me. Time's a great thickener of things.

Abraham Lincoln to William Seward in *Lincoln*, quoting from *Macbeth* (Act I Scene 3 in the traditional text)

I. INTRODUCTION

Steven Spielberg's *Lincoln* (2012) is about the relationship of time to history. The film's symbolism, its words, deeds, actions and characters all represent time. And not just any old time, but momentous time; the sort of time that gets documented by historians and talked about by cultural commentators. The sort of time that is meant to be worth remembering and charting; time that has a place in history; not just time that is slouching towards the next event or action and which will be quickly forgotten as the moment recedes, but time that is forever ingrained upon memory and remembrance. The sort of time Hollywood likes very much.

That Spielberg the director might want to document time through history in this manner is no great surprise. His historical movies – *Empire of the Sun* (1987), *Schindler's List* (1992), *Amistad* (1997), *Saving Private Ryan* (1998), and more recently *Bridge of Spies* (2015) – all make the viewer constantly aware of time as a marker of some historical substance. The moment things of import happen, the passing of time as momentous signifier, the establishment of monuments as frames of reference; so much in Spielberg's cinematic conscience means something timely. As he makes clear, talking about the background and production of *Lincoln*, 'history is always relevant'.[1] And by this Spielberg means to suggest, as his career has constantly framed it, that the past always re-embellishes and illuminates the present, offers allegory and metaphor even in its smallest fragmentary moments. In *Bridge of Spies*, Tom Hanks' character, the lawyer Jim Donovan, sent to Berlin at the height of the Cold War to negotiate the repatriation of the shot-down U2 pilot Gary Powers, is passing from east to west on an elevated train when he witnesses a night-time shooting of someone attempting to scale the putative Berlin Wall. The scene immediately recalls contemporary apogees of migration and desperate escape to a 'better' and 'free' west in our own age.

Time, then, intimately connects Spielberg's history across eras, and he's a smart enough filmmaker and historian of film to know that time as a measurement of cinema *and* history has been a fascination for scholars too, especially those of early film. As Mary Doane reminds us, 'the emerging cinema participated in a general cultural imperative, the structuring of time and contingency in capitalist modernity' (Doane 2009: 77). The moving image was always aware of itself as a spectacle of movement, a refraction of time caught and preserved in the amber of celluloid.

Steven Spielberg's *Lincoln* has thus been aligned with a number of contemporary analogies as metaphoric linkage, as this chapter goes on to detail. From the art of congressional bipartisanship and the object lesson in winning congressional votes, to the call for powerful oratory and titanic leadership in the wake of 9/11's calamitous impact. This chapter, though, equates *Lincoln* with more than just parable, more than just time as historical artefact. In seeking answers to that relative dimensional relationship, the following considers earlier films as clues to Spielberg's presentation of the president, theorises the way time and history has been analysed, and questions how and why time has been the constant iteration referencing 9/11's impact on the twenty-first-century world.

II. TIME AND LINCOLN

I suppose it is time to go, though I would rather stay.
Daniel Day-Lewis as the president making
his way to Ford's theatre in *Lincoln*

Up to 2015, *Lincoln* was Steven Spielberg's biggest commercial *and* critical success of the twenty-first century (only *War of the Worlds* [2005] and *Indiana Jones and the Kingdom of the Crystal Skull* [2008] had bigger box-office returns, but with far less plaudits). Tony Kushner's script documenting the road to ratifying the thirteenth Amendment to the Constitution as the Civil War lumbers towards its final months in 1865, subjects race to the test of political efficacy rather more than it does any strong moral or social alignment, and it is this which is the film's most striking facet for the present age; that equality before the law and little else piques the attention. For much of the movie, the president who will secure the legal freedom of African Americans isn't awe-struck by the realignment of the races at all. That black soldier Ira Clark (David Oyelowo) can recite the concluding line from the Gettysburg Address that his white counterpart has forgotten in the movie's first scene doesn't stir much response in Lincoln other than loquacious tales. He then asks his wife's assistant Elizabeth Keckley (Gloria Reuben), as the vote for the amendment in the House of Representatives looms, whether her people are afraid of the future, of the time that lies ahead. Keckley states bluntly that white people don't want African Americans in the country, asking of the president whether that is his opinion too.

Figure 9.1 Abraham Lincoln (Daniel Day-Lewis) speaks with African American Union soldiers in the first scene of *Lincoln* (2012).

'I don't know you Mrs Keckley,' the president states, 'any of you. I assume I'll get used to you.' What her people are to do with the amendment passed and freedom at her disposal, Lincoln isn't sure, not knowing or understanding black people in any real sense. Iwan Morgan reinforces this reading and Spielberg's supposed tone when he asserts that the problem of Lincoln movies has been that restorer of the union has been a far more forceful and attractive narrative than emancipator of the slaves has been (Morgan 2011: 6).

Nevertheless, the scene is a telling assessment from the past for a picture made in the modern age where post-racial America united under a black president was supposed to have lost the taint of sectionalism. Instead, the scenes recognise where prejudice, ignorance and disapproval, even the ripples of violence spread down from the midnineteenth century continue to circle out across the US societal pond in the age of Obama.

Indeed, these moments in the film, meant to signify ambiguity at best in Lincoln's equality of the races philosophy, have turned out far more prophetic for post-9/11 America than many would have thought when the film was released in 2012. Subsequent mass shootings, police violence, law and order skewed against perpetrators of colour, debates about the public place of the Confederate flag, disagreements over the continuing scandals about mass incarceration; all have focused the mind on who African Americans are, and in fact who any minority or ethnic group is in modern America. What place do they have, what place indeed does the Constitution have in its ostensible role as protector of rights and freedoms guaranteed to all?

Time has seemingly not healed old wounds by this analogy between film and wider representational culture. But it has proved crucial to many an assessment of arguably America's greatest president. The untimely death of Abraham Lincoln provides continuing counterfactual speculation as to what might have been if the president had been allowed to complete his second term in office. And films about Lincoln have always immersed themselves in that subjunctive condition by having time as an enemy of the man's life, work and accomplishments. From *The Iron Horse* (1924) to *Young Mr Lincoln* (1939), from *Abe Lincoln in Illinois* (1940) to *The Conspirator* (2010), from *Abraham Lincoln: Vampire Hunter* (2012) to Spielberg's *Lincoln*.

Melvyn Stokes' concise and striking appreciation of *Lincoln* in his book *American History Through Hollywood Film* confirms how ubiquitous Lincoln was to early film (thirty-nine appearances in silent movies between 1908 and 1915 alone), as though nascent Hollywood was desperate to fashion a future out of the past by returning again and again to the man's deeds and words. Stokes is at pains to suggest that this was less a confirmation of the president's saintly status, however, than it was a rehabilitation of him that had taken some while to gather momentum (Stokes 2013: 57). Indeed, many historians 'underestimated the time it took for Lincoln to secure his place in history', argues Stokes (Stokes 2013: 56). He cites Eric Goldman as one who saw the 1880s as the moment when things began to alter, but in reality points to Ida Tarbell's influential serialisation of the man's life in *McClure's Magazine* in 1897 when the tide really started to turn in favour of what Tarbell called 'the common Westerner', a pointed description that forsook the rather more recurrent epithets of inspirational leader or unionist saviour.

By the 1920s the mythological Lincoln had by now bedded himself in cinematically. Andrew Piasecki, for example, is unequivocal about Lincoln's presence in John Ford's silent masterpiece, *The Iron Horse*. Here, states Piasecki, Lincoln is a 'guiding force that brings unity and harmony out of chaos and struggle' (Piasecki 2003: 65). But he also reaffirms the film's central tenet: that the president, seen presiding over the signing of the Pacific Railroad Act in 1862 which will pave the way for the transcontinental railway to be built, is a force for progress: economic, political, social and moral. It's a role that had been assigned him early on in Hollywood's character construction, and it was one that subsequent portrayals found hard to deviate from.

At the close of *Young Mr Lincoln*, director Ford is still up to the same tricks. Henry Fonda's honest Abe impersonation is both pragmatic and progressive, cloaked as it is in portent. Lincoln the young lawyer takes on a seemingly unwinnable case, of two young men accused of murder at an Independence Day state fair with witnesses after the fact to prove the contention. The Clay brothers (Richard Cromwell and Eddie Quillan) are exonerated, however, because of time; the moon's cycle had moved on such that it wasn't 'full bright' the night of the stabbing, which means key witness Palmer Cass (Ward Bond) couldn't have seen the fight from the distance away he was as it was too dark. Tearing the testimony to shreds, Lincoln further succeeds in having Cass implicate himself in the crime, stabbing his so-called friend over a financial dispute.

Stephen Douglass (Milburn Stone), cast as the doubting Thomas, apologises to Lincoln at the close of the trial, saying he won't make the mistake of underestimating the young lawyer again. 'Well Steve, reckon neither one of us should underestimate the other, from here on in.' Lincoln's response, courtesy of screenwriter Lamar Trotti, gives a nod to their political battles and famous debates to come, conflicts that are all destined to intertwine as the years go by, fates that will consign Lincoln to the path leading to Ford's theatre.

Lincoln's magic-realist trip to the top of the hill in the very last scene – as if self-consciously stage set – with thunder and lightning crashing around him, is matched by Spielberg in the ethereal dream sequences in *Lincoln* three-quarters of a century later, that have the president fronting the prow of a steamship in dark waters seeking the light in the distance. Spielberg drapes these scenes in a muslin-covered sepia glow – complemented by Lincoln himself in other scenes being wrapped in the drapes of the White House curtains billowing beside the open windows – seemingly accelerating and decelerating time as if wishing to delay the inevitable, attempting almost to stop history and prevent destiny from reaching its natural conclusion, while at the same moment embracing the magnitude of the event that will shape the United States forever.

Figure 9.2 Abraham Lincoln shown at the front of a steamship in the ethereal dream sequence from *Lincoln*.

Spielberg's film plays with time in a more conventional sense as well. Its narrative is also that staple of cinematic drama: the race against time. Lincoln, worried in January 1865 that the Emancipation Proclamation may become redundant if the war ends and then the slave states are returned to the union without a constitutional amendment to reinforce the proclamation, urges for a passage of the thirteenth Amendment before the month is out. Complicating matters are colleague Preston Blair's (Hal Holbrook) instructions to negotiate a settlement with Confederate representatives that sees them bearing down on Washington as the bill reaches the House floor for the all-important vote; all of this a precursor to the Hampton Roads conference aboard the *River Queen* steamboat in Virginia on 3 February 1865 that Lincoln personally attends with Secretary of State William Seward (David Strathairn) and which forms part of the concluding aftermath in *Lincoln*.

Time, or timelessness, then, crosses both Spielberg's and Ford's films, as it does D. W. Griffith's *Abraham Lincoln* (1930), in a hurry to link the past with the present, and to add up circumstance and criteria with modern dilemmas and whims. In Doris Kearns Goodwin's book *Team of Rivals* (2005), upon which Spielberg's film takes inspiration though the actual events cover only a few pages of Kearns Goodwin's text, time spins on the axis of decision making, and sets decisions up on the understanding that the administration is in a process of becoming, even if the feeling of moving towards some inevitable date with destiny is never too far away. Politics likes portent; signs and signals of greatness to come. History largely provides it. It's why so many early films about Lincoln chose to focus on his pre-political life and formative years as a lawyer and public official. Spielberg has often remarked of the debt his own filmmaking owed to John Ford. In Joe McBride's biography of Spielberg, Ford's *The Searchers* comes up time and again as an influence (McBride 1997: 84, 263), and one sees in the latter's Lincoln film the similar notions of time as a state of learning, of gathering strength in preparation for the moments to come, as Ford employs it in *Young Mr Lincoln* as well as symbolically and apparitionally in *The Iron Horse* and then later in *How the West Was Won* (1962).

But these early movies and even later ones with the same actor reprieving the role (Raymond Massey played Lincoln a number of times throughout his career before his last, wordless, appearance in Ford's 1962 generational epic) projected the greatness at hand. Spielberg's film wonders what leadership even means, let alone what greatness eschews. 'There are lots of ways to talk about Abraham Lincoln', says Jim Cullen in his book *Sensing the Past* (Cullen 2013: 147) and not all of them necessarily about personal fortitude. For Cullen, Lincoln was above all a 'quintessential institutionalist', a man with an almost impregnable faith in the power of constitutional organisations to add value to society. It is a focus very much in tune with post-9/11 questions about establishment dependence and responsibility, about the ability of leaders to exude presence as well as manage crisis in an era of diminishing political faith.

III. TIME AND HISTORY

Are we fitted into the times we're born in?
　　　　　　　　　Lincoln to his Morse code operator, *Lincoln*

Mary Doane explains that the turn of the twentieth century saw time become palpable as a specific condition of modernity; measured, refined and locked intimately into the emerging technologies of first photography and then film (Doane 2009: 77). At around the same moment, French philosopher Henri Bergson was observing that time is always in a state of flux and that any fixed concepts of being were clearly false. As Laurel Harris describes it, quoting Bergson in the process:

> Thanks to the third dimension of space, all the images making up the past and future are . . . not laid out with respect to one another like frames on a roll of film . . . But let us not forget that all motion is reciprocal or relative: if we perceive them coming towards us, it is also true to say that we are going towards them (Bergson 1965: 142). Absolute time and space are historical products as are the concepts of 'time-space compression' and 'implosion', but their mediated and mediating reality is nonetheless crucial to the formation of lived experience. (Harris 2003)

Harris goes on to map time and space onto scientific, philosophical as well as cultural evolution, most obviously realised in the theoretical physics of Newton and Einstein, enlightenment thinkers like Descartes, and film theorists of the twentieth century such as Bazin and Metz. Doane's assessment of time's representability further references Walter Benjamin in asserting film's shock impact, the 're-thinking of temporality in modernity' in which cinema played such a significant role (Doane 2009: 80). Time was felt to be a source of anxiety and a pressing problem for representation. Doane relates the story of granddaughters looking at an old photograph of their grandmother, an example used by Kracauer in his work on photography. The shock is not in seeing their relation as they may once have appeared – younger, adolescent – but in recognising time in the photograph, its spatial contingency and intersection with what is known and what is seen (Doane 2009: 81). The phenomenon is familiar in the contemporary cultural frame too.

In Frank Spotnitz's 2015 television adaptation of Philip K. Dick's 1963 novel *The Man in the High Castle* (Amazon Video, 2015–), the Second World War has been won by the Axis powers and the Germans and Japanese occupy the east and west coasts of the United

States respectively, with a neutral zone buffering the two somewhere around the rocky mountain areas. In the Amazon Studios series, the interwoven plot revolves around the rumours and myths surrounding a set of – pointedly – newsreels known only by the ambiguous title 'The Grasshopper Lies Heavy'. In Dick's novel that title belongs to a *book*, not a set of films, a supposed reworking of history that has the Allies victorious instead and which is widely read in neutral areas but banned by the occupying powers. The book confronts the characters with the possibility of their history being misread and misrepresented, as not really existing at all, and they seek answers from the enigmatically residing 'man in the high castle' who in Dick's story is the author, Hawthorne Absendsen.

The television series, however, offers far more temporality than that, revealing that the newsreels show not just the possibility of Allied victory, but that history itself is misaligned and cannot be believed at any level. Joseph Stalin, executed in the series' history in 1949, is revealed to have been alive as late as 1954, having of course actually died in 1953 in the 'real' world. Meanwhile, the uncovered newsreel that climaxes the end of season one reputedly shows not only a nuclear attack on San Francisco a year before the action takes place (many preceding scenes as well as the one in which the film is being screened take place in the city, 'proving' that this newsreel must be false), but that two of the show's main characters, Frank Fink (Rupert Evans) and Joe Blake (Luke Kleintank), are in the city at that moment, and *in* the film. With the newsreel playing through a gymnasium projector in an empty school as he and fellow protagonist Juliana (Alexa Davalos) attempt to escape the clutches of the Japanese Kempeitai (secret police), Frank looks on in disbelief as he is shot by Blake (a Nazi spy in the story but one who has also ostensibly helped Juliana and Frank on occasion) in a German army uniform at the close of the newsreel. History is a lie, says the film. And yet in reality the show's conceit seen through the series' concluding scene really projects time as being unreliable; as memoir, as history, and as projection of one's very being and existence. Are these in fact moments to come rather than ones past; do they exist in another dimension; can time be bent to the whim of history?

Likewise, then, the dream-like celestial scenes in *Lincoln* are also close to Bergson's and Doane's theories. Like 'The Grasshopper Lies Heavy' newsreels, Spielberg constructs his own *mise en abyme* within the film while Lincoln dreams of another time and state of being. The picture becomes grainy, almost as though a signal is being fought for and lost, radio waves battling the elements in the depths of night intimating that the film's progress through the projector – or across each digital bit – is being interrupted as if time itself could be slowed down. Indeed, *Lincoln* is somewhat in awe of its temporality too, adjusting time in these sequences, removing itself from the 'present' as though the story of Lincoln were not real in the absolutist sense anyway, but more a fragment of the immortality and mythology previously constructed about the man. What film theorists call the 'contingent' or common, easily shared moment reveals its problematic circularity here for once filmed, isn't the event condemned to the past anyway, is it any longer contingent at all, isn't it defined by its very filmability and thus self-conscious historicity?

Previous work in this area has very usefully subjected periods of history in film (cinematic subgenres) to inquiry regarding their use of time and the linearity of that condition. Bettina Bildhauer's work on medieval films, for instance, suggests a 'co-presence of past, present and/or future in a single moment' (Bildhauer 2016: 407). Here she argues that time is interrupted, re-parcelled and non-linear in the modernist sense, in no small part because the Middle Ages saw time not as one continuous dimension but as eternal and not within one's grasp to determine or measure anyway. In the post-9/11 era, television shows like *The Man in the High Castle* (and before it *Lost* [ABC, 2004–10]), as well as *Lincoln*, reimagine a similar concept for more familiar ages, and ask where time and history begin and end, where provenance is always myth.

IV. TIME AND 9/11

Since 11 September 2001, time has been vitally important to the United States, indeed to the world. The events of that day have been relived more than any historical event since John F. Kennedy's assassination nearly forty years beforehand. And, like JFK's death, time is always the archivist of action. Over the years, the timed elements of 9/11, the breaking down and fragmentation of the events and parallel actions in real time, have been pored over more relentlessly, made more 'historic', and given greater weight and meaning to the force of the most momentous event in the world's modern, integratively communicated and technologically advanced era. After all, as David Holloway reminds us, 9/11 at the time and subsequently has been interpreted as privileging a whole series of crises – relationally with other nations/cultures, as well as in terms of national security and governance – periodically linked to American traditions of 'catharsis and renewal' that have been intermittently part and parcel of the nation's psychosis (Holloway 2008: 6).

The event, if not these crises, has also been important to Hollywood, to cinema's past as well as its advance into the twenty-first century. Across the internet, the conspiracists have had a field day with time, and especially 9/11 as a signal or reference point, as some sort of, presumably, code word. Then the Lord said to me, 'There is a conspiracy among the people of Judah and those who live in Jerusalem.' So says Jeremiah 11:9 in the Bible, or variations thereof of the phrase in different versions, and a passage that has become an enduring component of conspiracy theories about the events of that day. Hollywood has been by no means immune to such speculation. YouTube videos point out the number of timepieces in feature films roughly between 1978 and 2001 where hands are, coincidentally, often locked on dials at variations of '9' and '11'. In Tony Scott's conspiracy thriller *Enemy of the State* (1998), for example, character Brill's passport (Gene Hackman reinterpreting his earlier role as Harry Caul from Francis Ford Coppola's *The Conversation* [1974]) is seen in shot at one point registering his birthdate as . . . 11 September. Clocks have become monuments to 9/11 too as well as totems of reason and explanation, and the memorial museum at 'ground zero' even featured a clock counting down the moment to the exhibit's opening on the tenth anniversary of the attacks.

Time, to reinforce the point, has been an enduring measurement of 9/11. The time the planes struck the towers, the moment each tower collapsed, the response time of the emergency services, the amount of time President Bush spent in the elementary school in Sarasota, Florida he was visiting on that morning. Films made time their mantra too. Michael Moore's *Fahrenheit 9/11* (2004) made a facet of Bush's rigid indecision in the classroom by highlighting the time and even having a clock count the passing moments on screen before the president's advisors felt the need to usher him away was finally too great and pressing, though accounts of the time period in that moment have long been disputed as well. In the aftermath, Bush was often ridiculed yet occasionally praised too – especially from those in the room that day – for either sitting too long, fazed by the information coming his way or, alternatively, remaining calm, if pressured. For his supporters, the events became the making of him as a leader; for detractors, they exposed the limited capabilities that had long been thought a facet of his demeanour.

The dilemma of those few moments would come back to taunt Bush many times over as the events that unravelled in the wake of 9/11 increasingly haunted him. In Oliver Stone's bio-pic *W.* (2008), released towards the end of his presidency, Bush is less excoriated for his post-9/11 actions than he is pitied; 'a man who just didn't belong there', Stone said in an interview, a man who didn't fit in with the necessity of the times (Stone interviewed by the author, 7 December 2012, Santa Monica, CA).

In this context the resurrection of Lincoln in the 2010s seems perfectly in tune with the clamour for the return of heroes, not least those set in the supernatural fantasy world of *Abraham Lincoln: Vampire Hunter*. The demands for a reignition of political debate and depth, of rhetoric and poise allied to action hero routines that might slay, in this case, supernatural beings, offered all the metaphoric ambition one could wish for in an era where political scandal and Washington intransigence turned people away from conventional politics and politicians in the hope of renewal and reinvention found elsewhere.

If *Abraham Lincoln: Vampire Hunter* was allegorically chasing down blood-sucking prey, *Lincoln*, by Greg Frame's reading, is a film of far more serious portent, redemption, heroic posturing and righteous espousal for the commuting of the nineteenth century's – and enduringly today's – shibbolethic dividing cause in America: race. In a time of social and cultural strife early in the twenty-first century, little wonder, thinks Frame, that America's mythic saviour and redeemer should make a grand re-entrance (Frame 2014: 289–90). Little surprise too that he is ripe for recasting as saviour in some fantasy comic shoot-out that criss-crosses between an Anne Rice novel and the *Twilight* series (2008–12).

Director Timur Bekmambetov's vampire slayer president could happily escape historical verisimilitude. Stokes' analysis of *Lincoln*, on the other hand, concentrates somewhat on the predictable modern-day battles over accuracy, if not authenticity, in the film. Authentic in that the film's aesthetic pretensions – coins with Lincoln's image on them, the distribution of photographer Alexander Gardner's famous plates of slaves and the understanding that the Gettysburg Address might be recited by anybody almost at will – are all falsities that the film, allegedly, doesn't just get wrong, but piously indulges in (Stokes 2013: 81).

But *Lincoln* also 'conjures up a past', to use critic Michael Philips' phrase, as though it were unfussed about time and context. When Secretary of War Edwin Stanton (Bruce McGill) utters the immortal, and often disputed, line 'now he belongs to the ages' at the deathbed scene near the close of the film, Spielberg surely means within the framing of the text that Lincoln is not for *all* time, but for *any* time. His Lincoln's enduring relevance then is not merely the Hollywood staple of passion, power, redemption and renewal, since the beginning of cinema almost, but as a mythological figure that transcends history, and thus transcends time. Transcends not just in terms of remembrance or memory, but in the realms of practicality and progression. '9/11 changed everything' was the mantra often repeated in the years immediately after the attacks, and the refrain is still heard. *Lincoln* the film, though, conceives that everything and nothing changes when the weight of history bears down on time.

V. CONCLUSION: 'A LINCOLN FOR OUR TIMES'

Abraham Lincoln has always been a useful addendum for Hollywood from which to draw on other analogous moments in history. The spate of Lincoln movies in the 1930s, for example, starting with Griffith's eponymously titled survey of the president and culminating with John Cromwell's *Abe Lincoln in Illinois* (1940 with Raymond Massey, again, and released in the UK as *Spirit of the People*), the adaptation of Robert Sherwood's hit Broadway play, aligned themselves somewhat with liberty's defence against the encroaching forces of fascism (Stokes 2013: 79). For Stokes, critical of Spielberg's narrow racial and social focus in his film, similar analogous connections nevertheless reside from a contemporary perspective, albeit more in domestic politics than international affairs in *Lincoln*. He equates the storyline's battle for the thirteenth Amendment with a transformative leader coercing bipartisanship out of an unwilling congress, 'an ideal hero for the current era of gridlock', thinks Stokes (Stokes 2013: 6).

This perspective has reigned across scholarly and popular reception about the movie, and critic Marc Mohan was surely not the only one to state that Spielberg's film, and Daniel Day-Lewis' extraordinary performance, provided us with a 'Lincoln for our times' (Mohan 2012). Other presidents also poured forth throughout the post-9/11 period in films and TV series as part explanation, part rationalisation, part impersonation of Lincoln and/or the kind of steely reserve that was needed for the trying times ahead. The first, almost immediately after 9/11, was David Palmer (Dennis Haysbert), the United States' 'first' African American president in the hit television series *24* (FOX, 2001–14).

Beginning with Palmer, chief executives went through a litany of heroic poses in the post-9/11 era, led later by Aaron Eckhart as Benjamin Asher in *Olympus has Fallen* and Jamie Foxx as James Sawyer in *White House Down* (both 2013). Occasionally corrupted and or politically vacuous, some TV shows like *Scandal* (ABC, 2012–), *State of Affairs* (NBC, 2014–15), *Madam Secretary* (CBS, 2014–) and more also made chief executives morally compromised, rhetorically guarded, even hostile to the history paraded in the nineteenth century by Lincoln as though unable to match the expectations.

By this bearing, Lincoln re-emerged in the twenty-first century to guide a raft of fictional and factual presidents down the true path of leadership; he is everything post-9/11 leaders, including Obama, haven't been. The call to re-evaluate Lincoln in a post-9/11 world seems natural enough then. For all its metaphoric allusion to times of crisis, Steven Spielberg's film isn't dealing with traumatic events – even Lincoln's death – so much as it is dealing with aftermath. What to do next, how to heal, where to seek place and position. While its release was somewhat coincidental then – having taken Spielberg years to negotiate its final making – more than a decade after 9/11 it does chime with notions of assessment, of moving on, closing chapters, trying to advance past divisive conflict and, sometimes, catastrophic decision making and loss of life.

Time, though, ultimately determines Lincoln's triumph and burden in the film. He makes a surprise visit in one scene to his political 'fixers' led by W. N. Bilbo (James Spader), hired by Seward to twist arms and force lame-duck Democrats due to lose their seats when the Congress closes to vote in favour of the amendment. 'We have heard the chimes of midnight gentlemen,' the president states, 'the great day is nigh upon us.' Time is immeasurably moving towards the president's greatest achievement, and yet also his eventual mortality. In a later scene, on a visit to his general Ulysses Grant's headquarters at Petersburg, the military architect of the Union's victory remarks that 'by appearance you are ten years older than you were a year ago'. Time is running against Lincoln, physically and historically. Post-9/11 Hollywood cinema has therefore spent much time seeking out tell-tale signs of redemption and allegory in the years since that day, and *Lincoln* perceptibly contributes to that debate. But in reality its meaning is located not in the passing but in the transitory fragments of time, the space between the moment and history, between the myth and the reality.

NOTE

1. 'History is always relevant.' Steven Spielberg quoted from *In Lincoln's Footsteps* documentary, part of the extras to the Blu-ray disc edition of *Lincoln*.

REFERENCES

Bergson, Henri (1965), *Duration and Simultaneity*, trans. Leon Jacobson, New York: Bobbs-Merrill Company, Inc.

Bildhauer, Bettina (2016), 'Heart and Clock: Time and History in The Immortal Heart and other films about the Middle Ages', in Robert A. Rosenstone and Constantin Parvulescu (eds), *A Companion to the Historical Film*, London: Wiley.

Cullen, Jim (2013), *Sensing the Past: Hollywood Stars and Historical Visions*, Oxford: Oxford University Press.

Doane, Mary A. (2009), 'The Representability of Time', in Marnie Hughes-Warrington, *The History on Film Reader*, London: Routledge.

Harris, Laurel (2003), 'Space/Time', The Chicago School of Media Theory, last accessed 27 January 2016: https://lucian.uchicago.edu/blogs/mediatheory/keywords/spacetime/

Holloway, David (2008), *9/11 and the War on Terror*, Edinburgh: Edinburgh University Press.

McBride, Joseph (1997), *Steven Spielberg*, London: Faber & Faber.

Mohan, Marc (2012), '"Lincoln" review: An auteur's and actor's masterpiece', Special to *The Oregonian*, 15 November 2012 at 12.00 pm, updated 16 November 2012 at 12.34 pm: http://www.oregonlive.com/movies/index.ssf/2012/11/lincoln_review_a_hybrid_master.html

Morgan, Iwan W. (2011), 'Introduction', in Iwan W. Morgan (ed.), *Presidents in the Movies: American Politics on Screen*, New York: Palgrave.

Piasecki, Andrew (2003), 'Abraham Lincoln in John Ford's *The Iron Horse*: Both Trumpets and Silences', in Peter Rollins and John O'Connor (eds), *Hollywood's White House: The American Presidency in Film and History*, Lexington: University Press of Kentucky.

Phillips, Michael (2012), 'A Political Animal of a Different Kind', *Chicago Tribune*, 9 November 2012, last accessed 27 January 2016: http://www.chicagotribune.com/entertainment/movies/sc-mov-1106-lincoln-20121108-column.html

Stokes, Melvyn (2013), *American History Through Hollywood Film: From Revolution to the 1960s*,

CHAPTER 10

Foreshadows of the Fall: Questioning 9/11's Impact on American Attitudes

Stephen Joyce

I. INTRODUCTION

Given the shocking events of 9/11, many have seen the fall of the Twin Towers as the fiery birth of a new epoch, as revolutionary in its own way as the storming of the Bastille. This perception was heightened by Bush administration rhetoric, which used the attacks to frame a new sense of identity and purpose in the post-Cold War environment. Yet, in looking at films prior to 9/11, we find curious portents of this new world. In *Independence Day* (1996), we find not only heroic American responses to an evil assault but a president who dons a flight suit to lead the counter-attack and ends the film high-fiving his fellow warriors, just as President Bush did in 2003 when he declared 'Mission Accomplished' in Iraq. Even more perplexingly, in *The Siege* (1998) we find not only the USA threatened by Arab terrorism but the military and CIA torturing naked Arab suspects in images astonishingly reminiscent of Abu Ghraib. If these films had been made after 9/11, we would unhesitatingly see them as responses to a post-9/11 world; that they were made less than five years prior to 9/11 suggests that life has started imitating art to a disturbing degree. Indeed, Robert Altman declared after the attacks that 'Nobody would have thought to commit an atrocity like that unless they'd seen it in a movie . . . we created this atmosphere and taught them how to do it' (2001). Although it is improbable that terrorists stole ideas from Hollywood blockbusters, the similarities between pre-9/11 cinema and the public response to the atrocity suggest that Hollywood cinema of the 1990s helped shape pre-formed narratives of how the nation should respond to an attack.

This essay is therefore something of a devil's advocate in relation to the main currents of scholarship studying the impact of 9/11 on American popular culture because its argument is that the terrorist attacks of September 2001 did not cause a profound change in America's self-image, despite assertions to the contrary. As Terence McSweeney notes, 'It became common in the months and years after 11 September to suggest that 9/11 "changed everything", a phrase that echoed from politician to commentator and back again' (2014: 30). Even Pew Research, an organisation dedicated to carefully surveying American public opinion, felt compelled to announce without any evidence that 'America's view of the world changed dramatically, and perhaps permanently, on Sept. 11' (2001b). Pronouncements of a new era in history possess an emotional resonance equal to the shock of the event, yet the examples of *Independence Day* and *The Siege* should prompt us to ask what exactly changed: if pre-9/11 cinema anticipates the post-9/11 world, then in what sense is 9/11 a watershed?

To clarify, it is not that the events of that horrible day had no impact on American culture, but to date that impact has been more limited than many claim. McSweeney explains that 'the master narrative of the cultural trauma of 9/11 was quickly formed within a matter of days of the attacks' (2014: 10), but we should ask how a master narrative could form so quickly in a country of over three hundred million people spread across a continent; even given the mass media's reach and ubiquity, the speed is astonishing. Moreover, the essence of trauma is that the traumatic event refuses easy comprehension. As Cathy Caruth explains, 'trauma is described as the response to an unexpected or overwhelming violent event or events that are not fully grasped as they occur' (1996: 91). Yet despite the traumatic nature of 9/11, the American public was surprisingly quick to assimilate it into a master narrative. In this essay, I argue that the master narratives of both the 'War on Terror' and its opponents were pre-formed in the 1990s and thus available to hand when they suddenly became critical for American society. It is often argued that popular culture both reflected and shaped how the USA responded to 9/11, but what is overlooked is how popular culture shaped in advance American responses to 9/11 by creating consistent ideas about how Americans might respond to an external attack.

These narratives are tied to the long-standing belief that the USA is uniquely consecrated to the protection of liberty and democracy, yet this belief has produced two contradictory attitudes. As Henry Kissinger notes, 'The first is that America serves its values best by perfecting democracy at home, thereby acting as a beacon for the rest of mankind; the second, that America's values impose on it an obligation to crusade for them around the world' (1994: 18). Hellmut Lotz defines these attitudes as Isolationism and Leadership:

> Isolationism fears the vulnerability of America's uniqueness through exposure to an alien and corrupt environment . . . proponents of Leadership focus on America's moral strength and political power to spread and protect the American way of life . . . in less fortunate areas of the world. Like the American Dream, Leadership is optimistic and assumes equality among humans, while Isolationism is pessimistic and makes a qualitative distinction between Americans and foreigners. (1997: 82)

After victory in the Cold War, belief in American exceptionalism was reinforced and inspired visions of global leadership through the universality of the American way while simultaneously encouraging isolationist anxieties about the corruption of American values through contact with the outside world. These narratives would find new forms in the 1990s as the USA negotiated a world without the threat of the Soviet Union.

It is important, though, not to associate Leadership and Isolationism with political traditions of right and left. Douglas Kellner, for example, argues in *Cinema Wars* that 'film and culture in the United States has been a battleground between competing social groups, with some films advancing liberal or radical positions and others reproducing conservative ones' (2010: 1). Yet this rather binary division and Kellner's personal dislike of 'the noxiousness and lunacy of the rightwing extremists running the country' (2010: 8) clouds his understanding of both American cinema and how the traditions of Leadership and Isolationism are not isomorphic with conservatives and liberals. At different times, particular versions of Leadership and Isolationism have been deployed by both conservatives and liberals, depending on internal politics and external events, and thus the challenge is to understand how these shifts are represented in and shaped by popular culture.

This chapter will examine how Leadership and Isolationist narratives developed in Hollywood cinema of the 1990s; popular culture is a vital link between policy elites and the public because it represents, in Mark Lacey's words, 'a space where "commonsense" ideas about global politics and history are (re)-produced and where stories about what is acceptable behaviour from states and individuals are naturalised and legitimised' (2003: 614). It was these narratives the American public drew on after 9/11, leaning first towards the Leadership narrative before swinging back to a more Isolationist stance in the wake of the Iraq War and Guantanamo Bay. From this perspective, 9/11 did not fundamentally reshape views of America's place in the world but instead gave a violent push to the pendulum, causing public opinion to oscillate rapidly between the two available narratives.

II. THE JUST CRUSADER

The end of the Cold War concluded the meta-narrative of global resistance to communism that had framed US attitudes for two generations. As Henry Hyde, Chairman of the House International Relations Committee, said on 7 March 2001, 'the principal problem [for the US] is that we have no long-term strategy, no practical plan for shaping the future' (quoted in Cameron 2002: xv). In this vacuum, the publication of Francis Fukuyama's *The End of History and the Last Man* in 1992 generated an inordinate amount of attention as Fukuyama used Kojeve's interpretation of Hegel to conceive a historical dialectic which had now achieved its final synthesis: 'liberal democracy may constitute the "end point of mankind's ideological evolution" and "the end of history"' (1992: xi). All nations were thus heading towards the USA's shining city on a hill. Fukuyama's theory rested on the assumption that industrialisation creates similar social phenomena such as 'urbanization, bureaucratization, the breakdown of extended family and tribal ties, and increasing levels of education' (1992: 89), and so the 'enormously productive and dynamic economic world . . . has a tremendous homogenizing power' (1992: 108). This makes the world capitalist while man's 'natural' desire for recognition can only be satisfied by participation in liberal democracy. In the bullish atmosphere following the USSR's collapse, this argument solidified some key elements of the Leadership narrative: a) the USA's values really are universal; b) the USA is the natural global leader because it is the arc towards which history is bending; c) the USA should project its power to neutralise those on the wrong side of history and shepherd the weak through the valley of darkness.

What helped render this narrative a species of neo-conservatism in the 1990s was the nationalistic edge, the championing of the free market, and the implicit mandate to use force to make the world a better place. In popular cinema, these elements cohered into a master narrative for Leadership in the post-Cold War world. Across a range of popular blockbusters in the decade before 9/11, American cinema imagined the USA as a nation whose universal values sublimated its diverse people into a common unity, as a morally innocent country that could be provoked to justifiable violence by external attack, with the locus for national pride being the president, who would lead America as its Commander-in-Chief. Reflecting a distinctively American belief, the military was seen as emblematic of America's virtues. Whereas during the Vietnam War the military had a decidedly more mixed appraisal, by the 1990s popular culture tended to depict the army as a bastion of loyalty and honour amid the corruption of Washington. Politics was messy and compromising, whereas military action was noble and clear-cut. The films that most clearly illustrate this narrative are *Independence Day* (1996) and *Pearl Harbor* (2001).

A fundamental element of the Leadership narrative is that the USA should lead the world because, as its people are so diverse, it effectively is the world. As John Carlos Rowe has argued, this negates cultural and geopolitical differences by 'importing' the world in order 'to render global differences aspects of the US nation' (2004: 588). In Hollywood cinema of the 1990s, this manifested itself in two ways: celebrations of American diversity and minimisation of other nations' importance. The celebrations of diversity were apparent in the resurgence of the disaster movie ethos; disaster movies typically throw disparate people into a dangerous situation, forcing them to cooperate in order to survive, which affirms society's basic unity. In *Independence Day*, the main characters are an idealised cross-section of America: President Whitmore is an archetypal WASP, Captain Hiller is an African American fighter pilot, and David Levinson is a Jewish computer genius. The minor characters include an alcoholic veteran with three Hispanic children and Hiller's fiancée, Jasmine, a streetwise stripper who befriends the refined first lady, Marilyn Whitmore. The straightforward framing suggests equality between the characters and their individualism is contrasted with the homogenous aliens, implying that beneath America's diversity lies an immense communal strength that is greater than superficially more organised enemies. As Jude Davies argues, the film 'imagines the United States as fitted for global leadership and military pre-eminence by ascribing to it the status of *the* privileged site for the integration of racial and ethnic difference' (2005: 399). *Pearl Harbor* employs a similar disaster movie structure during the attack. Mechanics strive to get the fighter pilot protagonists, Rafe and Danny, into the air so they can fight back. Dorie Miller, an African American cook, mans the guns and shoots down a Zero, while nurses improvise tourniquets from stockings and collect blood donations in coke bottles as the wounded flood in. The Japanese army's organised and disciplined ranks contrast starkly with the anarchic individualism of the US forces, with Rafe and Danny flying to the rescue in hula shirts. This exaltation of *E Pluribus Unum* obscures deep divisions within American society. Although Dorie Miller laments institutional racism, no character is personally racist towards him. The film also ignores the fate of the Japanese American civilians we see in Hawaii because their internment would undermine the image of a diverse nation pulling together for survival. This disaster movie ethos was repeated in other films of the period, such as *Deep Impact* (1998) or *Armageddon* (1998), which showed ordinary Americans uniting to save a world which, through their own diversity, they also represent.

Where this became problematic for international audiences was the depiction of other nations as ancillary to American heroism. In a review of *Independence Day* for the BBC, Neil Smith derided 'an entire species of technically superior aliens bested in all departments by good old Uncle Sam and his can-do spirit' (2000). Max Herrmann for the German film magazine *Artechock* sarcastically noted that 'durch die extraterristriche Bedrohung bekommen wir einen Grund, uns alle, ob Chinesen oder Iraker, der Fuhrung der einzigen wirklichen Großmacht, God's Own Country, anzuschliessen' (1996).[1] Although the whole world is attacked, we rarely see non-Americans, who are peripheral to the main storyline. This reflected a general disregard of the outside world in the 1990s with 'coverage of foreign affairs in television . . . [down] by 50 percent since the 1980s' (Cameron 2002: 104). The three cities shown being destroyed are Los Angeles, New York, and Washington; foreign cities are assumed to be destroyed by extension but this omission implies that an attack on the USA is in itself an attack on humanity. The most striking example of this ego-centricity comes when the USA coordinates a counterattack among allies desperate for American leadership. As a British officer standing uselessly in the desert exclaims, 'It's about bloody time. What do they want us to do?' Yet the scorn for this was nothing compared to the response in Britain to the portrayal of the Battle of Britain in *Pearl Harbor*, which seems to be won single-handedly by Ben Affleck. As Rafe McCawley's British CO remarks, 'if there are many more back home like you, God help anyone who goes to war with America'. S. P. McKenzie, in *The Battle of Britain on Screen*, describes the film as giv-ing the impression 'that Britain is on its last legs and will fall without the likes of McCawley coming to the rescue' (2007: 133), and cata-logues some appalled British responses, of which 'putrid' may be the most concise. The depiction of allies waiting helplessly for American leadership conveniently combines unilateralism and multilateralism; the US leads and the rest willingly follow! This attitude both reflects how 'most Americans fundamentally doubt the relevance of international events to their own lives' (Pew 1997) and helped shape the idea of the 'coalition of the willing' to describe international cover for unilateral US actions during the 'War on Terror'.

In order for the US to remain morally innocent, it is vital that the attack on the USA be unprovoked. In *Independence Day*, the US attempts to make peace with the aliens until the president has a 'vision' that they are pure evil and must be destroyed; yet *Pearl Harbor* is even more egregious because it takes a well-studied historical event and nonetheless creates a nationalistic tale of innocence shattered by unprovoked aggression. In contrast to the complexity of *From Here to Eternity* (1953) or the balanced view from both sides of *Tora! Tora! Tora!* (1970), *Pearl Harbor* treats the subject in a jingoistic manner, simplifying history in order to present a 'portrait of the peaceful and idyllic world of Pearl Harbor before the attack, a world of camaraderie and innocence that is violated' (Landy 2004: 89). As the Zeros fly over Hawaii, they pass scenes of typical Americana. Boy scouts in the mountains and children playing baseball watch the planes with no clue as to their purpose. A number of scenes involving naval intelligence absolve it of failing to anticipate the attack. This construction of national innocence requires the film to ignore the complex background to the war. Admiral Yamamoto makes a brief reference to oil shortages but the war's primary cause is Japanese imperialism, which the US is totally justified in opposing in the name of freedom.

Even more interesting may be films from the period which absolve the American military of wrongdoing in Vietnam. In *Rules of Engagement* (2000), the film's excellent first act turns, oddly, into an absolution of the army's past. A Marine unit sent to evacuate the American embassy in Yemen comes under attack from demonstrators and in the confusion the commanding officer orders his men to open fire on the crowd, killing eighty-three people. Instead of exploring the difficulty of decision making amid chaos and violence, or the clash between moral and political imperatives, the trial of Colonel Childers hinges on a parallel situation in Vietnam and the absolution of Childers symbolically justifies any transgressions committed there, retrospectively turning the US army in Vietnam into the band of brothers seen in *Saving Private Ryan* (1998). This determination to construct a national sense of innocence was repeated after 9/11 with only 21 per cent of Americans believing 'that past US unfairness may have motivated the attacks' (Pew 2001a).

The locus of national pride in these narratives is the president and, in a peculiarly American twist, the president is never more presidential than when he is acting as Commander-in-Chief rather than as a politician.

In *Independence Day*, the difference between soldiers and politicians is represented by the characters of General Grey and Defence Secretary Nimziki. Grey is confident, purposeful and loyal; in contrast, Nimziki is 'a snivelling little weasel'. Stuck between these two is President Whitmore, a Gulf War veteran whose poll ratings are slipping because of 'too much politics'. However, at the beginning President Whitmore cannot lead because he is unsure whether he is a soldier or a politician. Only when he fires Nimziki can he become the ideal president, a warrior-chief, who personally leads the victorious counterattack. Clarity of purpose is associated with military action while politics requires too many compromises. *Pearl Harbor* similarly prefers to show Roosevelt as a commander and leader of the people rather than a politician. His speech to Congress about 'a day that will live in infamy' is intercut with shots of ordinary Americans listening on the radio, uniting FDR with the people, and he becomes their commander in the next scene when he asks the military to strike back. Later, as the Doolittle raid approaches Tokyo, we see FDR delivering a radio address that extols the virtues of America's armed forces. This trend of glorifying the president as a warrior-chief reached its peak with the success of *Air Force One* (1997), in which Harrison Ford's president is an action hero single-handedly defeating terrorists aboard Air Force One. One only has to imagine a British or German film portraying David Cameron or Angela Merkel respectively as action heroes to understand how ludicrous this would be for any other country. These popular portrayals of the president as decisive military leader were echoed by the 'extraordinary levels . . . of support for President Bush' (Pew 2001a) recorded after 9/11 as he, too, attempted to cast himself as Commander-in-Chief.

The crusader narrative that emerged in the 1990s thus depicted the USA as an innocent, peaceful nation with universal values and, if attacked, its diverse people will unite behind a strong president and apply the clarity and manly vigour of military force to defeat evil. This is identical to what McSweeney describes as 'the master narrative' of 9/11: 'a heinous and unprovoked attack on a virtuous and blameless nation, an attack that was impossible to anticipate and that brought about a reluctant "end of innocence" for the United States' (2014: 10). The reason this master narrative came into play so quickly has less to do with the Bush administration's PR campaign than that this narrative had already been forged on screen. Indeed, *Pearl Harbor* was released mere months before the September 11 attacks and can be seen as a template for the narrative that emerged in real life later that autumn. Similarly, Davies notes that *Independence Day*'s 'terms of reference' were applied wholesale in the wake of 9/11, 'making sense of it as the work of alien evil born of a hatred of civilised values, and defining the

Figure 10.1 President Whitmore (Bill Pullman) in *Independence Day* (1996) (upper) and President Bush in 2003 (lower). Public Domain Image. Photo by Tyle J. Clements.

United States as the natural world leader in combating such evil due to its longstanding status as a repository of those values' (2005: 403). Such attitudes pervade the official 9/11 commission report, which glosses over Bin Laden's criticisms of American policy in the Middle East by saying his 'grievance with the United States may have started in reaction to specific US policies but it quickly became far deeper' (2004: 51). The enemy is defined in opposition to American values and not in terms of political goals: 'its purpose is to rid the world of religious and political pluralism, the plebiscite, and equal rights for women' (2004: xvi). In contrast, the report praises Americans for 'their amazing resilience and courage as they fought back' (2004: xvii). Thus, as in the films discussed, the USA is blameless for an attack by evil external forces and the nation unites to combat the threat. In a time of crisis, the public turned to the president and the worst attacks ever suffered on American soil had the ironic effect of giving President Bush, in early 2002, 'unprecedented high (90 per cent) approval ratings for his conduct in office' (Cameron 2002: 189). Finally, there was a perceived sea change in America's attitude towards other nations. 'According to one European Foreign Minister, quoted by Reuters on 7 March 2002, "we are witnessing a phenomenon without precedent. We have never seen such disdain from Washington. Not only is there a complete absence of consultation, but there is an exaltation of unilateralism and the militarization of foreign policy thinking"' (Cameron 2002: 194). This phenomenon was not without precedent, however, for it merely extended attitudes repeatedly expressed in pre-9/11 cinema. Yet the master narrative of 9/11 was not the only one anticipated by cinema of the 1990s; alongside the blockbuster nationalistic hits were less popular films that dealt with Isolationist themes which would become more prevalent once the scandals of Abu Ghraib and the occupation of Iraq began to cast doubt on the simplistic master narrative.

III. THE TARNISHED CITY ON A HILL

While Fukuyama's 'end of history' thesis was hugely influential, it was immediately criticised in Samuel Huntington's controversial *The Clash of Civilisations*, which argues (contra Fukuyama) that industrialisation does not produce homogenisation; instead, different cultures seek a form of modernisation that is compatible with their fundamental beliefs. In place of a single model of liberal capitalism, Huntington sees the world dividing into seven or eight major civilisations. In Huntington's view:

It is sheer hubris to think that because Soviet communism has collapsed, the West has won the world for all time and that Muslims, Chinese, Indians and others are going to rush to embrace Western liberalism as the only alternative. The Cold War division of humanity is over. The more fundamental divisions of humanity in terms of ethnicity, religions, and civilizations remain and spawn new conflicts. (1998: 66)

US values are not universal. Indeed, 'the survival of the West depends on Americans reaffirming their Western identity and Westerners accepting their civilisation as unique not universal and uniting to renew and preserve it against challenges from non-Western societies' (1998: 20). This calls for a period of retrenchment rather than expansion. It is a measure of the left's confusion on foreign policy at this time that the major new ideas on the USA's place in the world are from differing strands of the conservative movement, but the fact that some ideas from both arguments are compatible with left-wing beliefs shows the difficulty of neatly dividing politics into opposing camps.

There is a persistent concern in 1990s cinema that American values face a threat from external engagement and internal corruption, yet the films that deal with these themes also struggle to advance any solution to the problems of the post-Cold War world. As Henry Kissinger argues, 'America is more preponderant than it was . . . yet, ironically, power has become more diffuse. Thus, America's ability to employ it to shape the rest of the world has actually decreased' (1994: 809). Many Americans worried about the USA abandoning its core values amid foreign entanglements, foreshadowing a growing isolationism. If the world cannot be shaped according to American ideals, then the US should withdraw and concentrate on improving its own society and protecting America's unique (but not universal) values. The potential for corruption leads to a lack of clear-cut villains and as flawed humans fall into a spiral of violence, military action is no solution but merely an escalation of aggression. No film exemplifies these concerns better than *The Siege*.

While *Independence Day* and *Pearl Harbor* depict the USA uniting under threat, *The Siege* depicts a country torn by internal power struggles. The kidnapping of an Islamic terrorist leader by the sinister General Devereaux initiates a wave of suicide bombings in New York. Anthony Hubbard and his partner Frank Haddad lead the FBI counterterrorism unit responsible for locating the terrorist cells, but their investigations are hampered by CIA agent Sharon Bridger, who conceals information and tenaciously defends her Palestinian source and lover, Samir Nazhde, from the FBI. Departmental infighting denotes a lack of unity. Sharon and Hubbard continually fight turf wars over access to evidence and sources while New York burns. Ironically, the only thing that can unite them is their opposition to Devereaux, who seizes control of the situation and proceeds to make it worse. The divisions between the three are visually depicted after the torture of an Arab suspect; as Devereaux emerges from the room wiping his hands, he looks at Hubbard and the two walk away in different directions while Sharon stays in place with her head bowed, unable to choose between right

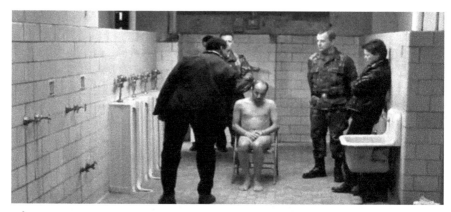

Figure 10.2 Torture scene from *The Siege* (1998) (upper) and photo from Abu Ghraib in 2003 (lower). Public Domain Image.

and wrong. The right-wing military villain is the flipside of the heroic ordinary soldier in 1990s cinema, and films as diverse as *Antz* (1998) or *A Few Good Men* (1992) picture the military's clarity and sense of purpose turning on a society whose disorder and weakness disgusts it. This character archetype surfaced in popular discourse after 9/11 both in criticisms of macho administration rhetoric and on the more extreme end from conspiracy theorists who believed 9/11 was a government conspiracy to justify increased military spending, government surveillance and war in the Middle East.

The absence of unity is partly caused by and most dangerous to vulnerable minorities. In *The Siege*, ethnic Arab enclaves in Brooklyn become sites where terrorists conceal themselves among the populace, which places even the good Arab American characters in an ambivalent position. A montage sequence shows Frank Haddad, Hubbard's partner, playing football with his son and Hubbard before cutting to a Muslim ceremony in his home which Hubbard and other FBI agents also attend. This shows how one can be both Arab and American, but the terrorist attacks create serious difficulties for him within both communities. Samir taunts Frank about not being a true Arab but he is not American either as his son is placed in a concentration camp, echoing the internment of Japanese Americans during the Second World War that was conspicuously ignored in *Pearl Harbor*. Furious, Frank quits the FBI, declaring, 'I am not their sand-nigger anymore', implying the persecution of Arabs is a product of racism. Ironically, many Arab Americans objected to *The Siege* on exactly these grounds; as Jack Shaheen argues, 'the movie not only reinforces historically damaging stereotypes, but also advances a dangerously generalised portrayal of Arabs as rabidly anti-American' (2007: 28). Although the film ends with a multicultural crowd cheering the end of martial law, this is 'an unconvincing resolution of a question that is rather more complex' (Prince 2009: 61), especially as the closing vision of unity is undermined by the internecine fighting and vulnerability of minorities. The changing make-up of multicultural America that *Independence Day* celebrates is treated in *The Siege* as a source of potential conflict with no clear resolution. The spectre of racism haunts other Isolationist-themed films such as *Three Kings* (1999), which connects the Iraq War with American racism, thus undermining the innocence and purity necessary to justify military conflict.

In Isolationist films, contact with other cultures contaminates America's unique values. In *The Siege*, the Arab world corrupts Americans who have prolonged contact with it. Sharon is an amoral liar whose licentiousness both attracts and repels Hubbard. Many reviewers criticised the negative portrayal of aggressive female sexuality but missed that it, in true orientalist fashion, signifies her corruption by the east. 'Orientals are inveterate liars' (Said 1978: 38) and practise 'the freedom of licentious sex' (1978: 190) in contrast to 'the clarity, directness, and nobility of the Anglo-Saxon race' (1978: 39). The film seeks to moderate its orientalist edge by having a black actor take the place of the Anglo-Saxon race, even though his character is an Establishment man 'of heroic proportions: an ex-paratrooper who studied law, a Catholic liberal who believes in the system' (Hollings 1999). His liberalism is contrasted with Devereaux's oriental despotism. Devereaux believes he can act with impunity because 'right here, right now, I am the law!' When he and Sharon torture an Arab suspect in a scene that eerily prefigures Abu Ghraib, they discuss methods employed by different Middle Eastern countries. In disbelief Hubbard asks, 'what if what they really want is for us to... put soldiers on the streets and have Americans looking over their shoulders? Bend the law. Shred the Constitution just a little bit. Because if we torture him . . . then everything we have fought and bled and died for is over.' The focus shifts from stopping the terrorists to preserving American values, a debate played out in real life over the question of torture. After the release of the Senate's torture report in December 2014, Obama said that torture was 'contrary to who we are' (quoted in Bruton 2014), while Senator Angus King paradoxically declared, 'This is not America. This is not who we are' (quoted in Beinart 2014), despite speaking about a 600-page report detailing exactly what American officials did during the 'War on Terror'. Implicit in the denials is the idea of a virtuous America that has somehow been corrupted through engagement with the outside world.

As the city succumbs to violence, Hubbard attempts to defend American values while Sharon warns him he cannot play by rules his enemies refuse to acknowledge. He responds by telling her 'this isn't the Middle East yet'. However, in *The Siege* New York is slowly turned into yet another violence-plagued Middle Eastern city. The film begins by depicting violence in the Middle East and then cuts to a muezzin calling the people to prayer. The camera then backs away to reveal the mosque is actually in Brooklyn, with the skyscrapers of Manhattan towering behind. Aerial tracking shots of New York are accompanied by haunting Arabic vocals that defamiliarise the well-known images. The military presence in Brooklyn is portrayed in images reminiscent of the occupied territories, such as Arabic youths throwing rocks at armoured cars. Yet the attempt to purge the city of foreign elements is more horrific as concentration camps are set up with internees freezing behind chain-link fences and barbed wire. As New York visually becomes a foreign city marked by violence and repression, the threat is no longer terrorism but how the fear of terrorism corrupts American values. In doing so, the film 'anticipates the extreme positions the Bush-Cheney administration would take and lays out counterarguments' (Kellner 18), arguments which would soon be used by the administration's opponents.

As the boundary blurs between good and evil, military action becomes not noble and decisive but part of an escalating spiral. Unlike in the Leadership narrative, the USA is not seen as innocent. *The Siege* portrays violence as cyclical so the US is partly responsible. The film opens with a montage of news reports on the bombing of an American barracks in Saudi Arabia, followed by footage of Bill Clinton pledging to punish those responsible intercut with the kidnapping of Sheikh Ahmed bin Talal, the man behind the bombing. The FBI receives a message saying 'Release him' but they don't know to whom it refers as the different agencies refuse to share information. The violence begins in New York when the terrorists blow up a bus. The FBI kills the remaining members of the first terrorist cell before a second blows up a theatre. Hubbard kills a terrorist in a standoff before a third cell blows up FBI headquarters and the government declares martial law. Sharon confesses America's complicity when she finally explains why they are attacking the USA. 'He was our ally. We were financing him. Then there was a policy shift . . . we just stopped helping them. They were slaughtered.' Hubbard responds in a disillusioned voice, 'you taught them how to make bombs . . . and now they're here, doing what you taught them how to do.' Like Bin Laden (on whom the character is probably based), the sheikh is an example of foreign policy blowback. Rather than being innocent, America suffers in Isolationist narratives as a consequence of immoral actions against enemies given a rare level of humanity in Hollywood cinema: 'it is exceptional for a Hollywood action-adventure film, especially for one that deals with Middle Eastern terrorism, to provide the film's antagonist with a backstory or any human feelings other than insanity or vengeance' (Vanhala 2008). Again, *Three Kings* offers a point of comparison as one of the few Hollywood films to humanise Arabs while pointing out how Americans sold out their own allies in Iraq. The complicity in the cycle of violence critiques military action, but it is unclear what the solution to the foreign policy problem should be.

The core of the Isolationist narrative in the 1990s is now clear: a lack of moral purity and unity in the USA, possibly contracted from foreign entanglements, undermines its global mission and in a world of moral confusion where both sides have committed atrocities the use of military force simply exacerbates the problem. In the ebullient 1990s, these themes were not as popular as the Leadership narrative; not only did *The Siege* do significantly worse ($40.9 million) at the US box office than *Independence Day* ($306 million) and *Pearl Harbor* ($198.5 million), but many audiences actually thought Bruce Willis' nationalistic General Devereaux was the hero: 'at a recent preview screening, the public cheered Willis almost to the end, even as he tortured a suspect and then calmly shot him' (Kehr 1998). Although marginal in 1990s cinema, Isolationist themes emerged forcefully with opposition to the Iraq War and pose the questions at the heart of such later films as *Munich* (2005) and *The Dark Knight* (2008).

IV. CONCLUSION

It is tempting to assert that everything changed on 9/11; however, the narratives that influenced the American public in its aftermath were not born on that day but pre-written by the history of American exceptionalism and engraved in the popular imagination by Hollywood cinema of the 1990s. On that morning in 2001, the American public had before it two visions, Leadership and Isolationist, which determined its response. The majority, by inclination and under the influence of White House rhetoric, embraced the vision of the US leading a global fight against an evil enemy. The protracted occupation of Iraq, however, revealed the limits of US power and the more realistic views of the Isolationists gained traction: 'The casualties of the Iraq Syndrome could be the Bush doctrine, unilateralism, preemption, preventive war, and indispensable-nationhood. Indeed, these once-fashionable (and sometimes self-infatuated) concepts are already picking up a patina of quaintness' (Mueller 2005: 5). In retrospect, it was only a matter of time before the Leadership ideal encountered reality and crumbled, while the Isolationist stance gained strength through interaction with a world that stubbornly refuses to conform to American values. These shifts in public opinion were charted in Pew's quadrennial 'America's Place in the World' survey, which in 2005 recorded 'a revival of isolationist sentiment among the general public'. Over a ten-year perspective from 1995 to 2005, the attacks of 11 September 2001 created a spike in interventionist sentiment before a return to the post-Cold War trend of isolationism. While their long-term impact is as yet unclear, it is too early to make sweeping statements about 9/11's impact on American attitudes.

It is tempting for people to attribute seismic shifts to a single dramatic event but, no matter how shocking, the event can only be interpreted within the framework of pre-existing beliefs. Before 9/11, a complacent public beheld opposing visions of Leadership and Isolationism but felt no urgency to choose. The terrorist attacks pushed the pendulum of public opinion violently into motion. Following the White House's lead, it initially swung towards Leadership but the Iraq War exposed this vision's shaky foundations. Since then, the pendulum has swung back towards Isolationism. Yet as the terrorist attacks themselves showed, it is no longer possible for the USA to retreat. In the long term, the 11 September attacks may come to be seen as dramatic proof of what Kissinger defined in 1994 as the USA's fundamental foreign policy problem: 'What *is* new about the emerging world order is that, for the first time, the United States can neither withdraw from the world nor dominate it' (19). The Bush administration's failed attempt to dominate underscored the limits of American power and encouraged a swing towards Isolationism, but no one today can seriously believe it is irrelevant for the USA if ISIS gains control in Syria or the Taliban return in Afghanistan. Perhaps the true legacy of 9/11 may one day be that it forced an end to both Leadership and Isolationist narratives and led to the construction of a new narrative, one that will be crafted not just in elite policy circles but through the emergence and acceptance of a new vision for the USA in Hollywood cinema. It is the emergence of that narrative that will truly mark the post-9/11 film.

NOTE

1. 'Through the extra-terrestrial threat, we get a reason, all of us, whether Chinese or Iraqi, to fall into line behind the leadership of the only true Great Power, God's Own Country' (my translation).

REFERENCES

Altman, Robert (2001), 'Hollywood "Inspired US Attacks"', BBC interview, 17 October 2001, last accessed 29 November 2015: http://news.bbc.co.uk/2/hi/entertainment/1604151.stm

Beinart, Peter (2014), 'Torture is Who We Are', *The Atlantic*, 11 December 2014, last accessed 29 November 2015: http://www.theatlantic.com/international/archive/2014/12/torture-is-who-we-are-cia-report/383670/

Bruton, F. Brinley (2014), 'President Obama: CIA's Post-9/11 Torture was "Contrary to Who We Are"', NBC, 10 December 2014, last accessed 29 November 2015: http://www.nbcnews.com/storyline/cia-torture-report/president-obama-cias-post-9-11-torture-was-contrary-who-n265276

Cameron, Fraser (2002), *US Foreign Policy after the Cold War: Global Hegemon or Reluctant Sheriff?*, London: Routledge.

Caruth, Cathy (1996), *Unclaimed Experience: Trauma, Narrative, and History*, Baltimore: Johns Hopkins University Press.

Davies, Jude (2005), '"Diversity. America. Leadership. Good over Evil." Hollywood multiculturalism and American imperialism in *Independence Day* and *Three Kings*', *Patterns of Prejudice*, 39.4, pp. 397–415.

Fukuyama, Francis (1992), *The End of History and the Last Man*, London: Penguin.

Herrmann, Max (1996), review of *Independence Day*, *Artechock*, July 1996, last accessed 29 November 2015: http://www.artechock.de/film/text/kritik/i/inday.htm

Hollings, Ken (1999), review of *The Siege*, *Sight and Sound*, February 1999, last accessed 29 November 2015: http://old.bfi.org.uk/sightandsound/review/41

Huntington, Samuel P. (1998), *The Clash of Civilizations and the Remaking of World Order*, London: Touchstone.

Kehr, Dave (1998), review of *The Siege*, 'Not Our Coup of Tea', *New York Daily News*, 6 November 1998, last accessed 30 November 2015: http://www.nydailynews.com/archives/nydn-features/not-coup-tea-army-takeover-plot-overshadows-threat-arab-terrorists-silly-civics-lesson-siege-article-1.810182

Kellner, Douglas (2010), *Cinema Wars: Hollywood Film and Politics in the Bush-Cheney Era*, Oxford: Wiley-Blackwell.

Kissinger, Henry (1994), *Diplomacy*, London: Touchstone.

Lacey, Mark (2003), 'War, Cinema, and Moral Anxiety', *Alternatives: Global, Local, Political*, 28.5, pp. 611–36.

Landy, Marcia (2004), '"America Under Attack": Pearl Harbor, 9/11, and History in the Media', in Wheeler Winston Dixon (ed.), *Film and Television after 9/11*, Carbondale: Southern Illinois University Press, pp. 79–100.

Lotz, Hellmut (1997), 'Myth and NAFTA: The Use of Core Values in US Politics', in Valerie M. Hudson (ed.), *Culture & Foreign Policy*, London: Rienner, pp. 73–96.

McKenzie, S. P. (2007), *The Battle of Britain on Screen: 'The Few' in British Film and Television Drama*, Edinburgh: Edinburgh University Press.

McSweeney, Terence (2014), *The 'War on Terror' and American Film: 9/11 Frames per Second*, Edinburgh: Edinburgh University Press.

Mueller, John (2005), 'The Iraq Syndrome', *Foreign Affairs*, November–December 2005, last accessed 30 November 2015: https://www.foreignaffairs.com/articles/north-korea/2005-10-01/iraq-syndrome

National Commission on Terrorist Attacks upon the United States (2004), *The 9/11 Commission report: final report of the National Commission on Terrorist Attacks upon the United States*, New York: W. W. Norton.

Pew Research Centre (1997), 'America's Place in the World II', *Pew Research*, 10 October 1997, last accessed 29 November 2015: http://www.people-press.org/1997/10/10/americas-place-in-the-world-ii/#introduction-and-summary

— (2001a), 'Military Action a Higher Priority than Homeland Defence', *Pew Research*, 27 September 2001, last accessed 29 November 2015: http://www.people-press.org/2001/09/27/military-action-a-higher-priority-than-homeland-defense/

— (2001b), 'The View Before 9/11: America's Place in the World', *Pew Research*, 18 October 2001, last accessed 29 November 2015: http://www.people-press.org/2001/10/18/the-view-before-911-americas-place-in-the-world/

— (2005), 'America's Place in the World IV', *Pew Research*, 17 November, last accessed 29 November 2015: http://www.people-press.org/2005/11/17/opinion-leaders-turn-cautious-public-looks-homeward/

Prince, Stephen (2009), *Firestorm: American Film in the Age of Terrorism*, New York: Columbia University Press.

Rowe, John Carlos (2004), 'Culture, US Imperialism, and Globalisation', *American Literary History*, 16.4, pp. 575–95.

Said, Edward (1978), *Orientalism*, London: Routledge.

Shaheen, Jack (2007), 'Hollywood's Muslim Arabs', *The Muslim World*, 90, pp. 22–42.

Smith, Neil (2000), review of *Independence Day*, BBC, 18 December 2000, last accessed 29 November 2015: http://www.bbc.co.uk/films/2000/12/18/independence_day_1996_review.shtml

Vanhala, Helena (2008), 'Civil Society under Siege – terrorism and government response to terrorism in *The Siege*', *Jump Cut*, 50: http://www.ejumpcut.org/archive/jc50.2008/Seige/index.html

PART III

Allegories of the 'War on Terror'

'Daddy, I'm scared. Can we go home?' Fear and Allegory in Frank Darabont's *The Mist* (2007)

Terence McSweeney

1.

This [The Mist] has become a rather potent metaphor for where I think humanity is poised at the moment. It becomes a total microcosm of our culture and what we're going through. The divisiveness. The fact that reasonable people are getting ground up in the machinery and agendas of the unreasonable people who are in power. The extremists are holding sway and the rest of us are just getting dragged along for the ride.

Frank Darabont (2007: 28)

At some point we may be the only ones left. That's okay with me. We are America.

George W. Bush (quoted in Woodward 2002: 81)

The science fiction and horror genres have often been read as manifestations of the prevailing fears and anxieties of the cultural moments in which they are made. Whether we consider Weimar-era German cinema (see Kracauer 1947; Kaes 2011), post-Second World War Japanese science-fiction film (see Yomota 2007; Tsutsui 2004) or the cycle of alien invasion narratives produced by the American film industry during the first decades of the Cold War (see Booker 2000; Starck 2010), genre films frequently emerge as visceral and potent cultural artefacts and not, as they are often regarded in the mainstream press, superficial and shallow frivolities. In a similar vein to the examples provided above, this chapter regards the science fiction and horror films produced during the 'War on Terror' period as profoundly affectual documents which bear a compelling testimony to the era. While on the surface they often appear to have no apparent connection to the tumultuous events of the decade, they function as telling allegories, able, for one reason or another, to engage with their turbulent age often in ways more resonant than many films which attempted to portray the period directly (see Lowenstein 2005). Thus, horror films like *The Village* (2004), *Hostel* (2005), *Land of the Dead* (2005), *28 Weeks Later* (2007), *I am Legend* (2008) and *Cabin in the Woods* (2012); and science fiction films like *The Forgotten* (2004), *War of the Worlds* (2005), *Cloverfield* (2008), *Avatar* (2009), *Knowing* (2009) and *Battle: Los Angeles* (2011), among others, regardless of how they were received on their release, or of the political perspectives they adopt, become far more than disposable pop culture artefacts; instead, they can be read and understood as vivid embodiments of the ideological conflicts of their times.

Despite a comprehensive body of work written on the value of allegory in literature and the arts, the allegorical form is still often considered lacking when compared to attempts at portraying reality 'directly' (see Benjamin 1977; Jameson 1981). Walter Benjamin suggested that allegory emerges most often in periods of crisis and uncertainty; correspondingly it is no coincidence that some of the most thought-provoking films to be produced by the American film industry in the new millennium are allegorical texts. It is the inherent malleability of the allegorical form which is ironically both its quintessential strength *and* its weakness. Perhaps the defining Cold War science fiction film, Don Siegel's *Invasion of the Body Snatchers* (1956), has been read as both an allegory of fears of communist influence spreading across the United States *and* of the encroachment of the House of UnAmerican Activities Commission on civil liberties in the same period; two seemingly paradoxical interpretations, yet both readings undoubtedly bind the film to the times in which it was made in ways hard to ignore (see Grant 2010). Of course, Jack Finney's 1955 novel on which the Siegel film was based has been adapted for the screen no fewer than three times in the subsequent decades, each version offering a dynamic engagement with the political climate in which it was produced: from Philip Kaufman's brilliantly cynical post-Vietnam, post-Watergate *Invasion of the Body Snatchers* (1978), to Abel Ferrara's visceral, body horror-esque *Body Snatchers* (1993), and Oliver Hirschbiegel's underwhelming *The Invasion* (2007), which contains repeated allusions to 9/11 and the 'War on Terror'. In their allegorical narratives these films do not simply metaphorically re-create specific historical moments from their respective eras, but are able to dramatise the prevailing moods of the times often in a provocative and articulate fashion.

One further reason that the allegorical form is met with such suspicion is that it can produce apophenic, almost Rorschachian, texts in which audiences are able to see that which they wish to see in the narratives and the imagery projected on the screen. Such was the impact of 9/11 on American culture and society that writers on new millennial film often found it reflected everywhere (see Pollard 2011) in a process I have elsewhere described as '9/11 apophenia' (see McSweeney 2014: 23). This chapter presents an analysis of a film which was widely interpreted as an allegory of the post-9/11 decade on its release six years after 11 September 2001, Frank Darabont's adaptation of the Stephen King novella *The Mist*, which was written in the late 1970s and published in 1980. In 2007 *The Mist* was one of many films in that year alone which seem to positively beat with the pulse of the decade. Films as diverse as *Michael Clayton, In the Valley of Elah, The Kingdom, Rendition, 300, The Bourne Ultimatum, There Will be Blood* and *The Brave One* were all released in 2007 and all are, I would argue, profoundly post-9/11 films regardless of what one's definition of the term encompasses.[1]

The cinematic adaptation of *The Mist* embodies several timely concerns of the 'War on Terror' era and a range of universal (although predominantly masculine) fears, while at the same time bearing the palimpsestic residue of the source novella's anxieties connected to the 1970s in which it was originally conceived and written.[2] On its release, reviews for the film were divisive: it was described by David Edelstein at *New York Magazine* as 'feeble-minded' and Chuck Wilson at *The Village Voice* labelled it a 'disaster', but others saw more to the tale of a disparate group of small-towners stranded inside a local supermarket plagued by what might be supernatural beasts outside and, perhaps even more dangerously, religious extremism inside. John Patterson in *The Guardian* went as far as to call it 'Darabont's masterpiece – a despairing, angry thriller, with the bleakest ending of any Hollywood movie in years'. He even postulated that it 'may one day be seen as America's definitive post 9/11 movie' (Patterson 2008: 7).

The film is certainly self-consciously designed to function as an allegory for the post-9/11 American experience, an interpretation that Darabont returned to as frequently in interviews as critics did in reviews of the film. Darabont draws richly from this source of cultural background throughout *The Mist*, and during the publicity drive for its release the tagline 'Fear Changes Everything' beckoned from posters.

Fear certainly is at the thematic centre of *The Mist*, as it is for much of the genre. Darabont remarked:

> It's an examination of fear. It's an examination of people oper-
> ating in a pressure cooker of fear where fear replaces reason.
> That's why I've always loved this story. It wasn't so much about
> the mist outside the windows with the groovy critters in it. It
> is about what the people are going through inside the market.
> (Quoted in Spelling 2008: 58)

After a seemingly harmonious small-town community is confronted by a traumatic event they could not have anticipated and cannot explain, the film explores what happens when the thin veneer of civilisation is fractured, revealing a Hobbesian world underneath, 'solitary, poor, nasty, brutish, and short' (62).

In the aftermath of the attacks on 11 September 2001 the concept of the political role of fear in modern society became widely discussed. Many suggested that America found itself living in a culture of fear which seemed to revolve around the phrase the 'War on Terror' itself. Zbigniew Brzezinski observed, 'The damage these three words have done – a classic self-inflicted wound – is infinitely greater than any wild dreams entertained by the fanatical perpetrators of the 9/11 attacks when they were plotting against us in distant Afghan caves' (2007). The propagation of this culture of fear proved beneficial for the Bush administration in gaining support from Congress, which would have been severely hindered without the links the administration drew between 9/11 and Iraq, whether concrete or symbolic. Indeed, Bush was subsequently propelled through the 2004 elections after success-fully portraying himself as the head of a nation both under siege and at war. Benjamin R. Barber, the author of *Fear's Empire. War, Terrorism, and Democracy* (2003), considered the future implications of such a methodology when he wrote, 'If Americans cannot find their way out of fear's realm, they are lost. No friendly European ally will dissuade them from the course of war, no adversarial rogue state will seem puny enough to ignore. Since fear is about perception not reality, the terror-ists can win without firing a shot' (2003: 217–18).

As one might expect, for a genre largely based around the concept of fear, horror films explored manifestations of this motif with par-ticular and sustained associations to the post-9/11 decade. Films like *The Village, Hostel, I am Legend, The Purge* (2013) and *Cabin in the Woods* returned to it with an eye on the developing 'War on Terror' narrative.[3] *The Mist* emerges as an uncompromising and visceral text that, on the whole, adheres closely to the narrative of the novella on which it is based. The changes it does adopt seem deliberately designed to situate the film much more emphatically in the post-9/11 era. The largest of these alterations is undoubtedly the ending which, as we will see, has been the source of much debate. *The Mist* was Darabont's fourth feature film as director and his third Stephen King adaptation after *The Shawshank Redemption* (1994) and *The Green Mile* (1999), both of which have narratives primarily set in prisons. On the surface *The Mist* seems very different to these two films both stylistically and thematically, yet as Stephen King himself wryly commented, 'It's still a story about people in prison. They're just in prison in a supermarket' (quoted in Magistrale 2009: 54).

II.

It is not terrorism but fear that is the enemy, and in the end, fear will not defeat fear.

Benjamin Barber (2003: 32)

The morning after a terrible storm has engulfed their Maine community, David Drayton (a familiar King archetype of the everyman artist) and his son Billy leave the home that has been in their family for generations to venture into the town for supplies at their local store, the Food House. On arrival they find the store crowded with what seems like the whole town seeking to do the same. Darabont quickly and efficiently introduces the cast as per the conventions of a disaster film, emphasising the normality of the environment and establishing the film's diverse cast of characters. As Maurice Yacowar wrote on the genre, 'The entire cross section of society is usually represented in the cast. The effect is the sense of the entire society under threat, even the world, instead of a situation of individual danger and fate' (1995: 268). Alongside their previously estranged neighbour Brent Norton (Andre Braugher), we meet the archetypal belligerent 'red neck' mechanics Jim and Myron (William Sadler and David Jensen), the quiet and unassuming store clerk Ollie (Toby Jones) and Mrs Reppler (Frances Sternhagen), the colourful septuagenarian teacher who finds time to criticise the government for its policies: 'We had damage at the school, wouldn't you know that's what we get for not fixing that roof when we should have, but with funds being cut every year. You'd think educating children would be more of a priority in this country but you'd be wrong. Government's got better things to spend our money on like corporate handouts and building bombs.' We are also introduced to Sally, the pretty checkout girl who informs David that electricity is down all over the town with only the store generators giving them power in the Food House. She prophetically adds, 'Only to keep the food cold, everything else, welcome to the Dark Ages and bring your chequebook.'[4] Perhaps most significantly Darabont introduces Mrs Carmody (Marcia Gay Harden), the local religious zealot who begins the film as a social outcast, taken seriously by no one, but who before long becomes a formidable and malicious presence.

The eponymous mist itself arrives just twelve minutes into the film, sweeping like an eerie blanket across the parking lot, blocking out the sun and only coming to a stop within a few feet of the doors of the Food House. While many writers on post-9/11 cinema have been too eager to see direct visual allusions to 11 September 2001 on the screens of new millennial American film, the way Darabont and his cinematographer Ronn Schmidt shoot the arrival of the mist seems a particularly explicit example. About the scene Kevin Wetmore in his *Post-9/11 Horror in America Cinema* (2012) wrote that the mist 'rolls through the town in a greyish cloud like the smoke, dust and debris on 9/11' (121), and Victoria McCollum suggested, 'The cloud of dust-like mist that rolls malevolently over the buildings, pavements, and vehicles, juxtaposed with the spellbound gazes of the citizens, is undoubtedly evocative of 9/11' (91). In the novella King writes, through David's first-person narration, 'I had a nutty feeling that I was watching some extra-good piece of visual effects, something dreamed up by Willis O'Brien or Douglas Turnbull', anticipating the repeated refrain that 9/11 was 'just like a movie' for those who witnessed it first-hand or vicariously through the television (see Usborne, quoted in Summers and Swann 70). In a single rather throwaway sentence King recognises that while experiencing something out of the ordinary, people reach to that which is familiar for a frame of reference. These connections are further emphasised in the film by the lingering close-ups of the incredulous faces of those within the supermarket and the image of a figure, Dan (Jeffrey De Munn), running from the mist with blood pouring down his face, screaming, 'Something in the mist! Something in the mist took John Lee!'

From this moment on the film becomes a horror-inflected siege film, with those inside the supermarket trapped as the Food House is transformed from a harmonious and communal space to something much more threatening.[5] The supermarket, like the shopping mall in *Dawn of the Dead* (1978), provides a convenient and socially relevant location for the site of societal breakdown post-9/11. The nature of the confined space and the apparent (though later confirmed) hostile forces outside is certainly similar to films like *The Birds* (1963) or *Dawn of*

Figure 11.1 How far the scenes of the mist spreading through the parking lot in *The Mist* (2007) evoke 11 September 2001 is up to audiences to decide.

the Dead, each of which have produced a range of profoundly allegorical readings (see Paglia 1998; Wood 1986). Darabont, as Hitchcock and Romero before him, is just as, if not more interested in the relationships between the people inside than what is transpiring outside, as the film proceeds to dramatise the fears and anxieties of a new millennial United States and project them onto the screen 'into a great white cloud of unknowing, one that comes with teeth, claws and tentacles' (Pilkington 2008: 64).

The responsibilities of a father (as David's wife Stephanie is quickly removed from the narrative) become the central thematic motif of the film, as David will attempt to shield his son Billy from the horrific events in which they are both forced to participate. David is one of many fathers (or father figures) in post-9/11 genre cinema to have their masculinity and status tested by events outside their control (see *War of the Worlds, Battle: Los Angeles, Taken* [2008], *Man on Fire* [2004], among others) as the masculinity in crisis trope saw itself updated for the 'War on Terror' era in the wake of Peggy Noonan's widely quoted plea for a return to traditional forms of the masculine ideal (see also du Toit's 'The Pussification of the Western Male'). What is perhaps most interesting about these films is how they are able to simultaneously represent both the prevailing fears *and* fantasies of American society post-9/11. In the vast majority of them this challenge is portrayed as an opportunity for ageing males to prove their masculinity both to themselves and to those around them, most often by saving the children in their charge (frequently although not always young, white, virginal girls). In this understanding the inherent *fear* is that of the father (and all that he represents) not being able to protect those close to him and the *fantasy* is that he will be able to meet the challenge and reconstitute both his masculinity and the patriarchal order by the end of the narrative. Of course, these fears have been a central part of the global cultural imaginary for decades, but the centralisation and frequency of these texts might be considered examples of the prevailing need after 9/11 to re-establish a sense of protection that was felt lost by America as a whole after 11 September 2001. About this sense of loss Susan Faludi wrote, 'The intrusions of September 11 broke the dead bolt on our protective myth, the illusion that we are masters of our own security, that our might makes our homeland impregnable, that our families are safe in the bower of our communities and our women and children are safe in the arms of their men' (2007: 12).

In the sequence where the mist emerges, quickly followed by what seems to be an earthquake, it becomes apparent that the visual style of the film is markedly different to the way the camera has been habitually employed in Darabont's earlier works, which are defined by their elaborate, beautifully lit compositions and their use of static or slow-moving cinematography. In stark contrast to this, Darabont has chosen a rough, hand-held style for *The Mist*. Such decisions have both budgetary and aesthetic implications; it is much cheaper to shoot fast and loose on two hand-held cameras running simultaneously, producing a ragged and confrontational aesthetic which brings an effective sense of urgency and immediacy to the film which I have elsewhere described as 'the quintessential new millennial marker of authenticity' (McSweeney 48). It is important to note that *The Mist* rejects the glibness of many contemporary horror films which seem self-consciously designed to titillate and eviscerate the young people who both star in and go to see them: films like *Scream* (1996), *Final Destination* (2000), *Resident Evil* (2002) and the franchises they inspired. *The Mist* is not filmed with a glossy MTV aesthetic, nor is it populated by nubile teenagers baring their breasts before being killed in graphic close-up. In fact, many of the cast are middle-aged and far from conventionally attractive (with the notable and perhaps problematic exception of Thomas Jane). The ensemble nature of the project and the fact that it is populated by a cast of non-traditional horror actors led Mark Pilkington to describe it as 'a rare beast: a mature, genuinely intense horror film that takes its improbable subject matter, and hence its audience, seriously' (2008: 64).

Explanations flow around the panicked customers as they speculate as to what could have caused such a mist: perhaps a pollution cloud, a chemical explosion at the local mill, or a poisonous gas? It is tempting to equate their confusion with that of those on the ground on 11 September 2001 but their bewilderment is accurately reproduced from King's original novella. Mrs Carmody almost immediately suggests that they are experiencing the rapture, but at this stage of the narrative she is still an object of ridicule and derision, the crowd laughing at her as they are not yet afraid enough to take her pronouncements seriously. However, they soon will be. Amanda Dunfrey (Laurie Holden), a local schoolteacher, even slaps her around the face, drawing blood which Carmody holds up for the crowd to see. Amanda adds, 'I'm sorry everybody, but this lady's perspective is a little bit too Old Testament for my taste.' Some locals even mention the existence of a mysterious military base not far from the town called the 'Arrowhead Project' about which King's novella is ambiguous but Darabont, to the film's detriment, reveals more.[6]

David Drayton's first confrontation with what might actually be inside the mist comes when he ventures into the darkness of the packing room at the rear of the store to retrieve a blanket for his already traumatised son. Hearing strange noises from outside, he discovers that the air conditioning has become blocked by something 'out there'. The mechanics Jim and Myron and a teenage bag boy called Norm (Chris Owen) laugh at him, questioning both his masculinity and his status within the community. Jim states, 'I know you're a big shot art-ist with connections in New York and Hollywood and all like that, but that don't make you better than anyone else, not in my book.' While David *is* a local (with connections to the town that go back genera-tions), both his education and his success have made him an outsider. It is Ollie who explains, 'They've lost their sense of proportion, out there in the market they were scared and confused. In here there's a problem they can solve so they're goddamn gonna solve it.' This is the first example in the film of a theme that emerges as a motif: the considerable impact fear plays on one's ability to make rational and logical decisions. However, almost as soon as they open the door to the outside, David is proved right and at just twenty-four minutes in *The Mist* shows the first of its impressively diverse array of creatures. Dan had warned the diegetic characters within the film and us the audience that there was 'something in the mist' and now we see it.

The Cthulhuian monster which appears and attacks them is best described in King's words, as Darabont has endeavoured to re-create the images from the novella as closely as possible on the screen:

> The tentacle tapered from a thickness of a foot – the size of a grass snake – at the point where it had wrapped itself around Norm's lower leg to a thickness of maybe four or five feet where it disappeared into the mist. It was slate gray on top, shading to a fleshy pink underneath, and there were rows of suckers on the underside. They were moving and writhing like hundreds of small, puckering mouths. (King [1980] 2007: 83)

The monster pulls Norm into the mist to his death, leaving the rest of the men shell-shocked. David is the most distraught and turns his anger towards Jim and Myron: 'You got that kid killed. Did you get a good look at it?' But their disbelief was perhaps understandable and is echoed in David's neighbour Norton's sceptical response a few moments later. Outside of a movie (or perhaps a novella), who could have conceived of such a thing?

When David and Ollie attempt to convince the rest of those in the supermarket that they might be experiencing something out of the ordi-nary, it is too far away from their experience to process. The only person in the supermarket who believes them, seemingly without a moment's pause, is the religious zealot and fundamentalist Mrs Carmody. David tries to convince his neighbour Norton but he refuses (again initially somewhat understandably) to entertain the story and sees this as a con-tinuation of the community's rejection of him as a well-educated and prosperous African American. Darabont's casting of Braugher emphasises an understated racial aspect to Norton's belief that the locals do not care for out-of-towners, and his delivery of the single line 'Y'all stick together' with the contraction sounding odd in his usually clipped diction adds a potent dimension to the scene which may not have been apparent on the pages of the script.[7]

After the packing room incident, three separate groups quickly emerge within the supermarket, each antagonistic towards the others and each with its own agenda and different way of responding to the crisis. David leads a group of pragmatic realists who understand that something very strange is happening even if they cannot explain it. The second is led by the pompous Norton who sets up camp as the opposition, refusing to believe the mist is anything other than a natural phenomenon despite compelling evidence to the contrary and criticising David's belief in 'tentacles from planet X'. Darabont makes it quite clear whose side we are supposed to be on as David, the film's hero, who like us has seen the creature in the mist, tells Norton 'get your head out of your ass' and Ollie comments, 'you cannot convince some people there's a fire even when their hair's burning. Denial is a powerful thing.' Despite this, some have seen something more in the characterisation and actions of Norton, further indication of the malleability and the allure of allegory to give form to what one wishes to see. Victoria McCollum, in a chapter entitled 'Rednecks, Racism and Religion: King and Darabont's Precarious Prophecy of Obama's Coming', as the title suggests, somewhat implausibly asserts that 'Darabont's depiction of Norton symbolizes an Obama: a maverick-defeating, coalition building newcomer' (97). She suggests that Norton is to be read by audiences as 'a beacon of hope and change amid catastrophe' (93). Yet this understanding egregiously ignores Norton's intransigence and the fact that his refusal to accept the new parameters of their situation results in him leading his group outside to what appears to be their deaths, as evidenced by off-screen screams and the fact that one of them is pulled back into the store only to reveal he has been cut in half.[8]

III.

We are being punished for going against the will of God. For going against the forbidden rules of old. Walking on the moon! Yes! Yes! Or splitting his atoms. Or stem cells and abortions! And destroying the secrets of life that only God above has any right to!

Mrs Carmody

The third group to emerge in the supermarket is led by Mrs Carmody, whose status begins to rise as the morale of those trapped in the supermarket depresses. In fact, unlike the rest of those stuck inside the Food House, she seems to flourish in the situation. In the novella King observes, 'Mrs Carmody looked younger somehow, and more vital. As if she had come into her own. As if . . . as if she were thriving on it' ([1980] 2007: 184), and this is certainly visualised in the film too. Darabont also brings her particularly fundamentalist Christian beliefs to the centre of the text, rather than the more general religious comments contained in the novella. Played with grim relish, Harden's performance as Carmody is characterised by her self-righteous belief that puts one in mind of a Pat Robertson or a Jerry Falwell with her ominous declaration that 'The end of times has come, not in flames but in *mist*', and the fact that she blames those who do not believe in God for causing what they are experiencing. Her diatribe of 'They mock us. They mock our God, our faith, our values, our very lifestyle. They mock our humility and our piousness. They piss on us and laugh' evokes Falwell's infamous attempt to blame 9/11 on 'the pagans, and the abortionists, and the feminists, and the gays and the lesbians who are actively trying to make that an alternative lifestyle, the ACLU, People For the American Way, all of them who have tried to secularize America. I point the finger in their face and say "you helped this happen".'[9]

That night the creatures within the mist do attack as Mrs Carmody had predicted. Large prehistoric bird-like beasts break through the glass windows at the front of the store and kill several people. A grotesque insect lands on Mrs Carmody but then flies off, leaving her alone (an incident which is not present in the novella). What could have been a coincidence is read as confirmation of her divinely chosen status by the crowd and as a consequence of this more followers begin to listen to her increasingly apocalyptic sermons. Even Myron and Jim, who had attempted to hit her at the start of the film and suggested that her 'tongue must be hung in the middle, so that it can waggle at both ends', are seen standing in front of her nodding in reverence. With the destruction of their previously held beliefs and norms in front of their very eyes and their growing sense of fear, the crowd turns to anyone that can offer guidance. While this transition seems rather abrupt (which is perhaps par for the course in the genre), a *Time* magazine poll conducted less than a year after 9/11 in June 2002 suggested that 59 per cent of Americans believed John's apocalyptic prophecies will be fulfilled and a further 36 per cent believed that the Bible is the literal word of God (Gibbs 2002). Darabont's adjustments to Carmody's character, specifically her identifiably Christian fundamentalism, evoke the pronounced religiosity of the Bush administration and Bush's own suggestion that he was 'driven with a mission from God' (quoted in MacAskill 2005).[10] It was these increasingly fundamentalist beliefs of large sections of American society that Chris Hedges described in his book *American Fascists: The Christian Right and the War on America* released in 2007, the same year as *The Mist*. Hedges wrote, 'It is a small step from this toxic rhetoric and exclusive belief system to the disempowerment and eradication of nonbelievers, a step a frightened and enraged population could well demand during a period of prolonged instability or a national crisis.' (92)

Darabont deliberately and repeatedly draws connections between the situation the community find themselves in and the 'War on Terror' era. He even has one of his characters, Dan, suggest, 'If you scare people bad enough you can get them to do anything. They'll turn to whoever promises a solution' (an exchange not present in the novella). This particular moment was criticised by Chris Hewitt in *Empire*, in his description of the scene as 'featuring dialogue so on-the-nose that it might as well come with a flashing subtitle "This is about the Bush administration"' (Hewitt 2008: 46). David Drayton recognises the seductive allure of such certainty in a crisis situation: 'By noon she'll have four more. Tomorrow night, when those things come back she'll have a congregation and then we can start worrying about who she's gonna sacrifice to make it all better.' Some of the others, including the young teacher Amanda, find it hard to believe that such a thing could happen, that a civilised small-town community could resort so quickly to such barbaric behaviour, but David is more pragmatic: 'As long as the machines are working and you can dial 911. You take those things away and you throw people in the dark, you scare the shit out of them, no more rules. You'll see how primitive they get' (also not featured in the novella). He is proven right as Carmody's sermons take a progressively more darker tone:

> It is time to declare yourselves. Take sides, the saved and the damned. Read the good book, it calls for expiation. Blood. Blood. Little Normy was first and now God calls the rest of us. The bill is due, it must be paid. As Abraham prepared to sacrifice his only son to prove his love for God.

Carmody has used the currency of fear as a potent weapon to control and manipulate what de Tocqueville called 'the tyrannical masses' (see Robin 2004: 79). One might suggest that this type of fear has been central to the American experience post-9/11, as political leaders capitalised and exploited real world threats to generate support for their ideas, policies and their party.[11]

Following Carmody's lead, it is no coincidence that the individual the crowd turns on in their demand for 'expiation' is a local young soldier, Jessup (Sam Witwer), a character who does not appear in the original novella. Jessup is one of four soldiers featured in the film who are entirely ineffectual and offer no help whatsoever in the crisis situation that the community find themselves in. Furthermore, when they realise the gravity of their situation, two of the soldiers commit suicide by hanging themselves. In another example of post-9/11 apophenia, Tony Magistrale suggested, 'Their choices of death are also notable, as the two men elect to hang themselves, ironically paralleling Saddam's form of execution for war crimes committed against his own people in Iraq' (56). When the crowd turn on Jessop they question him about his knowledge of the Arrowhead Project and he reveals that the government had been working on secret experiments which may or may not have caused the mist. Driven to a frenzy by Carmody's demand for bloody revenge, the mob repeatedly stab him and throw him outside the store to be eaten by whatever resides in the mist. Mrs Carmody crows with victory, 'The beast will leave us alone tonight. Tomorrow . . . Tomorrow we'll just have to wait and see . . .' Just twenty-four hours before they had been a quiet and law-abiding small-town community sharing complaints and anecdotes over the supermarket checkout, yet now individuals who had once been friends and neighbours prove themselves capable of human sacrifice. Billy asks his father to 'Promise you won't let the monsters get me', although this line of dialogue is left deliberately ambiguous for the audience to decide which monsters he is referring to.[12] David and the small group of rational-minded individuals left fear for their own lives at the hands of Carmody's flock and plot an escape, deciding they would rather face the monsters outside the walls of the supermarket than those within.

IV.

> The ending [of The Mist] will tear your heart out . . . but so will life, in the end. Frank Darabont's vision of hell is completely uncompromising. If you want sweet, the Hollywood establishment will be pleased to serve you at the cineplex, believe me, but if you want something that feels real, come here.
> Stephen King, Danse Macabre, 2011 edition (King xxx).

The next morning David's planned escape is thwarted almost immediately. As the crowd begins to move towards his group it becomes clear that Billy is their target as David's worst fears are realised. Carmody yells, 'Grab that boy, grab him. Get the whore too [referring to Amanda]. Kill them, kill them all!' It is the unassuming Ollie who steps forward and shoots her twice, once in the stomach and once in the head. She drops to the floor with a look of intense surprise on her face. The crowd is stunned by the death of their leader, giving David and his group time to flee outside and drive off into the mist and an uncertain future.

The predicament of the five remaining characters (Ollie having been killed on the way to the car) is now before them: they do not know where to go or how long their fuel will last, so they just begin to drive. Darabont sets the succeeding driving montage sequence to a hauntingly threnodic piece of music called 'The Host of Seraphim' taken from the 1988 Dead Can Dance album *The Serpent's Egg*, as they pass scenes of destruction and devastation, all the while driving through the never-ending mist. It is unclear how much diegetic time passes before Darabont visualises one of the most memorable moments in the novella, as a huge beast walks over their car reaching so high that it disappears into the mist above them. King wrote, 'For the moment it was over the scout I had an impression of something so big that it might have made a blue whale look like the size of a trout – in other words, something so big that it defied the imagination' ([1980] 2007: 227). The scene artfully emphasises the sheer hopelessness of their situation as it seems that the mist covers the whole world. What chance could they have of escape when creatures even larger than dinosaurs dwell inside it?

Figure 11.2 David Drayton (Thomas Jane) and the rare failure of the American patriarch in post-9/11 cinema.

Thus the scene is set for the climax of the film. In the original ending to the novella King chose to leave the narrative open-ended. David stops writing in the journal he had been recounting the story in, leaving the reader unsure of what will happen after his final sentence. Yet there is a small sense of hope as in the final line he writes, 'If only I really heard it. If only. I'm going to bed now. But first I'm going to kiss my son and whisper two words in his ear. Against the dreams that may come, you know. Two words that sound a bit alike. One of them is hope' ([1980] 2007: 230). Just a few pages before, King had written, through David's first-person commentary, on the nature of such an ending, 'It is, I suppose, what my father always frowningly called "an Alfred Hitchcock ending," by which he meant a conclusion in ambiguity that allowed the viewer to make up his own mind about how things ended. My father had nothing but contempt for such stories, saying they were "cheap shots"' ([1980] 2007: 228). It appears that Frank Darabont shares David's father's contempt for such inconclusive endings, as early on in the screenwriting process he decided to change it, explaining, 'As much as I love Steve's story, I remember the first time I read it back in 1980, going, "Oh really? There's not really an ending?"' (Darabont 2007: 26). Darabont elects to end his film with David's car finally running out of petrol, leaving the group stranded in the middle of the mist with no hope of survival. With only four bullets left in his gun they reluctantly decide to take their own lives on their own terms, instead of waiting for the beasts to kill them. Mindful of his earlier promise to Billy, David kills Dan, Irene, Amanda and finally his beloved son, sparing them from the horror of the monsters outside. Only the father is left alive with his pain. David gets out of the car hoping to be killed himself by the creatures in the mist, but just moments later a truck full of soldiers and survivors appear: miraculously and devastatingly, the mist has begun to clear. Had he only waited a few more minutes, they all would have been saved.

The potency of the ending is undeniable; the final destruction of the family unit at the hands of the father, one who had sought throughout the narrative to protect his child and yet becomes so overwhelmed by a lack of hope that he takes his own son's life. The last word in the novella was 'hope', but there is none here for David Drayton and Billy. What kind of life can he have now after what he has done? To make matters worse (if that is at all possible) in the back of a passing truck we recognise the face of a young mother (Melissa McBride) who had earlier elected to leave the supermarket and go to her children after the arrival of the mist, despite being warned by everyone not to. Unlike

David and those in his group, she had never given up hope while all around had lost theirs. It was perhaps the centrality of this hope motif which led Victoria McCollum to suggest that the film 'subtextually anticipates the longing for, and consequence of, a change of leadership amidst disaster' (90) in the form of the presidency of Barack Obama, whose presidential campaign at that time focused around the words 'hope' and 'change'. *The Mist* is one of many post-9/11 horror films to explore similar territory, as Kevin Wetmore argued: 'After 9/11, nihilism, despair, random violence and death, combined with tropes and images generated by the terrorist attacks began to assume far greater prominence in horror cinema' (2–3). The downbeat conclusion is far removed from not only that of the original novella but also Darabont's previous feature films as a director: from Andy Dufresne's daring prison escape and subsequent reunion with Red in *The Shawshank Redemption*, the spiritual illumination of Paul Edgecomb in *The Green Mile*, to Peter Appleton's rejection of his Hollywood career and return to the small-town community of Lawson, California in *The Majestic* (2001), where he is welcomed with open arms. In each of these films the main characters are rewarded for never giving up hope, despite the seemingly futile nature of their predicament.

The ending has certainly been the most discussed element of the entire film and Darabont stated that he had only agreed to the contract with Dimension Films because they promised not to change his proposed conclusion. He stated, 'It was a leap in the dark, a big risk. One big producer offered me a great deal and a $30 million budget – on the condition that I change the ending. So I went with Bob Weinstein, and a budget half that size' (quoted in Patterson 2008: 7). Subsequently Darabont has commented that 'much to my delight, SK [Stephen King] has been incredibly supportive . . . He loves the ending' (quoted in Hewitt 2008: 111). There is little doubt that it is one of the bleakest endings for a studio picture ever made and a rare example of a father (or father figure) failing in his mission to protect his child in a mainstream American film. Until the final scenes of the film David had done everything asked of him by the film's narrative: as do Ray Ferrier in *War of the Worlds* and Bryan Mills in *Taken*, each of whom save the child in their charge (and by implication themselves in the process) and are rewarded by at least a partial reconstitution of normalcy and patriarchy. David's alpha male status in the film is quite different to his depiction in the novella, where he is significantly less overtly masculine. With his movie star good looks and his history of heroic roles in films like *Deep Blue Sea* (1999), *Stander* (2003) and *The Punisher* (2004),

Jane's interpretation of the character lacks a sense of vulnerability that another less hard-bodied actor might have brought to the role. The novella's David Drayton is much more ambiguous and more human because of it: he has a one-night stand with the teacher Amanda Dunfrey, loses control in the packing room scene (where he decides to let go of the bag boy Norm to save his own life), is much less of a leader in the Food House and is considerably less heroic when the bird-like beasts attack at night, all of which Darabont chooses to remove from his cinematic adaptation, leaving Thomas Jane's David Drayton significantly more virtuous and dependable, although whether this makes the impact of the final scene of the film more or less resonant is a matter for audiences to decide.

The rejection of this return to patriarchal normalcy has been rare in post-9/11 cinema. Much more frequent was reconstitution of the "dead bolt" Susan Faludi suggested was removed by 9/11 (Faludi 12). Faludi suggested, 'No doubt, the fantasy consoled many. But rather than make us any safer, it misled us into danger, damaging the very security the myth was supposed to bolster. There are consequences to living in a dream' (289). In the post-9/11 decade American cinema played an important role in reconstituting this fantasy. One might argue that allegorical films like *The Mist* performed a particular social role in an age where explicitly critical dramatisations of the fears and anxieties of the post-9/11 era were rare. Like other cinematic allegories which emerged during turbulent moments of twentieth-century American history, these anxious periods are not mentioned by name within the diegetic frames of the films, but their presence is palpable. This refusal to adhere to the master narrative of the 'War on Terror' might be one of the reasons *The Mist* was largely rejected by audiences on its release on, of all dates, Thanksgiving weekend 2007, who preferred instead to see the fairytale fantasy of *Enchanted* (2007) or the cathartic videogame-style violence of *Hitman* (2007) and *Beowulf* (2007). Yet this very refusal is perhaps why the film continues to resonate and will be regarded in years to come as a compelling cultural artefact.

NOTES

1. *The Mist* was the second adaptation of Stephen King's work to be released in 2007 after *1408* directed by Mikael Håfström, which has its own connections to the fears and anxieties of the decade even though it was originally written in the late 1990s. Elsewhere in this edited collection, Jim Kendrick notes that 2007 was the biggest year of the decade for American horror films with thirty-one releases.

2. This sense of ambiguity of time frame is the focus of Aviva Briefel's interesting chapter on the film titled '"Shop 'Til You Drop": Consumerism and Horror' in the collection *Horror After 9/11: World of Fear, Cinema of Terror*. She suggests, 'It couches its obvious critique of the Bush administration within a form and content that herald classic Americana' (156). While seemingly set in the present, there are odd anachronisms which create an otherworldly aspect to the drama: the fact that there are no computers at the checkout, no one has mobile phones and the décor in the Food House is extremely dated. Interestingly, Darabont released a black-and-white version of the film on the special edition DVD release which further accentuates this sense of temporal ambiguity.

3. *The Village* is one of many cinematic texts that seem coded from the start with self-conscious allusions to the post 9/11 climate. Like much of Shyamalan's work, *The Village* is characterised by a narrative twist in the style of a *Twilight Zone* episode. In this case the reveal is that the film is not actually set in the year 1897, rather in a contemporary America in which the village elders, all of whom had suffered from trauma brought about by the modern world, had sought to create an idyllic society guarded and fenced in, the ultimate gated community. The film's narrative is a timely disquisition on the manufacture of a culture of fear which could not fail to resonate with American audiences in the middle of the 2000s.

4. In his book *The Dark Ages of America. The Final Phase of Empire* (New York: W. W. Norton, 2006), Morris Berman contends that the United States has entered a crucial and perilous stage of its development, asserting that like many empires before it has entered into a decline: 'For what we are now seeing is the obvious characteristics of the West after the fall of Rome: the triumph of religion over reason; the atrophy of education and critical thinking' (2).

5. Maurice Yacowar suggested that the disaster genre tends to follow sixteen key points and a close analysis reveals that *The Mist* adheres to thirteen out of the sixteen (1995).

6. In this volume Jim Kendrick suggests that the tendency to explain the roots of the monstrous becomes a trope of post-9/11 horror.

7. King's Norton is a slightly one-dimensional, overweight, middle-class, white lawyer, characterised as one of the villains of the piece by his repetitive swearing in front of Billy, his profession and the fact that he continuously stares at David's wife's breasts.

8. Wetmore writes, 'While Norton and Carmody both believe they have the answers and are doing the right thing, both are clearly doing damage and bring death to themselves and others as a result' (124).

9. See Jerry Falwell, Christian television programme *The 700 Club*, 'Falwell apologizes to gays, feminists, lesbians', CNN, 14 September 2001: http://edition.cnn.com/2001/US/09/14/Falwell.apology/. He later apologised.

10. Bush also asserted, 'I trust God speaks through me. Without that, I couldn't do my job' (quoted in Kamen 2005).

11. Of course, this is not something that can not only be applied to American leaders post-9/11, but it has been a key and enduring part of global power politics throughout history.

12. David's promise to his son is not part of the novella. See Gareth Edward's ambiguously titled *Monsters* (2010) for a further example of this.

REFERENCES

Barber, Benjamin (2003), *Fear's Empire. War, Terrorism, and Democracy*, London: W. W. Norton.

Benjamin, Walter (1977), *The Origin of German Tragic Drama*, New York: Verso.

Booker, Keith M. (2001), *Monsters, Mushroom Clouds, and the Cold War: American Science Fiction and the Roots of Postmodernism, 1946–1964*. Westport, CT: Greenwood Press.

Briefel, Aviva, and Sam J. Miller (eds) (2012), *Horror after 9/11: World of Fear, Cinema of Terror*, Austin: University of Texas Press.

Brzezinski, Zbigniew (2007), 'Terrorized by war on terror,' *The Washington Post*, 25 March 2007.

Chang, Justin (2007), review, *Variety*, 19 October 2007, pp. 37, 45.

Darabont, Frank (2007), interview, *Creative Screenwriting*, 14:6, November/December, pp. 26–8.

du Toit, Kim (2013), 'The Pussification of the Western Male', accessed 22 June 2013, http://talltown.us/guns/nancyboys.htm

Edelstein, David (2007), 'Savage Grace', *New York Magazine*, last accessed 15 May 2015: http://nymag.com/movies/reviews/41278/index1.html

Faludi, Susan (2007), *The Terror Dream: Fear And Fantasy in Post 9/11 America*, Melbourne: Scribe.

Falwell, Jerry (2001), 'Falwell apologizes to gays, feminists, lesbians', *The 700 Club*, CNN, 14 September 2001, last accessed 28 September 2016: http://edition.cnn.com/2001/US/09/14/Falwell.apology/

Gibbs, Nancy (2002), 'Apocalypse Now', *Time Magazine*, 23 June 2002.

Grant, Barry Keith (2010), *Invasion of the Body Snatchers*, London: BFI Classics.

Hedges, Chris (2007), *American Fascists: The Christian Right and the War on America*, London: Vintage Books.

Hewitt, Chris (2008), 'In conversation with Frank Darabont', *Empire*, 224, February 2008, pp. 111–16.

— (2008), review, *Empire*, 230, August 2008, p. 46.

Hitchens, Chris (2001), 'The ends of war', *The Nation*, p. 9.

Hobbes, Thomas (1651), *Leviathan Or The Matter, Form, and Power of a Commonwealth, Ecclesiastical and Civil*.

Jameson, Frederic (1981), *The Political Unconscious: Narrative as a Socially Symbolic Act*, Ithaca: Cornell University Press.

Kaes, Anton (2011), *Shell Shock Cinema: Weimar Culture and the Wounds of War*, Princeton: Princeton University Press.

Kamen, Al (2005), 'George W. Bush and the G-Word', *The Washington Post*, 14 October 2005: http://www.washingtonpost.com/wp-dyn/content/article/2005/10/13/AR2005101301688.html

King, Stephen (2007 [1980]), *The Mist*, New York: Signet.

— (2012 [1981]), *Danse Macabre*, New York: Gallery Books.

Kracauer, Siegfried (1947), *From Caligari to Hitler. A Psychological Profile of the German Film*, Princeton, NJ: Princeton University Press.

Lowenstein, Adam (2005), *Shocking Representations: Historical Trauma, National Cinema and the Modern Horror Film*, New York: Columbia University Press.

MacAskill, Ewan (2005), 'George Bush: "God told me to end the tyranny in Iraq"', *The Guardian*, 7 October 2005, p. 1.

Magistrale, Tony (2010), *Stephen King: America's Storyteller*, Santa Barbara: Praeger.

Maher, Kevin (2008), review, *The Times*, 3 July 2008, p. 18.

Malcolm, Derek (2007), 'Anyone got the foggiest?', *The Evening Standard*, 3 July 2007, p. 41.

McCollum, Victoria (2014), 'Rednecks, Racism and Religion: King and Darabont's Precarious Prophecy of Obama's Coming', in David Garret Izo (ed.), *Movies in the Age of Obama*, Lanham: Rowman & Littlefield, pp. 85–102.

McSweeney, Terence (2014), *The 'War on Terror' and American Film: 9/11 Frames per Second*, Edinburgh: Edinburgh University Press.

Noonan, Peggy (2001), 'Welcome Back, Duke From the ashes of Sept. 11 arise the manly virtues', *Wall Street Journal*, 12 October 2001, last accessed 12 May 2012: http://online.wsj.com/article/SB122451174798650085.html

Paglia, Camille (1998), *The Birds*, London: BFI Publishing.

Patterson, J. (2008), 'The human race is insane', *The Guardian*, 27 June 2008, p. 7.

Pheasant-Kelly, Francis (2013), *Fantasy Film Post-9/11*, London and New York: I. B. Tauris.

Pilkington, Mark (2008), review, *Sight and Sound*, 18:7, July, p. 64.

Pollard, Tom (2011), *Hollywood 9/11 Superheroes, Supervillains and Super Disasters*, Boulder: Paradigm Publishers.

Robin, Corey (2004), *Fear: The History of a Political Idea*, Oxford: Oxford University Press.

Smith, Kyle (2007), review, *New York Post*, 21 October 2007, last accessed 15 May 2015: http://www.nypost.com/p/entertainment/movies/the_mist_g4bYH4cLIhMWd2noI4igEK

Spelling, I. (2008), 'Fear Forecast', *Starburst*, 358, January, pp. 57–9.

Starck, Kathleen (ed.) (2010), *Between Fear and Freedom: Cultural Representations of the Cold War*, Newcastle upon Tyne: Cambridge Scholars.

Summers, Anthony, and Robbyn Swann (2012), *The Eleventh Day*, London: Corgi.

Tsutsui, William M. (2004), *Godzilla on My Mind: Fifty Years of the King of Monsters*, Basingstoke: Palgrave Macmillan.

Wetmore, Kevin J. (2012), *Post 9/11 Horror in American Cinema*, New York: Continuum.

Wilson, Chuck (2007), 'Condensation Nation', *The Village Voice*, 13 November 2007: http://www.villagevoice.com/film/condensation-nation-6424075

Wood, Robin (1986), *Hollywood from Vietnam to Reagan*, New York: Columbia University Press.

Woodward, Bob (2002), *State of Denial: Bush at War*, London: Simon & Schuster.

Yacowar, Maurice (1995), 'The Bug in the Rug: Notes on the Disaster Genre', in Barry Keith Grant (ed.), *Film Genre Reader*, Austin: University of Texas Press.

Yomota Inuhiko (2007), 'The Menace from the South Seas: Honda Ishirō's *Godzilla* (1954)', in Alastair Phillips and Julian Stringer (eds), *Japanese Cinema: Texts and Contexts*, New York: Routledge, pp. 102–11.

CHAPTER 12

The Terrible, Horrible Desire to Know: Post-9/11 Horror Remakes, Reboots, Sequels and Prequels

James Kendrick

1. INTRODUCTION

Given horror's persistent ties to cultural anxiety, it is not surprising that the genre experienced a significant rebirth in American cinemas post-9/11, an era indelibly marked by terrorism, war and near-constant global tensions. Even though horror is, by its very nature, a culturally marginalised genre, one that appeals primarily to a specific audience and has only rare mainstream crossover appeal, even a cursory glance at the theatrical marketplace in recent years shows that it has been growing in both popularity and production since 9/11. In 1995, for example, there were only sixteen horror films in wide release in the US, representing 2.78 per cent of the market share. Ten years later, in 2005, those numbers had increased to twenty-nine horror films in wide release and 5.73 per cent of the market share – a percentage increase of more than 80 per cent in terms of production and 106 per cent in terms of market share. And this elevated presence of horror films has persisted in subsequent years. From 2005 to 2015, there has been an average of twenty-seven horror films in wide release, the biggest year being 2012 with thirty-three releases, although those films commanded only 2.79 per cent of the market share. By that metric, 2007 was actually the decade's biggest year for horror films, with thirty-one releases accounting for 7.16 per cent of the market share ('Horror: Year-by-Year Market Share').

During this period, one of the dominant trends in the genre has been a cycle of remakes and reboots of earlier films and film series, which started most prominently by reworking the low-budget, independently produced horror films of the 1970s but quickly spread to both the independent and major studio-distributed films of the late '70s and 1980s. It is important here to distinguish between a *remake* and a *reboot*, as the terms are sometimes used interchangeably despite describing very different products. As William Proctor (2012) notes:

> Reboots and remakes share an abundance of commonalities, but this does not mean they are conjoined entities without distinction . . . a film remake is a singular text bound within a self-contained narrative schema; whereas a reboot attempts to forge a *series* of films, to begin a franchise anew from the ashes of an old or failed property. In other words, a remake is a reinterpretation of *one* film; a reboot 're-starts' a *series* of films that seek to disavow and render inert its predecessor's validity. (4)

Because many of the most commercially successful contemporary horror films exist within a series of sequels (and sometimes prequels), most of the post-9/11 horror films that reworked material from horror films of the '70s and '80s are best described as reboots, although a number of them failed to ignite a new series.[1] However, the commercial logic behind their creation was predicated largely on the fact that the original series had exhausted themselves through sequels of diminishing critical and commercial impact, hence the need to 'begin anew'.

Of course, the idea of remaking older horror films is not in any way new; as Rüdiger Heinze and Lucia Krämer point out, 'Remakes have been a common feature from the very advent of film-making', and the Hollywood remake 'flourished during the Classical Studio era and has never disappeared' (11). To wit, the era that produced the films that have been remade in the 2000s produced its own fair share, including remakes of *Invasion of the Body Snatchers* (1956) in 1978, *The Thing From Another World* (1951) in 1982 as *The Thing*, *The Fly* (1958) in 1986, and *The Blob* (1958) in 1988. Of those films, however, only *The Fly* and *Invasion of the Body Snatchers* produced follow-up films (1988's *The Fly II* and 1994's *Body Snatchers*, respectively). The era of the late 1970s and 1980s was also, not incidentally, a period of vastly increased horror film production on both the independent and major studio levels (Kendrick 2009: 137–8; Prince 2000: 298), which resulted in a plethora of horror titles and series that can now be remade or rebooted.

Aviva Briefel and Sam J. Miller (2011) argue that the flagging horror genre was reinvigorated by the real-world horrors of that day in

September 2001, and the resulting films have been 'darker, more disturbing, and increasingly apocalyptic' (1), partly because they provide 'a rare protected space in which to critique the tone and content of public discourse' (3) in the era of the 'War on Terror' and resulting debates about the invasions of Afghanistan and Iraq, the increasing powers of the federal government to spy on and detain citizens, the use of 'enhanced interrogation techniques' against suspected terrorists, and the revelations of outright abuse of prisoners at Abu Ghraib. Numerous post-9/11 horror films either dealt with themes pertaining to 9/11 and its aftermath or appropriated imagery associated with those events, often 'indirectly and elliptically' (Johnson 2011: E7). Kevin J. Wetmore Jr (2012) marks the distinction between pre- and post-9/11 horror in terms of hope: 'the former frequently allows for hope and the latter just as frequently does not. In pre-9/11 horror, there is almost always a way to stop the evil . . . After 9/11, nihilism, despair, random violence and death, combined with tropes and images generated by the terrorist attacks began to assume far greater prominence in horror cinema' (2–3).

However, an intriguing aspect to these films that has not been much discussed is their incessant desire to *explain*. While many horror films of the '70s and '80s were content with ambiguity and mystery, especially as it pertained to their depictions of monstrosity and evil, post-9/11 horror, despite its despair and sometimes outright nihilism, is frequently consumed with showing us *how* and *why*, which parallels the American culture's grasping for understanding following the terrorist attacks on the World Trade Center and the Pentagon. Even though the intent behind including psychological backstory and explanation was fully commercial in nature, a means of refreshing stale franchises and giving them a new identity without completely eliminating the traits and iconic elements that had made them popular in the first place, it is nonetheless curious that the genre would parallel real-world desire for knowledge in this manner.

II. AMERICAN HORROR IN THE 2000s

Throughout the first decade of the 2000s the horror genre was increasingly popular at the US box office, drawing in sizeable audiences that, while small when compared to the tens of millions that turn out for mega-budget studio-produced blockbusters, are nonetheless significant for films made on relatively low budgets, usually with no stars, and almost always with an inherently audience-limiting R rating and reputation for taboo flaunting. For example, in 2005 seven horror films debuted at the top of the US box office (*Hide and Seek, Boogeyman, The Ring Two, The Amityville Horror, The Exorcism of Emily Rose, The Fog* and *Saw II*), while in 2006 there were eight (*Hostel, Underworld: Evolution, When a Stranger Calls, Silent Hill, Snakes on a Plane, The Covenant, The Grudge 2* and *Saw III*). These films went on to be handsomely profitable, taking in a combined US and international average box office gross of $99 million against an average production budget of only $24 million.[2]

The horror remake/reboot cycle had a few notable predecessors prior to the 2000s, including the 1998 shot-for-shot colour remake of *Psycho* (1960), the 1999 remake of *The Haunting* (1963), and a pair of remakes of William Castle gimmick films: *The House on Haunted Hill* (1959, remade in 1999) and *Thirteen Ghosts* (1960, remade in 2001).[3] There was also a series of American remakes of recent Asian horror films, which began with *The Ring* (2001), a remake of 1998's *Ringu* that became a significant hit, earning $129 million at the domestic box office and spawning both a 2005 sequel and a series of other Asian horror remakes, including *The Grudge* (2004), *Dark Water* (2005), *The Eye* (2008) and *Mirrors* (2008).

However, the origin point of the remake/reboot cycle could be reasonably fixed with the visually slick 2003 version of *The Texas Chain Saw Massacre* (1974), which rebooted the series nearly nine years after the last instalment, the dismally received *Texas Chainsaw Massacre: The Next Generation* (1994). The reboot's successful run at the box office ($80.5 million domestic gross) showed that there was an eager audience for new versions of recent horror classics, so others quickly followed in its wake, starting with the 2004 remake of *Dawn of the Dead* (1978). Each subsequent year has witnessed a number of horror remakes and reboots, some drawn from familiar titles, some from films far more obscure. These include 2005 remakes of *War of the Worlds* (1953), *The Fog* (1980) and *The Amityville Horror* (1979); 2006 remakes of *Black Christmas* (1974), *The Omen* (1976), *When a Stranger Calls* (1979) and *The Hills Have Eyes* (1977); 2007 remakes of *Halloween* (1978) and *The Hitcher* (1986); 2008 remakes of *It's Alive* (1974) and *Prom Night* (1980); 2009 remakes of *The Last House on the Left* (1972), *Friday the 13th* (1980), *My Bloody Valentine* (1981), *The House on Sorority Row* (1983) and *The Stepfather* (1987); and 2010 remakes of *The Crazies* (1973), *I Spit on Your Grave* (1978), *Mother's Day* (1980) and *A Nightmare on Elm Street* (1984). In the subsequent five years there have been remakes of *Carrie* (1976, remade in 2013), *Piranha* (1978, remade in 2010 in 3D), *The Evil Dead* (1981, remade in 2013), *Poltergeist* (1982, remade in 2015), *The Thing* (1982, remade in 2011) and *Fright Night* (1985, remade in 2011 in 3D).

Several of these remakes have also spawned sequels and prequels of their own, including *The Texas Chainsaw Massacre: The Beginning* (2006) and *Texas Chainsaw 3D* (2013), *The Hills Have Eyes 2* (2006), *Halloween II* (2009) and *Amityville: The Awakening* (2016). There have also been belated sequels and prequels to previous horror films that have not been remade. These include a sequel and a prequel to *The Silence of the Lambs* (1991), both based on novels by Thomas Harris – *Hannibal* (2001) and *Hannibal Rising* (2007) – as well as *Red Dragon* (2002), a version of the Harris novel that was previously adapted in 1986 as *Manhunter*. And, following the successful theatrical release of an extended version of *The Exorcist* (1973) released in 2000, there were not one but two different versions of the same prequel, Paul Schrader's *Dominion: Prequel to The Exorcist* (2005) and Renny Harlin's *Exorcist: The Beginning* (2004), the latter of which was made after the film's producer, James G. Robinson, so disliked Schrader's version that he shelved it and hired Harlin to make it all over again.

This still-ongoing cycle of remakes, reboots and associated prequels and sequels differs significantly from the other major periods of horror film production in the United States in a number of ways. The Universal cycle of horror films in the 1930s tended to centre on iconic horrific characters drawn from either gothic literature (e.g. 1930's *Dracula* and 1931's *Frankenstein*) or long-standing mythology (e.g. 1932's *The Mummy* and 1941's *The Wolf Man*). The cycle of low-budget horror films produced in the 1970s such as *The Last House on the Left*, *The Texas Chain Saw Massacre*, *The Hills Have Eyes* and *Halloween* were almost uniformly original stories, sidestepping well-known iconic figures and familiar locations and drawing instead on social and political issues that were rooted in middle America. The same was generally true of horror films in the 1980s, with the exception of studio-produced efforts that tended to draw from popular literature (e.g. Warner Brothers' 1980 production of *The Shining*, based on the Stephen King novel, and 1981 production of *Wolfen*, based on the novel by Whitley Strieber). Rather than remakes, the name of the game in the 1980s was sequels, which encouraged the production of franchises built around monstrous 'stars' such as Michael Myers in the *Halloween* series (1978–2002), Jason Voorhees in the *Friday the 13th* series (1980–2003) and Freddy Krueger in the *A Nightmare on Elm Street* series (1984–2003). While all of these traits still remain in the genre to one extent or another – witness the continual adaptations of Stephen King's novels and short stories, including *1408*

(2007) and *The Mist* (2007), and the popularity of the serial killer Jig-
saw in the *Saw* series (2004–10) – remakes have emerged as a major
trend. Of the 50 highest-grossing horror films released between 2002
and 2015, seventeen of them (35 per cent) were either direct remakes/
reboots or one of their sequels. The trend is perhaps best exemplified
in the Museum of the Moving Image's 2007 film series 'It's Only a
Movie: Horror Films From the 1970s and Today', which consciously
paired 'politically charged horror movies of the 1970s and the literal-
minded, blood-soaked remakes many of them are receiving today'
(Kehr 2007: 22).

David Kehr's description of the remakes as 'literal-minded' is all
too appropriate given the prevalence of post-9/11 horror remakes
that explain the evils of their various monstrosities in ways that sacrifice ambiguity, one of the hallmarks of '70s cinema in general and
'70s horror in particular (see Wood 1986), in favour of a potentially
reassuring sense of understanding. However horrible the monsters
of twenty-first-century horror may be, many of them are ultimately
reducible to psychological explanation, which flies in the face of the
genre's foundation in the unknowable.

III. THE TERRIBLE, HORRIBLE DESIRE TO KNOW

In 'Why Horror?', his philosophical exploration of the horror genre,
Noël Carroll notes that the genre is fundamentally paradoxical: 'It
obviously attracts consumers; but it seems to do so by means of the
expressly repulsive' (2002: 33). In striving to explain the apparent
contradiction of how such repulsive films manage to draw in viewers,
Carroll posits the pleasures of narrative, specifically the way in which
narrative form generates and then answers questions via 'the processes
of discovery, proof, and confirmation' (36). As Carroll notes, 'All narratives might be thought to involve the desire to know' (35), and narrative theory is rooted in the idea that we as viewers are driven by
curiosity. Horror films are complex in this regard, as they reward such
curiosity through 'stories [that], with great frequency, revolve around
proving, disclosing, discovering, and confirming the existence of something that is impossible' (34). Thus, even though 'to a large extent, the
horror story is driven by curiosity' (35) and 'Horror stories, in a significant number of cases, are dramas of proving the existence of the monster and disclosing (most often gradually) the origin, identity, purposes,
and powers of the monster' (35), they are still predicated on the existence of something impossible and therefore functionally unknowable.

Horror stories therefore differ fundamentally from other stories with similar narrative form, especially detective stories and other sorts of mysteries, because they have at their centre 'something which is given as in principle *unknowable* – something which, *ex hypothesi*, cannot, given the structure of our conceptual scheme, exist and that cannot have the properties it has' (35).

Horror has often relied and even thrived on ambiguity because, after all, what is more terrifying than *not knowing*, which opens up all the darkest recesses of the mind and sets them to work filling in the blanks? Robin Wood alludes to this in his seminal essay 'The American Nightmare: Horror in the 70s' (1986), when he describes many horror films of this era as 'incoherent texts' and notes that 'overall, the genre itself [has moved] characteristically toward an unresolvable and usually unrecognized dilemma', which Wood then connects thematically with the quandaries of American identity in the troubled 1970s (70). Later, he notes a key distinction between horror in the classical era of the 1930s and horror in the 1970s: 'The typical ending of the former has the monster destroyed, the young lovers (sometimes the established family) united and safe; the typical ending of the latter insists that the monster cannot be destroyed, that the repressed can never be annihilated' (87). Hence, Leatherface is left angrily swinging his chainsaw in the middle of a backcountry road in *The Texas Chain Saw Massacre*; Larry Cohen's *It's Alive* ends with the portentous news that another monstrous baby has been born in another city; and *Halloween* ends with the mysterious disappearance of Michael Myers after he has been shot numerous times and fallen to his apparent death from a second-floor window. Each of these films – and many others – ends on notes of menace that underscore the fundamental ambiguity of the monsters themselves: Leatherface, whose violent rage and strange gender-bending are given only a cursory explanation via dialogue referencing the closing of the local slaughterhouses, which provided his family with both income and an identity; the deformed baby in *It's Alive*, the possible product of defective pharmaceuticals, is both monstrous and pathetic; and Michael Myers, whose murderous rampage and seemingly inhuman indestructibility are never explained.

The horror films that tend to be the most reassuring are the ones that ultimately dispense with ambiguity via explanation, thus rendering their monsters knowable. If monsters are, in Carroll's words, 'repelling because they violate standing categories', they are 'compelling of our attention' for the very same reason (39), and our inherent inclination is to consume them by understanding them. Explanation of horrific events, while not completely relieving us of those horrors, nevertheless ameliorates them to some extent because they are now contained within a sphere of understanding and categories. To put it even more directly, making monsters knowable means that they can be defeated. The monsters of the 'Golden Era' of Hollywood horrors all had their vulnerabilities that had to be discovered and then exploited – vampires with a stake to the heart or exposed to sunlight, werewolves pierced with a silver bullet, Frankenstein's monster repelled with fire – which they were with great success, as each film ended with the monster being explicitly and unambiguously dispatched.

Many of these same ideas can be applied to the real-life horrors of 9/11 and our response to it. The connection between horror and terrorism is quite clear, as Wetmore (2012) notes: 'the role of the horror film is to cause fear. The role of the terrorist attack is also to cause fear. Both the horror film and terrorism are rooted in the visual experience of horrifying images that cause dread and terror' (10). Some writers have even gone so far as to specifically frame the mediated experience of the 9/11 attacks as a horror narrative:

> When the second plane hit the South Tower, it became instantly clear that something deliberate was going on. It also became one of the most harrowing and tragically iconic moments in television history – a visual that is still seared into the collective consciousness ten years later. To watch the footage now is to experience something akin to the feeling of seeing a horror movie. We see the anchors fumbling to explain what is going on, even as we know all too well the terror and trauma they are about to experience. ('9/11: How TV Networks Broke The News')

Continuing the analogy, the hijackers can be viewed as monsters who elicited the same paradox of horror: an uncomfortable intermingling of abject disgust and morbid curiosity. Who were these men? Where did they come from? How could they do what they did? What drove them to homicidal acts of violence on such a grand scale? The extremity of the attacks, unprecedented on American soil, did not fit with Americans' pre-existing schemas, which tended to frame terrorism as something that happens 'over there', not in the heart of Manhattan on a sunny Tuesday morning. The days immediately following 9/11 were shrouded in mystery, confusion and fear, and it wasn't until three days later on 14 September that the FBI released the identities of the hijackers ('FBI Announces List of 19 Hijackers'). Newspaper, magazine, television and online journalists and pundits immediately sought to explain the hijackers by exploring their ethnic backgrounds, personal experiences, political and religious ideologies, and so forth.

We can see this most explicitly in the *New York Times* profile of Mohamed Atta, 'the suspected mastermind of 9/11'. Published a month after the attacks, the article was provocatively titled 'The Mastermind', although it is the subhead that is more revealing: 'A Portrait of the Terrorist: From Shy Child to Single-Minded Killer' (Yardley 2001). The article tracks 'Mr Atta's path to Sept. 11' via his personality ('meticulous, disciplined, and highly intelligent'), the psychodynamics of his upbringing ('His mother pampered him, but his disciplinarian father thought him girlish'), his vision of Islam ('embraced resolute precepts of fate and destiny and purity'), and his increasing frustrations with western incursion into the Middle East ('the target of his blame became the West, and especially America'). Interestingly, the article ends with the supposition that Atta purposefully allowed his luggage to be left at Logan Airport in Boston rather than make it onto the plane he crashed into the World Trade Center because 'the introvert, the meticulous planner, the man who believed he was doing God's will, wanted to make certain the world knew his name' (B1). This coda is particularly important, as it attributes to Atta a motivation that would be immediately recognisable to American readers immersed in a culture of celebrity and social media: the desire to be famous, to be known, to be remembered, even as a monster.

IV. ROB ZOMBIE'S *HALLOWEEN*: SHAPING MICHAEL MYERS' DERANGED PSYCHOLOGY

While there are numerous examples of post-9/11 horror films that could be examined in light of the genre's shift towards a desire to know and understand, the remainder of this chapter will focus on Rob Zombie's 2007 reboot of John Carpenter's *Halloween*. Zombie's *Halloween* is particularly intriguing because, as a reboot designed to maximise profitability without alienating the 'devoted, and already skeptical, horror and franchise fans' (Stam 2015: 55), it removes all the ambiguity that defined the original film by explaining in no uncertain terms how its monster, a hulking, silent slasher named Michael Myers, became a monster. Several other remakes, reboots and prequels of this era similarly create elaborate backstories where there previously had been none, including *Texas Chainsaw Massacre: The Beginning*, which elaborates events that are obliquely hinted at in the original, specifically the Hewitt clan's loss of their slaughterhouse jobs and turn to cannibalism for survival, and *Hannibal Rising*, a feature-length explanation of how Hannibal Lecter became a serial-killing cannibal after witnessing the murder and consumption of his beloved baby sister by desperate members of the SS during the Second World War. However, the concentrated and extreme differences between Carpenter's *Halloween* and Zombie's *Halloween* make it a particularly fruitful case study in the horror genre's shift towards explaining monstrosity post-9/11.

Regarding *Halloween*'s placement in the post-9/11 cinematic landscape, its release in late August 2007 is not insignificant, as Stephen Prince described late 2007 as

> a turning point in American cinema's response to the fallout from 9/11. The Hollywood studio-distributors embarked on their most expansive and ambitious package of films to date and nervously watched the box office response . . . This – 2007 – was the year when the floodgates seemed to burst, with films pouring out of Hollywood about terrorism and Iraq, most of them being released late in the year. (296)

These films included *The Kingdom*, *A Mighty Heart*, *Rendition*, *The Situation*, *In the Valley of Elah*, *Lions for Lambs*, *Home of the Brave*, *The Kite Runner*, *Monster's Ball* and *Charlie Wilson's War*. Interestingly, as noted earlier, 2007 was also the best year for horror films at the US box office since 9/11, with thirty-one major theatrical releases accounting for 7.16 per cent of the market share ('Horror: Year-by-Year Market Share'). In addition to *Halloween*, there were several notable hit horror films released that year: *I Am Legend* ($256 million), a big-budget apocalyptic horror-thriller; *1408* ($71 million), which was based on a Stephen King short story about a sceptical paranormal investigator who spends a night in a haunted hotel room; and *Saw IV* ($63 million), the fourth entry in the long-running series about a serial killer who traps victims in elaborate, grisly life-or-death games. Thus, even though Zombie has never explicitly linked *Halloween* with the post-9/11 environment, it was conceived, produced and released during the most significant years for Hollywood cinema following that national trauma, which makes it a part of that landscape, intentionally or otherwise.

Described by Zombie as half prequel, half reimagining of Carpenter's original (*Jimmy Kimmel Live!*), his *Halloween* takes place in the same fictional, Midwest town of Haddonfield, Illinois and follows the same general story as conceived by the original film's screenwriters, Debra Hill and John Carpenter: as a child, Michael Myers murders his sister Judith on Halloween night and then spends the next fifteen years in a psychiatric hospital from which he subsequently escapes and returns to Haddonfield on Halloween, where he murders a number of people, most of them teenage girls babysitting, before being stopped by one of the teen girls, Laurie Strode, and Myers' psychiatrist, Dr Sam Loomis (played by Donald Pleasance in the original and Malcolm McDowell in the reboot). While the second half of Zombie's film follows the original fairly closely, even replicating certain scenes, dialogue exchanges and killings nearly verbatim, the two films diverge radically in terms of how they present Michael Myers' backstory.

Carpenter's *Halloween* is purposefully vague about Myers' psychology, giving us very little information about his background and instead presenting him as faceless evil incarnate, which is why the blank white mask he wears is so visually and symbolically effective. It is a human face, no doubt, but one that has no discernible characteristics. As Carpenter put it in a 2011 interview:

> ... the main character, the guy in the mask, really isn't altogether human. He has no characteristics. He's, uh, almost like a machine. He was just pure evil. That was what I intended to do. It's evil out of nothing, evil from no background, which completely creeps me out as a human being, that evil could arrive at my doorstep without a purpose, without a past, without an origin. (Abramovitch 2015)

Rather than present a similar monster, one without explicit past or origin, Zombie's film goes the opposite direction by providing a lengthy origin story that purports to explain Myers' murderousness via a nexus of familial, institutional and psychological issues. In fact, Zombie uses thirty-eight minutes – more than one-third of the film's 120-minute running time – on Michael's childhood both before and after his first killings.

It is not surprising that Zombie would take this approach in rebooting *Halloween*, as creating a new origin story – depicting the process of *becoming* – is one of the quintessential characteristics of the reboot. As William Proctor (2012) notes,

> A reboot wipes the slate clean and begins the story again from 'year one,' from a point of origin and from an alternative parallel position: *Batman Begins* tells the story of the Dark Knight, who he is and how he came to be; Abrams' *Star Trek* depicts the original Enterprise crew in utero; and *Casino Royale* portrays James Bond's inauguration as a 00-agent with a license to kill. All these texts show the protagonist(s) in a process of 'becoming' (Arnett 2009: 4), and this is a fundamental feature of the reboot. (5)

Yet the difference in depicting Myers in the process of 'becoming' is not just one of structure but of fundamental meaning, as the extensive backstory that Zombie provides completely alters Michael Myers' character, his relation to other characters and the nature of his monstrosity.

In Carpenter's film, Myers starts as a six-year-old from an apparently normal, stable middle-class home. His murdering his sister in the film's opening sequence is never explained in any way, although some critics have read it from a psychoanalytic perspective that sees Michael's witnessing Judith going upstairs to have sex with her boyfriend as a traumatic sexual event that triggers his murderousness (Dika 1987: 96). Such a reading is certainly plausible and has helped shape the overall understanding of the slasher film (see Clover 1992; Dika), although it is not absolutely inherent to the film itself.

In this regard *Halloween* is purposefully vague about Myers' motivation, which enhances the horrific qualities of the protracted opening scene, which is shot entirely from Michael's point of view. First-time viewers are not aware that the eyes through which they are watching the action belong to a child, as Carpenter starts the film from Michael's perspective, thus hiding his identity until he exits the house after stabbing his sister and runs into his parents as they are getting out of their car. 'Michael?' his father says as he extends his hand to remove the mask Michael is wearing, at which point Carpenter cuts to a reverse angle, revealing a little boy in a shiny clown costume with a disturbingly blank look on his face and a bloody kitchen knife clutched in his hand. As the film's signature musical score begins to escalate on the soundtrack, Carpenter cranes back from the medium shot of Myers to a high-angle extreme long shot as the boy stands motionless, flanked on both sides by his unmoving parents, which gives the viewer the opportunity to fully digest the revelation of what s/he has just witnessed. Thus, rather than *becoming*, the opening of Carpenter's *Halloween* confirms that Michael already *is* and probably always has been.

It is interesting in this regard that, at the beginning of this sequence, the first thing we hear on the soundtrack are unseen children chanting over a black screen:

Black cats and goblins and broomsticks and ghosts,
Covens of witches with all of their hosts,
You may think they scare me, you're probably right
Black cats and goblins on Halloween night.
Trick or treat!

Figure 12.1 While the depiction of six-year-old Michael Myers in John Carpenter's *Halloween* (1978) suggests a figure who has always been evil, the depiction of the ten-year-old Myers in Zombie's reboot suggests a person who is in the process of becoming a psychopath.

In unison with the unseen children yelling 'Trick or treat!', the camera suddenly moves out from behind a tree, giving us a full view of the Myers house from what we will eventually learn is Michael Myers' point of view. While this chant helps to set the mood of the film's Halloween setting, it also explicitly associates Myers with elements of the supernatural (goblins, witches and ghosts) from the very beginning, which encourages us to see him as a monster outside the realm of logical explication – something that, in Noël Carroll's terms, cannot be.

Zombie's *Halloween* opens in much different fashion. The children's chanting about supernatural creatures is replaced instead with a quote from the book Dr Loomis has written about his experiences with Michael: 'The darkest souls are not those which choose to exist within the hell of the abyss, but those which choose to break free from the abyss and move silently among us.' While the quote bears a certain metaphysical weight with its mention of souls and hell, it still smacks of a psychiatrist waxing poetic about an extreme psychological case. The narrative proper begins with a series of scenes leading up to Michael killing not just Judith, but also her boyfriend and his mother's boy-friend. These scenes locate him within a deeply dysfunctional family suffering under economic hardship, domestic abuse and a general sense of depravity that is exhibited in both the characters' grimy appearances and their crude, vindictive demeanour towards each other. The family is led by Michael's mother, Deborah (Sheri Moon Zombie), a stripper whose live-in boyfriend, Ronnie (William Forsythe), is a vulgar brute whose already poison-bitter personality is not improved by his being temporarily disabled from an accident. Michael's sister Judith (Hanna Hall) is depicted primarily in terms of her callous sexuality and snide attitude, while ten-year-old Michael (Daeg Faerch) is already a budding psychopath who hides behind a plastic clown mask while killing his pet rat with an X-Acto knife before breakfast. The only sense of humanity and affection displayed in the Myers household is Deborah's warm and protective demeanour towards Michael (which raises the ire of both Ronnie and Judith) and Michael's affection for his baby sister Boo.

Zombie's depiction of the Myers house as deeply dysfunctional, brimming with emotional and physical violence amid the squalor of poverty, has a profound impact on the film's underlying politics as they relate to the horrific. In Carpenter's film, Myers' being a part of a seem-ingly stable middle-class family in the heartland of America made his abject evil all the more unnerving because it had no obvious, easily identifiable social, familial or economic cause. This lack of explanation doesn't absolve the American family or capitalist structure of any com-plicity in real-life horrors, but rather presents them as largely irrelevant in the face of genuine evil – a force that transcends social, cultural and economic bounds. Quite the opposite, the violence in Zombie's film is easily reducible to the fetid horrors of Michael's deranged family dynamic, which is clearly incapable of producing someone who is not depraved or, at the very least, socially maladjusted.

The opening scene is set in a filthy kitchen littered with clutter and dirty dishes; its yellow-tiled walls are suggestive of the inside of an institution, not a home. Members of the Myers family are introduced insulting and threatening each other as they engage in a back-and-forth of loud interpersonal torment. This tone carries through the rest of the film's opening scenes, as Michael is tormented at school by a bully (Daryl Sabara) who mocks his mother's profession as a stripper and beats him physically. Thus, if Carpenter's film planted the idea that the worst evil could emerge in the dullest of families, Zombie's film reassures us that psychotics emerge from depravity and economic squalor.

The difference in Michael Myers between the two films is fully cemented in the way he is discussed by Dr Loomis, the man who knows him best. In Carpenter's film, we first meet Dr Loomis in the scene immediately following Judith's murder. A title card informs us that it is fifteen years later, and Loomis is driving with a nurse to Smith's Grove Sanitarium where Myers has been committed. When the nurse asks if there are any special instructions in handling Myers, Dr Loomis replies, 'Just try to understand what we're dealing with here. Don't underestimate it.' The nurse is taken aback by his choice of the word 'it' to describe Myers, and Loomis acquiesces to her admonishment, 'Don't you think we could refer to "it" as "him"?', by simply replying, 'If you say so.' He also makes it clear that he 'never, never, never' wants Myers to be released, and the only reason they are going to pick him up to take him to a court hearing is 'because it's the law'. Much more explicitly, after Myers escapes and steals their car, Dr Loomis exclaims, 'He's gone! He's gone! The evil is gone!'

Later in the film, when Dr Loomis and Haddonfield's Sherriff Brackett (Charles Cyphers) are investigating the deserted Myers house, they come across a dead, partially eaten dog inside. When Loomis suggests that it is Myers' handiwork – 'He got hungry' – the sheriff scoffs and says, 'A man wouldn't do that', to which Loomis replies, 'This isn't a man.' Thus Dr Loomis' dialogue consistently denies Myers any kind of humanity, insisting instead on his existence as pure evil, a stance that would seem to fly in the face of his role as a psychiatrist, a profession that relies on proffering biological, psychological and neurochemical explanations for behaviours that would conventionally be described as 'evil'.

In Zombie's *Halloween*, Dr Loomis is first involved with Michael at his school when he gets into a fight in the bathroom with the aforementioned bully and is taken to the office after he says 'Fuck you' to the intervening principal multiple times. After a dead cat in a plastic bag is discovered in Michael's schoolbag along with a stack of photographs of dead animals that he likely killed and photographed, Dr Loomis tells his mother that killing and causing pain in smaller animals is an early warning sign for 'bigger and deeper problems'. 'He's a very disturbed young man . . . obviously it's a very deranged young mind that can do this to his pets', he is heard saying as Zombie cuts away to Michael running from the office. Thus, from the very beginning it is established that Michael is suffering from psychological issues that can only be exacerbated by his family situation.

After Michael is institutionalised for the murders of Judith, her boy-friend and Ronnie, Zombie spends a significant amount of time depicting his withdrawal into himself while at Smith's Grove, something that had already happened before the first frame of Carpenter's film. Over grainy black-and-white footage of Michael in the hospital, we hear Dr Loomis read his case notes, which become more and more despondent: 'To the untrained eye, there is nothing visually abnormal with this angelic young boy. But one must remember not to be fooled by his calm, unassuming façade.' Later, Dr Loomis intones, 'Michael's so-called "normal" moments are becoming fewer and fewer, and I'm particularly worried about this. I believe that these masks have begun to create a mental sanctuary in which Michael can hide within himself and from himself.' This is followed by 'Michael's downward slide into this hellish abyss continues. I fear he's on the verge of completely shutting down.' And finally, 'The child christened Michael Myers has become a sort of ghost, a mere shape of a human being. There's nothing left here now.'

These voiceover case notes are actually quite similar to what Dr Loomis says in Carpenter's film when he and Sheriff Brackett are investigating the deserted Myers house while looking for the escaped Michael:

> I met him fifteen years ago. I was told there was nothing left. No reason, no, uh, conscience, no understanding in even the most rudimentary sense, of life or death, of good or evil, of right or wrong. I met this six-year-old child with this blank, pale, emotionless face and the blackest eyes. The devil's eyes. I spent eight years trying to reach him, and then another seven trying to keep him locked up because I realized that what was living behind that boy's eyes was purely and simply evil.

It is crucial that, in Carpenter's film, the fact there is 'nothing left' has been presented to Dr Loomis as an assessment by someone else, rather than the result of his direct observation. Thus, there is the possibility that there was nothing there to begin with, meaning that Michael did not lose his humanity at some point, but was rather 'purely and simply evil' from the outset, a scenario that defies the logic, reason and order of psychiatry.

In Zombie's film, Dr Loomis is shown at a conference reading from a book he has written about his experiences working with Michael titled *The Devil's Eyes: The Story of Michael Myers*. As in Carpenter's film, he concentrates on Michael's eyes, but comes to a very different conclusion:

> These eyes will deceive you. They will destroy you. They will take from you your innocence, your pride, and eventually your soul.

These eyes do not see what you and I see. Behind these eyes one finds only blackness, the absence of light. These are the eyes of a psychopath. Michael was created by a perfect alignment of interior and exterior factors gone violently wrong – a perfect storm, if you will. Thus creating a psychopath that knows no boundaries and has no boundaries.

Whereas Dr Loomis in Carpenter's film concludes that Michael is simply evil, Dr Loomis in Zombie's film concludes that he is a psychopath, a bounded psychological category defined by objective, agreed-upon characteristics. There is some wavering in this assessment, as later in the film Dr Loomis tells the Haddonfield sheriff (Brad Dourif), 'Evil is here. It's walking amongst us.' When the sheriff says, 'Doc, it sounds to me like you're talking about the Antichrist', Loomis replies, 'Well, perhaps I am!' However, his temporary foray into supernatural terrain is quickly undercut by his assertion in a subsequent conversation with the sheriff that 'You have to stop thinking that we're dealing with a normal man here. We're dealing with a soulless killing machine driven by pure animal instinct', which returns us once again to the realm of human psychology. While Dr Loomis in Carpenter's film is resolute in his assessment of Myers as pure evil, Zombie's Dr Loomis wavers but is mostly consistent in presenting him as a case of psychological damage – the 'deranged mind' he described back when Myers was ten, but now worse.

Figure 12.2 In Rob Zombie's *Halloween* (2007), Dr Loomis (Malcolm McDowell) reads from a book he has written about his experiences working with Michael Myers, concluding that he was created 'a psychopath that knows no boundaries and has no boundaries' by a 'perfect alignment of interior and exterior factors gone violently wrong'.

Herein lies the fundamental difference between the two films: Carpenter insists on a kind of evil that defies reason and understanding, while Zombie's film falls back on understandable, objective psychological explanations. This does not make Myers not frightening, as he is still a terrifying, hulking killer, but there is some sense of comfort in knowing exactly what he is. Like Mohamed Atta and the other 9/11 terrorists, he may be capable of horrible acts of violence, but we can at least classify and somehow understand him, thus reassuring ourselves that order, logic and reason still exist. The evil that Michael Myers in Carpenter's *Halloween* represents is a complete breakdown of rationality, a figure of menace we cannot explain or understand and must simply destroy, even as he resists destruction.

V. CONCLUSION

Rob Zombie's decision to reboot the *Halloween* franchise by explicitly explaining Michael Myers as a psychopath via extended exposition of his backstory and its attendant familial violence, psychological trauma and economic hardship is only one example of the tendency of post-9/11 horror remakes, reboots, sequels and prequels to sacrifice ambiguity and mystery in favour of understanding. While this shift is partially explained by the film industry's propensity to refresh ageing or failed franchises by returning to the origin story, its overwhelming presence in the post-9/11 era also suggests that it is a reflection of the times.

Post-9/11 horror, despite its enhanced visual transgressions, thematic despair and sometimes outright nihilism, has often been intent on showing us *how* and *why*, which reflects the American public's need to understand the hows and whys of the terrorist attacks on the World Trade Center and the Pentagon. This wasn't always the case, as some remakes and reboots maintained a menacing air of ambiguity. To wit, the 2007 remake of *The Hitcher* (1986), which does not try to offer any explanations for its villain. John Ryder (Sean Bean), the murderous hitchhiker of the title, is sadistic, cruel, cunning and relentless, but there is no exposition about or rationale for his evil. At one point, a police investigator asks him why he has murdered numerous people and framed an otherwise innocent pair of college students for his crimes, and he replies simply, 'Why not?' This allows Ryder's villainy to work in deeply chilling ways, suggesting that such evil defies logical explanation and exists in a realm all its own – that it is, in Carroll's (2002) terms, "something which is given as in principle *unknowable* – something which, *ex hypothesi*, cannot, given the structure of our conceptual scheme, exist and that cannot have the properties it has' (35). In an era marked by terrorism, random violence and war all around the globe, *not knowing* may be the one thing that we are truly terrified to endure.

NOTES

1. For example, the 2009 version of *Friday the 13th* (1980) has, at least at the time of this writing, failed to produce even a single sequel, while the original film spawned seven direct sequels between 1981 and 1989. Similarly, the 2010 version of *A Nightmare on Elm Street* (1984) has also failed to produce any sequels, while there were six sequels to the original between 1985 and 1991. These films are arguably best thought of as failed reboots.

2. All of the box office information has been taken from Box Office Mojo (http://www.boxofficemojo.com). In the few instances when Box Office Mojo did not have numbers for the production budget, that information was compiled from the Internet Movie Database (http://www.imdb.com).

3. I should note that under the general category of 'remake' I am including both films that are based on previous films with original storylines and films that are based on previously published material from which an earlier film or films have been made. So, for example, *The Haunting* (1999) can be seen as a remake of the 1963 film and/or a new adaptation of Shirley Jackson's 1959 novel *The Haunting of Hill House*. Other such titles include *War of the Worlds* (2005), which is based on H. G. Wells' 1898 novel that was previously adapted in 1953, and *The Amityville Horror* (2005), which is based on the 1977 book by Jay Anson that was previously adapted in 1979. In some cases, such as *The Amityville Horror*, the earlier film and/or screenplay is cited in the credits as source material, while in other cases, such as *The Haunting*, they are not. Nevertheless, the presence of an earlier film version is significant, especially in terms of how these films were often framed by audiences and critics as remakes, rather than multiple adaptations of a single source text.

REFERENCES

'9/11: How TV Networks Broke the News', 11 September 2011: http://www.huffing-tonpost.com/2011/09/09/911-tv-coverage_n_940613.html

Abramovitch, Susan, (2015), 'John Carpenter Speaks: Directing Legend on Secrets of "Halloween," Plagiarism Case Against Luc Besson', *The Hollywood Reporter*, 26 October 2015: http://www.hollywoodreporter.com/news/john-carpenter-speaks-halloween-secrets-834754

Briefel, Aviva, and Sam J. Miller (eds) (2011), *Horror After 9/11: World of Fear, Cinema of Terror*, Austin: Texas University Press.

Carroll, Noël (2002), 'Why Horror?', in Mark Jancovich (ed.), *Horror: The Film Reader*, London: Routledge, pp. 33–46.

Clover, Carol (1992), *Men, Women, and Chainsaws: Gender in the Modern Horror Film*, Princeton: Princeton University Press.

Dika, Vera (1987), 'The Stalker Film, 1978–81', in Gregory A. Waller (ed.), *American Horrors: Essays on the Modern American Horror Film*, Chicago: University of Illinois Press, pp. 86–101.

Federal Bureau of Investigation (FBI) (2011), 'National Press Releases: FBI Announces List of 19 Hijackers', 14 September 2011: https://www.fbi.gov/news/pressrel/press-releases/fbi-announces-list-of-19-hijackers

Heinze, Rüdiger, and Lucia Krämer (2015), 'Introduction: Remakes and Remaking – Preliminary Reflections', in Rüdiger Heinze and Lucia Krämer (eds), *Remakes and Remaking: Concepts, Media, Practices*, Bielefeld, Germany: Transcript, pp. 7–22.

'Horror: Year by Year Market Share', 30 September 2008: http://the-numbers.com/market/Genres/Horror.php

Jimmy Kimmel Live!, ABC, New York, 23 June 2006.

Johnson, Reed (2011), 'How 9/11 Seared Itself Into American Culture', *Los Angeles Times*, 4 September 2011, E7.

Kehr, Dave (2007), 'It's Only a Movie: Horror Films From the 1970s and Today', *New York Times*, 15 June 2007, E22.

Kendrick, James (2009), *Hollywood Bloodshed: Violence in 1980s American Cinema*, Carbondale: Southern Illinois University Press.

Prince, Stephen (2000), *A New Pot of Gold: Hollywood Under the Electronic Rainbow, 1980–1989*, Berkeley: University of California Press.

— (2003), *Classical Film Violence: Designing and Regulating Brutality in Hollywood Cinema, 1930–1968*, New Brunswick, NJ: Rutgers University Press.

— (2009), *Firestorm: American Film in the Age of Terrorism*, New York: Columbia University Press.

Proctor, William (2012), 'Regeneration & Rebirth: Anatomy of the Franchise Reboot', *Scope: An Online Journal of Film and Television Studies*, 22 February 2012: https://nottingham.ac.uk/scope/documents/2012/february-2012/proctor.pdf

Stam, Ryan (2015), *Rob Zombie, the Brand: Crafting the Convergence-Era Horror Auteur*, dissertation, University of Western Ontario.

Wetmore, Kevin J., Jr (2012), *Post-9/11 Horror in American Cinema*, New York: Continuum.

Wood, Robin (1986), *Hollywood from Vietnam to Reagan*, New York: Columbia University Press.

Yardley, Jim (2001), 'The Mastermind: A Portrait of the Terrorist: From Shy Child to Single-Minded Killer', *The New York Times*, 10 October 2001, B1.

CHAPTER 13

Post-9/11 Power and Responsibility in the Marvel Cinematic Universe

Christine Muller

I. IN THE BEGINNING . . . POWER AS ORIGIN STORY

'It's about power. Who's got it. Who knows how to use it.' These words begin the first episode of the 1997 to 2003 television series *Buffy the Vampire Slayer*'s final season, and that same episode's concluding dialogue fully amplifies this meditation on 'what it's about' beyond a mere immediate concern with plot: '[W]e're going . . . right back to the beginning. Not the Bang. Not the Word. The true beginning . . . It's not about right. It's not about wrong. It's about power' (Whedon 2002: 'Lessons'). Joss Whedon, the show's creator and often director and writer, has explored the theme of power[1] throughout *Buffy the Vampire Slayer*[2] and across multiple other intermingled genres of fiction, known collectively as the 'Whedonverse'. In doing so, he has persistently drawn from the standpoint of a real world in which dominant western philosophies regard power as immanent rather than transcendent, leaving the matter of where power originates less pressing than questions about the conditions under which it emerges and operates. Across the Whedonverse, characters routinely wonder: Do I control the power to which I have access, or does it control me? Is this power to help or to harm? Does having this power necessarily bind me to any duties regarding its use? What distinguishes power as either benevolent or malevolent? With consistency, his narratives unfold a response that recognises notions of good and evil, without characterising power as intrinsically one or the other; embraces action as shaping and disclosing character; and endorses prosocial behaviour and community bonds. This ethic manifests – not coincidentally, since Whedon grew up reading Marvel comics – in both *The Avengers* (2012) and *Avengers: Age of Ultron* (2015), films he co-wrote and directed that serve as culminating nodes in a larger story arc that comprises the Marvel Cinematic Universe (MCU).

The MCU draws on decades of Marvel Comics stories and characters to sustain continuity across films, beginning with *Iron Man* in 2008 and including eleven other films at the time of the release of *Avengers: Age of Ultron*, with plans for more stretching until at least 2028 (Leonard 2014).[3] President of Marvel Studios Kevin Feige produces all of them, ensuring that the novel, ambitious project remains consistent and coherent over the years as different writers, directors and crews craft each individual release. As a result, unique worlds such as Captain America's Second World War-based emergence and Thor's distant-space Asgard home receive distinct treatments in stand-alone features, while still situated within the same larger imaginative space of the MCU, as signalled by nods within these stand-alone features to related films. Such nods, which tantalisingly include brief scenes embedded within the closing credits to hint at a direction a future film might take, help to affirm what Marvel through its comics and Whedon through his work have long envisioned as crucial storytelling components: that actions have consequences and choices produce effects, intended or otherwise, which characters cannot simply elude when the particular story portraying those actions and choices ends. With continuity across the MCU, what happens in one film can be seen to have lasting, reverberating repercussions that future films' stories and characters must at least acknowledge, if not address.

Such a format provides a rich opportunity to engage real world issues that, apropos of the real world, fail to resolve neatly within a single storytelling session. In particular, the MCU's development within the first two decades of the twenty-first century occasions an apt relationship between the superhero genre, which has long confronted questions about the possibilities and constraints that great power entails, and the 'War on Terror',[4] which has showcased never-fully-resolved crises about the very same questions. Born in horror, danger and a confounding of fundamental cultural assumptions about safety and agency, the 'War on Terror' traces its beginnings to trauma, much the way the Avengers themselves have been forged. Such structural, thematic and contextual alignments render cinematic portrayals of 'War on Terror' dilemmas in terms of long-standing superhero and Whedonverse principles, which attend critically to the circumstances within which power appears and is exerted, including the specific pressures that exigent danger engenders. Particularly within the MCU's dramatic switch points of the two Avengers films, superheroes serving as embodied power struggle under trauma's compromising duress to determine right from wrong, both in ethical terms and in the practical sense of knowing precisely what options will help rather than harm. For viewers, these fictive labours give form to ongoing considerations in the real world of whether and how to wield power under extremity, specifically in both just and effective ways.[5]

II. SUPERHEROES AS ETHICAL COMPASS

A 1962 comic introduced Marvel's Spider-Man with the caution, 'With great power, there must also come – great responsibility' (quoted in Fingeroth 2013: 125). While still associated with Spider-Man, this principle asserts the basic existential dilemma of all superheroes (Fingeroth 2013: 125). By nature, they possess great power and, therefore, their very existence continually prompts critical reflection not only about how their power should be used, but also about who they are as beings of power. Yet narrative attempts to work through such questions matter not only to these fantastic figures within their fictional worlds. If, as Peter Coogan elaborates on this idea, 'superhero stories concern the responsible use of extraordinary power in the service of justice' (Coogan 2013: 3), then thinking through what constitutes responsibility, what constitutes justice, and how power can be directed in the service of each proves a valuable exercise for readers and viewers in the real world, in which power is unevenly distributed across fraught terrain.

Features consistent across superhero stories evidence a common starting point for making such assessments. For example, superheroes 'fight evil and protect the innocent; this fight is universal, prosocial, and selfless' (Coogan 2013: 4). In distinguishing good from evil, Ivory Madison, writer of *Huntress: Year One* from DC Comics, argues that 'narcissism is the defining factor, perhaps even the core, of evil' (Madison 2013: 159). In effect, 'the superhero will sacrifice himself for others, whereas the supervillain will sacrifice others for himself' (Madison 2013: 159). In sum, superhero tales evoke an ethic of absolute altruism, understood as 'the good', in direct contrast to evil, which is marked by the opposite quality of selfishness. So, while both good and evil forces can wield considerable power, the stories clearly endorse which values should guide how that power is used.

The Whedonverse further elaborates these themes. For Whedon as well, evil is characterised by selfishness, seeking to foster discord and refuse culpability. In contrast, good embraces community bonds and responsibility for one's actions. Specifically, though, Richardson and Rabb identify Whedon's perspective as a 'virtue ethics grounded in care' (Richardson and Rabb 2007: 52), which urges that if you can act, then you must (Richardson and Rabb 2007: 44). Ultimately, for Whedon, the quality of power depends on the choices of those who wield it, who reveal themselves to be either heroic or villainous through their decisions over time to direct that power either selflessly, to help, or selfishly, to harm. But all of this should perhaps appear strange; in scenarios involving superheroes with extraordinary power, why would individualism and even narcissism not be endemic? Superheroes need not be good, and given their extreme power, who can require or demand anything of them? Yet these stories, certainly within Whedon's conceptualisation, feature protagonists for whom careless self-absorption is never a given. Rather, these powerful beings struggle continually, with themselves and with each other, to situate themselves in prosocial commitment to serve the larger communities of which they are, no matter how anomalously, a part. For Whedon, it is the choice to commit in this way that signals heroic status.

As a result, readers and viewers come to assume the best of intentions for superheroes. With such an assumption, it is then tempting to think that readily determined and easily endorsed decisions about how to act during a crisis are sure to follow. Yet this is when it becomes especially complicated. For example, within Marvel storylines, 'good guys' Iron Man/Tony Stark and Captain America/Steve Rogers have embodied distinct moral positions, with Iron Man inclined towards utilitarianism and Captain America disposed towards a deontological approach (White 2012: 6–10). In principle, this means that Iron Man decides how to act based on what would produce the best outcome for the most people, while Captain America prioritises the fulfilment of specific duties. In this case, one superhero directs his behaviour towards projected results, which cannot always be accurately predicted, and another is committed to preserving integrity within his actions, which risks failure to achieve a critical objective. When the two work together on the same team, such as the Avengers, their divergent priorities can complicate the conflict with their adversary by leading to friction among even the story's heroes. In both *The Avengers* and *Avengers: Age of Ultron*, this volatile dynamic periodically manifests, suggesting that like ordinary people, superheroes at times confront crises whose complex origins, manifestations and potential consequences can fuel vigorous dissension among those sharing a calling to respond.

Such moments of ethical dissonance present an opportunity for interactive viewership. In keeping with Whedon's vision of characters manifesting their moral positioning through their choices, those who encounter his work can do the same for themselves. David Baggett points out that Whedon produces tensions in his stories that he often does not fully resolve, avoiding simplistic portrayals of pure good winning handily over pure evil in favour of failings, frictions, mistakes, conflicting values and other narrative wrinkles that disturb a complacent reading of ethically challenging scenarios (Baggett 2011: 9–23). As Rabb and Richardson argue, his storytelling style enables multiple standpoints on issues to compete in what they term a process of 'narrative ethics' (Rabb and Richardson 2014: 312–24). While, within the Whedonverse, often the 'correct moral choice involves self-sacrifice' (Rabb and Richardson 2014: 315), and typically 'compassion, cooperation, community, and self-sacrifice seem to save the day' (Rabb and Richardson 2014: 322), ultimately sufficient irresolution persists to enable viewers to choose among multiple options to enact a narrative ethics of their own and form, through their choices, who they themselves will become (Rabb and Richardson 2014: 324). On these terms – with Whedon's moral compass pointing towards altruism in community and his narrative ethics inviting viewers to make their own decisions right alongside the superheroes as they confront complex, high-stakes quandaries – the Avengers films emerge out of a 'War on Terror' era characterised by fear, a pervasive aura of risk, and distant combat fought by few on behalf of many.

III. NOVEL THREATS AND VULNERABLE ACTORS: ENTER THE AVENGERS

11 September 2001 has often been characterised as having changed the world. The extent to which this might be true socially, politically, economically, militarily, historically or otherwise depends on careful, discipline-specific study. Yet, in the day's immediate aftermath, many people professed a general sense of the world having changed, suggesting something existential and visceral about what this characterisation might mean. Hijackers with neither prior notice nor publicly declared motives flew three passenger-filled commercial airliners into occupied buildings in Lower Manhattan and Arlington, VA, with a fourth downed in rural Pennsylvania by civilian intervention on board. For US television viewers, who watched the destruction live and through endless replays of the footage of planes crashing and the World Trade Center towers collapsing, the attacks presented a number of unfamiliar and unprecedented phenomena. Debate has surrounded the question

of whether the US government knew more and could have done more about the Al-Qaeda threat. However, for US civilians on 11 September, everything was unexpected, and 10 September felt like an entire world away. The way things would work in this seemingly new world had yet to be discerned and understood, with acute uncertainty about once taken-for-granted fundamental assumptions about day-to-day life marking 11 September 2001 as a cultural trauma.[6]

The US government's response to 11 September falls under the nebulous term 'War on Terror'. With the objective of eradicating foreign threats by targeting a tactic, the project's very premise poses problems of definition, practical implementation and resolution. Its own tactics have raised additional concerns, particularly those troubling notions of the just conduct of war and the parameters of civil liberties. While many US news consumers likely already have predispositions about where they stand regarding the basic contours of the 'War on Terror's practical and ethical dilemmas, many might also wonder whether a seemingly new situation demands a fresh standpoint. Without particular training, expertise or insight in policy matters, how does one judge what is right and what is wrong, what will work and what will not, and how questions of morality and practicality inter-relate? How do vulnerable subjects who participate civically in the power of government decide for themselves when and how that power should be used, particularly under the pressures of traumatic disruption? As noted earlier, these types of questions have long informed both superhero stories and Joss Whedon's own narrative preoccupations.[7]

The MCU provides a comprehensive canvas for exploring such issues. By the time *The Avengers* begins, the ordinary people of Earth have learned that beings with extraordinary abilities exist. Captain America/Steve Rogers (Chris Evans), missing since the Second World War, first pushed the boundaries of what a person could do after successfully enduring an experiment that gave him exceptional strength, stamina and healing capability to fight both Nazis and Hydra, a fictional fascist organisation. Rogers, a committed patriot during patriotic times, adheres faithfully to a Boy Scout-style code of conduct and has been considered the ultimate soldier (*Captain America: The First Avenger* 2011). Over time, others have emerged. Iron Man/Tony Stark (Robert Downey, Jr), the arrogant but genius CEO of defence contractor Stark Industries, develops an 'Iron Man' suit of armour enhanced with sophisticated flight and weapons technology and seeks to protect the vulnerable around the world against rogue military violence (*Iron Man* 2008). He remains vigilant about who, such as the government or foreign insurgents, has access to his superior devices (*Iron Man; Iron*

Man 2 2010). Then there is the Hulk. Ordinarily mild-mannered scientist Bruce Banner (Edward Norton) has undergone an experiment that unexpectedly and irrevocably alters his body, leaving him susceptible when angry to becoming a 'hulk', or monstrous creature, with profound strength fuelled by pure, irrational rage. The US military hopes to weaponise his condition, which Banner resists because of its uncontrollability. Caught between fear of his own power and a greater fear of that power falling into the hands of others who cannot be trusted with it, he seeks to isolate himself to facilitate the constant vigilance necessary to prevent the Hulk from appearing (*The Incredible Hulk* 2008). On a basic level, such figures individualise some of the most prominent projections of US might: the combatant, the military-industrialist and the scientist – all two-sided coins, personifying both the positive and the negative attributes and implications of their respective roles. When crisis calls these characters to immediate action, they each prove invaluable to the team effort that is the Avengers. But when circumstances call for proactive decision making about how to forestall prospective threats, these incarnate values and interests perform the complexly human dimensions contouring structures and systems of power.

In *The Avengers*, the appearance on Earth of even more exceptional beings has augured just such a prospective threat. Thor's (Chris Hemsworth) arrival from distant planet Asgard included a destructive battle with another Asgardian entity that levelled a small town in New Mexico (*Thor* 2011). To Nick Fury (Samuel L. Jackson) of the Strategic Homeland Intervention, Enforcement and Logistics Division (SHIELD), a high-tech intelligence agency focused on global rather than only national security, the fact that extraterrestrial life has reached Earth looms more critically than any immediate physical damage (*The Avengers*). Although Thor himself acted heroically, sacrificing himself to secure the safety of human beings, he did so in confrontation with a hostile force (*Thor*). For Fury, this development signals an existential peril, with the risk now palpable that even more hostile, even more powerful enemies could threaten humanity (*The Avengers*). If considered as a real world occurrence, the revelation of such extraterrestrials would be a game-changer; such knowledge and the insecurity it portends would be comprehensively conceptually transformative – culturally traumatic. As Agent Phil Coulson (Clark Gregg) tells Thor, 'You changed everything around here.' Of course, Fury has impressive options, with Phase 1 (his first choice) summoning to the world's defence an Avengers team of superheroes and Phase 2 focused on weaponising the Tesseract, a stone Loki (Tom Hiddleston) has described as 'power', possibly 'unlimited power'. But Fury has also admitted to antagonist Loki that he is 'desperate' (*The Avengers*). Such challenges resonate with contemporary concerns following the phenomenological crisis that 11 September changed everything: when human beings acutely aware of their own radical vulnerability have access to great power, what does and what should shape their decisions to act?

The Avengers poses no simple answer to this question. When members of the Avengers team learn about Phase 2, dissension erupts. Stark, Banner (Mark Ruffalo) and Rogers confront Fury, angered by the covert attempt to generate what Rogers calls 'weapons of mass destruction', a charged term naming the very thing a real world US accused Iraq of cultivating, providing a reason to go to war. In this exchange, Fury defends his actions by elaborating the potential crisis to which he is responding, pointing to how the Asgardian appearances on Earth demonstrated that 'we are hopelessly, hilariously, outgunned'. He argues that 'The world's filling up with people who can't be matched, who can't be controlled.' Rogers challenges that logic by questioning Fury's ability to control the Tesseract, to which Fury responds, 'You [Thor] forced our hand. We had to come up with something' (*The Avengers*). Fury's anxieties call to mind real world worries about a repeated 11 September (or a larger-scale crisis triggered by chemical, biological, radiological or nuclear weapons) which have pushed the parameters of acceptable forms of pre-emption and response. Within this fictional argument, each character asserts his own concerns and values, with Fury voicing a figurative combination of entities such as the US National Security Agency (NSA) and the Department of Defense and Rogers speaking within the discourse of the just rules of war.[8] No matter how earnest Fury's apparent intentions, he has pursued the dubious and dangerous path of developing proliferating, potentially unmanageable weaponry. Yet no matter how noble Rogers' objections to that weaponry might seem, he fails to satisfactorily neutralise the spectre of extreme vulnerability that Fury has raised. At this point, neither character concedes the argument and the narrative proffers no clear resolution.

Accordingly, this scene instantiates Whedon's narrative ethic by presenting multiple perspectives without unequivocally endorsing a particular position, leaving viewers to consider what they know and believe and take their own sides in the fictionalised debate. At the same time, though, Fury's preference for Phase 1, the eventually successful assembly of the Avengers to defend New York, and the final removal of the Tesseract to Asgard ultimately do signal an ethical stance in favour of prosocial fellowship over the pursuit of security by any means, no matter what the exigency might seem to impel.

Figure 13.1 The superheroes debate their objectives, methods and values in *Avengers: Age of Ultron* (2015). Steve Rogers/Captain America anchors the centre, while Tony Stark/Iron Man defends his aggressive choices. The mirroring of characters' faces on room surfaces underscores this moment of self-reflection.

IV. LEARNING CURVES OF THE BOTH WEAK AND POWERFUL

As the conflict above evidences, Fury's objective of defending the Earth invokes substantial resources, either of personnel (Phase 1) or of weaponry (Phase 2). However, while Rogers resists the menace of Phase 2, Fury's (and the narrative's) preferred vision of uniting a group of champions for Earth poses its own set of problems. Not only do the superheroes distrust him – and not without good reason – but they also distrust themselves and one another. Trauma by definition undermines a person's sense of safety and agency by violating both, and it inhibits community by confronting a person with isolating experience, even though shared bonds can provide salutary resources of comfort and solidarity. With their extraordinary powers manifesting and developing within contexts of violence and horror, Rogers, Banner and Stark must somehow find a way to make peace with past personal struggles if they are to join together constructively in a common purpose.

For Steve Rogers, trauma takes both conventional and unconventional forms. During the Second World War, he loses both his mentor Dr Abraham Erskine (Stanley Tucci) and his best friend Bucky Barnes (Sebastian Stan) to the secretive, totalitarian Hydra. After losing Barnes, Rogers finds he cannot even self-medicate by drinking, since his serum-enhanced metabolism processes the alcohol too quickly for him to get drunk; he cannot dull his emotional pain. In the end, he sacrifices himself in an aircraft that crashes into ice, where he is frozen, then found decades later and revived by SHIELD. A man out of time, his entire world has truly changed; nothing and no one is familiar (*Captain America: The First Avenger*). When viewers first see him in *The Avengers*, he is pummelling his memories into punching bag after punching bag. Alluding to unspecified political developments since his war, he tells Fury, 'They say we won. They didn't say what we lost', indicating disillusionment about what his country has done since his sacrifice.[9] Nevertheless, when Fury calls him to a new mission, he readily joins. Later, when Banner and Stark suggest that Fury is hiding something, Rogers remains more circumspect and insists, 'We have orders. We should follow them.' Yet his continued deference to authority wavers; he investigates on his own and discovers the covert Tesseract-derived weapon prototypes. To Rogers this means 'The world hasn't changed a bit', because para-governmental agencies persist in pursuing unwarranted kinds of power (*The Avengers*). As a result, following Agent Coulson's death, when Stark exclaims, 'I am not marching to Fury's fife!' Rogers replies, 'Neither am I! He's got the same blood on his hands as Loki does. Right now we've got to put that aside and get this done' (*The Avengers*). His response evidences a more nuanced sense of responsibility: Fury's approach might be suspect, but the threat is still real; yet, just because Rogers and Fury share a very real enemy, this does not mean Rogers must conform to Fury's questionable ethics.[10] Triggered by dismay, his new assertion of autonomy augurs a post-traumatic turn for Rogers. No longer living in the past, neither through memories nor through adherence to outmoded forms of unreflective allegiance, Rogers now enters his commitments with a critical eye, ensuring that he acts in accord with what he understands as just principles.

Bruce Banner's change into the Hulk, for the first time but possibly every time, constitutes his trauma. Wild and dangerous, the Hulk (Edward Norton) damages property and harms people in a haze that he only partially registers consciously. He comes to resist close relationships, since even physical intimacy can elevate his heart rate into a dangerous range, foreclosing his chances of creating a family (*The Incredible Hulk*). In *The Avengers*, Banner (Mark Ruffalo) reveals that he has even tried to kill himself, but the Hulk prevented his death. Yet Stark, who believes Banner should embrace the Hulk transformation, wonders whether the Hulk actually saved Banner's life during the initial experiment. In fact, Stark tells Banner he considers his own precarious yet power-enabling state 'a terrible privilege'. After damaging fights with Romanoff and Thor on board the airborne SHIELD helicarrier, the Hulk falls from the sky, but neither dies nor hurts anyone else. An onlooker (Harry Dean Stanton) says he witnessed Banner consciously landing in an unoccupied area, affirming that Banner can assert more control over the Hulk, which encourages him to feel more trust and confidence in his ability to self-regulate. With his anger now better in-check, he is ready to contribute to the team (*The Avengers*).

Tony Stark also has a history of war-related traumatic experience. The fellow captive and scientist Ho Yinsen (Shaun Toub) who helps him in Afghanistan dies aiding his escape, and Stark nearly dies there as well. His imprisonment catalyses his adoption of more altruistic aims in his business practices and in his Iron Man persona (*Iron Man*; *Iron Man 2*). However, Rogers accuses Stark of naïve self-absorption during the heated Phase 2 argument, contending that 'The only thing you really fight for is yourself. You're not the guy to make the sacrifice play, to lay down on a wire and let the other guy crawl over you.' Stark retorts, 'I think I would just cut the wire', but Rogers smiles, 'Always a way out ' Rogers soon revisits this theme when Stark angrily blames Agent Coulson for his own death, calling him an 'idiot' for confronting the more powerful Loki instead of waiting for back-up. Rogers advises Stark that 'Sometimes there isn't a way out.' Yet, when Loki uses the Tesseract to open a wormhole over New York and expose the Earth to a superior invading force, at the same time that a nuclear missile is heading to the city as the World Security Council's effort to contain the invasion, Stark (as Iron Man) grabs the missile to redirect it into the wormhole and guide it towards annihilating the alien multitude. Rogers (as Captain America), who had been criticising Stark about his narcissism and unrealistic optimism about combat options, asks, 'Stark, you know that's a one-way trip' (*The Avengers*)? Stark confronts the reality of the no-win scenario and finds within himself the ability to sacrifice himself to save others.

Taken together, these transformations mark how Whedon not only envisions an entity such as the Avengers, but also the possibility of the judicious use of might under duress. Each hero wrestles with his own particular challenge, with Rogers learning to question authority,

Banner learning to control his rage, and Stark learning that no-win scenarios exist, in which no amount of money, arms or intelligence can prevent a problematic outcome, yet some action must be taken. In a text contemporary with the 'War on Terror', the maturation of these personifications of US power could prompt further reflection, positing alternative principles that temper reactions to trauma and channel them towards more constructive modes, with the existence of threat not denied but rather processed through cautious deliberation. After all, each hero's struggle occurred not in isolation, but through interaction with each other, with Banner and Stark precipitating Rogers' suspicions about Fury, Stark prompting Banner's re-evaluation of the Hulk, and Rogers helping Stark to understand his capacity for heroism. Only through social support do these individuals with superhuman abilities realise their full, authentic potential, an ethic of altruistic community in keeping with Whedon's other work. And so, when Black Widow asks during the Battle of New York, 'How do we do this?', Captain America replies, 'As a team' (*The Avengers*).

V. CONTINUITY, TRAUMA AND *AVENGERS: AGE OF ULTRON*

Avengers: Age of Ultron begins with the Avengers attacking a remote Eastern European target – the fictional Sokovia – while tracking Hydra and now Hydra-affiliated components of SHIELD to secure Loki's sceptre, missing since *The Avengers*.[11] Once it appears that the assault might endanger civilians in a nearby city, Iron Man deploys his Iron Legion, drone-type Iron Man-style suits, to warn everyone to take shelter.[12] Yet the armoured suits broadcast their message of safety in English, and the atmosphere in response to them seems hostile. Later, we learn that two occupants of the targeted stronghold, twins Wanda/Scarlet Witch (Elizabeth Olsen) and Pietro/Quicksilver (Aaron Taylor-Johnson) Maximoff, endured experiments to generate capabilities to seek revenge against Tony Stark, having lost their parents and almost their own lives when Stark Industries missiles struck their home. Altogether, this opening scene with its backstory efficiently demonstrates how continuity across the MCU enables viewers to appreciate links between actions and consequences. Once-secured weapons like Loki's sceptre can fall again into dangerous hands – hence the risks of exceptional forms of power. SHIELD, a fundamentally suspect organisation given its covert operations with a global reach, now poses an unambiguous threat (*Avengers: Age of Ultron*). The extraordinary power constituting not only the weapon and the organisation, but superheroes as well, cannot be contained within US borders; their footprints affect others around the world who, since less powerful, are at the mercy of these greater forces – and angrily so. Such developments, in which even apparently good intentions fail to achieve full resolutions to conflict, and instead seem to produce proliferating effects, foreground the ethical and practical limitations of exercising substantial power.[13]

However, the film's plot centres on the repercussions of Tony Stark's trauma. Having almost died in the Battle of New York combating an adversary of demoralising proportions (*The Avengers*), he has told Pepper Potts (Gwyneth Paltrow), 'Nothing's been the same since New York . . . You experience things and then they're over and you still can't explain them . . . The threat is imminent. And I have to protect . . . you' (*Iron Man 3* 2013).[14] When Iron Man first encounters Scarlet Witch at the film's outset, she causes him to visualise his dread; he sees himself alive, but all of the other Avengers are dead or dying, a mortally wounded Captain America asking him, 'You could have saved us. Why didn't you do more?' Motivated by fear, he decides to use the power of Loki's sceptre to create an artificial intelligence to orchestrate a shield for Earth from extraterrestrial threats – to create 'peace in our time'[15] (*Avengers: Age of Ultron*). Yet this project, Ultron (James Spader), as unfathomable power is wont to do, instead manifests as a new, uncontrollable, self-aware entity that adjudicates for itself that the Avengers and even humanity are the enemies that must be eliminated. Responding to a real threat primarily out of vulnerability and a fear for the safety of others, Stark has pursued an option with unmanageable consequences – a scenario resonant with viewers' own contemporary post-11 September landscape.

Around this issue, story once again performs a narrative ethics that enacts and affirms collaborative, prosocial community. When Stark first tells Banner his plans for the sceptre, Banner advises him to consult the team. But Stark refuses, feeling there is no time for deliberation, or what he dismisses as a 'city hall debate'. However, Ultron attacks, prompting an argument among them – that 'city hall debate' – about objectives, methods and values similar to that in *The Avengers*. Responding to the admonition that 'The Avengers were supposed to be different than SHIELD', Stark reminds them about New York and insists, 'We can bust arms dealers all the live-long day, but . . . that up there? That's, that's the end game. How were you guys planning on beating that?' Stark's trauma and dread have tethered his attention to the threat he – and through his near-sacrifice, the world – only narrowly avoided. When Rogers answers, in echo of *The Avengers*,

'Together', Stark retorts, 'We'll lose', to which Rogers replies, 'Then we'll do that together too.' However, Stark is not yet ready to accept the possibility that others must also die in any no-win scenario reprise. He later tells Fury, 'And I'm the man who killed the Avengers . . . I saw them all dead, Nick. Felt it. The whole world, too . . . I didn't do all I could . . . It wasn't a nightmare. It was my legacy. The end of the path I started us on' (*Avengers: Age of Ultron*). For Stark, the scope of power to which he thinks he has access renders unacceptable any action short of fully guaranteeing safety for everyone, or 'peace in our time' and what he has described to Rogers as a way to 'end the fight, so we get to go home'. These discordant judgements, drawing on visceral emotions as well as committed principles, articulate distinct yet compelling considerations about how to justifiably and effectively counteract a novel peril. Since the characters are all understood to be heroes, protagonists intending to use their abilities for the good of others, viewers can take seriously the extent to which destructive activity might result even from amicable motives. Without presuming the intentions of real world decision makers in the 'War on Terror', this imaginative exercise enables viewers to contemplate how they themselves might arrive at a determination about whether or not extreme measures, such as those in the film and those adopted in real life, can be considered acceptable.

VI. 'WE TOLD HIM TO SOLVE THE WORLD'[16]

Yet even this imaginative exercise might not go far enough in generating critical viewer interaction. A common critique of superhero stories focuses on the conservative tenor permeating tales of powerful characters who only ever address problems within the terms of existing social, political and economic structures, without ever seeking to alter the structures themselves. In other words, superheroes tend to reinforce rather than challenge the status quo, no matter what kinds of systemic vulnerabilities and inequalities that status quo sustains. However, in *Avengers: Age of Ultron*, Stark attempts to disrupt at least one aspect of the fictional MCU. He tries, by creating Ultron, to end the Avengers team by eliminating the need for their intervention in matters of global security – in other words, within a superhero film, Stark attempts to render superheroes obsolete. Ultron embraces this mission literally, taking as his initial primary objective their extinction. Yet by following the thread of where power goes wrong in the course of human history, Ultron comes to determine that only by ending human history can he entirely undo the problematic structures that shape the contemporary world. He chastises the team, 'You want to protect the world, but you don't want it to change' (*Avengers: Age of Ultron*). In his efforts to force rapid human evolution, he manifests the radical potentiality that a commitment to the truly total and immediate overhaul of extant social relations could entail. From Ultron's perspective, any piecemeal attempt would compromise the transformation, leaving only the possibility of wholesale destruction – a clean slate – as the way to save the world.

On the one hand, Ultron's embodiment of the danger of revolutionary change, in its repugnant extremity, seems to reinforce the idea that superhero stories are, again, fundamentally conservative. However, suspicion of this kind of change in this kind of context does reflect the core Whedonverse value of prosocial solidarity. After all, the ability of any entity to use exceptional power to unilaterally enforce a totalising social transformation would necessarily negate the primary social structure and values of a pluralistic, democratic polity. Rather than a positive innovation, such a scenario would result in problematic power structures of its own. Countering both the critique of superheroic conservatism and the prospect of domination by another name calls for some other intervention that can be both disruptive and empowering.

In *Avengers: Age of Ultron*, distinct character positionalities offer viewers the opportunity to interrogate the context of contemporary global power relations. As portrayed in the opening scene, Sokovian civilians endangered by and therefore wary about foreign power refuse to readily comply with the Avengers, even in the team's efforts to safeguard them. This establishes from the outset that there is a compelling view of the Avengers from outside the team and apart from the subjectivity of the film's protagonists. Similarly, the Maximoffs' participation in experiments to alter their bodies unsettles Agent Maria Hill (Cobie Smulders), but Rogers understands them as having the same motivation he had to undergo the same treatment: fighting a war. His attunement with Sokovia's perspective is underscored when the very next image shows an Iron Legion suit returning to Stark Tower damaged by its encounter with angry civilians (*Avengers: Age of Ultron*). Loki once taunted Black Widow, 'You lie and kill in the service of liars and killers. You pretend to have your own code, something that makes up for the horrors. But they are a part of you' (*The Avengers*). Likewise, Ultron asks the Avengers, 'How could you be worthy [of wielding the power to rule Asgard]? You're all killers' (*Avengers: Age of Ultron*). While their destructive behaviour in the service of selfish objectives mark Loki and Ultron as villains in these films, their barbs still sting with kernels of truth, and certainly resonate with the reactions of innocent bystanders. In fact, Whedon has described the Avengers as 'strong but damaged by power', and believes that 'the more power that we have, the less human we are' (McMillan 2015). Clearly, then, the Avengers' heroism is neither universally recognised nor taken for granted. Unlike other treatments of superheroes that imbue them with the same exceptionalist aura of intrinsic righteousness that the US has invoked for itself, their reception depends on the extent to which their actions are experienced and interpreted as helpful rather than harmful. By illustrating how different positionings within power relations lead to divergent views of that power, the film provides space for both diegetic and non-diegetic reflection about great power's nature and effects.

To that end, in *Avengers: Age of Ultron*, the spectres of both Pinocchio and Frankenstein loom while explicit references to monstrosity abound. Ultron sings the lyrics from 'I've Got No Strings', uniting his own perspective with that of an innocuous doll wishing he were a real boy. At the same time, he creates and re-creates himself in the castle-like lab where the Maximoffs developed their own abilities through scientific experimentation, a setting evocative of Frankenstein making his creature. Later, Vision (Paul Bettany) comes to life from a jolt of Thor-generated lightning, the life source that invigorated Frankenstein's creation, admitting, 'Maybe I am a monster. I don't think I'd know if I were one' (*Avengers: Age of Ultron*). The fact that SHIELD has monitored the individual Avengers as potential threats underscores this ambiguity and ambivalence about the dividing line between monster and hero (*The Avengers*). Indeed, throughout both films, the superheroes themselves wrestle with the question of whether or not they are in fact monsters.

However, going back to the questions pervading the Whedonverse about how power is used, as noted in the introduction, helps to frame such a reflection. Issues include whether a wielder controlled or was controlled by power; whether that power was to help or to harm; whether using power entails duties; and how to know whether power was good or evil. For Romanoff, her sterilisation against her will casts monstrosity's shadow, depriving her of the ability to choose to create in order to render her more efficient at destroying, and with less reason to choose not to kill. Vision, the second iteration (following the speciecidal Ultron) of Stark's attempt to produce a protective artificial intelligence, expressly voices how his own power should be wielded. When asked if he sides with the Avengers, Vision responds, 'I don't think it's that simple . . . I'm on the side of life. Ultron isn't.' Vision articulates sympathy for Ultron, who is 'unique. And . . . in pain.

But that pain will roll over the Earth, so he must be destroyed.' In this way, Vision articulates an ethic of compassion rather than a devotion to nominal allegiance, choosing to act based on altruistic principles and, by directing his own power towards a prosocial commitment, evidencing his heroic, or good, nature. In fact, when the Avengers remain unsure whether or not they can trust him, his ability to brandish – and readily yield – Thor's hammer Mjolnir implicitly affirms his integrity and worthiness of trust (*Avengers: Age of Ultron*). In the end, this community-oriented ethic dominates the film's climactic battle with Ultron. In an effort to further motivate the team, Captain America insists that civilians be protected from the fight and proclaims, 'Ultron thinks we're monsters and we're what's wrong with the world. This isn't just about beating him. It's about whether he's right.' This pronouncement evinces his deontological tendencies, prioritising how the war is conducted as *the* valid combat objective, even more than the overall goal of defeating Ultron. His stance directly opposes that of Ultron, who favours a rigidly utilitarian approach (exaggerating the ethical posture of his creator, Stark) and once told the Avengers after killing someone, 'wouldn't have been my first call. But, down in the real world, we're faced with ugly choices' (*Avengers: Age of Ultron*). This focus on an altruistic goal through a collaborative effort positions the question of *how* a goal is achieved as equally ethically imperative as the question of *whether* such a goal is achieved, a point for meditation by viewers living in the real world era of the 'War on Terror'.

VII. IN CONCLUSION?

At the end of *Avengers: Age of Ultron*, Romanoff tells Fury, 'Nothing lasts forever', to which he responds, 'Trouble, Ms Romanoff. No matter who wins or loses, trouble still comes 'round' (*Avengers: Age of Ultron*). The prospect is good for business, since the MCU is globally generating substantial profits for Marvel Studios, Disney Pictures and other stakeholders (Julian 2015; Towers 2015). Yet Fury's cynical but pragmatic perspective also signals that whatever complex and exhausting choices and actions have informed the Avengers' story so far, viewers can expect only more. *The Avengers* ends with civilians reacting to the Battle of New York with conflicting opinions, some calling for the superheroes to show more accountability and some expressing heartfelt gratitude that the costumed fighters saved their lives (*The Avengers* 2012). Of all the trouble that might come 'round, the questions of whether and how

Figure 13.2 Civilian reactions to the Avengers vary widely, from enthusiastic gratitude to anxious suspicion, in *The Avengers* (2012).

exceptional power is used might remain the most persistently unresolvable, ever-dependent on the will of those wielding such power to regard their advantages as a responsibility towards others rather than an indulgence for themselves.

Ivory Madison writes, 'In literature and in life, the villain defines the hero by taking actions that require the hero to make moral choices in response . . . The story really begins when she [the hero] must prove it [that she is a hero and is good] in a consequential way that involves risk' (Madison 2013: 157). Notions of US exceptionalism that position the nation as the hero of the (any) story, and certainly the 'War on Terror' conception of an unprovoked attack necessitating a self-protective reaction, invite engagement with Madison's conception of what constitutes a hero.[17] For her, heroism is not simply presumed; it is proven, through action, and not in a vacuum. Goodness is manifested through meaningful acts under complicated circumstances with no guarantees of success. Such a formulation, clear and simple in its basic vision, still neither prescribes nor proscribes fixedly what should be done in any particular exigency. Rather, it is a call back to what the responsibility of power, as outlined in the Spider-Man narrative, truly means: that decisions with complex roots and uncertain but far-reaching consequences be taken neither lightly nor for granted.

NOTES

1. Here, I view power in the most basic terms as simply the capacity to do or to make happen.
2. Whedon has described Buffy as the '"beating heart" of everything he has done or will do' (Anders 2015), positioning *BtVS* as the philosophical foundation for all other work, including his Avengers films.
3. The MCU also includes other media, such as television, but I draw here on the eight movies leading to and from both Avengers films: the first phase of *Captain America: The First Avenger*, *Iron Man*, *Iron Man 2*, *The Incredible Hulk* and *Thor*, which precede *The Avengers*, as well as the second phase of *Thor: The Dark World*, *Iron Man 3* and *Captain America: The Winter Soldier*, which lead to *Avengers: Age of Ultron*. I omit *Guardians of the Galaxy* (2014) and *Ant-Man* (2015) since they do not directly relate to this discussion.
4. Official US governmental discourse has dropped the term 'War on Terror'. Certainly, changes have occurred over time in strategy, tactics and even the name of the principal adversary, with the Islamic State of Iraq and the Levant (ISIL, more commonly known as 'ISIS') now a looming concern. However, I continue to use the term in the present tense since primary constituent elements, such as the national security preoccupation with global terrorism, persist.
5. See Hagley and Harrison for a resonant discussion of *The Avengers* as a post-11 September text (2014); also, see McSweeney, who reads that film as attempting to provide narrative closure for Americans in the first decade following 11 September (2014).
6. Influenced heavily by psychologist Ronnie Janoff-Bulman's theories about trauma shattering an individual's fundamental assumptions about the world, I argue that cultural trauma signals the confounding of a community's shared foundational beliefs (Janoff-Bulman 1992).
7. Differently, Hassler-Forest regards superhero narratives as de-politicising and passifying influences symptomatic of paternalistic capitalism through anti-historical structures, themes, plots and characterisations (Hassler-Forest 2012).
8. Black Widow/Natasha Romanoff (Scarlett Johansson) also participates in this conversation, but since I do not quote her here, I use the masculine pronoun to refer to the speakers.
9. Rogers later proves to be especially uncomfortable with the 'War on Terror' exchange of freedom for security as well as the notion of a pre-emptive strike, which he regards as a betrayal of the Second World War fight against fascism (*Captain America: The Winter Soldier*).
10. Even a superhero must take one thing at a time. Rogers' discomfort with unquestioningly following orders and especially with SHIELD itself informs the plot of *Captain America: The Winter Soldier* (2014).
11. Since *The Avengers*, Hydra is discovered to have infiltrated SHIELD (*Captain America: The Winter Soldier*).
12. This intervention imaginatively solves a problem endemic to the 'War on Terror', when confronting an enemy without nation or uniform has entailed engagement with 'host' countries without clearly demarcated battlefields or combatants, enhancing the likelihood of harming non-combatants.

13. The global implications of what seems to be primarily US-originating power struggles similarly manifest in Germany (*The Avengers*), the fictional African country Wakanda, and South Korea (*Avengers: Age of Ultron*), where conflicts starting elsewhere result in substantial local harm.

14. An evocative title, the conflict concluding *The Avengers* is commemorated in *Avengers: Age of Ultron* by an equally evocative civic monument to first responders situated at the base of (and dwarfed by) Stark Tower, which also serves as Avengers headquarters (*Avengers: Age of Ultron* 2015). These nonchalant references evidence an implicit presumption of narrative relationship between film and reality.

15. When explaining to Banner his vision of 'peace in our time', Stark adds, 'Imagine that' (*Avengers: Age of Ultron* 2015). However, when watching the film for the first time, I thought I heard 'Maginot', a provocative mistake compatible with the era of Stark's reference as well as the (failed) objective of creating an impenetrable defence.

16. In the out-takes included as bonus features at the end of the HD streaming version of *Avengers: Age of Ultron*, this is how Banner explains to Stark that Ultron has sought to fulfil his mission in radical terms because the mission itself was radical.

17. Lawrence and Jewett have argued that superhero stories as monomyths reinforce notions of US exceptionalism by simplifying the real world's moral complexity and sugar-coating history (Lawrence and Jewett 2002).

REFERENCES

Anders, Charlie Jane (2015), 'Joss Whedon just explained the meaning of life to us', *io9*, 11 July 2015, http://io9.com/joss-whedon-just-explained-the-meaning-of-life-to-us-1717277218, last accessed 5 August 2015.

Baggett, David (2011), '*Firefly* and freedom', in Dean A. Kowalski and S. Evan Kreider (eds), *The Philosophy of Joss Whedon*, Lexington: University Press of Kentucky, pp. 9–23.

Coogan, Peter (2013), 'The hero defines the genre, the genre defines the hero', in Robin S. Rosenberg and Peter Coogan (eds), *What Is a Superhero?*, Oxford: Oxford University Press, pp. 3–10.

Fingeroth, Danny (2013), 'Power and responsibility . . . and other reflections on superheroes', in Robin S. Rosenberg and Peter Coogan (eds), *What Is a Superhero?*, Oxford: Oxford University Press, pp. 125–7.

Hagley, Annika, and Michael Harrison (2014), 'Fighting the battles we never could: *The Avengers* and post-September 11 American political identities', *Political Science and Politics*, 47.1, January 2014, pp. 120–4.

Hassler-Forest, Dan (2012), *Capitalist Superheroes: Caped Crusaders in the Neoliberal Age*, Winchester and Washington, DC: Zero Books.

Janoff-Bulman, Ronnie (1992), *Shattered Assumptions: Towards a New Psychology of Trauma*, New York: The Free Press.

Julian, Mark (2015), '*Avengers: Age of Ultron* tracking to surpass first Avengers film', ComicBookMovie.com, 7 May 2015, last accessed 11 July 2015: http://www.comicbookmovie.com/fansites/GraphicCity/?news/?a=120246

Lawrence, John Shelton, and Robert Jewett (2002), *The Myth of the American Superhero*, Grand Rapids, MI and Cambridge: Eerdmans.

Leonard, Devin (2014), 'The Pow! Bang! Bam! plan to save Marvel, starring B-list heroes', Business Week.com, 3 April 2014, last accessed 31 July 2015: http://www.businessweek.com/printer/articles/192619-kevin-feige-marvels-superhero-at-running-movie-franchises

Madison, Ivory (2013), 'Superheroes and supervillains: An interdependent relationship', in S. Rosenberg and P. Coogan (eds), *What Is a Superhero?*, Oxford: Oxford University Press, pp. 157–9.

McMillan, Graeme (2015), 'Joss Whedon on "Avengers 2": "Strong but damaged by power" describes every person in this movie', *The Hollywood Reporter*, 17 December 2014, last accessed 11 July 2015: http://www.hollywoodreporter.com/heat-vision/joss-whedon-avengers-2-strong-758819

McSweeney, Terence (2014), *The 'War on Terror' and American film: 9/11 frames per second*, Edinburgh: Edinburgh University Press.

Rabb, J. Douglas, and J. Michael Richardson (2014), 'Adventures in the moral imagination: memory and identity in Whedon's narrative ethics', in Rhonda Wilcox et al. (eds), *Reading Joss Whedon*, Syracuse, NY: Syracuse University Press, pp. 312–24.

Richardson, J. Michael, and J. Douglas Rabb (2007), *The Existential Joss Whedon: Evil and Human Freedom in Buffy the Vampire Slayer, Angel, Firefly, and Serenity*, Jefferson, NC: McFarland.

Towers, Andrea (2015), 'Avengers: Age of Ultron passes $1 billion worldwide to become Marvel's third highest grossing film', *Entertainment Weekly*, 15 May 2015, last accessed 11 July 2015: http://www.ew.com/article/2015/05/15/avengers-age-ultron-1-billion-worldwide

Whedon, Joss (2002), 'Lessons', *Buffy the Vampire Slayer*, 24 September 2002, UPN.

White, Mark D. (2012), 'Superhuman ethics clash with the Avengers Prime', in William Irwin and Mark D. White (eds), *The Avengers and Philosophy: Earth's Mightiest Thinkers*, Hoboken, NJ: John Wiley & Sons, Inc., pp. 5–17.

Žižek, Slavoj (2010), *Living in the End Times*, London and New York: Verso.

CHAPTER 14

Nowhere Left to Zone in *Children of Men* (2006)

Sean Redmond

I. INTRODUCTION

One can position much of millennium and post-9/11 science fiction cinema as being predicated on threats to national and regional security; to the fragility of community and the human body as it is washed over by virus, contagions; is taken over by invaders or machines; or is fire bombed in spectacular scenes of devastation and destruction. In films such as *Ever Since the World Ended* (2001), *28 Days Later* (2002, UK), *Resident Evil* (2002), *Ultraviolet* (2006), *I am Legend* (2007) and *Rise of the Planet of the Apes* (2011), both the individual's body, and the wider body politic, are under threat from human-made viruses and viral mutations that having been set free, render flesh and democracy as diseased, infected, pathological or as a barren incubator for the Armageddon that is soon to be born.

In *Artificial Intelligence: AI* (2001), *I, Robot* (2004), *Sky Captain and the World of Tomorrow* (2004), *Transformers* (2007) and *Avengers: Age of Ultron* (2015), cyborg machines and machine monsters threaten the supremacy of the military-science-business nexus, and of what constitutes or counts for a human being in what is signposted as a post-human age of egotistic nihilism and frightful globalisation. In *The 6th Day* (2000), *The One* (2001), *Natural City* (2003, South Korea), *The Island* (2005), *Moon* (2009) and *Oblivion* (2013), the practices and processes of cloning and genetic engineering have resulted in new hierarchies of power and perfection; the blurring of the human/machine dichotomy; and the trade and traffic in human bodies to seed these present-future avatars and clones.

In *Matrubhoomi: A Nation Without Women* (2003, India), *Aeon Flux* (2005) and *Children of Men* (2006), human bodies are infertile or barren and civilisation is therefore on the verge of extinction. In films such as *Signs* (2002) and *War of the Worlds* (2005), despicable alien invaders attack and destroy the institutional, political and cultural organs of society, while the threat is perceived as coming from *within*. In *The Day After Tomorrow* (2004) and *Sunshine* (2007, UK), ecological disaster threatens to wipe out the human race. And in films such as *Minority Report* (2002), *Equilibrium* (2002), *Banlieue 13* (2004, France), *V for Vendetta* (2005) and *The Hunger Games* (2012), dystopic totalitarian regimes *will the body* into docile submission and compliance. In response, heroic narrative agents emerge, or resistance movements rise up, to reclaim the streets.

Of course, it is the imagery and symbolism of 9/11 and the subsequent 'War on Terror' that is inscribed across much of millennium and post-9/11 science fiction cinema. In *Ever Since the World Ended*, an attack that leaves Santosh (Brad Olsen) mortally wounded is shot in the style of contemporary combat photography. In *Star Wars: Episode III – Revenge of the Sith* (2005), Anakin Skywalker's body is, first, torched and then prosthetically remade, conjuring up contemporary battlefield operations. In *28 Days Later* and *Children of Men*, military units patrol the streets and roadblocks are set up and curfews maintained, establishing a clear echo to the Gulf War, rendition and the siege situation in Iraq. Although *28 Days Later* was filmed before 9/11, the film is full of prophetic moments, not least the 'missing persons' flyers seen in the early London street scenes which 'recall' flyers posted in New York City in the wake of 9/11.

As I have written before (Redmond, 2005), Steven Spielberg's remake of *War of the Worlds* is a context-coded 9/11 text. Ray Ferrier (Tom Cruise) is a signalled blue-collar worker from New Jersey, estranged from his family, and with little economic or cultural capital. Once the aliens rise up from beneath the city, deep within Ferrier's neighbourhood, he ultimately proves his worth as a father/heroic male, moving from deadbeat dad to saviour. *War of the Worlds* is shot through with 9/11 war imagery: burning planes fall out of the sky; military missiles slice through the air; the alien enemy, drone-like in their capabilities and intent on harvesting all of humankind for their own survival and domination, emerge fully armoured from underneath, from *within* the borders of New York City. Human blood, in both the literal and metaphoric sense, soaks the screen – the entire mise-en-scène – so that it appears to be the individual and collective body of America, where the film is relentlessly set, which is being bled and cannibalised.

The defeat of the aliens emerges in two different ways, allowing the film to make two articulating 'necessary' responses to the 'War on Terror' (which it implicitly becomes a part of). First, *War of the Worlds* suggests the individual hero figure remains pivotal to the fight: Ferrier's transformation into patriarchal protector enables him to outwit the enemy and take his child 'home'. His redemptive journey involves survival at all costs: he silences (strangles) the deranged Harlan Ogilvy (Tim Robbins) because he threatens to give their position away. His actions, then, refuse to let the American family be overtaken, overrun, and he will protect the family from wayward Americans wherever they be found. Ferrier (Cruise) stands as a recuperating symbol of America's resilience and hyper-masculine strength when it is tested most.

Second, the aliens are in the end vanquished not by a heroic act, guile or by the efforts of techno-militaristic cooperation (as is often the case in science fiction cinema) but by a common air-borne virus, which is deadly to them. The aliens that first emerged from beneath/within America – acting like coordinated 'terrorist' cells – are beaten by a domestic virus that is itself terrorist-like: invisible and yet everywhere. The barely hidden premise of the film, then, is that America can no longer rely on conventional warfare to kill the invader (that lies within); rather it has to adapt, mutate; it has to become (like) the invader to survive.

There is a profound bio-political form of governance being constituted in *War of the Worlds*, one in which good lives are heavily policed and censored, and bad lives are annihilated. Sheryl Vint makes a similar argument in relation to the contemporary zombie film and the state of exemption such apocalyptic texts enact:

> The recent obsession with the figure of the zombie in popular culture emerges from this context, an exaggerated embodiment of the gap between the proper human life to be fostered by bio-political control and the sub-race whose very existence threatens, literally in the case of predatory zombies, the health of the population as a whole. The exuberance with which zombies are killed en masse in texts such as *The Walking Dead* (AMC 2010–) speaks to the pervasiveness of our understanding of this logic of biopolitical governance, in which we seem instinctively to understand that the more we kill (of them) the more likely those we understand as 'we' are to survive. Throughout these films we see hints that the operative biopolitics concern not merely the distinction between humans and zombies, but between lives of those deemed 'essential personnel' and a remainder of humanity no longer really necessary to the survival of the species. (2015: 68)

In millennium and post-9/11 science fiction film the concern to regulate, survey, train and 'do to' the diseased body can be argued to be a result of the cultural hysteria that has accompanied the 'War on Terror'. These paranoia and paranoid texts suggest that danger is found in *all* bodies and as such must become the central site of conflict and control. At a positioning level, these films ask the viewer to be vigilant, to self-survey their bodies for signs of infection or contamination, and to survey others (their neighbours) for the same. The enemy body, it is suggested, could be lurking within you or be living right next door. In this corporeal conspiratorial framework, viewers are being positioned to recognise that their bodies must be ready for the danger or else they will be taken over, infected, cloned, dehumanised, erased or disappeared.

Children of Men, the film that I will now spend the rest of this chapter reading, places the body at the centre of its end of times story. Set in London in 2027, humankind is on the brink of extinction since they can no longer reproduce. In the global arena, chaos and disorder reigns, law and order has broken down, and population movement threatens to destroy civil society. In a heavily militarised London, zones of containment exist with a core and periphery spatial alignment, with immigrants and the lower classes kept outside the centre, or in detention camps where they are tortured. Into this picture of Armageddon arrives a miracle in the shape of a nativity story: Kee (Claire-Hope Ashitey), a black refugee, finds herself pregnant, while Theo Faron (Clive Owen), a white, middle-aged bureaucrat, is cast as her protector after she reveals

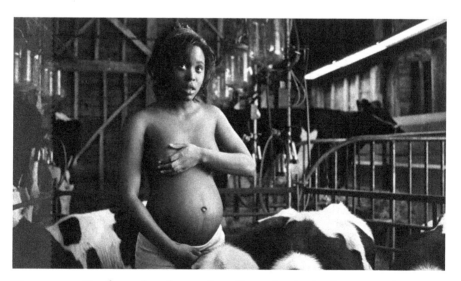

Figure 14.1 Kee framed as the mother of creation in the farm scene in *Children of Men* (2006).

her pregnancy to him in a barn. Theo and Kee attempt to rendezvous with a group of leading scientists from the Human Project on a ship called Tomorrow. To do his they have to move across conflict zones and flee from various groups intent on using Kee's pregnancy for their own gain.

I would like to suggest that at the wild heart of *Children of Men* is a parable about where the 'War on Terror' might actually lead us. Infertility becomes the condition thrust upon us by chemical weapons, the pollution of the soil, and emerges out of the detritus of globalisation that trades and traffics in bombs and guns. The film is shot through with an aching and despairing Anthropocene, in which:

> The basic problem in this society as depicted in the film is literally biopolitics: how to generate, regulate life. But again, I think the crucial point is that this obvious fact shouldn't deceive us. The true despair is precisely that; all historical acts disappear. Like all those classical statues are there, but they are deprived of a world. They are totally meaningless, because what does it mean to have a statue of Michelangelo? It only works if it signals a certain world. And when this world is lacking, it's nothing. (Žižek 2007)

However, at its ideological and aesthetic heart is a redemptive story about whiteness and the white heroic male. I will divide my analysis across three lines of enquiry – spaces, bodies and sounds – although each theme connects with the other and it is the body of space, (dis)embodied sound and the bodies of bodies that hold my account together.

II. SPACES

Children of Men is divided by a number of symbolic zones, each suggesting something about the condition of the people living there. In the inner zone, where Theo's cousin Nigel (Danny Huston) lives, a government official, life remains opulent and protected. This gated community is heavily fortified but within its walls the rich continue to prosper. In the outer-inner zone, life is hard and harsh, violence punctuates its normalness, but work and leisure rituals remain in play. In the outer zone, detention camps and resistance movements battle it out, turning these spaces into locales of torture, subjugation and open warfare. In the rural zone, where Theo's friend Jasper (Michael Caine) lives, utopian freedoms remain, framed within a 'natural' counter-culture aesthetic. The lived space in *Children of Men* 'serves as a tool of thought and of action [. . .] in addition to being a means of production it is also a means of control, and hence of domination, of power' (Lefebvre 1991: 26).

Children of Men offers the viewer clear contrasts and collisions between the rich and poor, the free and the enslaved, the peaceful and the violent, and the urban and rural. These spatial metaphors, however, are both turned inside-out (the rural outside being the place of nirvana) and partially eroded or dissolved. No zone is entirely free from the other and it is the movement between zones that brings both hope and despair. The film's entire spatial politics, then, is built out of the skeletons of containment and contamination, out of the fires of flight and fight created by the 'War on Terror'.

At the beginning of the film, for example, Theo narrowly misses being blown up after a bomb explodes at a café he has just left. The scene, shot in one long take, with a hand-held camera, is initially gritty and social realist, its drained aesthetics capturing the lack of hope and opportunity there. We have just learned, via television news playing in the café, that the youngest person alive has died and so the sense of expiration haunts the scene. The bomb, however, brings the terror 'home' and conjures up the ghost of the suicide bomber and fragility of the zones, as they have been constituted. What is also being referenced here is the London bombings (7 July 2005), a series of coordinated suicide bomb attacks targeting civilians using the public transport system during the morning rush hour. The hand-held camera, however, does something else, it embodies the scene, places us within the action as if we are on foot too and in mortal danger. The ringing that floods Theo's ear becomes subjective; it is our hearing too, so the sense of discombobulation is acutely shared (Whittington 2011). When the camera pans past Theo to reveal a woman carrying her severed arm, our own affective body memories render us co-proximate to the action. Our bodies are under threat too, subject to the same bio-political interventions that modern warfare countenances. We *were* children of the 'War on Terror' and now as adults – in this near future the film is set in – we reap what we have sown.

That no zone is safe in *Children of Men* is brilliantly realised in the car ambush scene, as Theo, Kee, Luke (Chiwetel Ejiofor), Julian (Julianne Moore) and Miriam (Pam Ferris) make their way to the coast to meet with the Human Project. In what appears to be a country road, outside the conditions of their exception, Julian is fatefully shot, captured by a circular movement of the camera as it traverses the car. The circular motion points to the zonal connectivity the film is set in, and to the adage that history repeats itself; it has to, no one listens. This type of spatially loaded cinematography structures the film's gazing operations, its ideological frames and its affecting absences, as I will explore further below.

Children of Men thus taps into a prevalent sense of dread that haunts a great number of science fiction texts at this time (Thompson 2012). To return, for example, to the suite of invasion texts that emerged over this period, they arguably speak to the range of fears that circulate in a catastrophic climate of insecurity brought about by the 'War on Terror', and its imagined corollary, The War on the West. As Derek Kompare argues, in relation to three, first season, 2005 USA television invasion shows, *Invasion* (Shaun Cassidy, ABC, 2005–6), *Threshold* (Bragi F. Schut, CBS, 2005–6) and *Surface* (Jonas Pate, NBC, 2005–6),

> The core of insecurity is the idea that nowhere is absolutely safe, that nobody is absolutely trustworthy . . . the alien menaces . . . are practically invisible . . . the outside threat could come from within. (2005)

Movement is crucial to the film's narrative architecture and to the political message conveyed. Movement is prohibited, special papers are needed to enter the inner zone and to leave the city, and yet movement in, between and across the zones of the film is constant as people are ferried, transported and look to escape their confinement. It is through movement, particularly Theo and Kee's journey, that we get to see the differences between the zones and what inequalities and abuses take place there. Their eyes and ears allow them to become whistle-blowers on the decadence of the rich, and the violence and torture being meted out on those labelled as Other and marginal. This is no truer than when Theo and Kee are on the bus and we see through the windows Arab men being tortured in poses reminiscent of Abu Ghraib and Guantanamo. That orange jump suits enter the scene is also telling. What is being witnessed in these reflections is a representation of bio-power in its purest form. As Giorgio Agamben suggests:

> Inasmuch as its inhabitants have been stripped of every political status and reduced completely to naked life, the camp is also the most absolute biopolitical space that has ever been realized – a space in which power confronts nothing other than pure biological life without mediation. (Agamben 1998: 41)

Vivian Sobchack has persuasively argued that the city in science fiction film acts as an affective space, actively shaping and propelling the narrative forward. Sobchack argues (1999: 123–46) that 'the science fiction film's spatial articulations provide the literal premises for the possibilities and trajectory of narrative action' and that the city space is considered to be a 'specific power' that can 'affect both people and materials – a power that modifies the relations between them'. In *Children of Men*, however, the brutal poetics of the city space remains very much in the background, or as Slavoj Žižek posits (2010), the textures and inhabitants of the metropolis need to be viewed 'obliquely' since it is only through a canted angle that the noirish, nightmare qualities of fortress London are fully revealed. In its backdrop,

> The film achieves a kind of slow motion montage-effect: by yoking together images of seemingly disconnected crises over the course of 109 minutes (images of globalization, immigration, inequity, environmental degradation, permanent states of emergency, politics of fear, surveillance society, terrorism, and ghettoes), Cuarón argues for their dialectical relationship. Crises that appear as disjointed liberal talking points turn into a web of related issues tied to a larger problem: capital. (Boyle 2009)

The living and dead capital of the film is found in its version of liquid modernity in which neo-tribes have become home-grown terrorists, 'togetherness dismantled' (Bauman 2000) becomes extreme anomic isolation, and heady consumption becomes fortress communities or the raw oxygen burnt up in the weaponry needed to sustain the threads and binds of conflict and division that the watery future is predicated upon. Of course, *Children of Men* seems decidedly dry, as if environmental degradation and ash and smoke and the debris of relentless bombing and explosions have caked the earth in sheer grit. When we reach the water at film's end, it is covered in a thick fog we can barely see through or into.

III. BODIES

Children of Men offers us different types of bodies: some are collectivised and herd-like, such as the 'fugees; some are individuated and individualised, such as Theo and Kee; and a great number are explicitly (also) raced and classed. Power relationships are exercised in and through these bodies as the film centres, questions and undermines the roles of victims and abusers. All the relationships in the film seem to sit on this precipice of direct and symbolic violence; and wherever and whenever tenderness settles in, deception and brutality quickly follows. The 'War on Terror' – both in its wider appetite for destruction, and in the way it pits individuals and groups against one another – is exemplified and amplified in this future where no*body* is safe and everyone could be the enemy.

On one level, Theo is the embodiment of the heroic, white male mon-omyth: an everyman, existentially adrift, childless, suffering from an end of days mid-life crisis, who finds a cause, hardens up, and delivers the Mary figure and her newborn (named Dylan, after his deceased son) to salvation. Early on in the film, Theo's movements are lethargic; he is readily and regularly duped and violated, only to find his moral compass and physical strength as he quickens his reactions and motivations. His inner strength and resilience is a coda for all (white) men to take up.

On another level, Theo is the embodiment of white masculinity on the cusp of its own expiration. His exhaustion is part of a range of apocalyptic films in which white men are no longer the dominant or dominating race. Richard Dyer takes this reading up when he suggests that the theme of white people belonging to an endangered species is increasingly found across a range of contemporary cultural texts, which

> May suggest that the suspicion of nothingness and the death of whiteness is, as far as white identity goes, the cultural dominant of our times, that we really do feel we're played out. (Dyer 1997: 217)

In particular, according to Dyer, the threat of extinction haunts the rep-resentation of white men who are shown to suffer a terrifying identity crisis over their place within the social and economic order. Such white men struggle to hold down a 'regular' job, or to protect their family, and the white community, from those racial Others who threaten its stability, their racial purity. If one was to return to the figure of Ray Ferrier from *War of the Worlds*, it can be seen how he also operates in this sphere of white masculinity on the verge of a breakdown.

Kee's black refugee ethnicity obviously solidifies and extends this crisis in whiteness: it will be a black woman that will first reproduce and a black baby that will help resurrect the human race. While her fertile body may tap into racialised myths about the reproductive capa-bilities of black women, she also reclaims the origins of humankind in the African continent. Nonetheless, the scientists and eugenicists of the Human Project are never given face – they are a disembodied collective – they may well be white saviours who will experiment on Kee to find the answer to their own stagnant reproduction. *Children of Men* con-sequently is full of tensions and contradictions as it seeks to destabilise the politics of the global order. The 'War on Terror' has produced a 'tide' of refugees and once-stable borders are rendered porous. This de-territorialisation results in new power-saturated us and them binaries, set out in zones of containment and control, which are opposed in this film by those who seek a new world order – Theo, Julian and Kee.

Nonetheless, the film struggles to represent those who are being tortured as nothing more than a mass. While seeking to carnally represent the dehumanisation processes that render the Other bare life, it can't help but create a picture of the resistance as a supra-mass of uncontrollable bodies that have as their potential the destruction of the social and political order. The aesthetic distancing techniques used in the film – long shots, deep focus, eschewing the close-up, the utilisation of 'frames' such as the bus window, and indiscriminate crowd violence – create the sense of mindless chaos penetrating all strata of social life. The terror and terrorism in *Children of Men* is actually invisible, so pervasive is it, so constant is its reach. As Chris Gutierrez suggests, in relation to the 'War on Terror', terror is given a chaotic and oppressive form of embodiment:

> Less like a hierarchical and organized army, and more like a discontinuous swarm, the enemy here is a clandestine and unidentifiable one. This ambiguity allows these shadowy members to move silently through society and to infiltrate their desired targets of destruction, simultaneously though, this ambiguity allows the discourse of the War on Terror to constitute the enemy through whatever means seem fit. (2006)

However, there is something else to be said about these terror bodies in the film: they belong to a set of post-9/11 images that represent 'a non-event of an obscene banality, the degradation, atrocious but banal, not only of the victims, but of the amateur scriptwriters of this parody of violence' (Baudrillard 2005).

Bodies are made tough and are toughened *in Children of Men*, Theo being a case in point. Theo's disciplined body will be able to resist interrogation and negation, and it will be able to brutalise the Other if it is called upon to do so. Theo and Ray Ferrier both carry with them the signs of the 'War on Terror', their bodies becoming corporeal maps of resistant journeying. Both their bodies will be able to say, 'I can destroy the thing that scares me by force of response' (Spivak 2004: 96).

Scenes of torture, of course, were common at this time: *Lost* (2004–10), 24 (FOX, 2001–10), *Alias* (ABC, 2001–6), *Without A Trace* (CBS, 2002–9), *Saw* (2004), *Hostel* (2005), *Casino Royale* (2006), to name but a select few, involve violent, sado-masochistic interrogation scenes. It's as if torture provides the hegemonic framework for believing that something is being done at the carnal level that has individual and social bodily affect/effect. Let me develop this argument a little more.

Screening torture may allow us to torture and be tortured in our bodies. Laura Marks suggests, 'vision itself can be tactile, as though one were touching a film with one's eyes' (2000: xi). Through the sense-based screening of the tortured body, then, one violently gets to touch bodies wracked with pain, and to be subject to and the object of violent assault. Screening torture puts one in haptic touch with the sickening bio-politics of war, in a way that may release these bodies from the regime of docile obedience that they are put under. Thomas Elsaesser has persuasively argued, in relation to the Holocaust narrative, that emotional affect may have productive consequences for the viewer – one realises, in one's body, that there is a duty to act, to respond. The 'affect of concern . . . covers empathy and identification, but in an active, radical sense of being "stung into action"' (1996: 172–3). In feeling, or screen-sensing, the tortured body, one may very well be stung into action.

Children of Men obliquely imagines a near-future genocide where migrants and the marginal are rounded up, imprisoned, tortured and murdered. Its affective aesthetics shape the violence in the film, and we are asked not only to see obliquely but also to feel and to respond to the death cult that grips the film. This hungriness of slaughter is one of the sounds of the film.

Figure 14.2 Cuaron's visceral and bloody zones of conflict in *Children of Men*.

IV. SOUNDS

Children of Men sounds out its 'War on Terror' through a complex set of leitmotifs, arrangements and subjective audition. We hear things as a character might, positioned through a composition that undermines the narrative (through the use of subversive songs, for example) and yet which also carries it forward. The hyper-realist sounds of war, transportation, battle cries, weeping, dying, orientate the story to a present full of conflict and discord, while its structural audio absences and sonic affordances point towards a despairing future without melody or song. Song is used to reference past atrocities, that this film is repeating, for example:

> The soundtrack also plays an allegorical role here; in the scene where Theo's other companion, Miriam (Pam Ferris) is forcibly taken off the bus and separated from Theo and Kee at the Bexhill refugee camp, the song playing in the background is by the British rock band – The Libertines and is titled – Arbeit Macht Frei. (Whittington 2011: 9)

The slogan *Arbeit macht frei* or 'work makes you free' was placed at the entrances to a number of Nazi concentration camps during the Second World War.

There are also sound shapes that offer hope, such as the epiphany that Theo begins to undergo in the forest as he begins to hear the world differently as Zen-like sound effects fill the spaces of the trees. The transcendental score also anchors the drama in terms of its redemptive and recuperative qualities: Theo becomes a changed man as much through the way he hears as sees the world anew.

Theo is often at the centre of the way the soundscape orientates itself, and the tinnitus that he suffers following the film's opening bomb blast becomes his leitmotif in times of danger and crisis. The barely audible ringing that cuts through the film is literal and metaphoric – it is found, for example, in the sound of gunfire and the bell that sounds out the closing of the film. The ringing we hear is Theo's own battle fatigue and the film's frame for creating a destabilising sound-image for the 'War on Terror' it is shaped by. As William Whittington argues,

> The ringing is accentuated by a muting of the overall sound track through the use of high-pass audio filters, which dampen the fidelity of the ambient sounds as if we are hearing them through a pane of thick glass. As a result, the audiovisual field takes on a

detached and dreamlike quality, which supports Theo's despondent demeanour and establishes the theme of alienation, mapping it as both an external and internal condition. (2011: 8)

The sound that is carried within and by Theo is not constant, however. The nativity play that the film's narrative architecture is built around involves a musical score that suggests a possible redemption for Theo and the world at large. As a Christ-like figure, with stigmata wounds, Theo's movements are also orchestrated by John Tavener's accompaniment music, 'Fragments of a Prayer'. The score suggests a (coming) transformation in Theo, and in the world as it might be (if only he/we/ they hears its possibilities). William Whittington again suggests that,

> Theo's sense of loss and despair through the introduction of a musical score that connects with various spiritual traditions from around the world, including Christianity, Hinduism, and Buddhism. The orchestrations, placement and emotive impact of the compositions by John Tavener evoke a sense of transformation and transcendence within the character. (2011: 9)

The mixture of religious tones and valences found in the score suggests both a world where global intersections (already) exist, and where if they are carried forward to Tomorrow, will lead to the redemption of the human race. However, it is Theo's theology that will save the world: he becomes a salvic white hero not simply through mythic characterisation but the way he unites the fragments of all (acceptable) religions together into one transcendental song.

The apocalypse of *Children of Men* is of course haunted by another set of sounds or – at least initially – by their absence. At the beginning of the film there are no children's voices and thus none of the innocence and purity that one senses when those voices are heard, and those bodies are seen. When we later visit an abandoned school where children should be studying and playing we only hear the sounds of dead, decaying objects and silent passageways. These 'haunted spaces . . . bear the traces of repressed personal or national traumas' (Thompson 2012: 129). This is where Dylan, Theo's son, should be present, and where children should be growing up together. Laughter and learning should be filling the air and not the nothingness of the paranoid present. Wars enter playgrounds and shut schools – this is not simply, then, an absence of reproduction but the presence of genocide.

The next time we hear the sound of an infant, it is through the cries of Kee's newborn baby. This scene plays out in a siege, in a building in

Bexhill under heavy attack by the military. As soon as the baby is heard crying, the attack is suspended and a hush and stillness descends on the scene. This miracle baby drowns out the sounds of war and the cries of people dying. It's sounding momentarily re-enchants the world, brings to the fore the repressed sounds that the film has struggled to mute. As William Whittington writes, 'the audio effect (a variation of the "found sound") reintroduces a long-absent voice that fosters a sense of unity, renewal and hope for both Theo and humanity' (2011: 11). This new-born will fill the world with song again, or at least has the potential to.

The second and final time we hear the sound of children is over black space and the title card, as the film ends. What we hear are the repressed sounds of the child Dylan might have been, of the absent children that should have been in the school, and of the future children that soon will be born since Tomorrow is now in reach. As Zahid Chaudhary suggests,

> As we see the words 'Children of Men,' we hear the sound of children's laughter and playing, a sound that contains no recognizable words but the prattle of child sounds: giggles, screams, exclamations, happily agitated involuntary noises, and shouts . . . Since the camera does not show us any images of these children, the film avoids here the visual economies of difference on which it has relied thus far. Given the optimistic thrust of the film's final sequence, these inarticulate sounds are coming from Utopia, a world in which alterity no longer signifies because the acquisition of language has not yet constituted otherness – or burdened the spirit with language, to use Karl Marx's figuration from the first epigraph. (2009: 75)

Unlike Chaudry, however, I am not sure alterity has been fully vanquished. While it is true that Theo dies, and the (African) baby that is born carries the name of his lost child, suggesting an intersectional future, Kee and Dylan will find themselves at the mercy of scientists. While we do not see this group in the film, the reverence with which they are treated suggests a long tradition of privileging white scientists as salvic figures (Redmond 2011). *Children of Men* may offer us a way out of this 'War on Terror' but its final solution may well be whiteness inspired.

V. CONCLUSION

Children of Men is a wonderfully complex 'War on Terror' film: it is full of ideological tensions and thematic contradictions, is progressive in its representational and affective ethics, but ultimately seems to privilege the white salvic hero and the team of (white) scientists who wait on the ship *Tomorrow*. It achieves its complexity through the way space, body and soundscape intersect to create thick representations of power, conflict and control. The film is energised by movement, by a journey that takes Theo and then Kee from city to country to sea. For almost the entire duration of the film they are on the run, looking for refuge, for a safe harbour in a world at war. At each zone they seem to have nowhere left to run but manage each time to escape their impending containment or death. When they reach the sea, of course, there is nowhere left to run: this is the end point for Theo, who dies, and the point of no return for Kee, who has to become a boat person to escape the terror behind her. Both Kee and Theo have been stung into action, the affective power of the issues they face demanding they act upon the world rather than be enacted upon. For Kee, however, it is the white hero who has led her to salvation.

REFERENCES

Agamben, Giorgio (1998), *Homo Sacer: Sovereign Power and Bare Life*, trans. Daniel Heller Roazen, Stanford, CA: Stanford University Press.

Baudrillard, Jean (2005), 'War Porn', trans. Paul A. Taylor, *International Journal of Baudrillard Studies*, 2, No. 1, last accessed 27 July 2007: http://www.ubishops.ca/baudrillard/vol2_1/taylor.htm

Bauman, Zygmunt (2000), *Liquid Modernity*, Cambridge: Polity.

Boyle, Karen (2009), '*Children of Men* and *I Am Legend*: the Disaster-capitalism Complex Hits Hollywood', *Jump Cut*, No. 51, Spring, last accessed 1 July 2015: http://www.ejumpcut.org/archive/jc51.2009/ChildrenMenLegend/text.html

Chaudhary, Zahid R. (2009), 'Humanity Adrift: Race, Materiality, and Allegory in Alfonso Cuarón's *Children of Men*', *Camera Obscura*, 24.3, pp. 72, 73–109.

Dyer, Richard (1997), *White*, London: Routledge.

Elsaesser, Thomas (1996), 'Subject Positions, Speaking Positions: From *Holocaust, Our Hitler* and *Heimat* to *Shoah* and *Schindler's List*', in Vivian Sobchack (ed.), *The Persistence of History: Cinema, Television and the Modern Event*, New York: Routledge, pp.145–83.

Gutierrez, Christopher M. (2006), *Bodies of Terror/ Terrorizing Bodies*, dissertation, Concordia University (unpublished), http://spectrum.library.concordia.ca/8758/1/MR14200.pdf

Kompare, Derek (2005), 'We Are So Screwed: Invasion TV', *Flow 3*, No. 6, 18 November 2005, last accessed 23 March 2007: http:// jot.communication.utexas.edu/flow/?jot=view&id=1304

Lefebvre, Henri (1991), *The Production of Space*, London: Blackwell.

Marks, Laura U. (2000), *The Skin of the Film: Intercultural Cinema, Embodiment, and the Senses*, New York: Duke University Press.

Redmond, Sean (2005), 'When Planes Fall Out of the Sky', in Karen Randell and Sean Redmond (eds), *The War Body on Screen*, New York: Continuum, pp. 22–35.

Sobchack, Vivian (1999), 'Cities on the Edge of Time: The Urban Science Fiction Film', in Annette Kuhn (ed.), *Alien Zone II*, London: Verso, pp. 123–46.

Thompson, Kirsten Moana (2012), *Apocalyptic dread: American Film at the Turn of the Millennium*, New York: State University of New York Press.

Spivak, Gayatri Chakavorty (2004), 'Terror: A Speech after 9/11', *Boundary 2*, 31, No. 2, pp. 81–111.

Vint, Sheryl (2015), 'Biopolitics and the War on Terror in *World War Z* and *Monsters*', in Sean Redmond and Leon Marvell (eds), *Endangering Science Fiction Film*, New York: AFI Film Reader series, pp. 66–80.

Whittington, William (2011), 'Sound Design for a Found Future: Alfonso Cuarón's *Children of Men*', *New Review of Film and Television Studies*, 9.01, pp. 3–14.

Žižek, Slavoj (2007), *Children of Men*, last accessed 11 September 2015: http://www.youtube.com/watch?v=pbgrwNP_gYE

Traumatise, Repeat, Finish: Military Science Fiction (Long) after 9/11 and Doug Liman's *Edge of Tomorrow* (2014)

Steffen Hantke

1. ARE WE STILL POST-9/11?
THE COLD WAR PARADIGM

While literal representations of the events of 11 September 2001 have rarely garnered commercial rewards to match critical accolades – *United 93* (2006) comes to mind – horror and science fiction films have thrived in the aftermath of the attacks. In fact, the events of 9/11 have initiated a cultural cycle that retains its hold on the popular imagination to the present day. From the safe distance of the two genres' more hyperbolic signature tropes – among them most notably the zombie apocalypse and the alien invasion – horror and science fiction cinema have often come to rely on 9/11 as a topical reference point. The iconography of 9/11 would grow into a reference system equivalent in evocative intensity and cultural universality only to the Cold War and its preoccupation with nuclear anxieties. A few well-chosen images, a clichéd reference to a certain technology – radioactivity in the case of the Cold War, international terrorism in the case of the post-9/11 period – would be sufficient to subsume diverse political, social and cultural phenomena under a single historical paradigm.

The example of the Cold War as a point of reference is not arbitrarily chosen. Not long after the attacks on the World Trade Center, post-9/11 America seemed to acquire quite a few traits uncannily reminiscent of the 1950s. From the sudden spike in xenophobia, as a backdrop to both domestic and foreign policy, to the 'us versus them' attitude by which the Bush administration rhetorically divided friends and enemies, the paranoia accompanying the enforcement of political and ideological conformity, and the demonisation of an enemy that was everywhere and nowhere at the same time – the early years of the Cold War seemed like a fair approximation of what it felt like to live in the aftermath of 9/11. Depending on one's political position, the historical analogy with the 1950s communicated either the valour of newly rediscovered American greatness, the continuation of the 'American Century' in the hands of the 'Project for the New American Century', or the more dystopian version of a 1950s America in the grip of hysterical McCarthyite witch-hunts and apocalyptic end-times visions.

The analogy between the Cold War and the post-9/11 period might have been politically useful, but it would quickly prove itself to be skewed in two crucial respects. For one, Cold War audiences could, to one degree or another, disavow the explicit recognition that the creature features and alien invasion flicks they were watching were allegories of the Cold War. Many early Cold War science fiction and horror films were dismissed as adolescent fare. The slew of B-movie productions from the period further discredited the genres. It would allow for a casual critical dismissal that would throw the topical baby out with the tepid bathwater of low production values, bad acting and preposterous premises. Burdened with the self-awareness that tends to come with historical belatedness, popular culture in the post-9/11 period could claim no such innocence. History being 'thinly disguised' behind the zombie apocalypse and the alien invasion: this idea applied all the more since so much post-9/11 horror and science fiction would take its cues directly from the blueprints of Cold War culture. The popular culture of the post-9/11 period brought back Cold War horror and science fiction with a vengeance. This time around, however, the intertextual evocation of these historical precursors made it impossible to disavow the recognition of their historical topicality. A few members of the audience for *Invaders from Mars* (1953) may have seen the film as an allegory of Cold War anxieties – very few members may not have seen post-9/11 anxieties writ large across *War of the Worlds* (2005), *The Invasion* (2007), *I am Legend* (2007) or *Battle: Los Angeles* (2011).

The second, and more important, distinction between popular culture in both periods would be that the Cold War, for the duration of its existence, was not predicated on a single catastrophic origin – like 9/11. Of course the origins of the Cold War can be pinpointed with considerable historical accuracy. What is not possible, however, is to assign its start to a single event on a specific day, captured in images that would go around the world and burn themselves into the global collective consciousness. As a result, the duration of the Cold War was never subject to questioning in regard to its origins and the steadily increasing historical distance from this point of origin. Only in retrospect, from the safe perspective of its aftermath, would there ever be a 'late period' of the Cold War. Unlike the post-9/11 period, the Cold War would never produce the question: when has enough time passed before we can put all this behind ourselves? Fifteen years after 9/11, this is the crucial question: at what moment in time have we crossed the threshold into something other than the 'post-9/11' period?

To the extent that horror and science fiction have participated in the effort of trying to produce an answer to this question, post-9/11 texts have increasingly departed from the structures and concerns they had originally inherited from their Cold War antecedents. It is in asking the historical question 'When have we reached the point where we no longer live in the post-9/11 period?' that more recent post-9/11 horror and science fiction has begun to take on idiosyncratic shape. In fact, this question has, slowly but surely, begun to emerge as the key concern worked out in text after text. While films like *I am Legend* (2007) or television series like *Invasion* (ABC, 2005), *Threshold* (CBS, 2005) and *Surface* (NBC, 2005) are still firmly entrenched in a vision of the world defined by 9/11, a television series like *Battlestar Galactica* (Universal TV, 2004–9) would turn, in its final phase, towards the paradoxical question of how to end an eternal war.[1] Hence, it invests considerable efforts in its final season imagining a form of narrative closure for its extended and highly complex multiple storylines in which the two early mandates of the post-9/11 period – never to forget the events of 9/11 on the one hand, and defying terrorism by returning to normality as quickly as possible on the other hand – are equally acknowledged and their inherent contradiction is resolved. As the Bush administration yielded the White House to Barack Obama in 2008, alien invasion narratives on television (*V* [ABC, 2009–11], *Falling Skies* [TNT, 2011–15]) would retain the 9/11 iconography yet reroute its global terrorist paranoia towards domestic right-wing anxieties projected onto the incoming administration and its political figurehead.[2] In regard to 9/11, *Falling Skies* moved the narrative forward by showing little interest in the traumatic event that legitimised the prolonged narrative that was to follow; relegated to a montage sequence in the opening credits, the alien invasion itself had almost dropped off the radar, yielding to the aftermath imagined as a period of prolonged military occupation.

Despite these signs of decline, the alien invasion narrative has clearly not lost its cultural relevance. From among the films in its most recent cycle, Doug Liman's *Edge of Tomorrow* (2014) provides a fascinating example of where the alien invasion film stands – aesthetically and politically – around the fifteenth anniversary of 11 September 2001. Like *Falling Skies*, *Edge of Tomorrow* seems to announce the end of the cycle when it shows little interest in the original trauma of 9/11 (i.e. the alien invasion, similarly relegated to an opening montage). Yet it abandons the paranoid domestic reading of alien invasion typical of the Obama-period texts and returns to a more aggressive militarism. For this most recent transformation, the film deserves closer critical scrutiny.

II. *EDGE OF TOMORROW: GROUNDHOG DAY* (1993) WITH GUNS

Edge of Tomorrow is a perfect Hollywood product, worked on tirelessly by three different screenwriters (Christopher McQuarrie, Jez Butterworth and John-Henry Butterworth), drawing on a Japanese novel as source material (*All You Need Is Kill* [2004] by Hiroshi Sakurazaka), and showing off the considerable action film credentials of its director, Doug Liman. Despite these various credentials, the film is primarily driven by the charismatic presence of Tom Cruise, a star with links to the science fiction genre, but also with a star persona that adds interesting complications to the film's subtext.

The film's plot involves an alien invasion, by a species referred to as the Mimics (and then never discussed in any further substantial detail), which begins with a landing in Germany, spreads rapidly across Europe, and is finally brought to a temporary halt, after a decisive military victory at the Battle of Verdun, at the beaches of Normandy. All this is compressed in a montage sequence over which the opening credits are played. As an international army is readying itself for an invasion of Normandy from the British Isles, our protagonist, William Cage (Tom Cruise), flies into London for what he believes is a public relations mission. To his dismay and against considerable personal resistance, he is forced into combat duty and joins the invasion. During the battle on the beaches of Normandy he is killed, only to wake up at the start of the previous day, pressed into combat duty and on his way to the same beach to be killed yet again. The daily repetition, triggered each time by his death, brings him to the attention of Rita Vrataski (Emily Blunt), a highly decorated soldier, who explains Cage's condition to him and to the audience. Once infected with the enemy's blood, Cage shares the Mimics' ability to 'reset time', which entraps him in the cycle of repetition but also puts him in the privileged position to penetrate, anticipate and foil the Mimics' invasion plans. Together with Rita, Cage defeats the Mimics and saves the world.

As a piece of post-9/11 science fiction, the film retains some of the crucial iconography that reaches back to the Cold War. Part of the by-now-familiar post-9/11 iconography is the fact that the Mimics tend to burrow underground before they attack, investing otherwise familiar or idyllic landscapes with a latent sense of danger. During the Cold War, this was the trope of the fifth column, reincarnated for the 'War on Terror' as the trope of the terrorist sleeper cell. In post-9/11 science fiction, the trope is anticipated by Spielberg's *War of the Worlds*, which imagined the Martian war machines already buried beneath American urban centres a long time before the start of the actual invasion. There is also the fact that the Mimics are a hive mind controlled by nodal entities which must be destroyed for the entire invasive species to be eliminated. Like the fifth column/sleeper cell, the hive mind metaphor harks back to that old Cold War chestnut that communism eliminates the individual, a trope ubiquitous in 1950s science fiction. Then there is the absolute otherness of the enemy. The Mimics are purely a product of computer-generated imagery: no human actors are used in front of the camera for their visual representation. They are a mixture of mechanical and biological tropes: they are slithery yet composed of gunmetal-black segments. Some variants are vaguely reminiscent of animals, while the Mimic that represents their collective hive mind's central node looks like a sea anemone, softly undulating in the waters beneath the flooded Louvre parking garage. The vast majority of Mimics are absolutely non-anthropomorphic, a tangle of black tentacles. Their extremely rapid movements, writhing and flailing in spiky excrescences, recapitulate the transformation of the cinematic zombie from a slow shambling ghoul (with George Romero's films [1968, etc.] providing the original conceptual model) to the hyperactive and self-destructively hyper-aggressive creature post-9/11 audiences have been habituated to (from Snyder's *Dawn of the Dead* remake [2004] to *World War Z* [2013]). Almost a decade and a half after 9/11, the Mimics are that figure of absolute otherness again, that enemy that cannot be negotiated with.

To emphasise this point even further, the film not only fails to provide a motivation for the Mimics' invasion; it explicitly condemns the search for such a motivation as a pointless distraction. In a scene devoted exclusively to making this point, Cage escapes from the gruelling and unsuccessful series of repetitions and decides to turn his back on the war. In a pub in London, he interrupts a conversation between some of the patrons who are arguing about the reason for the invasion. 'What does it matter?' is his question – a question that not only remains unchallenged but also reinforced by the realisation that, having walked away from the war, Cage now is responsible for the Mimics swimming up the Thames and overrunning the last bastion of humanity. The world of the film is simultaneously one of ethical absolutes, and one operating beyond morality altogether. Compared to the cautious challenging of these absolutes creeping into science fiction during the second term of the Bush administration (*Threshold, Invasion, Surface, Falling Skies*), *Edge of Tomorrow* positions itself among the earlier and more conservative and militaristic texts in the larger cycle.

If this adherence to well-established conventions seems to render *Edge of Tomorrow* a tired retread of earlier, more original films, Liman and his team come up with a central narrative conceit that differentiates their product from its immediate predecessors. This is the cyclical repetition of the crucial twenty-four hours of the invasion: Cage, together with the audience, reliving the same day over and over.[3] This looping repetition becomes *Edge of Tomorrow*'s marketing hook – what one might think of as its version of 'high concept' to distinguish it from other alien invasion films. In the medium of cinema, reviewers were quick to pick up on the similarity to *Groundhog Day*, though science fiction's pulp tradition may have cleared the path much earlier.[4] Infused with the enemy's blood, Cage receives the enemy's ability to 'reset the day'. What starts with him helplessly trapped within the 24-hour loop gradually develops into him understanding his condition, mastering it, and deploying it to his advantage. With every pass through the loop, Cage learns from his mistakes, acquiring the (to others) uncanny ability to anticipate the enemy's next move, which (to others) comes across as total control and mastery over his material environment. To the extent that, within the social environment, this mastery retains all the negative connotations of arrogance, Cage's learning curve inevitably leads him from self-containment to his collaboration with Rita and, eventually, to his social engagement with his fellow soldiers in J-squadron. The same team that initially despises and marginalises Cage ends up joining him on his mission and sacrificing their lives for him.

For most viewers, this looping repetition will be an invitation to read the film as a therapeutic response to the trauma of 9/11. Each time Cage relives the botched invasion on the beaches of Normandy, the film obsessively returns him and us to the site of the original trauma. With each therapeutic revisiting of the wound, our hero familiarises himself with the unexplored territory, and gradually overcomes his hesitation

to return. Just as this cyclical return threatens to tilt over into the opposite symptom of trauma – the compulsive return to the wound to the
exclusion of all else – the film grants Cage, first, a temporary leave
from the repetition (as he goes AWOL for a while). Then, in the final
sequence, he is relieved from the compulsion for good when, thanks to
a blood transfusion, he loses the ability to 'reset the day' and must now
re-enter linear time, which will eventually deliver him to the closure of
the final scene. The film abandons the cyclical repetition just before the
audience grows tired of it; this is, after all, an action film, not *Last Year
at Marienbad* (1961). Manohla Dargis explicitly links the film's central conceit to the (strictly prescribed) pleasures of genre cinema: 'the
movie's clever tagline, "Live, Die, Repeat", she reminds us, 'echoes the
faith that every film genre fan embraces: live, watch, repeat'. But this
meta-commentary remains submerged beneath the film's more obvious appeal to the vastly more popular narrative of trauma. Read in
this psychologising manner, *Edge of Tomorrow* traces its protagonist's
progress of compulsive repetition to transcendence and closure.

While this may make sense for the traumatised individual, the culture at large may need a storyline that reads Cage's progress not as a
move towards closure but as a reflection whether, collectively, such a
move is possible. In this context, it is difficult, if not altogether impossible, not to read the plot contrivance of looping repetition as part of a
figurative inquiry into the nature of history. With every walk-through
of the traumatic moment, the film reads the opportunity provided
by the repetition differently. Cage starts incompetent, then gradually
grows into a super-soldier. Cage starts isolated, then gradually reaches
out to his comrades-in-arms to aid in his mission. Cage gets frustrated
by the endless drudgery of training and the repeated experience of failure, then walks away from the war. Cage is motivated by accepting
responsibility for the fate of the world, then switches over to a romantic
attachment to Rita, his mentor and fellow soldier.

As each repetition tries out a variant of the basic plot, the film
transposes Cage's personal story onto the national learning curve. As
a representative American, Cage enacts that old question asked so
poignantly by Sylvester Stallone's character in *Rambo: First Blood
Part II* (1985): 'Do we get to win this time?' It concedes that 'mistakes
were made' in the conduct of the post-9/11 wars – from the futile
search for weapons of mass destruction to the decommissioning but
not disarming of the Iraqi military. It transforms this concession into
the recognition that the US is constantly learning from its mistakes.
All this serves as an underhanded assertion that US foreign policy
in its more egregious consequences is a matter of well-intentioned

failures rather than the pragmatic, self-interested weighing of strategic options. Herein lies perhaps the film's most ideological assertion – an assertion that is fairly common, though it has grown increasingly difficult to make: that the US after 9/11 has been dragged into conflicts for which it neither asked nor showed itself equipped for. Cage's transformation from a public relations officer, talking a good game but untested in battle, into an experienced soldier lends this trajectory from innocence to experience the sheen that comes with military self-confidence. Military dominance is arrogance, the film argues, as long as it is owned but not earned.

In the final instance, *Edge of Tomorrow* fails to explore its interesting basic premise to its full extent when it returns, for the final confrontation between humanity and the Mimics, from cyclical to linear time. The conversion is achieved at the expense of narrative consistency; a final cyclical move – this one after Cage has supposedly lost the ability to reset time – brings us back to the opening sequence, only that this time the helicopter flyover across the London cityscape is accompanied by church bells ringing in the victory over the Mimics. A brief coda even reunites Cage with Rita, achieving the consummation of a romantic subplot that, throughout the film, has been kept largely in the background (and is inconsistent with Rita's character). Against Rita's earlier prediction that Cage must die to defeat the enemy, the final victory is achieved without sacrifice. It is a pat ending, inconsistent and unsatisfying. Even if read as a mechanically conventional gesture of closure imposed upon an unconventional narrative, the full potential of which it falls short of containing, this ending abandons all pretence of being part of a thought-out historical allegory. The best it has to offer in pursuit of an answer to the question of how to escape from the endless cycles of violence in the post-9/11 world is an adolescent power fantasy. Disappointed with this ending, viewers will have to turn elsewhere for a more rewarding commentary the film might have to offer on that very question.

III. *EDGE OF TOMORROW:* THE REMASCULINISATION OF AMERICA OR THE GREATEST GENERATION

Viewers in search of a more consistently developed ideological position in *Edge of Tomorrow* will inevitably – and somewhat paradoxically – come upon the film's intense intertextual overcoding. *Edge of Tomorrow* achieves a peculiar kind of originality by ransacking the history of science fiction cinema, and especially the alien invasion narrative.

Clearly the film is tailored to fans of the genre, but it also recombines familiar elements in new and surprising ways for a broader audience. The range of the textual poaching is considerable, so that the question arises as to whether the film merely recycles the cinematic and ideological past, or whether it might actually succeed in moving beyond the Cold War frame of reference typical of so much other post-9/11 science fiction.

For one, there is the long tradition of the alien invasion narrative itself, ranging from the various adaptations of H. G. Wells' *The War of the Worlds* (1898) – from Orson Welles, to George Pal and Steven Spielberg – to 1990s blockbusters like *Independence Day* (1996) and the 2015 television miniseries based on Arthur C. Clarke's *Childhood's End*. Beyond this broad generic horizon, the film references more specific hallmarks of science fiction cinema. There is, for example, an extended training sequence, in which Rita helps Cage transform himself into an efficient soldier, which references the training sequence in *Star Wars* (1977). The film's final battle takes place in a flooded underground space beneath the Louvre in Paris, a space that allows for an action sequence reminiscent of that in *Alien: Resurrection* (1997), which has a band of survivors trying to dive to safety through an obstacle course with hostile aliens in pursuit. When Cage discovers that a rogue scientist has invented a device that allows him to tap into the Mimics' communication network, temporarily sharing the alien perspective, the conceit and its execution recall the mind-melding technology portrayed in *Pacific Rim* (2013). Meanwhile, the Mimics themselves, with their black multi-tentacled fluidity, reach back to similar designs for the so-called Sentinels in the *Matrix* franchise (1999, etc.), as filtered through alien invader technology in *Battle: Los Angeles*. *Edge of Tomorrow*'s exoskeletal fighting suit goes back all the way to *Starship Troopers* (1997) and, in the genealogy of Heinlein's source novel, to Joe Haldeman's novel *The Forever War* (1974), as well as its various cinematic incarnations, from James Cameron's loaders, used first in *Aliens* (1986) before being repurposed as military technology in *Avatar* (2009), all the way to Neill Blomkamp's more recent *Elysium* (2013). With similarities in production design dominating the film's surface, some of Liman's casting choices also enrich the film's dense intertextual fabric. Seeing actor Bill Paxton in the part of Sergeant Farell conjures up memories of Paxton as Hudson in Cameron's *Aliens*. As to the musical soundtrack, *Edge of Tomorrow* appropriates both the idiosyncratic five-note drumbeat of the *Terminator* franchise, amped up with the droning brass motif that has run across science fiction soundtracks ever since Christopher Nolan's *Inception* (2010).

While critics of the film might read this high density of intertexual borrowing as a symptom of its lack of originality and creative exhaustion, more dispassionate viewers might wonder whether the film is not engaged in a deliberate summarising of its own cinematic tradition. Instead of dismissing the film in this manner, I would like to propose a reading that positions the film late in the cinematic cycle of post-9/11 military science fiction. This late occurrence in the cycle has two consequences, both of which oddly intertwine with each other. On the one hand, the high degree of intertextuality might register as a baroque overloading of its essential structures. As cinematic cycles go, following the initial period in which thematic and formal structures emerge and solidify is a period characterised by amplification. Films in this period tend to get faster, louder, longer, more colourful, graphic and excessive. To some extent, the intertextual density of *Edge of Forever* registers as such baroque excess: if *Saving Private Ryan*'s (1998) first fifteen minutes were what made the film famous, how much better would a film be that replayed those famous fifteen minutes over and over? What is crucial about this baroque excess in *Edge of Tomorrow*, however, is its articulation not only in terms of amplification and repetition, but, more specifically, in the register of intertextuality. It imbues the film with a kind of 'knowingness' that ties audiences to their favourite genres and fans to their favourite franchises. Without dismissing the film as derivative, such an audience might, in fact, appreciate the basic familiarity that hides behind the superficial novelty as a sign of the film's faithfulness not to a branded franchise but to a spirit, a basic ideological position, inherent in military science fiction and how it interfaces with the larger culture.

Those in search for what this basic ideological position might be will quickly settle on one particular strand of intertextual citations which the film begins to foreground from the moment of its opening news montage. In this montage, we learn that the alien invasion begins with a landing in Germany. An accompanying map visualises the multiple tentacles by which the invasion spreads out from this Central European hub to the rest of the Europe. In case the Second World War reference is not explicit enough, newscasters remind us that there is an Eastern and a Western Front in this war, and that the decisive battle is stacked up with two massive armies – the human United Defence Force in Britain, and the Mimic defenders of the continent in France – along the coasts of the Channel. As in the Second World War, the US is crucial to increasing British troop strengths, and has finally done the right thing in entering the war only 'after exhausting all other options' (to paraphrase Winston Churchill). The film's protagonist, arrogant and

Figure 15.1 'We will fight them on the beaches . . .' All Over Again: Ending the War on Terror by Mobilizing the Greatest Generation in *Saving Private Ryan* (1998) (upper) and *Edge of Tomorrow* (2014) (lower).

cowardly William Cage, embodies this lingering resentment against reluctant American intervention.

As the film translates this historical analogy into the register of cinema, its primary point of reference is not American cinema during the Second World War – it is its reimagining by Steven Spielberg with

Saving Private Ryan, easily *the* most influential war film released in the last thirty years. With its basic conceit – that Cage is reliving the day of the invasion over and over again – *Edge of Tomorrow* has the liberty of replaying the signature scene from *Saving Private Ryan* again and again: quite a rewarding proposition for an action film! Liman's staging of the repeated beach landing sequence follows Spielberg's lead closely: Cage's landing craft may not be a water vehicle but, like the vehicle in the opening scene in *Saving Private Ryan*, its complement of soldiers barely has a fighting chance as they get hit before making the beach. Liman also follows Spielberg's immersive aesthetic, the camera weaving and bobbing as it traces its path through a bewildering over-kill of visual and auditory stimuli.

What is important to note about this intertextual use of *Saving Private Ryan* is that it infuses *Edge of Tomorrow* with the Second World War combat film. Jeanine Basinger's description of the combat film as a cinematic form uniquely attuned to the American experi-ence of the Second World War is based on a series of characteristic features, many of which are shared by *Saving Private Ryan* and *Edge of Tomorrow*. Both films structure their narrative around 'a mission which will accomplish an important military objective' (Basinger 68): while Spielberg's film must arrive at the significance of the mission by way of sacrifice and negotiation, Liman's film posits the importance of Cage's mission in hyperbolic terms typical of adolescent adventure – it is up to Cage to save not a single man, but the world. With Upham (Jeremy Davies), Spielberg's film uses 'an observer or commentator', while Liman's film splits this function between Rita and Cage, both of whom alternate in being insiders/outsiders to the mission (68). Most importantly, both directors adhere to the conclusion Basinger posits for the Second World War combat film: 'The audience is ennobled for having shared [the unit's] combat experience, as they are ennobled for having undergone it. We are all comrades in arms' (69).

With this descriptive statement, Basinger also ties the combat film to its interpellative function. Regardless of whether the film registers as pro- or anti-war, the demand for audience immersion to the point of 'sharing' the fictional characters' combat experience ties in directly with Spielberg's and Liman's immersive visual aesthetic. Like *Saving Private Ryan*'s famous first fifteen minutes, *Edge of Tomorrow* presents Cage's military service as an ordeal for character and audience alike. What Spielberg accomplished with the sheer length of the Normandy Invasion sequence, Liman accomplishes by the number of its repeti-tions in the course of the narrative. Both films ultimately try to con-tain the visual excess and affective intensity of these combat sequences:

Spielberg follows the overkill of the first fifteen minutes with a highly sentimental and conventionally narrated fable about the patriotic and personal value of sacrifice, while Liman eventually liberates Cage from the endless cycles of repetition and launches him, in the final assault on the enemy's headquarters underneath the Louvre, into a linear narrative with a satisfying sense of closure.

In the final instance, viewers might come away from both *Saving Private Ryan* and *Edge of Tomorrow* with a sense that both films' attempts at containing and contextualising the immersive overload of the combat sequences have actually fallen short of their goal. Or, as Samuel Fuller has famously stated, no film will ever be able to capture the experience of being in combat (short of having someone with a gun take shots at the patrons in the theatre during the screening).[5] Elisabeth Bronfen has made the same point in a more academic fashion. She argues that it is the 'irrepresentability of any actual experience of war' (109) – i.e. the audience's affective 'detachment from the heightened anxiety of battle' (108) – which allows 'the war film to pass as movie entertainment [. . .] regardless of how realistic it strives to be' (108–9). Cinema can restage or re-enact the original trauma in a 'scenic reconstruction' of what must inevitably be 'fragmented internal images' (110). These images can be 'unequivocally perceived as being different from the original experience' (110), and thus reintegrated into a coherent narrative. Narrative externalisation and reintegration allow for a representation of trauma – not trauma itself – to be communicated from the affected subject to a cinematic audience, a process that is always and inevitably ideological in nature. Just as *Saving Private Ryan* needs the full two hours of running time following those traumatic first fifteen minutes to make sense of the overwhelming experience, *Edge of Tomorrow* revisits the traumatic moment in order to resolve the trauma by transitioning its endless self-consuming cycle into a coherent sequential narrative that ends with our hero's triumph.

Reaching back to the Second World War as a historical reference point for its imaginary alien invasion, and accessing this reference point by way of *Saving Private Ryan*, *Edge of Tomorrow* also makes a play for a broader cultural discourse: it mobilises the trope of the 'Greatest Generation' fifteen years after its entry into popular parlance.[6] At the time of its inception, the discourse of the Greatest Generation reflected political manoeuvring around partisan politics that were framed around generational change. With Bill Clinton, a baby boomer, defeating Bob Dole, a veteran of the Second World War, in the presidential elections in 1996, the traditional values associated with the Greatest Generation took on even greater significance. However, while Americans seemed more than willing to pay tribute to what this generation had come to represent, they proved reluctant to vote for or pragmatically support one of their number. While demographically accurate, the incessant framing of the Greatest Generation as a vanishing breed (in films like *Saving Private Ryan* or *Flags of Our Fathers* [2006], which both frame the Second World War experiences with images of old men on the verge of death) acquired a note of the American Jeremiad – a lament over the selfishness and softness of the post-baby boomer generation. While the turn of the millennium rendered the Greatest Generation discourse as a commentary on the political attribution of conservative values if projected backwards throughout the 1990s, it also rendered this discourse as a convenient recruitment tool for the American wars in the wake of 11 September 2001. The willingness to sacrifice in stoic silence celebrated by the discourse of the Greatest Generation prepared the ground for the state's demand on the US military for the first decade of the new millennium.

As if all this audience interpellation into the discourse of the Greatest Generation is not enough, there is a secondary intertextual level at which *Edge of Tomorrow* selectively embraces cultural discourses of American military culture. The way to access this level is via the film's star, Tom Cruise. Though Cruise has, in recent years, attempted to diversify his star persona (*Magnolia* [1999], *Lions for Lambs* [2007], *Valkyrie* [2008]), it has remained firmly rooted in a particular narrative established with the early commercial successes of his career in the 1980s, the most notable of which, incidentally, is the military adventure *Top Gun* (1986).[7] Cruise's character in *Top Gun*, Maverick, starts out as a brilliant yet arrogant fighter pilot. Beyond the sheen of charisma, the character is not entirely likeable. The plot then puts this character through a series of experiences, most importantly the death of his co-pilot and best friend Goose, from which he is officially exonerated but for which he feels personally responsible. This ordeal strips Maverick of his arrogance, leaves his charisma undiminished, and thus transforms him into a thoroughly likeable person in the end.[8]

Across the chasm of thirty-odd years, it is not difficult to discern exactly this character in exactly this plot in *Edge of Tomorrow*. Cruise's William Cage starts out as a cocky, arrogant and – worst of all – cowardly public relations specialist, recruited from the private sector into the military where he serves as the shallow self-important public face of the war. As dramatic evidence of this character flaw, the film presents his refusal to serve as embedded journalist with the first wave of the invasion. Only the series of humiliations at the hands of his more experienced fellow-soldiers, the repeated failures on the battlefield leading to him dying over and over, and the obvious dis-advantage opposite Rita's fighting skills and demoted crack scientist Carter's (Noah Taylor) scientific comprehension of the enemy, add up to the beneficial humbling the character needs to undergo. Much like Maverick in *Top Gun*, the story revolves around Cage's return from humiliation a better man.[9]

Among the most iconic action films of the 1980s, *Top Gun* is not commonly counted as one of the films Susan Jeffords so famously tasked with the 'remasculinisation of America', the cultural reflection of the Reagan years and the attempt to compensate for the military and political humiliation of the US in the Vietnam War. Given his dimin-utive stature, Tom Cruise also fails to qualify alongside those actors Jeffords identifies with the conservative agenda of the 1980s action film – Arnold Schwarzenegger, Sylvester Stallone and Chuck Norris. With the help of prosthetic technology to amplify the power of Cruise's 'insufficient' body, the basic narrative trajectory in *Top Gun* and *Edge of Tomorrow* follows that enacted by these more heavily muscled stars in 1980s action cinema. To the extent that Cruise's star persona has consistently aligned itself with this narrative trajectory, therefore, *Edge of Tomorrow* imports, by way of Cruise as the film's central star, the historical allegory of the post-Vietnam remasculinisation of America as well. Like America at the beginning of the Second World War, Cage must abandon all hesitation to assume the messianic military role assigned to him by providential happenstance. And like America emerging humili-ated from the Vietnam War, he must shed the arrogance that led to his failure, the arrogance that came with the unshakeable belief in his own infallibility. In embracing this failure by reliving it over and over as a process of therapeutic cleansing, he will transcend his crisis of confi-dence and ultimately earn his dominance.

What *Edge of Tomorrow* suppresses in its idiosyncratic mobilisa-tion of historical discourses by way of citing cinematic predecessors is an alternative tradition of war films with its own ideological frame-work. Though the Vietnam War produced formally and ideologically conservative war films (most notoriously perhaps *The Green Berets* [1968]), its dominant cinematic and ideological heritage will be defined more by formally inventive films like *MASH* (1970), *Catch-22* (1970), *Slaughterhouse-Five* (1975) and *Apocalypse Now* (1979), all informed to varying degrees by the literary post-modernism the Vietnam War had helped to create.[10] *Edge of Tomorrow* cleverly screens out this alterna-tive tradition by accessing both the Second World War combat film and the Vietnam War film by way of belated conservative (one might be tempted to say: reactionary) responses to both historical events.[11]

IV. ARE WE THERE YET? STRATEGISING THE HISTORICAL ENDGAME

Despite its intriguing central conceit – the looping repetition – *Edge of Tomorrow* ultimately fails to imagine an extrication of the culture from the paradigm of 9/11, not just in its iconography but also in the narrative and thematic deployment of that iconography. Much like alien invasion narratives that precede it, the film struggles to reconcile the two opposing aspects of imagining an end to the 'War on Terror'. On the one hand, the prospect of emerging from the post-9/11 world into a new historical period – whatever that period might be – is liberating; finally, the burden of the past, claustrophobically weighing us down and preventing us from moving ahead, has been lifted. This liberation from the past's oppressive power then clears the path for new challenges (and of course for new anxieties). On the other hand, much like the Cold War, the 9/11 narrative has shaped conceptions of historical continuity so drastically for so long that the prospect of abandoning it is unsettling, not to mention the guilt that might be incurred by what may feel like betraying the historical mandate derived from all the casualties of 9/11. What is to follow once we have broken the power of the cultural master narrative?

Edge of Tomorrow is just a single film, and may thus not be representative of larger cultural trends. Still, read as a harbinger of possible things to come, the film opens up interesting interpretive venues. For one, its overloading of the alien invasion trope with intertextual references from the history of the science fiction film and the various social discourses in response to actual wars might come across simply as part of the search for originality – a polite way of calling it a gimmick. Nearly fifteen years of post-9/11 discourse has exhausted the available reservoir of tropes to the degree that films must resort to gimmicks like the endless looping repetition of time travel to keep things interesting. This is what I've been referring to as the baroque stage of the cinematic cycle, a stage in which ornament disconnects from, and even obscures, function. The problem with this explanation is that it asserts the appearance of symptoms of this creative exhaustion without being able to explain why a specific set of symptoms occurs and not another. This moves the looping repetition in *Edge of Tomorrow* back on the interpretive agenda: might this not be a meta-textual component that allows the filmmakers to imagine the reconciliation of staying true to the responsibilities of the past with the imperative of having to move forward?

More important than the film's 'high concept' is its highly selective mobilisation of two specific discourses that weave in and out of cinema history: the remasculinisation of America in the wake of the Vietnam War during the 1980s on the one hand, and the concept of the Greatest Generation rising to popularity in the generationally polarised 1990s on the other. Both discourses include a strongly interpellative component geared towards conservative values: the return to national self-confidence and strength, tied to traditional ideas of masculinity, in the wake of the Vietnam War, and the faith, honour, austerity and traditional social values associated with the veterans of the Second World War. Given its release date in 2014, *Edge of Tomorrow* faces an audience for which the Cold War has already been fully absorbed into the discourse of the 'War on Terror'. For a post-millennial audience with no personal memory of the years before 1991, the Cold War may be only, or at least primarily, accessible through the popular culture of the post-9/11 period. This shifts attention to the other two historical options in *Edge of Tomorrow*. Mobilising two historical discourses that aim at *re*writing historical failure, *re*visiting historical greatness, *re*committing national resources to military strength, and *re*newing traditional values, *Edge of Tomorrow* might have hit upon an original way after all to *re*-enlist its audience into the 'War on Terror'. When it talks about 'resetting the day', it means business! While the film's success in moving away from the Cold War analogy could be considered a sign of progress, there is still that irony about the film's title. When it comes to moving the post-9/11 discourse into its endgame after a decade and a half, we might be disappointed to discover that the edge of tomorrow looks a lot like a return to yesterday.

NOTES

1. See Hantke, 'Bush's America and the Return of Cold War Science Fiction: Alien Invasion in *Invasion*, *Threshold*, and *Surface*'; 'Exit Strategies: Narrative Closure and Political Allegory in *Lost* and *Battlestar Galactica*'; and 'Historicizing the Bush Years: Politics, Horror Film, and Francis Lawrence's *I Am Legend*'.

2. See Hantke, 'Aliens versus Tea Party Patriots: *Falling Skies* and the Post-Apocalyptic Survival Narrative in the Age of Obama' and '"We Are of Peace, Always": ABC's Remake of *V*, Alien Invasion Television, and American Paranoia After Bush'.

3. In regard to this trope, the most obvious influence on *Edge of Tomorrow* is digital gaming. Cage's ability to 'reset the day' by dying (suffering death passively or embracing it as a deliberate means of retaining control over the situation) mirrors that of players in a digital game saving, revisiting and thus mastering crucial gaming junctures. In the afterword to the novel on which the film is based, *All You*

Need is Kill (2004), Hiroshi Sakurazaka makes this link to the logic of gaming explicit: there is 'not a drop of hero's blood in my whole body [. . .] I'm just an ordinary guy, and proud of it' (268). Sakurazaka compares the process of writing a novel with the game's inherent ability to fail and repeat: 'I reset the game hundreds of times until my special attack finally went off perfectly. Victory was inevitable. So please, hold off on all the hero talk' (269).

4. Manohla Dargis, for example, starts her review with the clever line, 'Tell me if you've heard this one before', and then moves on to quote Robert Heinlein's novel *Farnham's Freehold* (1964) on the subject of time travel before, in the next paragraph, hitting upon *Groundhog Day*.

5. 'See, there's no way you can portray war realistically, not in a movie nor in a book [. . .] If you really want to make readers understand a battle, a few pages of your book would be booby-trapped. For moviegoers to get the idea of real combat, you'd have to shoot at them every so often from either side of the screen. The casualties in the theater would be bad for business' (Fuller, *Third Face*, 123).

6. The single idiosyncratic exception to this citing of the Second World War is the presentation of Rita as the heroine of the Battle of Verdun – an explicit reference to the First World War (and, implicitly, to the myth of the 'Angel of Mons'). This happens to be the battle at which humanity believes to have stemmed the tide of the alien invasion; we discover later that the Mimics' defeat was actually a ploy to lure humanity into the 'endgame' of the Normandy invasion.

7. Apart from franchises humming along on the strength of their brand name recognition alone (*Mission Impossible*, 1996–), Cruise's career at middle age has increasingly moved towards science fiction. While action films like *Knight and Day* (2010) and the inauspicious launch of a new franchise, *Jack Reacher* (2012), have been resounding commercial and critical failures, Cruise's association with director and producer Steven Spielberg (*Minority Report* [2002], *War of the Worlds* [2005]), as well as his more recent film *Oblivion* (2013), have situated his star persona more closely in relationship to the genre.

8. Reviewing the film for the *Village Voice*, Amy Nicholson has linked Cruise's star persona explicitly to the question of military recruitment. 'In 1986, peaceniks were mad at Tom Cruise', she reminds her readers. 'That year, the Navy thanked *Top Gun* for boosting enlistment another 20,000 recruits. Since then, he's made more critiques of military than advertisements, most of which (*Lions for Lambs*, *Born on the Fourth of July* [1989], *The Last Samurai* [2003], *Valkyrie*) j'accuse bad leadership of wasting the lives of a few – or a million – good men. With *Edge of Tomorrow*, Cruise comes full circle.'

9. The narrative takes on special poignancy at the present moment when Cruise's public persona has retained damage from his close association with Scientology. Cruise's star persona – relatively stable for most of the duration of the actor's career since the mid-1980s – began to unravel with his firing of his publicist of twelve years, Pat Kingsley, in 2004. On 23 May 2005, Cruise made an ill-fated appearance on the *Oprah Winfrey Show*, where his lack of emotional containment over his recent involvement with Katie Holmes was to set the stage for odd talk show appearances to come, as well as for leaked footage from Scientology events, culminating in the coverage of his involvement with Scientology in the HBO documentary *Going Clear: Scientology and the Prison of Belief* (Alex Gibney, 2015).

10. For the post-modernism connection, see Hantke, 'The Uses of the Fantastic and the Deferment of Closure in American Literature on the Vietnam War', pp. 63–82. See also Susan Jefford's discussion of the New Journalism and the Vietnam War, '"Facts No Longer Exist"', in *The Remasculinization of America*, pp. 30–35. M. Keith Booker's argument that the roots of this post-modernism actually go back to the 1950s (and thus are traceable specifically in the science fiction of the decade) does not invalidate this historical connection but expands its reach to a period 'even before postmodernism was recognized as a phenomenon' (Booker 21).

11. This is what Robert Kolker has in mind when he calls *Saving Private Ryan* 'a much more traditional war film than *The Hurt Locker*' (303).

REFERENCES

Basinger, Jeanine (2003), *The World War Two Combat Film: Anatomy of a Genre*, Middletown, CT: Wesleyan University Press.

Booker, Keith M. (2001), *Monsters, Mushroom Clouds, and the Cold War*, Westport, CT: Greenwood Press.

Bronfen, Elisabeth (2012), *Specters of War: Hollywood's Engagement with Military Conflict*, New Brunswick, NJ: Rutgers University Press.

Dargis, Manohla (2014), 'Killed in Action by Aliens, Over and Over Again: Tom Cruise Battles Invaders in "Edge of Tomorrow"', *New York Times*, 5 June 2014: http://www.nytimes.com/2014/06/06/movies/tom-cruise-battles-invaders-in-edge-of-tomorrow.html

Fuller, Samuel (2002), *A Third Face: My Tale of Writing, Fighting and Filmmaking*, New York: Knopf.

Hantke, Steffen (2001), 'The Uses of the Fantastic and the Deferment of Closure in American Literature on the Vietnam War', *The Rocky Mountain Review*, 55.1, Spring, pp. 63–82.

— (2010a), 'Bush's America and the Return of Cold War Science Fiction: Alien Invasion in *Invasion*, *Threshold*, and *Surface*', *The Journal of Popular Film & Television*, 38.3, Fall, pp. 143–51.

— (2010b), '"We Are of Peace, Always": ABC's Remake of V, Alien Invasion Television, and American Paranoia After Bush', *AAA: Arbeiten aus Anglistik und Amerikanistik*, 35.2, pp. 143–63.

— (2011), 'Historicizing the Bush Years: Politics, Horror Film, and Francis Lawrence's *I Am Legend*', in Aviva Briefel and Sam J. Miller (eds), *Horror After 9/11: World of Fear, Cinema of Terror*, Austin: University of Texas Press, pp. 166–86.

— (2013), 'Exit Strategies: Narrative Closure and Political Allegory in *Lost* and *Battlestar Galactica*', *ZAA: Zeitschrift für Anglistik und Amerikanistik*, 61.2, Spring, pp. 375–90.

— (2014), 'Aliens versus Tea Party Patriots: *Falling Skies* and the Post-Apocalyptic Survival Narrative in the Age of Obama', *The Journal of Language, Literature and Culture*, 61.2, August, pp. 117–32.

Jeffords, Susan (1989), *The Remasculinization of America: Gender and the Vietnam War*, Bloomington: Indiana University Press.

Kolker, Robert (1980 [2011]), *A Cinema of Loneliness*, 4th edn, Oxford and New York: Oxford University Press.

Nicholson, Amy (2014), 'The Smart Edge of Tomorrow Keeps Killing Its Star: Tom Cruise Is Back! (And Back! And Back!)', *The Village Voice*, 4 June 2014: http://www.villagevoice.com/2014-06-04/film/edge-of-tomorrow/

Sakurazaka, Hiroshi (2004 [2009]), *Edge of Tomorrow* (previously published as *All You Need is Kill*), San Francisco: Haikasoru.

Selected Filmography

The 6th Day (Roger Spottiswoode, 2000)

28 Days Later (Danny Boyle, 2002)

28 Weeks Later (Juan Carlos Fresnadillo, 2007)

300 (Zack Snyder, 2006)

Abraham Lincoln: Vampire Hunter (Timur Bekmambetov, 2012)

Aeon Flux (Karyn Kusuma, 2005)

A Few Good Men (Rob Reiner, 1992)

Air Force One (Wolfgang Petersen, 1997)

Alien: Resurrection (Jean-Pierre Jeunet, 1997)

Aliens (James Cameron, 1986)

AmericanEast (Hesham Issawi, 2008)

American Sniper (Clint Eastwood, 2014)

Armageddon (Michael Bay, 1998)

Artificial Intelligence: AI (Steven Spielberg, 2001)

Avatar (James Cameron, 2009)

Avengers: Age of Ultron (Joss Whedon, 2015)

Apocalypse Now (Francis Ford Coppola, 1979)

Banlieue 13 (Pierre Morel, 2004)

Batman Begins (Christopher Nolan, 2005)

Battle for Haditha (Nick Broomfield, 2007)

Battle: Los Angeles (Jonathan Liebesman, 2007)

Beowulf (Robert Zemeckis, 2007)

The Birds (Alfred Hitchcock, 1963)

Body of Lies (Ridley Scott, 2008)

Body Snatchers (Abel Ferrara, 1993)

Born on the Fourth of July (Oliver Stone, 1989)

The Bourne Identity (Doug Liman, 2002)

The Bourne Legacy (Tony Gilroy, 2012)

The Bourne Supremacy (Paul Greengrass, 2004)

The Bourne Ultimatum (Paul Greengrass, 2007)

The Brave One (Neil Jordan, 2007)

Bridge of Spies (Steven Spielberg, 2015)

The Cabin in the Woods (Drew Goddard, 2012)

Captain America: The First Avenger (Joe Johnston, 2011)

Captain Phillips (Paul Greengrass, 2013)

Casino Royale (Martin Campbell, 2006)

Catch-22 (Mike Nichols, 1970)

Children of Men (Alfonso Cuarón, 2006)

Cloverfield (Matt Reeves, 2008)

The Dark Knight (Christopher Nolan, 2008)

The Dark Knight Rises (Christopher Nolan, 2012)

Dawn of the Dead (George Romero, 1978)

Dawn of the Dead (Zack Snyder, 2004)

The Day After Tomorrow (Roland Emmerich, 2004)

Deep Impact (Mimi Leder, 1998)

The Deer Hunter (Michael Cimino, 1978)

Diamonds are Forever (Guy Hamilton, 1971)

Die Another Day (Lee Tamahori, 2002)

Die Hard (John McTiernan, 1988)

Django Unchained (Quentin Tarantino, 2012)

Do the Right Thing (Spike Lee, 1989)

Edge of Tomorrow (Doug Liman, 2014)

Elysium (Neill Blomkamp, 2013)

Equilibrium (Kurt Wimmer, 2002)

Extremely Loud and Incredibly Close (Stephen Daldry, 2011)

Ever Since the World Ended (Calum Grant and Joshua Litle, 2001)

Final Destination (James Wong, 2000)

Flags of Our Fathers (Clint Eastwood, 2006)

The Forgotten (Joseph Ruben, 2004)

For Your Eyes Only (John Glen, 1981)

From Here to Eternity (Fred Zinneman, 1953)

From Russia with Love (Terence Young, 1963)

Going Clear: Scientology and the Prison of Belief (Alex Gibney, 2015)

Goldeneye (Martin Campbell, 1995)

The Green Berets (Ray Kellog, 1968)

The Green Mile (Frank Darabont, 1999)

Green Zone (Paul Greengrass, 2010)

Groundhog Day (Harold Ramis, 1993)

Halloween (John Carpenter, 1978)

Halloween (Rob Zombie, 2007)

Halloween II (Rob Zombie, 2009)

The Hateful Eight (Quentin Tarantino, 2015)

The Happening (M. Night Shyamalan, 2008)

Hitman (Xavier Gens, 2007)

Home Alone (Chris Columbus, 1990)

Hostel (Eli Roth, 2005)

The Hunger Games (Gary Ross, 2012)

The Hurt Locker (Kathryn Bigelow, 2008)

I am Legend (Francis Lawrence, 2007)

Inception (Christopher Nolan, 2010)

The Incredible Hulk (Louis Leterrier, 2008)

Independence Day (Roland Emmerich, 1996)

Indiana Jones and the Kingdom of the Crystal Skull (Steven Spielberg, 2008)

Inglourious Basterds (Quentin Tarantino, 2009)

Invaders from Mars (William Cameron Menzies, 1953)

The Invasion (Oliver Hirschbiegel, 2007)

Invasion of the Body Snatchers (Don Siegel, 1956)

Invasion of the Body Snatchers (Philip Kaufman, 1978)

The Interview (Seth Rogen and Evan Goldberg, 2015)

In the Valley of Elah (Paul Haggis, 2008)

I, Robot (Alex Proyas, 2004)

The Iron Horse (John Ford, 1924)

Iron Man (Jon Favreau, 2008)

Iron Man 2 (Jon Favreau, 2010)

Iron Man 3 (Shane Black, 2013)

The Island (Michael Bay, 2005)

Jackie Brown (Quentin Tarantino, 1997)

Jack Reacher (Christopher McQuarrie, 2012)

Jaws (Steven Spielberg, 1975)

Kill Bill: Volume One (Quentin Tarantino, 2003)

Kill Bill: Volume Two (Quentin Tarantino, 2004)

The Kingdom (Peter Berg, 2007)

Knight and Day (James Mangold, 2010)

Knowing (Alex Proyas, 2009)

Land of the Dead (George Romero, 2005)

The Last Samurai (Edward Zwick, 2003)

Last Year at Marienbad (Alan Resnais, 1961)

Licence to Kill (John Glen, 1989)

Lincoln (Steven Spielberg, 2012)

Lions for Lambs (Robert Redford, 2007)

Little Big Man (Arthur Penn, 1970)

The Living Daylights (John Glen, 1987)

Lone Survivor (Peter Berg, 2013)

Magnolia (Paul Thomas Anderson, 1999)

The Majestic (Frank Darabont, 2001)

Man on Fire (Tony Scott, 2004)

Man of Steel (Zack Snyder, 2013)

The Man with the Golden Gun (Guy Hamilton, 1974)

Marvel Avengers Assemble (Joss Whedon, 2012): US title *The Avengers*

MASH (Robert Altman, 1970)

The Master (Paul Thomas Anderson, 2012)

Matrubhoomi: A Nation Without Women (Manish Jha, 2003, India)

Michael Clayton (Tony Gilroy, 2007)

Minority Report (Steven Spielberg, 2002)

The Mist (Frank Darabont, 2007)

Moon (Duncan Jones, 2009)

Moonraker (Lewis Gilbert, 1979)

Monsters (Gareth Edwards, 2010)

Munich (Steven Spielberg, 2005)

Natural City (Byung-Cheon Min, 2003, South Korea)

Oblivion (Joseph Kosinski, 2013)

On Her Majesty's Secret Service (Peter R. Hunt, 1969)

Pacific Rim (Guillermo del Toro, 2013)

Pearl Harbor (Michael Bay, 2001)

Platoon (Oliver Stone, 1986)

Psycho (Alfred Hitchcock, 1960)

Psycho (Gus Van Sant, 1998)

Pulp Fiction (Quentin Tarantino, 1994)

The Punisher (Jonathon Hensleigh, 2004)

The Punisher: War Zone (Lexi Alexander, 2008)

The Purge (James DeMonaco, 2013)

Quantum of Solace (Marc Forster, 2008)

Redacted (Brian De Palma, 2007)

Rambo: First Blood Part II (George P. Cosmatos, 1985)

The Reluctant Fundamentalist (Mira Nair, 2012)

Rendition (Gavin Hood, 2007)

Reservoir Dogs (Quentin Tarantino, 1992)

Resident Evil (Paul W. S. Anderson, 2002)

Rise of the Planet of the Apes (Rupert Wyatt, 2011)

The Road to Guantanamo (Michael Winterbottom, 2006)

RoboCop (Paul Verhoeven, 1987)

RoboCop (José Padilha, 2014)

Rules of Engagement (William Friedkin, 2000)

Saving Private Ryan (Steven Spielberg, 1998)

Saw (James Wan, 2004)

Scream (Wes Craven, 1996)

The Shawshank Redemption (Frank Darabont, 1994)

Shooter (Antoine Fuqua, 2007)

The Shootist (Don Siegel, 1976)

The Siege (Edward Zwick, 1998)

Signs (M. Night Shyamalan, 2002)

Sky Captain and the World of Tomorrow (Kerry Conran, 2004)

Skyfall (Sam Mendes, 2012)

Slaughterhouse-Five (George Roy Hill, 1972)

Sniper (Luis Losa, 1993)

Soldier Blue (Ralph Nelson, 1970)

Source Code (Duncan Jones, 2011)

Spectre (Sam Mendes, 2015)

The Spy Who Loved Me (Lewis Gilbert, 1977)

Stander (Bronwen Hughes, 2003)

Starship Troopers (Paul Verhoeven, 1997)

State of Play (Kevin Macdonald, 2009)

Star Wars: A New Hope (George Lucas, 1977)

Star Wars: Episode III – Revenge of the Sith (Lucas, 2005)

Stop-Loss (Kimberly Peirce, 2008)

The Sum of All Fears (Phil Alden Robinson, 2002)

Sunshine (Danny Boyle, 2007)

Super 8 (J. J. Abrams, 2011)

Taken (Pierre Morrel, 2008)

The Taking of Pelham 1 2 3 (Tony Scott, 2009)

The Texas Chain Saw Massacre (Tobe Hooper, 1974)

The Texas Chain Saw Massacre (Marcus Nispel, 2003)

Texas Chainsaw Massacre: The Next Generation (1994)

There Will be Blood (Paul Anderson, 2007)

The Thing (John Carpenter, 1982)

The Thing From Another World (Howard Hawks, 1951)

Thor (Kenneth Branagh, 2011)

Three Kings (David O. Russell, 1999)

Top Gun (Tony Scott, 1986)

Tora! Tora! Tora! (Richard Fleischer, Kinji Fukasaku and Toshio Masuda, 1970)

Transformers (Michael Bay, 2007)

True Romance (Tony Scott, 1993)

Ulzana's Raid (Robert Aldrich, 1972)

Unforgiven (Clint Eastwood, 1992)

United 93 (Paul Greengrass, 2006)

Unstoppable (Tony Scott, 2011)

Valkyrie (Bryan Singer, 2008)

V for Vendetta (James McTeigue, 2005)

The Village (M. Night Shyamalan, 2004)

The Walk (Robert Zemeckis, 2015)

The War Within (Joseph Castrello, 2005)

The War of the Worlds (Byron Haskin, 1953)

War of the Worlds (Steven Spielberg, 2005)

The Wild Bunch (Sam Peckinpah, 1969)

The World is Not Enough (Michael Apted, 1999)

World War Z (Marc Forster, 2013)

X-Men (Bryan Singer, 2000)

Young Mr Lincoln (John Ford, 1939)

You Only Live Twice (Lewis Gilbert, 1967)

Zero Dark Thirty (Kathryn Bigelow, 2012)

Notes on the Contributors

Karen Bennett is Assistant Professor (*Professora Auxiliar*) at the Universidade Nova de Lisboa, where she lectures in Translation. She also researches in the area of Translation Studies with the Centre for English, Translation and Anglo-Portuguese Studies (CETAPS) and University of Lisbon Centre for English Studies (ULICES/CEAUL). She has published extensively on topics such as: knowledge in translation; inter-semiotic translation (literature, music, dance, film); inter-cultural communication; power and discourse in translation.

Vincent M. Gaine is an independent researcher based in Norwich, England. His research focuses upon liminality in contemporary film, with particular focus on auteurs including James Cameron and Christopher Nolan, as well as the thriller, superhero and science fiction genres. He has published a monograph, *Existentialism and Social Engagement in the Films of Michael Mann* (2011), as well as articles in *Cinema Journal* and the *Journal of Technology, Theology and Religion*, and chapters in multiple edited collections.

Steffen Hantke is author of *Monsters in the Machine: Science Fiction Film and the Militarization of America after World War II* (2016), as well as editor of *Horror: Creating and Marketing Fear* (2004), *Caligari's Heirs: The German Cinema of Fear after 1945* (2007) and *American Horror Film: The Genre at the Turn of the Millennium* (2010), and co-editor of *War Gothic* (2016).

Robert Jewett is Professor of New Testament at the University of Heidelberg in Germany. With John Shelton Lawrence he co-authored *The American Monomyth* (1977), *Captain America and the Crusade against Evil* (2003), and *The Myth of the American Superhero* (2002), which won the John Cawelti Best Book Award.

Stephen Joyce is Visiting Associate Professor at the Department of Communication and Culture at Aarhus University, Denmark, where he teaches media, literature and cultural studies. He has published numerous articles on contemporary media and is the author of *A River of Han: Eastern Tragedy in a Western Land* (2015).

James Kendrick is an associate professor in the Department of Film & Digital Media at Baylor University. He is the author of three books, most recently *Darkness in the Bliss-Out: A Reconsideration of the Films of Steven Spielberg* (2014). He is also the film critic for the website Qnetwork.com.

Geoff King is Professor of Film Studies at Brunel University London, and author of books including *American Independent Cinema* (2005), *Indiewood, USA: Where Hollywood Meets Independent Film* (2009), *Indie 2.0: Change and Continuity in Contemporary American Indie Film* (2013) and *Quality Hollywood: Markers of Distinction in Contemporary Studio Film* (2015).

Adam Knee is Chair in Film and Media Studies and Head of the School of International Communications at the University of Nottingham Ningbo China. He has published widely in the areas of US and Southeast Asian popular film.

John Shelton Lawrence is Emeritus Professor of Philosophy at Morningside College. With Robert Jewett he co-authored *The American Monomyth (1977), Captain America and the Crusade against Evil* (2003), and *The Myth of the American Superhero* (2002), which won the John Cawelti Best Book Award.

Terence McSweeney is Lecturer in Film and Television Studies at Southampton Solent University and the author of *The 'War on Terror' and American Film: 9/11 Frames per Second* (2014) and *'Beyond the Frame': The Films and Film Theory of Andrei Tarkovsky* (2015). In 2015–16 he was a Visiting Research Fellow at the University of Oxford's Rothermere American Institute.

Ana Cristina Mendes is Research Fellow at the University of Lisbon Centre for English Studies (CEAUL/ULICES). Her areas of specialisation are cultural and post-colonial studies, with an emphasis on the representations of alterity in the cultural industries and reception in the global cultural marketplace. Her latest publications include the monograph *Salman Rushdie in the Cultural Marketplace* (2013) and *Walls and Fortresses: Borderscapes and the Cinematic Imaginary* (2015), a special issue of *Transnational Cinemas*.

Christine Muller is dean of Saybrook College and lecturer in American Studies at Yale University. Her research interests are film, television and other forms of US popular culture from the first decade of the twenty-first century. She focuses particularly on fractures and ambivalences within dominant, post-11 September cultural understandings of subjectivity, agency and responsibility.

Paul Petrovic is an assistant professor of English at Emmanuel College in Georgia. He has edited a collection on post-9/11 narratives since 2007 entitled *Representing 9/11: Trauma, Ideology, and Nationalism in Literature, Film, and Television*, published on Don DeLillo, and is working on a monograph on Arab American literature since 9/11.

Sean Redmond is Associate Professor in Media and Communication at Deakin University, Australia. He has research interests in film and television aesthetics, film and television genre, film authorship, film sound, and stardom and celebrity. He convenes the Melbourne-based Eye Tracking and the Moving Image Research group, and the Science Fiction Research group at Deakin University. He has published ten books, including *A Companion to Celebrity* (2015), *The AFI Film Reader: Endangering Science Fiction Film* (2015), *Celebrity and the Media* (2014) and *The Cinema of Takeshi Kitano: Flowering Blood* (2013). With Su Holmes, he edits the journal *Celebrity Studies*, shortlisted for best new academic journal in 2011.

Andrew Schopp is Professor of English at SUNY Nassau Community College. He is the co-editor of, and contributor to, *The War on Terror and American Popular Culture: September 11 and Beyond* (2009). His research and scholarship focus is on post-9/11 film and culture, gender/sexuality studies and fear in American/popular culture.

Ian Scott is Senior Lecturer in American Studies at the University of Manchester. He has published widely on the topics of American politics, history and culture and is the author of *In Capra's Shadow: The Life and Career of Screenwriter Robert Riskin* (2006) and *American Politics in Hollywood Film* (2000).

Guy Westwell is Senior Lecturer in Film Studies at Queen Mary University of London, author of *War Cinema – Hollywood on the Front-line* (2006) and *Parallel Lines: Post-9/11 American Cinema* (2014), and co-author of *The Oxford Dictionary of Film Studies* (2012).

Index

Note: Page numbers in **bold** denote a figure

CPSIA information can be obtained
at www.ICGtesting.com
Printed in the USA
LVHW081913031221
705197LV00002B/49

9 781474 413817